WAR
AT THE
END
OF THE
WORLD

WAR
AT THE
END
OF THE
WORLD

Douglas MacArthur *and the* Forgotten
Fight *for* New Guinea, 1942–1945

JAMES P. DUFFY

NAL
CALIBER

NAL CALIBER
Published by New American Library,
an imprint of Penguin Random House LLC
375 Hudson Street, New York, New York 10014

This book is an original publication of New American Library.

First Printing, January 2016

Copyright © James P. Duffy, 2016
Maps by Chris Erichsen
Front jacket photographs: planes © Everett Historical/Shutterstock Images; mountains
© Minden Pictures/Getty Images; soldier © Getty Images. Back jacket photograph © Corbis.
Penguin Random House supports copyright. Copyright fuels creativity, encourages diverse voices,
promotes free speech, and creates a vibrant culture. Thank you for buying an authorized
edition of this book and for complying with copyright laws by not reproducing, scanning, or
distributing any part of it in any form without permission. You are supporting writers and
allowing Penguin Random House to continue to publish books for every reader.

NAL Caliber and the NAL Caliber colophon are trademarks of Penguin Random House LLC.

For more information about Penguin Random House, visit penguin.com.

LIBRARY OF CONGRESS CATALOGING-IN-PUBLICATION DATA:

Duffy, James P., 1941–
War at the end of the world: Douglas MacArthur and
the forgotten fight for New Guinea, 1942–1945/James P. Duffy.
p. cm.
Includes bibliographical references and index.
ISBN 978-0-451-41830-2
1. World War, 1939–1945—Campaigns—New Guinea.
2. MacArthur, Douglas, 1880–1964. I. Title.
D767.95.D84 2016
940.54'265—dc23   2015019828

Printed in the United States of America
10 9 8 7 6 5 4 3 2 1

Designed by Laura K. Corless

PUBLISHER'S NOTE

While the author has made every effort to provide accurate telephone numbers and Internet addresses
at the time of publication, neither the publisher nor the author assumes any responsibility for errors,
or for changes that occur after publication. Further, publisher does not have any control over and
does not assume any responsibility for author or third-party Web sites or their content.

Penguin
Random
House

To the memory of Mary Gallagher

In addition to all our other difficulties,
there was New Guinea itself,
as tough and tenacious an enemy as the Japanese.

—GENERAL DOUGLAS MACARTHUR

Heaven is Java; hell is Burma;
but no one returns alive from New Guinea.

—SAYING POPULAR AMONG JAPANESE SOLDIERS

CONTENTS

MAPS

INTRODUCTION

It was four years of some of the worst warfare in history. Fought in monsoon-soaked jungles, debilitating heat; impassable mountains; torrential rivers; animal-, insect-, and disease-infested swamps—the combat raged across what one American soldier called "a green hell on earth."

The war for New Guinea is perhaps the least-known campaign of World War II, yet was one of the most crucial. Gaining control of New Guinea was the cornerstone of the Japanese war strategy. So badly did the Japanese want the island that they dramatically depleted their defense of their other strongholds by pulling tens of thousands of troops, dozens of warships, and hundreds of aircraft into the quagmire of New Guinea. The more resources they committed, the more important the campaign became to the Imperial General Staff.

For the Americans, victory in New Guinea was pivotal in breaking the Japanese war machine, the vital first step in a long march through the South and central Pacific to the Japanese Home Islands and the ultimate destruction of the Japanese Empire. The vast number of troops, ships, and warplanes that the Japanese pulled away from other fronts to commit to New Guinea contributed directly to Allied successes at places such as Guadalcanal, Tarawa, Saipan and Iwo Jima. Japanese generals themselves, interrogated after the war, concluded that the New Guinea campaign had contributed a good deal to their losing the war.

This book is the story of the almost four-year campaign for control of New Guinea. From January 23, 1942, when the Japanese first landed on New Guinea, until the last holdouts in the mountain jungles surrendered on September 11, 1945, the fighting was virtually nonstop.

Emboldened by easy successes throughout the Pacific and Southeast Asia, the Japanese could not know that the world's second-largest island would ultimately break them. New Guinea would halt their juggernaut, just as the attempt to take Moscow broke both Napoleon and Hitler. Similarities between the events in Russia and those in New Guinea are striking. After sweeping across Europe in a succession of victories, the Germans were stopped at the Moscow suburbs by a combination of heavy snows, subfreezing temperatures, difficult terrain, a breakdown in their supply system, and militia-type defenders who fought ferociously until regular army units could arrive from Siberia. In New Guinea, the Japanese were slowed by monsoons that turned tracks and paths into raging streams and difficult terrain that drastically reduced their ability to resupply units in the field, before being stopped by militia and volunteer units who inflicted severe losses on the invaders until American and Australian regular army troops could arrive.

Winning the war in New Guinea was of personal importance to Allied commander in chief General Douglas MacArthur. His avowed "I shall return" to the Philippines could be accomplished only after taking New Guinea. For MacArthur, there was no way around New Guinea. He could not bypass the island and leave tens of thousands of enemy troops in his rear. The road to Manila was through New Guinea.

PROLOGUE

Historians differ on the start of World War II in the Pacific-Asia theaters. The earliest any can agree on is September 18, 1931, when soldiers of the Imperial Japanese Army stationed as guards along the Japanese-owned South Manchurian Railway in the Chinese province of Manchuria set off a minor explosion along the railway that did little damage. They quickly blamed the incident on "Chinese bandits" and used it as an opportunity to fire a series of artillery shells into a nearby garrison of the Chinese army. The Chinese returned fire. Fighting broke out and grew in intensity as it spread, leading finally to the Japanese occupation of all of Manchuria. They soon renamed the province Manchukuo, and installed a puppet government.

When news of the incident reached the West, United States secretary of state Henry Stimson urged President Herbert Hoover to impose economic sanctions on Japan. General Douglas MacArthur, then chief of staff of the U.S. Army, supported Stimson, but to no avail, as Hoover decided not to provoke Tokyo.[1]

A second date used by some for the start of World War II is July 7,

3

1937, when Japanese soldiers stationed in north China used the temporary disappearance of one of their own to open fire on Chinese troops across the Marco Polo Bridge that spanned the Yunting River near Peking. Local Japanese commanders wanted control of the vital bridge for their planned occupation of Peking. Following a series of failed cease-fires and truces, serious fighting broke out between Nationalist Chinese troops and Japanese forces, leading ultimately to the bloody battle for Shanghai in August 1937.[2]

Japanese expansion continued from there, based largely on the country's economic and resource needs. As General MacArthur later described it, "They lacked sugar, so they took Formosa; they lacked iron so they took Manchuria; they lacked hard coal and timber so they invaded China. They lacked security so they took Korea."[3]

With all this land captured, they still needed the nickel and other minerals from Malaya, and the oil and rubber from the Dutch East Indies. In fact, Japanese plans called for complete hegemony over much of China, Southeast Asia, and the western Pacific, which included the Philippines. They desired to establish the Greater East Asia Co-Prosperity Sphere, with a defensive perimeter running from the Kuril Islands in the north to the island of New Britain, off the coast of New Guinea, then turning west to include northwestern New Guinea and ultimately ending around Malaya, Burma, and Thailand. As Japanese planners viewed the situation, the greatest dangers to meeting their goal were the Pacific Fleet of the United States Navy, stationed at Pearl Harbor, and the United States Far East Air Force, headquartered in the Philippines. To negate these risks, they boldly launched near-simultaneous attacks at Pearl Harbor and the Philippines on December 7 and 8, 1941.[4]

Following the devastation on Pearl Harbor and the Philippines, the Japanese blitzkrieg swept across the western Pacific and Southeast Asia, scoring one victory after another. In December 1941 a pair of American possessions in the Pacific, Guam and Wake Island, fell to Japan. The following months saw Imperial forces conquer Hong Kong, Malaya, Singapore, Burma, the Dutch East Indies, and the Philippines.

To retain their authority over these lands, Tokyo's war planners knew they had to prevent American forces from building up in Australia. How to do this was the overarching question that dominated Japan's military policies throughout the South Pacific. The Imperial Japanese Navy and the Imperial Japanese Army heatedly disagreed on the answer. The navy was in favor of occupying at least Australia's northeastern portion, but the army was against it. Close to one million army troops were already committed to the war and occupation of China, Southeast Asia, and Manchuria, where they were worried about a possible Soviet invasion. Even if they succeeded in invading and taking control of a portion of the Australian continent, Japan would inevitably face a continuing war of attrition there. The army favored instead a naval blockade that would sufficiently isolate Australia from the United States. Either way, the key to driving Australia out of the war was New Guinea, from which bombers could threaten and even attack Australian cities, and from which Imperial ships could patrol the entrances to Australian ports.

When war came to the southwest Pacific in January 1942, Australia could not have been less prepared. The four combat divisions of the Australian Imperial Force were serving alongside other British Empire troops in North Africa and on the Malay Peninsula, as were nine squadrons of the Royal Australian Air Force. The five cruisers—two heavy, three light—of the Royal Australian Navy were returning to Australian waters following several months of service in the Indian Ocean and the Mediterranean. With the exception of one armored division that had no tanks, virtually no trained soldiers were left to defend a nation of slightly over seven million people. The defense of Australia was left to militia troops who required several months of training before they were ready to face Japanese combat forces. Air defenses for the nearly three-million-square-mile nation amounted to twenty-nine Hudson medium bombers and fourteen Catalina flying boats. Defense against air attacks would rely to a large degree on a small number of Australian-built training planes called Wirraways, which were almost useless in air combat.[5]

Such was the condition of the forces charged with the defense of Australia and New Guinea in January 1942, as a large Japanese war fleet steamed south.

Part One

1942

CHAPTER 1

"This Is War,
Not a Sunday School Picnic"

As the huge four-engine flying boat roared in over the lagoon, Truk Harbor below bristled with activity: massive warships steamed in and out, while dozens of freighters unloaded their cargo into massive warehouses. Rich green jungle reached out into the deep blue waters of the lagoon. Presiding over all, shore batteries of antiaircraft guns jutted from dozens of volcanic and coral islands that dotted the area. Truk defied an enemy to approach.

A triumphant wave of attacks across the South Pacific had further energized an already-confident Imperial Navy. Now, on January 3, 1942, just four weeks after the bombing of Pearl Harbor, an assembly of top army officers were flying in for a rare meeting with their naval counterparts, with whom they seldom agreed on anything. Aboard the plane, Major General Tomitaro Horii, commander of the Imperial Japanese Army's South Seas Detachment, and several of his regimental and battalion commanders braced for landing. As the flying boat skimmed the glittering waters, the officers were quiet and tense.

Truk was part of the Carolines, a string of tiny islands which had been mandated to Japan by the League of Nations following the First World War. Now, Truk Island was home to the Japanese Empire's southern military base. Known as the Gibraltar of the Pacific, it was Japan's most formidable base in the South Pacific.

Within minutes of landing, the army officers clambered off the aircraft into the bright morning sunlight and onto a boat that ferried them to Admiral Shigeyoshi Inoue's flagship, the *Katori*. The fifty-three-year-old admiral, who had earlier served as military attaché to several European nations, was bringing the two services together to discuss plans for the invasion of New Guinea, which lay just eleven hundred miles to the southwest. Governed primarily by Australia, with a smaller portion under Dutch rule, New Guinea would be their largest and most challenging target to date. The immense island, off the northern coast of Australia, was notorious for its hostile terrain: impenetrable shorelines, dense jungles, steep mountains, rain that seemed never to stop, and a native population rumored to include cannibals. Yet as the officers all knew, New Guinea was the gateway to Australia, an Allied nation that must be neutralized—either through invasion and occupation, or by cutting her supply and communication lines to the United States.

General Horii had been selected to lead the New Guinea invasion, his last and most fateful assignment. At age fifty-one, Horii was a seasoned and respected commander, a combat officer who often personally led his men into battle. During the 1930s, he had served in China, fighting in the Shanghai Incident of 1932, which had left ten thousand Chinese civilians dead. The Japanese atrocities had affected Horii deeply, and they would influence him as he took command in the Pacific War.[1]

In 1940 the Imperial Army had promoted Horii to major general and assigned him command of the South Seas Detachment, an elite amphibious landing unit that was part of the Imperial Navy's South Seas Force. After the attack on Pearl Harbor, the detachment participated in the successful battle for Wake Island against U.S. forces, then joined in on the swift move south that conquered island after island. During this period, Horii distinguished himself from his contemporaries, many of whom either ordered despicable acts or looked the other way when they were committed. Disturbed by his colleagues' atrocities, he issued a written order to his men, titled "Guide to Soldiers in the South Seas," that explicitly forbade "looting, violating women, and the needless killing or injuring of local inhabitants."[2]

Now, Horii's first targets were two smaller islands east of New Guinea: New Britain and New Ireland. Gaining control of New Britain's town of Rabaul was key. Ideally situated as a prospective base of operations, Rabaul was nestled snugly inside the deep-anchorage Simpson Harbor, protected on three sides by mostly mountainous terrain. The only entrance was through Blanche Bay, which opened into the St. George's Channel, separating New Britain and New Ireland. From Rabaul, Japanese warships could control the surrounding sea, including the Solomon Islands to the southeast. What was more, the town's two operating airports would enable Japanese aircraft to dominate the skies.

A plan developed by Imperial General Headquarters in November 1941, known as the First Operational Stage, had identified Rabaul as the key element in the defensive perimeter around Truk. Japanese planners believed that Truk, Japan's most important base in the South Pacific, would not be safe from enemy attack as long as Rabaul was in Allied hands.[3]

In the crowded wardroom, the army and navy officers shared intelligence reports gleaned from photographic reconnaissance flights and on-the-ground spies. They discussed several possible landing sites, but finally selected the town's waterfront inside Simpson Harbor as offering the best access to the airfields. Intelligence reported that the port and town were lightly defended, with fewer than two thousand troops, including volunteer militia.[4]

Nonetheless, Horii planned for an overwhelming invasion. A fleet of bombers would destroy any enemy aircraft before the 5,300 men of the South Seas Detachment launched a three-pronged attack. Two prongs would head toward the two airports outside Rabaul in an attempt to limit sabotage and secure landing sites for carrier-based aircraft. The center prong would go directly into the town itself. Orders from Tokyo were that all defenders were to be "annihilated."[5]

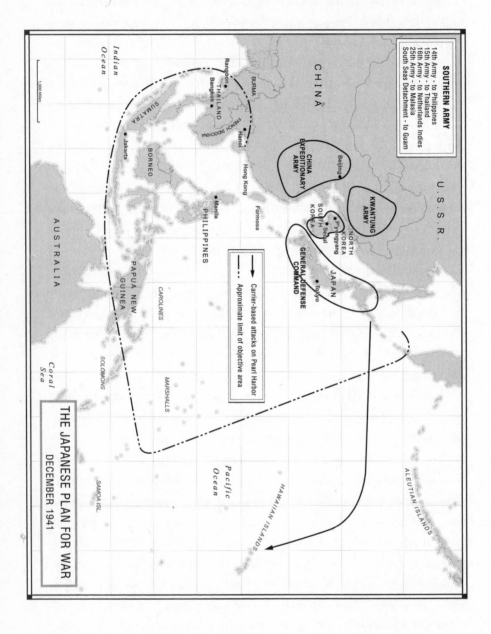

THE JAPANESE PLAN FOR WAR
DECEMBER 1941

SOUTHERN ARMY

14th Army - to Philippines
15th Army - to Thailand
16th Army - to Netherlands Indies
25th Army - to Malasia
South Seas Detachment - to Guam

→ Carrier-based attacks on Pearl Harbor
-·-· Approximate limit of objective area

CHINA EXPEDITIONARY ARMY

KWANTUNG ARMY

GENERAL DEFENSE COMMAND

CHINA

U.S.S.R.

NORTH KOREA

SOUTH KOREA

Beijing

Pyongyang

Seoul

Tokyo

JAPAN

Formosa

Hong Kong

Hanoi

FRENCH INDOCHINA

THAILAND

Bangkok

Rangoon

BURMA

SUMATRA

Jakarta

BORNEO

PHILIPPINES

Manila

CAROLINES

MARSHALLS

PAPUA NEW GUINEA

SOLOMONS

SAMOA ISL.

AUSTRALIA

Coral Sea

Pacific Ocean

Indian Ocean

HAWAIIAN ISLANDS

ALEUTIAN ISLANDS

1,000 Miles

The officers assumed that Rabaul's shore batteries could keep some of their ships out of the harbor. Fifty-one-year-old Rear Admiral Kiyohide Shima, whose warships were to escort the invasion's troop transports, expressed concern over reports that the Australians might have as many as ten coastal guns defending Rabaul. To lessen the danger to ships that would be clearly visible in daylight, the navy decided on a night assault. Several army officers, including General Horii, were unhappy about landing on a mostly unknown shore in the dark, but the final decision was the navy's.

With a population of five thousand, composed of fewer than a thousand of European ancestry, a thousand Asians (mostly Chinese), and three thousand members of local Melanesian tribes, Rabaul had once been a cosmopolitan town, with several hotels, a movie house, department stores, a well-stocked public library, a variety of restaurants, several druggists, a baseball field, and a cricket field. Simpson Harbor had boasted modern wharves, warehouse facilities, and a seaplane base. Yet in May 1937 a series of volcanic eruptions had buried the entire city under several inches of wet ash, destroying many of its buildings. These eruptions had transformed a formerly flat island in Blanche Bay into a seven-hundred-foot-tall conical mountain within which volcanic rumblings continued. Rabaul was just starting to reestablish itself when the war started.

The town's defenses were slim, numbering only fifteen hundred men and women, even less than the figure reported to Horii. Some were civilians—clerks, planters, miners, bankers, lawyers, and government employees—who had enlisted for training with the recently formed New Guinea Volunteer Rifles. They had signed up expecting to serve in support of regular Australian Army forces, not as frontline troops. However, a few had experience from the Great War, and most took to their training with enthusiasm and energy.

New Britain's main defense was Australia's 2/22 Infantry Battalion, known as Lark Force, under the command of fifty-two-year-old Colonel John Scanlan from Tasmania. Scanlan was a decorated veteran of the

Great War and a holder of the French Legion of Honor. His Lark Force was a mixed bag of infantry and artillery units, along with a medical detachment that included female nurses and a twenty-five-member band.

The defenders' weapons were out-of-date and inadequate. Among them were two old three-inch antiaircraft weapons—one deeply cracked— that gunners had dragged up the slope of a nearby sixteen-hundred-foot mountain following the attack on Pearl Harbor. They looked like two huge, grotesque lawn ornaments. Of the fifty-three members of the antiaircraft battery, only six had ever witnessed a shot fired by an antiaircraft gun. Their drills consisted of having one person, usually someone who had violated a rule and been dubbed the "pilot officer," run back and forth in front of the guns holding a long bamboo pole with a model airplane attached to one end.[6]

Two outdated six-inch breech-loading Mark VII coastal guns constituted the Rabaul shore battery. Made in 1901, they bore the marking VR, dating their manufacture to Queen Victoria's reign. The infantry carried mostly Lee-Enfield rifles manufactured before the Great War. There was also a mix of Bren guns, light machine guns, some mortars, and numerous handguns. Such was the force the Australian government had supplied Rabaul to defend the fifteen-mile-long coast on either side of the town.

Unknown to Rabaul's defenders, the Australian chiefs of staff had already decided to make the town a sacrificial lamb to the greater cause of slowing down the expected invasion of New Guinea. On December 15, 1941, Herbert Evatt, the Australian minister for external affairs, sent a secret cable to Washington, D.C., in which he outlined the decision not to reinforce Rabaul, nor to provide any large ships for its evacuation in case of a Japanese invasion. Evatt wrote that the government recognized that Rabaul was an important target for the Japanese and that any concentrated Japanese attack would be "beyond the capacity of the small garrison to meet successfully." With most of Australia's armed forces fighting alongside the British in North Africa, the Middle East, and Malaya, there was little the government could do to defend New Britain.[7]

Perhaps to soothe its conscience over leaving the defenders "hostages to fortune," the government did transfer fourteen Royal Australian Air Force (RAAF) aircraft to Rabaul. These included four coastal reconnaissance light bombers and ten Wirraway fighter-trainers that were less "fighters" than "trainers." The bombers were a military version of the twin-engine Lockheed Electra passenger plane made famous by Amelia Earhart, who was piloting one when she vanished in 1937. The Wirraways were the Australian version of North American Aviation's NA-16 trainer and all-purpose craft. This makeshift air force contingent, given the designation 24 Squadron, was under the command of twenty-nine-year-old wing commander John Lerew, a former race car driver and civil engineer.

A message distributed to all members of Lark Force on January 1, 1942, concluded with this sentence: "There Shall Be No Withdrawal." They were to fight to the last man.[8]

The situation was even worse on the neighboring island of New Ireland, which the Japanese planned to attack at the same time as Rabaul. One hundred fifty enlisted men and officers of the 1st Independent Company were the sole defenders of the 3,300-square-mile island. Their commander, Major James Edmonds-Wilson, a thirty-five-year-old farmer from South Australia, was instructed to resist an enemy invasion long enough to destroy all fuel supplies and military stores in and around the town of Kavieng, the island's chief port, and to sabotage the small airport to render it unusable for the Japanese. Edmonds-Wilson's force was to then escape the island in a small schooner and head for Rabaul. The 1st Independent Company had initially trained, as did many of the defenders of Rabaul, for combat in the open country of the Middle East; none had training in the tropical jungles that covered the islands they were now expected to defend.

The Australians in Rabaul were not idly waiting for an enemy attack. Following several December high-altitude reconnaissance flights over the town by Japanese flying boats, Wing Commander Lerew set out to accomplish a directive from the RAAF regional headquarters at Townsville on the northeastern coast of Australia: "To strike at Japanese bases and shipping wherever possible."[9]

On New Year's Day, Lerew led his four bombers on a mission against a Japanese seaplane refueling station on Kapingamarangi, a tiny atoll at the southern end of the Caroline Islands, approximately four hundred miles from Rabaul. It was the only potential target within range of the Hudsons, but only if they cut their thousand-pound bomb loads in half and added extra fuel tanks. The attack resulted in damage to several slipways used by seaplanes and flying boats and set a large fuel storage area aflame. Smoke from the burning fuel rose to about ten thousand feet. The four crews were airborne for five and a half hours.[10]

The plan in place, General Horii and his staff returned to their flying boat for the 630-mile trip back to their headquarters on Guam. The next day, January 4, 1942, Tokyo issued orders that the simultaneous invasions of New Britain and New Ireland, known as Operation R, were to take place in the second half of January. According to meteorologists, there would be little or no moonlight during the third quarter of the month. General Horii immediately ordered his staff to begin loading vehicles, fuel, weapons, nonperishable foodstuffs, and other supplies aboard nine transport vessels at Guam's Apra Harbor. Troops and horses would be the last to board.

That same day, sixteen bombers from the Imperial Japanese Navy's 24th Air Flotilla took off from Truk and headed south for Rabaul.

At ten thirty on the clear, bright Sunday morning of January 4, Cornelius Page, known to his friends as "Con," watched in shocked disbelief as sixteen airplanes passed high over his coconut plantation on the small island of Tabar, twenty-five miles of off the northeast coast of New Ireland. Page was a sublieutenant in the Royal Australian Navy Volunteer Reserves and an unpaid member of the Coastwatchers, trained to report unusual or suspicious events; sightings of strange ships, aircraft, floating mines; and anything else that might be of interest to the Royal Australian Navy, under whose auspices they operated.[11]

Con, whom the Japanese would later hunt down and kill, quickly identified the planes as Japanese bombers, rushed inside his house, cranked up his wireless radio, and reported what he had seen to military headquarters at Port Moresby, on the southwest coast of New Guinea. Port Moresby radio operators instantly transmitted the report to members of Rabaul's Lark Force, who assumed their town was the likely target. They immediately blasted the air-raid sirens, shattering the Sunday-morning peace. For a few minutes confusion reigned. Was it a drill or the real thing? A few daring souls waited in the open to find out, while others rushed to take cover in air-raid shelters.

As the bombers finally roared overhead, many of the antiaircraft gunners, most of whom were under nineteen years of age, began pointing skyward, yelling like schoolchildren until one finally asked the commander, Lieutenant David Selby, for permission to fire. Selby, a tall, thin attorney from New South Wales whose pencil mustache and bearing gave him the appearance of an aristocrat, watched the planes for a few seconds as the naive young men clamored around him. He suddenly turned and said, perhaps more harshly than he meant, "For heaven's sake, shut up. This is war, not a Sunday school picnic." Momentarily abashed, the young men collected themselves before rushing to the guns, now determined to display their professionalism. To everyone's surprise, the damaged three-inch gun fired without difficulty. Yet even with the fuses set at maximum height, the shells fell far short of the bombers, which maintained an altitude of eighteen thousand feet.[12]

Japanese planes took only minutes to pattern-bomb the Lakunai Airdrome, just outside of Rabaul along the coast, with fifty high-fragmentation bombs the Australians called "daisy-cutters." These released thousands of pieces of shrapnel intended to maim or kill anyone within reach. Only three bombs hit the runway; seventeen landed in a nearby tribal compound, killing fifteen people instantly and seriously injuring fifteen more. The rest of the bombs fell harmlessly into the sea. Wing Commander Lerew rushed two Wirraways up to try to intercept the bombers, but the Japanese planes were gone by the time the frustrated Australians reached fighting altitude.

Rabaul's defense forces remained on alert throughout the day as rumors spread of a possible enemy landing. The rumors finally gave way when reports made clear that there were no Japanese ships in the area. Life was settling back to relative routine when, just before dusk, eleven Japanese flying boats appeared overhead and bombed the Vunakanau Airfield, eleven miles south of the town. One person died, but the runway suffered only slight damage. Once again, the enemy owned the skies.

Rabaul was quiet on Monday, with only the sound of an occasional Wirraway passing overhead on patrol. Tuesday morning, January 6, the flying boats returned for another devastating attack on the Vunakanau Airfield, destroying a Wirraway and significantly damaging the field, its tiny air force station, and one of the Hudson bombers. Early the next morning a flight of twin-engine bombers flew in for the kill, pelting the airfield with more bombs, this time destroying a Hudson and a Wirraway, and heavily damaging two more Wirraways. Now only eight or nine Australian airplanes remained.

The tension in Rabaul grew. Few people in the town had any idea of what to do when the enemy arrived. The highest-ranking government official on the island, Deputy Administrator Harold Page (no relation to Con), had arranged a month prior to evacuate many of the women and children to Australia. Unfortunately, the nation's racial immigration policies had limited the evacuation to those of European descent. Now, as enemy bombers arrived almost daily, Page desperately cabled officials in Canberra, the Australian capital, asking for permission to evacuate the remaining civilians, including males. His requests went unanswered.[13]

With no intelligence or help from Australia, the Lark Force defenders decided to launch a reconnaissance flight against the Japanese. On Friday, January 9, a Hudson equipped with extra fuel tanks took off from the field near Kavieng on New Ireland and headed north to Truk. Flight Lieutenant Robert Yeowart, a twenty-seven-year-old accountant from Brisbane, and his six-man crew had volunteered for this dangerous mission. The Japanese dominated the skies over the entire length of the nearly fourteen-hundred-mile round trip. After dodging antiaircraft fire and defending fighters at Truk, Yeowart returned with photographs of a massive ship and aircraft buildup that looked to Scanlan and Lerew like an invasion force soon to be heading south.

Back on Guam, General Horii continued to oversee the final loading of his men and horses aboard the transport ships. Flying boats overhead kept a watch for enemy submarines. In the early afternoon of January 14 the transports sailed from Guam with Horii and his staff aboard the *Yokohama Maru*, a 6,143-ton armed passenger and cargo ship. The 5,300-man invasion force consisted of three infantry battalions, a regiment of engineers, three battalions of sailors from the Special Naval Landing Forces, a cavalry company, and a battalion of antiaircraft guns. There was also a fully staffed field hospital, a signals company, and a transportation company to monitor and repair the detachment's hundreds of vehicles. Finally, there was a veterinary unit to care for its five hundred horses.

As protection, three light cruisers, nine destroyers, and two minelayers steamed with the transports, while planes swept the seas in advance of the fleet in search of enemy ships and submarines.

In Rabaul, life settled into a tense monotony. The last bombing raid had been on January 7, and the only enemy spotted since were daily Japanese reconnaissance aircraft, presumably taking photographs. These planes flew beyond the maximum altitude of the Wirraways, frustrating the courageous pilots who took off in pursuit. Deputy Administrator Page continued to send urgent pleas to Canberra for an evacuation of civilians, but his pleas were left unanswered.

On January 8 an event occurred that should have alerted Page, and the others in authority at Rabaul, that the Australian government had all but abandoned them. Almost immediately upon arriving, the cargo vessel M.V. *Malaita*, carrying a full shipment of military supplies for Rabaul, received orders from Canberra to leave and return her cargo to Australia.

More frustration followed the next week, when six PBY Catalina bombers from Port Moresby flew into Kavieng to refuel before setting off to bomb Truk. Strong swells buffeted one of the planes when it tried to lift off the water, and somehow its bomb load ignited. The plane exploded and quickly sank. Another pilot, Lieutenant George Hutchinson, a U.S. Navy officer on loan to the RAAF, set his plane back down on the water to look for survivors. His efforts were in vain; all eight crew members perished. Of the remaining planes, only one actually found Truk in the bad weather that blanketed the Carolines. The single bomber dropped its sixteen bombs, but poor visibility prevented the crew from seeing whether they hit anything.[14]

Five days later Lieutenant Hutchinson became the first American combat casualty in the war for New Guinea. Hutchinson was flying a patrol along the north shore of New Guinea when he encountered a flight of Japanese fighters. He immediately radioed the Port Moresby operator that he was "being attacked by five fighters." In the uneven battle that followed, Hutchinson's Catalina, despite being riddled with bullets, managed to remain flying on autopilot. The last signal received from the American pilot was the ominous "On fire!"[15]

Hutchinson's tail gunner, Corporal T. H. Keen, discovered that the entire crew of ten was dead. With no knowledge in piloting the aircraft, Keen realized his only chance of surviving was to parachute out before the plane exhausted its fuel. He did not know if he would be landing in enemy territory, but jumping over land was safer than over the open sea, where he would likely become lunch for some sharks. Luckily, the Catalina was over the main island of New Guinea when Keen dropped out of the hatch. On the ground, local villagers took him to a nearby mission station.[16]

On January 14 the townspeople of Rabaul were surprised when a ship steamed into their harbor. It was the Norwegian-owned *Herstein*, now under charter to the Australian government. At the main dock, the crew unloaded her cargo, which included two thousand bombs for the now nearly nonexistent bomber force. Captain Gottfred Gundersen then moved the *Herstein* to another wharf to begin loading as quickly as possible several thousand tons of copra, the meaty inner lining of coconuts used primarily to make coconut oil. Gundersen scanned the sky for Japanese airplanes; the faster he could load his ship and get out of there, the better. Government officials in Canberra had refused him permission to leave Rabaul without a full load of copra.[17]

Deputy Administrator Page again cabled Canberra, pleading for permission to put some three hundred civilians aboard the *Herstein* for evacuation. When the response came in, Page stared at it in disbelief. The authorities wrote that all essential personnel must remain at their posts in Rabaul, and nonessential personnel could not board the freighter. The orders were explicit: "No one is to take the place of the copra aboard the *Herstein*." Page crumpled the cable in his hand. That settled it. No one was getting away before the invasion.[18]

———

About the same time the *Herstein* was loading her cargo, Vice Admiral Chuichi Nagumo sailed from Truk with a large and powerful fleet that included four aircraft carriers, two battleships, two heavy cruisers, one light cruiser, and nine destroyers. Always a cautious commander, Nagumo sent two squadrons of submarines ahead to patrol the St. George's Channel. The fifty-four-year-old Nagumo, who suffered from severe bouts of arthritis, was described by one contemporary as "an officer of the old school." Although he had disagreed with the attack on Pearl Harbor, he had carried out the mission as commander of the First Air Fleet. Nagumo was gruff and often uncommunicative, but many of his junior officers looked up to him as a father figure. Navy officers who knew him considered the pug-faced admiral to be Japan's leading advocate of combined sea and air operations. His carrier pilots were fresh from their Pearl Harbor victory and anxious for more combat. As the First Air Fleet sailed south toward its rendezvous with General Horii's transports, Nagumo obsessively studied the operational plans for the invasion and conquest of New Britain and New Ireland.[19]

———

Life aboard Horii's transports was miserable—cramped and hot. Temperatures inside the holds that housed most of the ranks often reached one hundred degrees Fahrenheit. Nevertheless, senior officers kept morale high with speeches that reminded the men of their samurai heritage and their absolute obedience and devotion to the emperor.

The monotony was briefly broken at 6:25 p.m. on January 17. A lookout on the minelayer *Tsugaru* reported seeing the mast of a ship under sail on the horizon, about eighteen miles distant. The *Tsugaru*'s captain later wrote, "At first . . . we suspected it to be MacArthur fleeing from the Philippines to Australia in a small vessel." The minelayer picked up speed and "pursued it with great excitement." Crew members rushed to the rails to catch sight of the enemy general as the small, distant vessel put on more sail in an attempt to escape. In the end, however, it turned out to be Japanese fishermen who had thought the pursuing warship was an American destroyer. The fishermen were so relieved that they gave the *Tsugaru*'s crew four large tuna from their catch.[20]

In the early-morning hours of January 20, the South Seas Detachment became the first Japanese army in the nation's history to sail across the equator. The crews marked the event with celebrations and praise for the emperor. That afternoon Horii's and Nagumo's fleets rendezvoused according to plan, and more than one hundred aircraft took off from the decks of the four carriers under the command of Japan's top pilot, Commander Mitsuo Fuchida, the commanding officer of the squadrons that had attacked Pearl Harbor.[21]

Once all aircraft were airborne, they separated into three formations. Based on the plan prepared by Fuchida, they were to approach Rabaul from three directions: east, west, and north.

––––––––––

At 12:48 p.m. that same day, January 20, Con Page informed Port Moresby by wireless that he had seen a formation of twenty bombers heading toward Rabaul. Port Moresby relayed Page's message to Lark Force, which again sounded the air-raid siren. People ran for cover or to battle stations. The seven remaining Wirraways took off and flew east, in the direction of Page's plantation on Tabar Island.

Suddenly a second group of thirty-three enemy aircraft appeared, approaching from the west. Minutes later another fifty Zero fighters approached from the north. The sky filled with a mix of fighters, bomb-ers, and dive-bombers. According to their commander, Lieutenant Selby, Rabaul's antiaircraft gunners were awestruck that "the Japs had a plane capable of anything like three hundred miles an hour."[22]

The Wirraway pilots were quickly under attack from all directions. Despite a daring and aggressive defense, the pilots were doomed. Selby later wrote that he and his gunners watched in stunned silence as their compatriots fought with "desperate gallantry" against the enemy. They all knew that "there could be only one conclusion to this fantastically uneven combat."[23]

In a matter of minutes, Japanese aircraft commanded the skies over Rabaul. Three Wirraway pilots perished in dogfights against the much faster and more maneuverable Zeros. Two others crashed while trying to land. One other plane did land successfully, but could no longer fly, with a portion of its tail shot away. Only one of the defenders managed to touch down safely and intact. All that was left of the squadron were two Wirraways and one Hudson bomber.

Now without defending aircraft, the members of Lark Force fought on with the weapons they had, although they knew that their rifles and Bren guns were no match for the high-flying bombers. For more than a half hour, the bombers circled far out of range and dropped their loads at will, targeting the two airfield runways and buildings, as well as any aircraft on the ground. The dive-bombers and the Zeros focused their attention on the waterfront, looking for ships, wharves, docks, and anything that resembled a military installation.

Once the enemy planes departed, the gun crews fell silent. Gone were the clamoring schoolboys. They were now subdued veterans who had witnessed one of the worst days in Australian military aviation.

Unbeknownst to them, however, their two antiaircraft guns had done some damage. Ensign Haruo Yoshino, who had commanded a torpedo bomber at Pearl Harbor, reported nearly fatal damage to his aircraft from the two old guns and serious damage to five planes in his group as he limped back to the carrier *Kaga*. He later described that day's mission as "frightful." Tokyo radio reported, "Seven of our planes failed to return."[24]

The courageous performance of Selby and his young gunners came to the public's attention a few months later when ABC war correspondent Haydon Lennard wrote, "Military officers in New Guinea are still talking about this man Selby and his unit. Selby's fate is unknown. But one thing is certain: Selby and his men behaved like heroes."[25]

From high above the action, Commander Fuchida had watched and realized with regret that he could have taken the port town's air defenses with far less airpower. The attack, he later said, was "like a hunter sent to stalk a mouse with an elephant gun."[26]

Historian Gordon W. Prange, who interviewed Fuchida in 1947, reported that the pilot, on his return to the carrier *Akagi*, told Admiral Nagumo that it was "ridiculous" to use so many aircraft against the target. He believed it was a waste of "time, gas, and bombs, none of which Japan had to spare."[27]

At the time the attack began, the *Herstein* had already loaded two thousand tons of the highly flammable copra. Three "Val" dive-bombers swept down on the ship, each dropping a single bomb. All three hit the target. One slammed into the engine room, and a fuel fire erupted, quickly reaching the cargo. Trained crew members operating the two old antiaircraft weapons mounted on the freighter kept up a continuing fire at the airplanes until the spreading flames forced them to jump overboard and swim to shore. Captain Gundersen was ashore meeting with the shipping agent when he saw his vessel explode.

The ship's steward, Karl Thorsell, ran down the gangway to escape. He almost succeeded, but suddenly turned and inexplicably ran back to the ship, vanishing into the inferno. The lines tying the *Herstein* to the wharf caught fire, and the vessel drifted free into the harbor. She burned all night and into the next morning.[28]

Wing Commander Lerew radioed RAAF headquarters in Townsville about the attack. "Waves of enemy fighters shot down Wirraways. Waves of bombers attacking aerodromes. Over one hundred aircraft seen so far. Will you now please send some fighters?" The response was not what he hoped to hear: "Regret inability to supply fighters. If we had them you would get them."[29]

Lerew's reply was straightforward. "Wirraways and Hudsons cannot be operated in this area without great loss and sacrifice of skilled personnel and aircraft. As fighters cannot be obtained only one course of services of trained personnel valued." The wing commander informed his headquarters that he planned to withdraw what personnel he had left from Rabaul with the hope they would live to fight another day. At this time, he had only three undamaged aircraft left, two Wirraways and one Hudson. He planned to use the Hudson to fly wounded men to Port Moresby for treatment.

A follow-up order the next day, January 21, instructed Lerew to send "all available aircraft" to attack a Japanese fleet reported to be sixty-five miles southwest of Kavieng on course for Rabaul. This meant Lerew should send his one remaining bomber to attack a Japanese fleet reported to include two aircraft carriers, three or four cruisers, a large number of destroyers, and between five and seven transports packed with Japanese soldiers.[30]

Despite the foolhardiness of the order, Lerew and his men, along with about a hundred local tribesmen, managed to push and pull the one patched-up Hudson and one Wirraway from their hiding place beneath a grove of trees. The second Wirraway was found to be too damaged for flight. They moved the planes slowly along a taxiway and onto the bomb-cratered muddy remains of the Vunakanau runway as the day neared its end, reducing the likelihood of further enemy attacks until the following day. With no bomb racks, the Wirraway was to fly as cover for the bomber. A short time later, both aircraft took off on what was a suicide mission. The Japanese carriers were sure to have a dozen or more fighters on their decks, ready to lift off and oppose any approaching planes. Fortunately, the darkness set in quickly and eliminated any possibility that Squadron Leader John Sharp and his crews on the two Australian aircraft would find their targets, so they soon returned to the field.[31]

Before making a final decision on evacuating his remaining air and ground crews, Lerew met with Colonel Scanlan to determine whether his men could be of assistance to the army. Scanlan told him the unarmed and untrained airmen would serve no purpose, and, besides, he had only about a thousand inexperienced men left to defend against what was likely to be between fifteen and twenty thousand combat-hardened enemy veteran fighters. The colonel did agree to send some army engineers to both airfields to blow up anything the Japanese might find useful, including the runways themselves.

A new order arrived shortly after Lerew and Scanlan met that instructed Lerew to use his men to "assist Army in keeping aerodrome open." Lerew had had enough of this foolishness and sent a now famous response, which the RAAF cipher clerks could not immediately understand until they realized it was in Latin. It read, "*Morituri vos salutamus*," which means "Those who are about to die salute you," quoting doomed Roman prisoners forced to fight in a mock naval battle before Emperor Claudius in A.D. 52.[32]

Meanwhile, fifty-two fighters and dive-bombers lifted off the decks of the Japanese aircraft carriers *Kaga* and *Akagi* on January 21 and attacked the harbor facilities at Kavieng on New Ireland. There they seriously damaged the island's escape vessel.

That same day, seventy-five planes from the carriers *Zuikaku* and *Shokaku* attacked Australian positions on the coast of New Guinea at Lae, Salamaua, Bulolo, and Madang.[33]

On the morning of January 21, the Lark Force radio operator picked up a transmission from a patrolling Catalina, which had sighted a large enemy naval force west of New Ireland heading directly toward Rabaul. Colonel Scanlan gave orders for all companies to prepare to move out on a moment's notice and for the troops stationed on a promontory overlooking the harbor to withdraw immediately. He did not intend, he told his second in command, Lieutenant Colonel Howard Carr, to allow his troops to be "massacred by naval gun fire."[34]

When the surviving crew members of the *Herstein* learned of the impending Japanese invasion, they held an impromptu meeting to discuss their future. Captain Gundersen and one other man wanted to leave Rabaul when the Australian forces withdrew, but all the others thought that because Norway was not at war with Japan, the Japanese might send them home as neutrals. They were badly mistaken—those who remained would suffer harshly as slave labor during the next five months, and then perish when an American submarine sank the vessel on which they were being shipped to Japan.[35]

Following the invasion, Gundersen joined a group of Australians that spent seventy-eight days trekking over three hundred miles along the New Britain coast in search of rescue vessels. When the motor yacht *Laurabada* from New Guinea found them, half the party had perished from hunger or illness, and several had died in Japanese ambushes. Gundersen joined Lieutenant Selby and 155 other escapees aboard the vessel. The captain was the only member of the *Herstein*'s thirty-six-man crew to survive and return to Norway.[36]

Thursday, January 22, dawned with showers and dense clouds, limiting visibility for lookouts aboard the Japanese invasion fleet. An unwarranted fear mounted among the invaders that enemy submarines or aircraft sent from Port Moresby might attack their ships from out of the gloom. Rear Admiral Shima wrote in his diary, "We were very much worried about being taken unawares by the enemy. Indeed, it was truly by the aid of the gods that we were not troubled by them." That they were not troubled was due less to the gods than it was to the defenders' lack of weapons.[37]

The admiral's concerns about an enemy attack were seconded by the intelligence officer of the South Seas Force, Major Toyofuku Tetsuo, who in March 1941 had slipped into New Guinea on a spy mission disguised as a merchant seaman. "We didn't fear attack from enemy naval units because we had control of the sea at the time. It was suspected, nevertheless, that attacks would come from submarines."[38]

In the predawn hours of the same day, Wing Commander Lerew had as many injured and sick men as he could removed from the army hospital and placed aboard the last Hudson bomber. He ignored an order to relinquish his command to Flight Lieutenant Brookes and return with the Hudson to Port Moresby to assume command of a newly formed squadron. Brookes was to place himself and his men under Colonel Scanlan to serve as infantry to defend the airfield.[39]

From their perch on the mountaintop, Selby's gunners caught sight of the enemy fleet's smoke through their gun telescopes. They sent a message to Colonel Scanlan, who sent two officers to investigate. By the time the two arrived and peered through the lenses, they were able to count twenty-two ships of all sizes heading straight toward them. The Japanese invasion was only a matter of hours away.

After the two officers rushed back to Scanlan and explained what they had seen, the colonel began withdrawing the thin defense line he had placed along the beaches. Scanlan recognized that such a large assembly of ships had to be bringing more troops than his small force could hope to stop. Besides, there was not much for his men to defend when the enemy arrived. They had heavily mined both airfields with bombs to prevent the Japanese from using them immediately; the coastal defense guns had been lost to bombing raids; and virtually all the radio transmission equipment had been destroyed in explosions. All that remained were the two old antiaircraft guns manned by Selby's gunners. Scanlan ordered Selby to destroy the guns and withdraw.[40]

When Selby inquired about transport vehicles for his men and their equipment, he was told no vehicles were available. This meant he would have to load his Vickers light machine gun, an antitank rifle, and as much ammunition as possible, along with all his men, into two decrepit trucks and drive the twenty miles of "bad road" to a rendezvous place before nightfall. Selby later wrote, "With a heavy heart I supervised the preparations for the destruction of the guns." He went on to describe them as "faithful friends" that had never let him down. Sadly, the men placed charges in each gun's muzzle and chamber and ran wires to a nearby shelter. Unable to give the order to fire, Selby simply nodded to the two men holding the ends of the wires. The resulting explosion split each barrel open for several feet. Painful as the act was for men who had pushed and pulled and nursed the two guns up the mountain, and watched them perform flawlessly, it was better, Selby wrote, than the "deep disgrace of letting them fall intact into enemy hands."[41]

Watching the enemy fleet approach from the Mission Station high above the harbor, a party of nurses, Catholic sisters, and priests were shocked. "We couldn't believe our eyes," said twenty-six-year-old army nurse Lorna Whyte from New South Wales. "There were submarines, aircraft carriers, troop ships." Within days, Whyte, along with seventeen other nurses, would be prisoners of the Japanese invaders and transported to Yokohoma. Known as the "Lost Women of Rabaul," for three years and nine months their fates would remain unknown.[42]

By ten thirty that night, all the Japanese ships were poised at their assigned anchorages, ready for the landings. The westerly wind had died down, the sea was calm, the night moonless, just as the planners in Tokyo had predicted. It was an ideal night for an amphibious assault.

CHAPTER 2

"Every Man for Himself"

At 10:35 p.m. on January 22, the order to "commence landing operations" passed between the ships in the anchorage. Twenty-five minutes later the troopships began lowering their landing barges into the quiet sea.[1]

Packed together in the landing barges, Japanese soldiers looked toward the land ahead of them, but could see little in the pitch-black. A few small fires still burned from that day's air raid, and a nearby volcano periodically spewed flames and smoke into the air. Gray volcanic dust laid a thin blanket on the ships, the barges, and the men.

Troopers of the 1st Battalion of the 144th Infantry Regiment under the command of Lieutenant Colonel Hatsuo Tsukamoto were the first to land at their objective a few minutes after one a.m. This was a beach near a place known as Praed Point, the site of the two now-destroyed coastal defense guns. The Japanese planners had considered it an ideal location for landing, with an accessible beach, but the feat proved to be more difficult when the soldiers found there was a six- to ten-foot-high cliff behind the beach, with dense woods beyond. It took the men more than thirty minutes to find a way through to the road leading to the Lakunai Airfield, one of their two primary objectives.[2]

Luckily for the invaders, Colonel Scanlan had decided that since the bomber attacks had wrecked the two 1901 coastal defense guns, there was nothing in the area to defend, so the landing went unopposed.

Events were radically different at the other two landing sites: At Raluana Beach, Lieutenant Selby and his antiaircraft gunners joined a company he described as "the odds and ends," made up of men from a postal unit, mess hall waiters, and office clerks. No one, including Selby and his men, had any real experience fighting as infantry soldiers. He had hoped they would not be sent to the beach to act as the first line of defense, but that was exactly what happened. A short time after three o'clock in the morning, the Australians heard the sounds of steel hulls scraping coral and the rumble of diesel engines as the landing craft approached the beach and began unloading their human cargo. Suddenly the beach was full of rifle and machine-gun fire and orders shouted in Japanese. A few minutes later word came for the Australians to withdraw immediately, since the beach was now in enemy hands. The "odds and ends" group, grossly outnumbered and outgunned, and now subjected to fire from the warships, began their long and arduous withdrawal to the rear. It would last weeks for those lucky enough to survive.[3]

Not far to the north of Raluana Beach, two companies of Japanese soldiers were to land south of Mount Vulcan and race toward the Vunakanau Airfield. However, one group, the 9th Company, missed the proper landing site and put its men ashore north of Mount Vulcan, right in front of a well-prepared defensive position. Major William T. Owen had ordered his reinforced rifle A Company to dig in just beyond the beach, where it had a clear line of fire. Owen's men then piled thick coconut logs in front of their positions for added protection. About eighty members of the New Guinea Volunteer Rifles, who had been called to active duty two days earlier, joined them. The company's single Vickers machine gun crew found a good spot from which it could rake the area, and the antitank and mortar teams set themselves up behind the infantrymen. Owen's company had also stretched barbed wire across the beach to slow down the invaders.

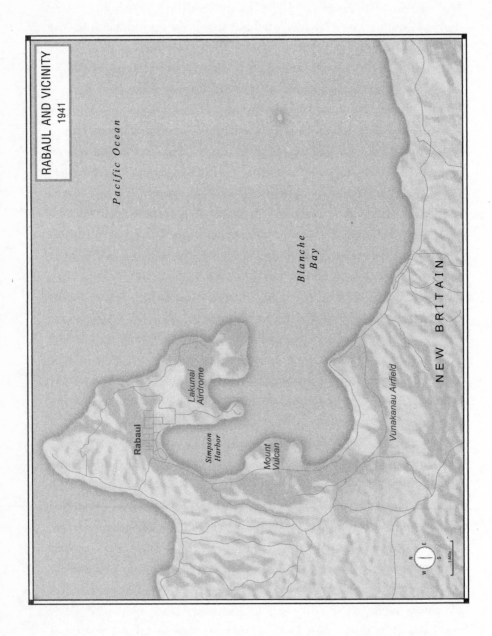

RABAUL AND VICINITY
1941

Pacific Ocean

Blanche Bay

Rabaul

Lakunai Airdrome

Simpson Harbor

Mount Vulcan

Vunakanau Airfield

NEW BRITAIN

N
W   E
S

1 Mile

Across the bay several buildings and a boat were burning. It was against the backdrop of these fires that the Australians suddenly caught sight of landing craft heading straight for them. The sound of diesel engines filled the quiet night as the defenders held their breath and waited for what would be for many of them their first combat encounter.

Corporal Kenneth Hale, a printer from Victoria, later described the scene as the invaders swarmed onto the beach: "As they landed the Japanese were laughing, talking and striking matches . . . one of them even shone a torch. We allowed most of them to get out of the boats and then fired everything we had. In my section, we had one Lewis gun, one Tommy gun, eight rifles. The Vickers gun also opened up with us. We gave the mortars the position . . . and in a matter of minutes they were sending their bombs over."[4]

Shaken by the intensity of the defense, especially when they had expected none, the Japanese at first fell back, and then made two attempts to breach the barbed wire. Both failed as Japanese soldiers fell by the dozens from the concentrated Australian fire. Unable to cross the wire, they moved south along the beach until they were no longer within range of Company A's weapons, and then started inland.

Meanwhile, following the unopposed landing at Praed Point, most of the 1st Battalion of the 144th Infantry Regiment raced toward the Lakunai Airfield, but the 1st Squad quickly moved up the side of the mountain. Its objective was to capture or destroy the ten coastal artillery guns that Japanese intelligence officers claimed were located there. Their orders were to take the battery by four a.m. If this was not accomplished, the ships in the harbor would have to withdraw five kilometers, out of range of the enemy guns, before daylight. The squad commander's instructions were grim: "If you cannot occupy the battery by four a.m., then you must cut open your bowels and die!"[5]

Given such an incentive, the squad found the first two guns, but its members frantically searched in vain for the remaining eight. Once the guns were located and either captured or neutralized, the squad was to fire three white flares over the harbor. When this signal did not appear by four a.m., the commanding officer of the invasion fleet ordered his ships to prepare to withdraw. Finally, the men of the squad realized there were no additional guns. There had been only two. The three flares lit up the night sky a few minutes late, but in time for the fleet commander to rescind his order to withdraw.

Meanwhile, Japanese landing craft continued to pour onto the beaches, discharging thousands of troops. Soon there were so many invaders that the small groups of defenders were in danger of being surrounded and wiped out. At every location, Australian soldiers and those fighting with them slowly gave way under the weight of the well-armed enemy.

To make matters worse, most of the radio communications equipment used by the Australian units was destroyed in the fighting, so messengers who often risked death before reaching their goal passed orders by word of mouth. Soon instructions about breaking up into small parties, and every man for himself, began to circulate. These were indicative of a cessation of organized control.[6]

Despite many examples of heroic defense, the Australians were badly outmanned and outgunned. At dawn, the situation grew worse when the warships began lobbing shells into the small concentrations of Australian soldiers, and the sky filled with Japanese dive-bombers and fighters intent on machine-gunning any retreating Australian.

Nearly out of ammunition and severely short of food supplies, the men of Lark Company withdrew from the town and headed into the jungle in search of a way off New Britain. The Battle for Rabaul was over. Japanese troops occupied the entire town, and units rushed into the nearby jungles to pursue the fleeing Australians.

Lieutenant Commander Minoru Genda, a classmate and close friend of pilot Commander Fuchida, described the conquest of Rabaul as accomplished "with ridiculous ease."[7] While the description was truthful, it is somewhat unfair to the members of Lark Force and the New Guinea Volunteer Rifles. Many of them fought gallantly against a much more experienced and better-equipped enemy force outnumbering them by nearly fourteen to one. It was a force supported by an armada of twenty-five ships, and what one historian described as a sky "filled with Japanese aircraft."[8]

Having sent most of his gunners to join the retreating infantry, Lieutenant Selby headed toward the wooded area beyond the Vunakanau airfield in search of Colonel Scanlan for instructions. Arriving at what was euphemistically called the Rear Operational Headquarters, which was little more than a small cluster of tents, a sergeant major informed him that the colonel had issued orders that "each man is to fend for himself."[9]

Simultaneously with the landings at Rabaul, nearly four thousand Japanese Special Naval Landing Force troops went ashore at two places near Kavieng on New Ireland. They arrived aboard several converted merchant ships, escorted by two cruisers and three destroyers. The invaders found that the small force of Australians had already withdrawn into the jungles and fled southeast in hopes of finding a safe way off the island. Within a few hours, the Japanese had fully occupied Kavieng.

On the day following the invasions, January 24, Imperial General Headquarters proudly announced to the world its twin successes. The *New York Times* reported, "An Imperial Headquarters communiqué late today said Japanese Army and Navy forces conducted successful landing operations on both New Britain and New Ireland, islands off British New Guinea early yesterday."[10]

Despite Tokyo's bragging, the war news from the southwest Pacific area was not all good for Japan. An American naval squadron comprising two cruisers and four destroyers under the command of Rear Admiral William A. Glassford was patrolling the sea between eastern New Guinea and Bali when word was received that a Japanese troop convoy was heading toward the oil-producing center of Balikpapan on Borneo. The convoy consisted of sixteen transports, escorted by the cruiser *Naka* and seven destroyers. Although the four U.S. destroyers—*Paul Jones, Parrott, Pope,* and *John D. Ford*—arrived too late to prevent the troops from landing, they did succeed in sinking four transports and a patrol boat, and damaging two other transports. Royal Dutch Martin B-10 bombers sank a fifth transport. A sixth met a similar fate when attacked by the Dutch submarine *K XVIII*. It was the heaviest loss suffered by a Japanese convoy since the start of their offensive into the southwest Pacific. It was also the first surface engagement in the southwest Pacific by the U.S. Navy since Commodore George Dewey's Asiatic Squadron attacked Spain's Pacific Squadron on May 1, 1898, in Manila Bay, the Philippines.[11]

Meanwhile, as Australian forces were fleeing the Japanese across New Britain, events occurring in the Philippines would have a profound impact on the coming war for New Guinea. The Japanese 14th Army, commanded by General Masaharu Homma, had pushed American and Filipino forces back onto the Bataan Peninsula. This resulted in a presidential order to the Allied commander in the Philippines, General Douglas MacArthur, to leave Bataan and go to Australia.

With Rabaul firmly under the control of his troops, Major General Horii instructed his commanders to hunt down the enemy and either kill or capture them. Japanese patrols ran along jungle paths in pursuit of the Australians, throwing hand grenades at them and shooting them. As daylight broke, fighter planes took to the air and circled clearings in the jungle canopy, waiting for Australians to come into the open so they could attack them with their machine guns. Soon dive-bombers joined the search and hundreds of enemy soldiers and civilians fell victim to the chase. By late morning, Japanese planes were covering a large portion of the eastern end of New Britain with leaflets calling on the Australians to surrender. The claim was that if they surrendered they would be treated humanely; otherwise, they would be killed by the emperor's soldiers or die of starvation in the mountain jungle that lay ahead. Few willingly surrendered. To say that those who did or those who were captured faced less than humane treatment is a gross understatement.

An Australian journalist provides one example, involving ten men, including several from a field ambulance unit wearing Red Cross armbands, indicating they were noncombatants. "A Japanese officer used his sword to cut the first man in the line loose and he gestured to him to get up and go with a Japanese soldier into the trees. A moment later the others froze as a blood-curdling cry of agony came from the man and shortly afterwards the soldier came back alone, wiping blood from his bayonet with a piece of rag. One by one the other prisoners were taken away, each by a different soldier, and butchered."[12] Such a story is emblematic of the fate of so many.

Few Australians survived to return home and tell of the horrors they had witnessed. Most members of 2/22 and the New Guinea Volunteer Rifles, as well as civilians and missionaries, died at the hands of the Japanese, or during weeks of attempting to find their way through the nearly impenetrable jungle crossed by numerous rapidly moving streams and rivers, some infested with crocodiles.

Confirmation of the invasion had reached the Australian capital by midday on the twenty-third, prompting Australian prime minister John Curtin to include the following in a cablegram to British prime minister Winston Churchill: "The heavy scale of the Japanese attack on Rabaul, where including other parts of the Bismarck Archipelago there is a force of 1,700, and the probability of its occupation, if such has not already occurred, presage an early attack on Port Moresby. The strength of Australian troops at Port Moresby is 5,500. Great importance is attached to this centre by our Chiefs of Staff as it is the only base in this region from which control can be exercised of the Torres Strait, which is the most direct line of supply to Darwin, the Dutch East Indies and Malaya, for which it is extensively being used."[13]

Curtin was angry that he had been unsuccessful in obtaining Churchill's agreement to release some of his forces to return to Australia. Three of Australia's best divisions were fighting the Germans and Italians in North Africa, and a fourth was engaged along with British and Indian troops in trying to stop the Japanese advance down the Malay Peninsula toward the fortified island of Singapore. With their country virtually defenseless, the Australian cabinet feared a Japanese invasion of their own country if both the Philippines and Singapore fell to Imperial troops.[14]

The Australian prime minister alluded to this situation when, in the same cablegram, he said: "The trend of the situation in Malaya and the attack on Rabaul are giving rise to a public feeling of grave uneasiness at Allied impotence to do anything to stem the Japanese advance. The Government, in realizing its responsibility to prepare the public for the possibility of resisting an aggressor, also has a duty and obligation to explain why it may not have been possible to prevent the enemy reaching our shores." Curtin's message was clear: the Australian people feared invasion while their own army fought elsewhere. They were angry at having to wait for the return of their forces to defend Australia after "having volunteered for service overseas in large numbers" in defense of the British Empire.[15]

For his part, Churchill was angry with Curtin, and had been since the day after Christmas, when the Australian prime minister publicly acknowledged that his government understood that Australia was not critical to the survival of Great Britain and might be considered expendable. Curtin added that his government was determined that Australia would not fall to the enemy. To prevent this, the government "shall devote all our energies towards shaping a plan, with the United States as its keystone, which will give to our country some confidence of being able to hold out until the tide of battle swings against our enemy."[16]

The Australian prime minister was cutting his nation's historic ties with Great Britain, which was obviously unable to help defend his country, and establishing a new relationship with the United States. He had taken the first step on December 10, 1941, when he cabled both Churchill and President Franklin D. Roosevelt, proclaiming that Australia would gladly accept a United States officer as commander in the Pacific area.

It is clear who Curtin had in mind, since he had already established radio communications with General Douglas MacArthur in the Philippines.[17]

The situation on New Britain had gotten worse since the successful Japanese invasion. The following month witnessed the massacre of about 160 men—military and civilian—at a place called Tol Plantation, after the Japanese gathered them there. Hundreds more were killed as they either surrendered or were captured while in flight. About four hundred members of the military force at Rabaul managed to escape. The RAAF sent two flying boats to a secret coastal position and removed about 120 members of 24 Squadron and a handful of army engineers who had joined them. Colonel Scanlan eventually surrendered after receiving a message from the enemy that he would be responsible for the deaths of any remaining soldiers unless he did so. Taken to Japan, he spent the remainder of the war in POW camps. He was so embittered that the government had abandoned his force with no real chance of escape that upon his return to Australia he refused to contribute to the official history of events.[18]

On June 22 approximately 209 civilians and 849 military prisoners left Rabaul on board the decrepit Japanese cargo ship *Montevideo Maru* and headed toward Japan. The ship had recently arrived with a load of soldiers and war supplies. The *Montevideo Maru* had no markings that it was a POW vessel, so when on July 1 it sailed into the crosshairs of an American submarine off the Philippine coast, it looked like any other enemy ship. The ship's starboard hull was ripped open by the first of four torpedoes, and in just over ten minutes, the vessel went down, taking the entire prisoner population with it. While some of the crew and the guards managed to escape in lifeboats, there is no indication that any of them unlocked the hatches to the holds where the prisoners were held so that some might have a chance of surviving.[19]

Meanwhile, Lieutenant Selby, refusing to surrender, led the remaining members of his gun crews and an assortment of other soldiers through the swamps and across the mountains of New Britain. Throughout February and March, they battled malaria, hunger, and the fear of capture by roving patrols of Japanese soldiers. At last, they arrived at what looked to be a safe haven, a plantation at Palmalmal on the south coast of New Britain. After days of anxious waiting, on April 9 a yacht arrived from Port Moresby and took aboard 137 troops and 20 civilians. Designed to carry eight passengers in its four cabins, it was quickly overcrowded. Four days later, the yacht arrived at Port Moresby, where its passengers transferred to the M.V. *Macdhui* for the final leg of their trip home to Australia. The ship was one of two from Burns, Philp & Co. that had evacuated hundreds of women and children from Rabaul on December 22. It now delivered the remnants of the survivors from that doomed town to safety.[20]

Within hours of the invasion, thousands of Imperial soldiers and sailors began pouring into Rabaul. Construction battalions immediately set about repairing the two airfields and building others. Buildings were converted to barracks and officers' quarters. Once the target of Japanese bombers, Rabaul quickly became the target of Australian bombers. Virtually every other day a small group of Catalina flying boats from Port Moresby attempted a bombing run on the Rabaul harbor and military installations. Based five hundred miles southwest of Rabaul, the American-built Catalinas were the only aircraft the Australians had that could carry a full bomb load, usually four thousand pounds, on that long a journey with any hope of returning to base. Unable to cross the mountains of New Guinea with such a heavy load, they had to fly around the island and across the Solomon Sea to reach their targets.[21]

Rabaul soon attracted attention from the U.S. Navy. Admiral Chester Nimitz, commander of the Pacific Fleet at Pearl Harbor, had few resources with which to strike a serious blow at the enemy. Instead, he settled for a series of harassing hit-and-run raids by the three operational fleet carriers he had—*Enterprise, Lexington,* and *Yorktown.* On January 31, Task Force 11 under Vice Admiral Wilson Brown left Pearl for the South Pacific. *Lexington* was the centerpiece of the task force, which included four heavy cruisers and ten destroyers.

Admiral Brown's first target was Rabaul, where intelligence reports claimed the enemy was gathering forces for attacks against American bases in New Caledonia and New Hebrides in order to cut the supply line from America to Australia. Brown's plan of attack was to launch his aircraft 125 miles from Rabaul in what he hoped would be a surprise strike. The launch would take place at four a.m. on Saturday, February 21.

From Rabaul, four Kawanishi Type 97 long-range flying boats were sent out each day to search an area five hundred miles out. At dawn on February 20, *Lexington* launched its own scouts, composed of six dive-bombers, to patrol three hundred miles out from the task force. At 10:15 a.m., the carrier's radar detected an intruder roughly thirty-five miles away. It was one of the Japanese flying boats. Grumman F4F Wildcat fighters scrambled from the deck in pursuit. Meanwhile, the pilot of the flying boat reported seeing the task force en route to Rabaul. The pilot, Lieutenant Noboru Sakai, then took his plane into a thick cloud cover for protection. Two of the Wildcat pilots, Lieutenant Commander John S. Thach and Ensign Edward R. Sellstrom, following instructions from the *Lexington*'s Flight Director Officer, Lieutenant Frank Gill, chased Sakai into the cloud. When the big four-engine plane exited the cloud cover, both fighters opened fire. The Japanese aircraft burst into flames and crashed into the sea below.

In a few minutes, a second intruder appeared on the radar. With Thach and Sellstrom returning to refuel, Gill sent Lieutenant (j.g.) Onia B. Stanley Jr. and Ensign Leon W. Haynes in pursuit. Aboard this flying boat, Warrant Officer Kiyoshi Hayashi was ordered to confirm the sighting reported by Sakai. Those orders cost Hayashi and his crew their lives as the two Wildcats sent their plane down in flames.

Admiral Brown realized he had lost the element of surprise; rather than subject his ships to an attack from land-based bombers, he decided to postpone the attack until he could obtain the assistance of a second carrier. Meanwhile, at Rabaul, unable to send fighters because the enemy strike force was beyond their range, the Japanese instead sent seventeen new Mitsubishi G4M1 Type I, Model 11 twin-engine bombers without fighter protection. Known to the Allies as Bettys, each bomber sported four machine guns and a 20mm cannon in its tail for protection. Although structurally sound, the absence of armor and self-sealing fuel tanks caused it to catch fire when struck by enemy shells. American fighter pilots nicknamed the bomber the "flying Zippo."[22]

The *Lexington* continued rotating planes for combat air patrol over the fleet, and sending search planes farther out for the next few hours. At 4:15, a six-fighter relief patrol lifted off her deck to replace the existing patrol that was running low on fuel. Just as it prepared to land, radar revealed a number of enemy planes heading directly for the patrol. Lieutenant Gill instructed the patrol to remain aloft and join the new patrol to intercept the approaching aircraft. The Japanese bombers came under fighter attack and most went down before they could reach the ships. Four managed to drop their bombs, but none came closer than three thousand yards from the carrier. Three of these then fled with the American fighters in pursuit. Three went down in flames while one managed to escape.

The final bomber tried a strafing attack on the carrier, but gunfire from the ship brought it down.

Suddenly radar detected a second group of nine bombers coming in from a slightly different direction than the first. Since most of the fighters were chasing the remnants of the first wave of bombers, only two were available to attack the second wave, and they were running low on fuel. As they turned to attack the bombers, the guns on one of the fighters jammed, leaving only the Wildcat piloted by Lieutenant Edward H. "Butch" O'Hare of Chicago to stop them. O'Hare shot down two bombers almost immediately; three others received damage serious enough to turn back. O'Hare continued to press his attack despite the explosions of antiaircraft shells around him, putting two more into the sea. A third crashed for reasons unknown.

Two American fighters were lost in the battle. Search and rescue crews succeeded in recovering only one pilot. Japanese losses were two four-engine flying boat patrol planes and sixteen two-engine bombers. For his actions that day, "Butch" O'Hare received the Medal of Honor, the first awarded a naval aviator in the war.[23]

Lieutenant Commander Thach told an American journalist on board *Lexington* that the battle with the bombers had demonstrated that the Japanese pilots attempted to carry out their mission "with great determination. The first lot went right for the *Lex*. They never hesitated a second, despite our attack, until their leader was shot down. The second nine never faltered and came right on in to the bitter end, even though O'Hare was eating them up from behind and we were coming in from ahead."[24]

Rear Admiral Matome Ugaki, chief of staff of the Combined Fleet, referred to the battle between the bombers and the American fighters as "most regrettable."[25]

At Rabaul, the loss of so many new bombers forced Admiral Inoue, who had planned an invasion of Lae and Salamaua on New Guinea, to delay the action by one week. Concerned he did not have enough fighter protection for the invasion, he also demanded the addition of at least one aircraft carrier to the invasion fleet.[26]

CHAPTER 3

First Landings in New Guinea

Converting Rabaul into a major air and sea base required that the Japanese protect it from enemy air attacks, which, launched from Port Moresby and airfields in New Guinea and Australia, had begun almost immediately after the town had fallen. The Japanese plan was to encircle the entire island of New Britain with a defensive ring. A major component of this ring was denying access to the Bismarck Sea to the Allied forces in Australia.[1]

Two villages on the northeastern coast of New Guinea, across the Solomon Sea from the western end of New Britain, were the anchors for this protective ring: Lae and Salamaua. Created in response to the gold rush era of the 1920s and '30s, both had been staging areas for thousands of miners and prospectors heading to the gold mines of the central mountain area around Wau, forty-six miles southwest of Lae and over 3,500 feet above sea level. Lae briefly gained international fame when Amelia Earhart took off from its small airfield on July 2, 1937, and headed east to America. It was the last time anyone reported seeing the famed aviator.[2]

The Japanese invasion and occupation of Lae and Salamaua was code-named SR Operation. Planning for the invasion began in early February. The primary objective was the airfield near each village. Each airstrip was between 2,600 and 3,200 feet long and 328 feet wide. Both served as forward bases for Allied aircraft from Darwin and Townsville attacking Rabaul and other targets on New Britain. Major Tadashi Horie, commanding officer of the 2nd Battalion of the 144th Infantry Regiment of the South Seas Detachment, whose troops were among those scheduled for the invasion of Salamaua, was told these "important bases" were only lightly "guarded by approximately 100 volunteer troops."[3]

The invasion force led by Rear Admiral Sadamichi Kajioka's 6th Torpedo Squadron (six destroyers, one light cruiser, one seaplane tender, three minesweepers, and five troop transports) left Rabaul at one p.m. on March 5 and sailed along the south coast of New Britain, heading west to New Guinea. Aboard the transports were three thousand troops, including Major Horie's battalion, one company of mountain artillery, and the Maizaru 2nd Special Naval Landing Force. Three hours later the three heavy and two light cruisers and two destroyers of the support group of Rear Admiral Aritomo Goto's 6th Cruiser Division followed. Air cover included two reconnaissance planes from the seaplane tender *Kiyokawa Maru* and fighters from the 24th Air Flotilla at Rabaul.[4]

On the afternoon of March 7, an RAAF Hudson bomber from the 32 Squadron piloted by Flying Officer Alfred Hermes was returning from a photoreconnaissance mission over Rabaul when Hermes and his crew were shocked to see the ships of the invasion convoy below. Unfortunately, the ships were only fifty-five miles from the New Guinea coast, so there was not enough time for Allied bombers staging out of Horn Island Airdrome off the coast of Queensland to attack them before they reached their destination. Other RAAF aircraft flying a routine reconnaissance over Rabaul reported that the harbor, jammed with warships a few days earlier, was virtually bereft of them now.[5]

At nine that evening, the convoy separated into two divisions. The transports carrying the naval troops headed toward Lae, while the army transports went to Salamaua. Escorting warships accompanied both groups of transports and began shelling Lae and Salamaua as soon as they arrived. Despite increased rain and a violent storm, with winds exceeding thirteen miles per hour, and coastal seas running eleven feet, the army transports lowered their landing barges at eleven p.m. Horie's soldiers hit the beaches at 12:55 a.m., just as a single aircraft took off from the Salamaua airfield. They rushed toward the field, which they fully occupied by three a.m. The entire Salamaua town and surrounding area were under complete Imperial control by four thirty a.m.

The naval troops went ashore at Lae two thirty a.m., also in a driving rainstorm. They immediately occupied the town and the nearby airfield.

It was soon determined that the Australian forces had withdrawn up the Francisco River valley toward Wau, as had most of the civilian inhabitants of both villages. The only route to the mining center was a single path called the Black Cat Track. After he had become a world-famous film actor, Errol Flynn described his ten-day trek as a gold prospector through the leech-infested jungle rife with typhoid and black water fever: ". . . You tried to sleep, and fought off mosquitoes, leeches, bugs, giant roaches, even New Guinea bats, night bloodsuckers. I have seen Central Africa, but it was never anything like the jungle of New Guinea."[6]

Bad weather over the airfields at Rabaul had prevented the arrival of Zero fighters from acting as air cover for the invading forces. Therefore, there were no Japanese aircraft in the area when Squadron Leader Deryck Kingwell, along with five RAAF Hudsons of the 32 Squadron from Horn Island, arrived at midday on the eighth and made a desultory bombing run that caused only minor damage to one of the transports at Salamaua.[7] Another bombing run, by three U.S. Army B-17 Flying Fortresses from Townsville, also produced negligible results.[8]

The Japanese landings had been unopposed because the Australian units at both locations included only members of the New Guinea

Volunteer Rifles and a handful of soldiers from the 2/22 Battalion who had survived Rabaul and managed to escape from New Britain. They had no guns big enough to resist the enemy troops sweeping ashore.[9]

After destroying anything of military value they could not take with them, including the RAAF radio station at Salamaua, the Australians had withdrawn ahead of the invasion forces and headed into the nearby hills. From a safe distance, they watched as Japanese engineers at both villages immediately went to work repairing and expanding the nearby airstrips. In thirty-six hours, the strip at Lae was able to welcome fighter aircraft from the 4th Air Group at Rabaul. The airfield at Salamaua was ready soon after.

In a bit of irony, the senior Australian officer at Salamaua when the Japanese invaded was Captain Alan G. Cameron of the 2/22 Battalion. After surviving the invasion of Rabaul, Cameron had retreated west with twelve of his men. On February 20, they boarded a twenty-one-foot boat with a two-stroke engine and made for the New Guinea coast. After eleven days at sea with minimum rations, the party arrived at Salamaua on March 3, just four days ahead of the Japanese.[10]

Cameron was at the airfield when he received word the Japanese were invading. He immediately told the pilot of the only plane at the field, a Hudson, to take off and fly to Port Moresby. He had members of the New Guinea Volunteer Rifles set fire to rags that had been soaked in kerosene on each side of the runway so that the pilot could take off in the dark. Once the plane was airborne, the fires were extinguished and the NGVR men spread out to blow the nearby fuel storage tanks. In a final act of defiance before retreating, Cameron and three of his men ambushed a party of Japanese soldiers, killing their officer. This is believed to be the only Japanese casualty from land action at either landing site. They then blew the previously prepared demolitions laid around the airfield and hangars before slipping away into the jungle.[11]

Most of the fleeing Australians crossed the rope swing bridge over the Francisco River, cutting the bridge's support ropes behind them so it dropped into the river. They left one man, Sergeant Hilary Farr, on the enemy's side of the river to round up several men who were staffing observation posts. Farr's group would move upstream and cross via a smaller hidden bridge.[12]

Unknown to the Japanese at Lae and Salamaua, serious danger lurked on the other side of New Guinea. Approaching Port Moresby from the Coral Sea was a powerful fleet that included the aircraft carriers *Lexington* and *Yorktown* and eight cruisers and fourteen destroyers. Commanded by Vice Admiral Wilson Brown, this force had just completed escorting a transport convoy of eight ships, mostly former luxury liners, taking fifteen thousand American soldiers from Melbourne, Australia, to the island of New Caledonia, 750 miles to the east on the far end of the Coral Sea. The Americans, who had spent a week in and around the Australian city during a stopover, would soon form the heart of the new Americal Division. They would later join the U.S. Marines in the fighting on Guadalcanal.

Still feeling the sting of his failed attempt at a surprise attack on Rabaul the previous month, Brown was planning a new approach to the Japanese stronghold when he learned of the invasions at Lae and Salamaua and received reports that few ships remained at Rabaul. This necessitated a change in plans, with new targets. There was a genuine sense of urgency throughout the entire Allied command structure that the Japanese not develop secure bases on New Guinea itself. The first obvious plan of attack would be for the two-carrier fleet to sail across the Solomon Sea and along the northeastern New Guinea coast between New Guinea and New Britain. The problem with this plan was the inability of the ships to make this passage without being subjected to attack by enemy ships and land-based bombers out of Rabaul. The element of surprise was important to a successful attack: catch the enemy while he is still busy preparing his bases and defenses.

Brown decided the best approach to strike the beachheads while protecting his ships from detection and counterattack was to continue northwest through the Coral Sea toward Port Moresby and launch his assault from the southwest coast of New Guinea. This would put the fleet beyond the reach of Rabaul bombers, and avoid exposure to

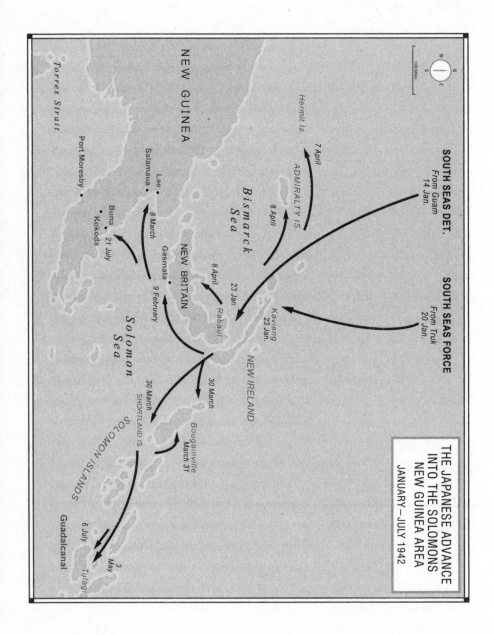

THE JAPANESE ADVANCE
INTO THE SOLOMONS
NEW GUINEA AREA

JANUARY–JULY 1942

patrolling enemy ships and planes. However, it also meant his pilots would have to fly across New Guinea from coast to coast, and over the Owen Stanley Range. With some peaks reaching a height of nearly thirteen thousand feet, Brown's air group commanders were concerned that their heavily loaded planes would not make it across in the thin air above the mountains.

Having little useful knowledge about the New Guinea east coast, much less the interior, Brown sent two officers on March 9 in search of information before the fleet arrived at the planned launch site some forty-four miles off the southern New Guinea coast. The *Lexington*'s air group commander, William Ault, flew to Port Moresby, while Commander Walton W. Smith, a member of Brown's staff, hitched a ride on a dive-bomber to Townsville. Both men were looking for a way through the uncharted mountains. They both learned valuable information, but Ault had the luck to speak with several Australian civilian pilots who had routinely flown between Port Moresby and Lae before the war. They explained that they had used a pass that cut through the mountains at 7,500 feet. The downside was that there was only a small window of opportunity when clouds and mist did not reduce visibility to dangerous levels that closed the pass entirely. This usually happened at about ten a.m. each morning, and meant the carrier aircraft would have to complete their missions and return to the western side of the mountains before that time.[13]

At ten minutes before eight the following morning, March 10, *Lexington* began launching her attack planes and fighters. Less than fifteen minutes later, *Yorktown* did the same. In all, 104 planes sped toward the pass through the mountains, guided and controlled by Commander Ault. As the overall commander, Ault orbited his plane above the pass, reporting weather and route conditions to the pilots passing below him. The attack group consisted of sixty Douglas Dauntless dive-bombers, twenty-six Douglas Devastator torpedo bombers, and eighteen Grumman F4F Wildcat fighters.[14]

The attack caught the enemy by complete surprise as the American planes swept down out of the misty mountains and bombed and machine-gunned Salamaua and Lae. The Japanese cruisers and destroyers that had escorted the troopships responded by quickly raising their anchors and heading to open water. Several dive-bombers gave chase, scoring some hits and near misses on the warships. The ships threw up a thick smoke screen to help cover their escape. Antiaircraft fire at Salamaua accounted for the only loss by the attackers when it knocked a Dauntless out of the sky. The pilot managed to make a landing in the harbor and had a good chance of reaching shore, but his fate remained unknown.[15]

Crashing into the waters along the New Guinea coast in the area of the beachheads brought its own special dangers. A Japanese fighter pilot related how he had pursued and machine-gunned an American B-26 Marauder medium bomber over Lae that resulted in an event that "sickened" him. Just before the plane burst into flames he saw four men parachute out of it. Their plane hit the water and exploded, sinking out of sight. The pilot continued to watch as a "small bright life raft popped up. As I circled the raft, I saw them clung to its sides. Since they were only two miles from Lae air base, it was only a matter of time before a boat would pick them up and make them prisoners. Suddenly one of the men thrust his hands high above his head and disappeared. The others were beating fiercely at the water, and trying to get into the raft. Sharks! It seemed that there were thirty or forty of them; the fins cut the water in erratic movements all about the raft. Then the second man disappeared. I circled lower and lower, and nearly gagged as I saw the flash of teeth, which closed on the arm of the third man. The lone survivor, a big bald-headed man, was clinging to the raft with one hand, and swinging wildly with a knife in the other. Then he, too, was gone. When the speedboat (sent to pick them up) returned to Lae, they reported that they found the raft empty and bloodstained. Not even a shred of the men was visible."[16]

The euphoric U.S. Navy carrier pilots returning from the early-morning attack on Lae and Salamaua reported sinking two heavy cruisers, a light cruiser, one destroyer, one minelayer, and five transports, and the probable sinking of two more destroyers and a gunboat. The attackers were awarded a total of fourteen Navy Crosses and eight Distinguished Flying Crosses, and President Roosevelt is reported to have told Prime Minister Churchill about the attack, calling it "the most cheering thing that happened in the Pacific so far." No sooner had the naval aircraft flown back through the pass than eight U.S. Army Air Force B-17 Flying Fortresses from Townsville made high-level bombing runs on both beachheads. The Army pilots claimed to have left two ships sinking, four on fire, and one beached.[17]

The attackers were in luck that morning because they faced no air opposition. Zero fighters from the 24th Air Corps at Rabaul, scheduled to move to Lae once the airfield was prepared, were on the ground awaiting word when they learned of the Allied assault. The first of these arrived over the beachheads at one p.m., long after the enemy was gone.[18]

As usual, when reports relied on excited pilots engaged in combat, the reality proved less successful than originally believed. Japanese records note that four transports were sunk and that one cruiser— Admiral Kajioka's flagship *Yubari*—received light damage, as did the seaplane tender *Kiyokawa Maru* and a fifth transport. Five additional ships, including two destroyers and a minesweeper, had minor damage done to them. Killed in the attack were 126 naval personnel and 6 soldiers. Wounded were 240 naval personnel and 17 from the army.[19]

Though more than one hundred aircraft attacked an enemy base, with total surprise as their ally, the results were less than spectacular. One reason was the inexperience of many of the pilots, but another, even more important factor was the poor performance of some of the weapons they used, especially the torpedoes, which should have taken a heavy toll on the ships. In an interview long after the war, then-Admiral Jimmie Thach, a Wildcat fighter pilot off the *Lexington*, explained: "You could see streaks of torpedoes going right to the side of those cruisers and nothing happened. Some obviously hit the cruisers and didn't explode. I saw one or two go right on underneath, come out the other side and bury themselves in the bank on the shore."[20]

Although the unexpected attack from carrier-based aircraft stunned Japanese commanders, they did not alter their original schedule. On the following day, troops from the South Seas Detachment occupied Finschhafen, fifty miles up the coast from Lae on the Huon Peninsula, and quickly set about expanding a small airfield north of the town. On

March 12, General Horii's army troops that had landed at Salamaua handed over the garrison to the troops of a naval landing force, as previously agreed, and returned to Rabaul. Soon after, Horii sent his evaluation of the plan for the seaborne invasion of Port Moresby in which his troops would be the main invasion force. He pointed out that the attack on the Lae and Salamaua by carrier aircraft revealed the presence of at least two Allied aircraft carriers in the region. This meant great difficulty in protecting an invasion fleet with several thousand valuable troops on transports unless Imperial Navy aircraft carriers were part of the plan.

General Horii made the following three points in his recommendation for what would soon be code-named MO Operation, the invasion of Port Moresby through the Coral Sea:

1. When considering the experience of the Salamaua-Lae operation, particularly the appearance of the enemy's carrier task force, then I believe it will be very difficult to assign protection for the transport convoy by land-based air units, and to protect the air base establishments and the landing point after disembarkation. I would like to see discussion during a central agreement to doubly ensure the strengthening of land-based air units and the cooperation of a fully equipped aircraft carrier for the coming operation. The carrier *Shoho* [actually a converted light carrier] currently assigned to the Fourth Fleet is not sufficient by itself.

2. I would like to see an increase by one in the number of transports exclusively assigned to antiaircraft duties (fitted out at Ujina for this operation).

3. I would like consideration for the use of an advanced force of paratroopers to disrupt the enemy and occupy the airfield near the landing point. The capture of air base installations prior to landing would be extremely beneficial.[21]

Horii got what he wanted on the first two points. First was the assignment of two fleet aircraft carriers as part of the protection for the invasion. In response to his second point, a specialized high-speed ship equipped with six antiaircraft guns, *Asakayama Maru*, also joined the fleet. As for the use of paratroopers, it is probably a good thing they were not used, for as events transpired, had they dropped into Port Moresby, they would likely not have survived.

Assigning the fleet carriers and the antiaircraft ship, as well as replacing the transports lost at Lae and Salamaua, delayed the planned invasion of Port Moresby until early May, laying the groundwork for the Battle of the Coral Sea. Fought between American and Japanese fleets from May 4 to May 8, 1942, this was the first naval engagement in history in which the opposing ships never actually sighted or fired directly at each other.

General MacArthur, who soon took over as commander in chief of all Allied forces in the South West Pacific Area ordered additional strikes on Rabaul, Lae, and Salamaua by his Townsville-based B-17s throughout the month of April, and the expansion of air facilities at Port Moresby. Despite these harassing raids, the Japanese continued to build and expand the bases they acquired at the two beachheads and elsewhere along the New Guinea coast. It would require herculean efforts to dislodge them.

With these strong footholds on the coast, especially around the Huon Peninsula facing New Britain, the Japanese effectively blocked the entrance to the Bismarck Sea, preventing MacArthur's forces from having a direct route from Australia to the Philippines. They added to their protective ring around Rabaul by occupying several islands north of Lae, including Manus Island in the Admiralties. Japanese airfields staffed with powerful land-based bombers were under construction in all directions.

CHAPTER 4

A General in Search of an Army

General Douglas MacArthur was the most widely recognized officer in the United States Army when Japan struck Pearl Harbor. His popularity among the American people and press was so great that at one point President Roosevelt judged him a potential rival for the White House.[1] He was the son of a Congressional Medal of Honor recipient who fought in the Civil War, the Spanish-American War, and the Philippine-American War. In addition to rising to the rank of lieutenant general, Arthur MacArthur Jr. had served as military governor of the Philippines.

On June 11, 1903, Douglas MacArthur graduated first in his West Point class of ninety-three students, having achieved the third-highest academic score ever recorded at the academy. Commissioned a second lieutenant in the Army Corps of Engineers, he served for one year as an engineering officer in the Philippines, then spent several months touring military installations in Asia, including Japan. Returning to the United States, he served as an aide at the request of President Theodore Roosevelt. Following the death of his father in 1912, Douglas was assigned as a young captain to the staff of Army chief of staff Major General Leonard Wood.

MacArthur's service under General Wood was marked by increased tensions with Mexico. Relations between the administration of Woodrow Wilson and the Mexican government of General Victoriano Huerta, who had used a military coup to take control of the country from a democratically elected president in February 1913, had plummeted to the point that Wilson demanded Huerta step down and allow democratic elections to select the next president. Huerta ignored Wilson's demand. When soldiers from Huerta's army briefly arrested nine U.S. sailors, Wilson ordered the Navy to occupy Mexico's most important port city, Veracruz, on April 21, 1914.

Occupied by a brigade of American soldiers, the city was soon surrounded by eleven thousand Mexican troops loyal to Huerta. Without informing Brigadier General Frederick Funston, the American commander on scene, Wood sent MacArthur to Veracruz. His assignment was to collect intelligence on the enemy and the neighboring countryside should the president order the Army to send a substantial expeditionary force into Mexico. Along with three Mexican civilians he hired, MacArthur penetrated some thirty-five miles behind the Mexican lines and gathered the intelligence requested. On the return trip, armed and mounted Mexicans, probably bandits, attacked MacArthur's party three times. He killed or wounded seven attackers. An examination of his uniform found bullets had pierced it at least four times, though none had found flesh.

A grateful General Wood, with the support of General Funston, recommended that MacArthur be awarded the Medal of Honor for completing the secret mission "at the risk of his life." An awards board, which was required to approve such a request, turned it down on the rather flimsy grounds that he undertook the mission without the knowledge of the local commander.[2]

During the First World War, MacArthur served with the 42nd Division, known as the Rainbow Division. The name came from the fact that it was composed of National Guard troops from twenty-six states and the District of Columbia. He started the war as an infantry colonel and chief of staff for the division. The 42nd entered the Allied lines in France in

February 1918, and over the next nine months, until the armistice that ended the fighting, MacArthur could always be found at the front. Promoted to brigadier general and placed in command of the 84th Infantry Brigade, he had the unique experience of being taken prisoner by soldiers from another American division who mistook him for a German general. By the end of the war, MacArthur had been awarded seven Silver Stars for gallantry, two Distinguished Service Crosses, one Distinguished Service Medal, and two Purple Hearts, along with nineteen awards from Allied nations, including two Croix de Guerre from France. For the second time MacArthur was recommended for the Medal of Honor, and again, the awards board rejected him.[3]

MacArthur's peacetime service included three years as superintendent of West Point, where he introduced many reforms. This was followed by three years as commander of the Military District of Manila, during which he developed a lifelong attachment to the Philippines and its people. He served as the president of the American Olympic Committee for the 1928 Summer Games, and then chief of staff of the United States Army under President Herbert Hoover and President Franklin D. Roosevelt.

In 1935, Manuel Quezon, soon to be elected president of the Philippines, asked MacArthur to help organize an army for the newly semi-independent commonwealth. President Roosevelt, perhaps eager to be rid of a possible election opponent, thought that a good idea and appointed MacArthur military adviser to the new commonwealth government. Two years later, MacArthur retired from the United States Army but retained his rank of field marshal of the Philippine Army.

With war on the horizon, Roosevelt recalled MacArthur to active duty effective July 26, 1941, and appointed him "Commanding General of the United States Army Forces in the Far East." Perhaps the president was recalling his last meeting with the general before the latter departed for Manila, when he told him, "Douglas, if war should suddenly come, don't wait for orders to return home. Grab the first transportation you can find. I want you to command my armies."[4]

MacArthur originally estimated it would take about ten years at a cost of five million dollars per year to build an army that could defend the Philippines. Given the funds and the time, the army MacArthur envisioned included hundreds of thousands of well-trained reservists built around a small professional army that would provide regular training in peacetime and leadership in war.[5]

As events transpired, the commonwealth had neither the money nor the time before Japanese forces invaded. War came to the Philippines within hours of the attack on Pearl Harbor. Although the defenders outnumbered the invaders, most of the 100,000 Filipino soldiers had no weapons, or in some cases, only obsolete World War I rifles, and few had completed training. Over the next two months, the Allied forces withdrew, according to a prewar plan, to occupy the Bataan Peninsula and await resupply and reinforcements. They had little choice, as the Japanese had almost total control of the sea and the air around the Philippines. During this time, some of the worst fighting in the war took place between the Japanese and the American/Filipino forces on Bataan. Unfortunately, very few supplies arrived by submarine and no reinforcements. The plan had been for the U.S. Navy's Pacific Fleet to drive the Japanese out, but a good portion of that fleet now lay at the bottom of Pearl Harbor, or was being towed back to the States for repair.

Throughout January and February 1942, the American press contained daily reports on the fighting on Bataan and the conditions on the small, fortified island of Corregidor at the peninsula's tip (known to the American troops as "the Rock"). MacArthur's headquarters were inside a vast tunnel on the island. As the situation grew steadily worse, with no hope of relief for the beleaguered forces, journalists and members of Congress began calling for the president to order MacArthur to evacuate. No one wanted American's most famous general killed or captured by the Japanese.

A U.S. submarine evacuated President Quezon, along with members of his family and government who were on Corregidor, on February 20, 1942. Also aboard were United States high commissioner to the Philippines, Francis B. Sayre, and his wife.

Officials in Washington were of two minds about MacArthur and his eighty thousand Filipino and American troops, as well as the thousands of civilians who had fled the invaders for what they thought would be the safety of Bataan. Chief of Staff General George Marshall recognized that all the talk in Washington about a relief expedition to Bataan was a waste of time. The Navy, on which such a task would rest, had too few capital ships to escort troop and supply vessels through the Japanese blockade of the Philippines. Several times Marshall urged MacArthur to take his wife and young son and evacuate Corregidor while there was still time to do so. Each time the general either ignored the request or answered that "they and I have decided that they will share the fate of the garrison."[6]

For his part, President Roosevelt opposed either a capitulation of the forces or the evacuation of their commander. He repeatedly sent optimistic messages to both MacArthur and President Quezon intimating that help was on the way. He reportedly told Secretary of War Henry L. Stimson that the evacuation of MacArthur "would mean the whites would absolutely lose all face in the Far East. White men can go down fighting, but they can't run away."[7]

Stimson was in full agreement, writing in his diary on February 2, "There are times when men must die."[8] This was an interesting comment coming from a man who had served only three weeks at the front as an artillery officer in a "quiet" sector in the last war, and, as one biographer described it, "never faced the actual combat" he reportedly sought.[9]

The newest member of Marshall's staff, Lieutenant Colonel Dwight Eisenhower (almost universally called Ike), was intimately familiar with both MacArthur and the Philippines, having served there as a member of MacArthur's staff. Marshall asked Eisenhower his opinion of what should be done for MacArthur. Ike studied the situation and options and responded, "It will be a long time before major reinforcements can go to the Philippines, longer than any garrison can hold out without any direct assistance . . . but we must do everything humanly possible. The people of China, of the Philippines, of the Dutch East Indies will be watching us. They may excuse failure, but they will not excuse abandonment. Their trust and friendship are important to us." He went on to recommend that Australia be the American base in the area through which support for the forces in the Philippines could flow.[10]

The relationship between these three men—MacArthur, Marshall, and Eisenhower—was complicated. Despite being lifetime members of the U.S. Army, Marshall and Eisenhower, as historian William Manchester wrote, "didn't belong to the same fraternity [as MacArthur]. The issue had nothing to do with personality, ability, or even performance. To MacArthur they were all officers who fought wars at desks far from the firing line and had little idea of what combat was like—who were, to use the derisive GI word, 'chairborne.'"[11]

This did not mean the experienced combat general did not respect their talents and abilities. MacArthur once wrote in a fitness report on Eisenhower, "This is the best officer in the Army. When the next war comes, he should go right to the top."[12] Clearly Marshall agreed with MacArthur, since he jumped Eisenhower over some forty officers senior to him, promoting Ike from lieutenant colonel in 1941 to major general by March 1942, then to commander of the European theater in June 1942. As one noted historian explained, Eisenhower "received extraordinarily fast promotion."[13]

The inner circle at the White House contained at least one influential voice in opposition to allowing MacArthur to remain in the Philippines: Major General Edwin M. Watson, known to all, including Roosevelt, as "Pa." A decorated soldier in the Great War, Watson had served as aide to President Wilson at the Versailles conference and now served two posts for Roosevelt. He was the president's military aide, and perhaps more important, his appointments secretary, controlling all access to the president. Watson and his wife were also close friends of Roosevelt's, who often stayed at their home in Virginia. As far as General Watson was concerned, MacArthur was worth "five army corps," and must be ordered out of the Philippines.[14]

Secretary Stimson remained of a different opinion. In early February, he drafted a message the president sent to MacArthur, instructing him to "continue to keep our flag flying in the Philippines so long as there remains any possibility of resistance." He said it was imperative that the United States not "display weakness in fact or spirit anywhere." The American determination to win, Roosevelt told MacArthur, must carry "down to the last unit."[15]

That MacArthur was prepared to die in the final battle for Corregidor is without question. He told Washington that several times, and made no plans for the evacuation of his family. Among the few in the government who opposed this was General Marshall. The American chief of staff told his British counterparts, "If one commander were designated out there [the Pacific theater], it couldn't be anybody but MacArthur, on the basis of pure competence alone."[16]

Marshall realized that only a direct presidential order could get MacArthur to leave Corregidor. However, despite Marshall's best efforts, Roosevelt resisted ordering him out.

On February 15, 1942, Allied forces in Singapore—mostly British, Indian, and Australian—surrendered to the Japanese in what Churchill described to Roosevelt as "the greatest disaster in our history."[17] Among the eighty thousand men taken prisoner were over fifteen thousand members of the Australian 8th Division. When the news reached Australia, it set off shock waves among the population and the government. The loss of so many soldiers at once was bad enough, but now the Japanese were slowly closing in on Australia.

The gravity of the Japanese success so far in the war became even starker four days later, when 188 Japanese carrier-based aircraft attacked the northern Australian port of Darwin at 9:58 in the morning. Commander Fuchida led the raid, directed at the forty-five ships in the port and the portside facilities. It lasted until ten thirty. Less than thirty minutes later, fifty-five land-based bombers made a second attack, this one targeted primarily at the nearby airfield. The two attacks cost 243 lives and injured between 300 and 400 more defenders. The American destroyer Peary and the transport Meigs, along with six other ships, sank.

The two raids destroyed twenty-four aircraft, including three U.S. Navy Catalinas, ten Kittyhawk fighters, one Liberator bomber, and three RAAF Hudsons.

Now that there had been the first "physical contact of war within Australia," as Prime Minister Curtin described it, the Australian War Cabinet wanted its army back to defend the country. Curtin fired off a cablegram to Churchill, demanding the return of the 6th, 7th, and 9th Infantry Divisions from the Middle East. The two prime ministers engaged in a heated exchange of cables, with Churchill resisting the loss of the three experienced combat divisions that he believed necessary to continue the fight against the Axis commander in North Africa, General Erwin Rommel.

Few recognized at the time that the Australian government was about to save MacArthur's life, for, in the words of biographer William Manchester, "it is almost certain that he would have been left to die on the Rock had Australia not interfered."[18]

Churchill turned to Roosevelt for help with the Australian prime minister. The president cabled Curtin, asking him to reconsider his decision to withdraw all three divisions "in the interests of our whole war effort in the Far East." Taking into account Curtin's desire to strengthen ties with the United States, Roosevelt told him that in addition to the American troops and forces now en route, a further 27,000 men, fully equipped in every respect, were to be sent from the United States to Australia.[19]

However, the Australians still had a strong hand to play. Of course they wanted American troops, but most of all they wanted an American commander who would ensure that the fight to save Australia from invasion would become an American fight. They wanted MacArthur. On February 21, the Australian cabinet met in a special session to discuss the request for the return of the three divisions. It decided to change its demand to the return of only two divisions if an American general were named supreme commander of their theater, along with a promise that more American troops would be sent to Australia. Churchill forwarded the proposal to Roosevelt.[20]

Robert Sherwood, a presidential speechwriter and close adviser to

Roosevelt, explained what happened next: "It was this strained relationship [between Churchill and Curtin] and the desperate predicament of Australia that caused it, which influenced the orders to MacArthur. Roosevelt knew full well that the departure of MacArthur from Corregidor would be a grievous blow to the heroic men of his command and thus to the whole United States. It was ordering the captain to be the first to leave the sinking ship. But Roosevelt had to weigh these considerations against the fact that no move he could make [other than sending them MacArthur] would be so well calculated to bolster the morale of the people of Australia and New Zealand." It would also allow Churchill to keep one Australian division in North Africa.[21]

President Roosevelt met with General Marshall, Admiral Ernest King—commander in chief of the United States Fleet and soon to be named chief of naval operations—and close presidential adviser Harry Hopkins on Sunday afternoon, February 22, to discuss MacArthur's fate. At that meeting, the president decided to send a coded message to MacArthur instructing him to leave Corregidor for the Philippine island of Mindanao. He was to remain there no longer than a week to determine the feasibility of a prolonged defense of the island. He was then to proceed to Australia, where he would take command of the U.S. forces building there. Following much soul-searching and discussions with his senior officers, MacArthur decided he had no choice but to obey. Perhaps Bataan, or at least Corregidor, could hold out long enough for him to return with a force large enough to drive the Japanese out.

After turning command over to Major General Jonathan M. Wainwright, who had been commander of the North Luzon Force, MacArthur and his party of nineteen persons slipped aboard four PT boats and headed to Mindanao after sunset on Wednesday, March 11. The group had several narrow escapes from Japanese warships that were probably searching for him, for word had leaked from Washington that he would be leaving. During the voyage, MacArthur's wife, Jean, became seasick and lost her purse overboard. They arrived at Mindanao at seven a.m. on March 13. Two B-17s from the 40th Reconnaissance Squadron of the 19th Bombardment Group flew them out on the morning of the seventeenth,

headed to Darwin, Australia, some five and a half hours away, over territory under complete control of the Japanese. Before departing, the lead
pilot, Lieutenant Frank P. Bostrom, drank eight cups of black coffee to
help him stay awake while local mechanics repaired one of his plane's
turbochargers. He had already flown nearly six hours to Mindanao and
would be heading back in a few hours with his valuable passengers.

MacArthur's plane had some engine trouble as it sped down the
runway, but managed to get off the ground safely. Everyone's luggage,
limited to one small piece each when they left Corregidor, had to be
left behind to reduce the weight. As for the general, he had left his island
fortress with nothing more than the khaki clothes on his back. He even
had to borrow a razor in order to shave. Except for the anxiety of flying
so close to Japanese-held airfields on the islands of Timor and Celebes,
the flight was without incident. Bostrom's navigator, Lieutenant Bob Ray
Carruthers, later wrote of the mission: "We had delivered our precious
cargo safe and sound and we all felt pretty swell about it."[22]

Unable to land at Darwin, which was under attack by enemy bombers, the two B-17s touched down some fifty miles to the south at Batchelor Field. It was here that MacArthur received the first clue that the
great American army he expected to be waiting for him in Australia,
based on his interpretation of Roosevelt's order, did not exist. When
he asked an American officer stationed at Batchelor Field about the
buildup of American forces, the man responded, "So far as I know, sir,
there are very few troops here." MacArthur was shocked and thought
the man must be incorrect.[23]

A small group of reporters approached MacArthur and asked him for
a statement. The general's promise to the people of the Philippines was
soon repeated throughout the Allied world. "The President of the United
States ordered me to break through the Japanese lines and proceed from
Corregidor to Australia for the purpose, as I understand it, of organizing
the American offensive against Japan, a primary object of which is the
relief of the Philippines. I came through, and I shall return."[24]

Many of the general's critics attacked him over the last three words,
attributing them to his ego. Yet the phrase actually came from Carlos

Romulo, a Filipino journalist and soldier who would later serve as president of the United Nations General Assembly. When, while still on Corregidor, one of MacArthur's staff officers told him their slogan would be "We shall return," the Filipino objected, telling the officer that "America has let us down and will not be trusted. But the people still have confidence in MacArthur. If he says he is coming back, he will be believed."[25]

Following the harrowing flight from Mindanao, the MacArthurs flew to Alice Springs, the nearest railway station, to catch a train to Melbourne, their ultimate destination.

Located in the middle of the continent, more than a thousand miles from Melbourne, Alice Springs was an outback village as remote as a frontier town in the American West. MacArthur's party put up at the only hotel and spent most of its time fighting off swarms of black flies that infested the area during Australia's sweltering late summer. The arrival of Brigadier General Patrick J. Hurley, an old friend of MacArthur's, aboard his own aircraft briefly cheered everyone's spirits. Hurley, who had served as secretary of war under Herbert Hoover, was now in Australia as a special representative of General Marshall. He told MacArthur that the entire nation was hailing him as a hero, like Dewey or Lindbergh, but the tired, gaunt escapee from Corregidor—he had lost twenty-five pounds since the invasion—only wanted to know where his army was. Hurley replied that he had no idea.[26] He then offered to fly the entire party to Melbourne. Jean, who had had enough of flying, responded, "No, thank you, we're going by train."[27]

After lunch on March 18, seven days after they left Corregidor, the MacArthur family, including Ah Cheu (Arthur's amah), Major Morehouse, young Arthur's doctor, and two other officers, boarded a train that one American journalist referred to as "the tiny Toonerville train that ran across Australia's barren core."[28] The locomotive slowly chugged along across the vast, open, mostly desert countryside toward Melbourne.

In the meantime, an American army officer had given Prime Minister Curtin a message from FDR informing him that General Douglas MacArthur had arrived in Australia. The president proposed that the

Australian government nominate MacArthur as the supreme commander of all Allied forces in the southwest Pacific. When Curtin asked exactly where in Australia the general was, the officer responded truthfully that he did not know.[29]

Perhaps Roosevelt thought this message accomplished two goals. First, he was giving the Australians the American general they wanted, expecting them in return to leave one division of their army in North Africa. Second, FDR may have believed that by moving quickly to make MacArthur the supreme commander of all Allied troops in the theater, the general might forget about the optimistic yet empty assurances of help he had received from Roosevelt and others in Washington while trapped on Corregidor. The promises included "streams of bombers" and troop reinforcements that never materialized.[30]

As the little train crept across the center of Australia, America read news of MacArthur's escape from Corregidor and his appearance in Australia. Under the headline "Pleased Australia Greets a 'Fighter,'" the *New York Times* quoted an Australian newspaper editorial as saying that MacArthur's arrival "will be regarded as the best single piece of news since the outbreak of the Pacific War. His gallant stand in the Philippines has fired the imagination of Australians, who love a fighter, and his command of Australians in addition to American troops will be an inspiration to the fighting forces."[31]

President Roosevelt issued a statement to the press explaining why he had ordered MacArthur out of the Philippines. He acknowledged the people's admiration for MacArthur's commitment in the archipelago, and asked them to consider the long-term success of the war in putting the general where he could best serve his country.[32]

The rest of the world quickly heard the news of MacArthur's arrival in Australia. Journalists in London reported that his appointment meant the Allies "intended to substitute offense for defense in the Far East." Some thought the appointment also indicated a change in the "Europe first" policy decided on by Roosevelt and Churchill. They were wrong, as would become apparent over the next few months.[33]

One American historian described the convergence of arrivals in

Australia in this way: "As it was, Japan suffered from the worst of two worlds. MacArthur came to Australia at the same time a crack Australian infantry division arrived from Europe."[34]

At Adelaide, MacArthur's party changed to a standard-gauge railroad and made grateful use of a private coach sent for them by an Australian railroad official. While this improved spirits, the arrival of MacArthur's deputy chief of staff, Brigadier General Richard Marshall, brought bad news. He had flown to Melbourne aboard Hurley's plane to gather information on what American troops were in the country and their location. Meeting his boss in Adelaide, Marshall explained that the army they all expected to be awaiting MacArthur's arrival was virtually nonexistent. There was no great American troop concentration. Instead, Marshall reported, there were less than twenty-five thousand American soldiers in the entire country. Making matters worse, he told MacArthur there were "no infantry or tanks; only two National Guard Coast Artillery antiaircraft regiments, a regiment or two of field artillery, and two regiments of engineers and some scattered Air Corps personnel." The total number of Allied planes was 250, but fewer than 100 were actually serviceable at the moment. The only trained combat troops in all of Australia was a single brigade—less than 7,000 men—from the Australian 6th Division, which had returned from North Africa. In addition, the February 27 Battle of the Java Sea had left the greater part of the Allied naval forces in the area destroyed.[35]

MacArthur's knees buckled a bit under the weight of this news and the realization that he had left three times as many troops, all combat experienced, trapped on Bataan and Corregidor. "God have mercy on us," he mumbled as he turned away from Marshall. As his new train sped toward Melbourne, the general spent most of the night pacing back and forth in his car, planning how he was going to create an army and liberate the Philippines, while Jean struggled to get him to rest. "It was," he later said, "the greatest shock and surprise of the whole damn war."[36]

Speaking later of those dark hours, speeding toward Melbourne and an army that did not exist, Jean told a friend that the news made Douglas "a lonely, angry man."[37]

One can only imagine how MacArthur felt while pacing the railroad car. In his heart, he knew many would view his evacuation from Corregidor as abandoning his troops, even though he had done so reluctantly and as ordered by his commander in chief. For long weeks, officials in Washington had been promising, or at the least intimating, that help was on the way, and he had passed that optimistic news to his troops, but he now realized it would never come. Washington had just wanted him and his army to keep the enemy occupied for as long as possible until they were killed or taken prisoner. Then had come vague promises of an army assembling in Australia that could be used to retake the Philippines. The truth was, he did not have enough actual combat troops to defend even one Australian port if the Japanese invaded, much less liberate the Philippines.

Winston Churchill nearly made the situation even worse for MacArthur. While the 6th and 7th Australian Divisions were being convoyed across the Indian Ocean and back to Australia, as Churchill, Roosevelt, and Curtin had agreed, in exchange for the American general, the British PM violated the agreement. He unilaterally ordered the ships carrying the 7th Division to change course and head to Burma to aid in the defense of Rangoon. When Curtin learned of this, he countermanded Churchill's instructions and ordered the ships to Australia. British historian Max Hastings agreed with Curtin. "The Australians, fine and experienced soldiers though they were, could not have turned the tide in a doomed campaign."[38]

Seventy-two hours after departing from Alice Springs, MacArthur's train arrived at Melbourne's Spencer Street Station a few minutes before ten on the sunny morning of Saturday, March 21, 1942. The *New York Times* described the greeting he received from the Australians as "a tumultuous welcome."[39]

At the station to greet the new commander was a party of Australian government officials and military officers. Heading the delegation was Army Minister and Deputy Prime Minister Francis M. Forde. The military men were "resplendent in gold braid" and a bit taken aback when MacArthur stepped off the train in plain khakis, his "old bush jacket" hiding the stars on his shirt collar, the only indication he was actually an officer. American journalist John Hersey wrote that among the well-turned-out, high-ranking Australian officers, MacArthur "looked like business."[40]

The American general wasted no time demonstrating to the highest-ranking Australian official present that he in fact meant business. He told Forde that although things looked "black" at the moment, he was "absolutely confident that with the backing and cooperation of the government and people of my country, and the wholehearted support and cooperation of the government and people of Australia, in the very near future naval vessels and airplanes, fighting personnel and weapons of war will be in Australian waters."[41]

In a sense, MacArthur and the Australian leadership were whistling past the graveyard. The general hoped the Australians might influence Washington to begin immediately sending men and supplies to the country so that he could start organizing his forces. The Australians, as Forde later explained, believed that "MacArthur was the man who would influence his government along the right lines."[42]

A cordon of Victoria state constables surrounded MacArthur's party as they detrained. Some five to six thousand people crowded the outer ring of the platform, from which the Australian police had barred them, and cheered as they caught sight of the man they all hoped would save Australia from the Japanese.

Before departing the station, MacArthur made a brief statement for the 60 correspondents gathered behind the constables and 360 American soldiers, some of whom were actually Filipinos flown earlier to Australia to have their wounds treated. An Australian Broadcasting Company microphone picked up his comments and broadcast them to radio sets across the vast country. "I am glad indeed to be in immediate cooperation with the Australian soldier. I know him well from World War days and admire him greatly. I have every confidence in the ultimate success of our joint cause." He then explained that success required more than personal courage and a willingness to die. It required, he said, "sufficient troops and sufficient material to meet the known strength of the potential enemy."[43]

MacArthur was clearly making a plea to the governments in Washington and London to not abandon him there in favor of their "Europe first" policy, which called for a defensive holding action against Japan while the majority of American resources were devoted to fighting Germany. One reason it did not turn out quite as Churchill and Roosevelt expected was that over the next few years, MacArthur and his supporters in the American Congress never ceased pressuring Roosevelt, both privately and publicly, for additional resources to fight an aggressive offensive campaign against the Japanese.

Among the journalists at the station was John Lardner, who described the effect MacArthur had on the officials, soldiers, and reporters forming a semicircle around the general as mystical. "More than a record, military or otherwise, goes to form this effect. There is a facile but genuine magic in such men. There is magic in MacArthur."[44]

Press reports indicated thirty thousand people lined the streets of Melbourne, cheering and waving small American flags as a military escort drove MacArthur to the Menzies Hotel.

An Australian war correspondent claimed, "The arrival of MacArthur has done more to lift morale on the mainland than anything else that has happened in this war."[45]

The *Melbourne Herald* celebrated the arrival of the man many Australians saw as their "national savior." It opined that the "United States would not send its greatest contemporary soldier to a secondary war zone, and the fact that it regards Australia as a sphere of supreme importance is by far the most heartening circumstances which the Commonwealth Ministers have encountered since Japan's entry into the war."[46]

Unfortunately, the Melbourne paper was incorrect. As far as Washington was concerned, Australia was simply a backwater that could be used to stop or slow the Japanese advance while the newly formed United Nations focused on the primary task of fighting Germany. More than ten thousand miles from Washington, MacArthur's influence on war policy was limited, even though most of the public and many members of both parties in Congress clamored to have him put in charge of the entire war. Prime Minister Curtin had even less influence. His statement in December altering Australia's relationship with Britain in favor of the United States had angered Roosevelt, who thought it "smacked of panic" and was an attempt to subvert the "Europe first" policy.

The MacArthur magic carried over to his meeting with Curtin. On March 26, MacArthur's escort drove him to the Australian capital of Canberra to meet Curtin and his government. After spending a few minutes together alone, they quickly came to not only like and respect each other but also to agree on how they were going to fight their war. Leaving Curtin's office to meet with the Advisory War Council, MacArthur put an arm around the prime minister's shoulder and said, "Mr. Prime Minister, we two, you and I, will see this thing through together. We can do it and we will do it. You take care of the rear and I will handle the front."[47]

MacArthur, who generally did not befriend politicians, had found one he could like and trust. As for the prime minister, he had found the experienced military leader he had sought, and was willing to turn over to him all his country's resources to fight the Japanese.

Following his meeting with Curtin, MacArthur met with the Australian Advisory War Council, where he expressed his opinion that the Japanese would not invade Australia because he doubted they had the available troops for such a large undertaking, considering their commitments elsewhere. He predicted they would attempt to seize airfields in New Guinea from which they could raid Australian cities, but as for an actual invasion, the "spoils [from occupying the vast empty reaches of northern Australia] are not sufficient to warrant the risk."[48]

That evening at an official banquet in MacArthur's honor sponsored by the prime minister at Government House, the general was treated like a conquering hero. The assembled dignitaries cheered when the American ambassador, Nelson T. Johnson, rose to read a cable he had received a few hours earlier from Washington announcing that MacArthur was to finally receive his country's highest recognition, the Medal of Honor. The citation accompanying the award, written by George

Marshall himself, read: "For conspicuous leadership in preparing the Philippine Islands to resist conquest, for gallantry and intrepidity above and beyond the call of duty in action against invading Japanese forces, and for heroic conduct of defensive and offensive operations on the Bataan Peninsula. He mobilized, trained, and led an army which has received world acclaim for its gallant defense against tremendous superiority of enemy forces in men and arms. His utter disregard of personal danger under heavy fire and aerial bombardment, his calm judgment in each crisis, inspired his troops, galvanized the spirit of resistance of the Filipino people, and confirmed the faith of the American people in their Armed Forces."[49]

Clearly affected by the award and the response to it by the Australian officials present, MacArthur rose to toast his hosts. He was, he said, "deeply moved by the warmth of greeting extended to me by all of Australia. Although this is my first trip to Australia, I already feel at home." He then explained his war goal directly: "There can be no compromise." He added slowly and emotionally, "We shall win or we shall die, and to this end I pledge you the full resources of all the mighty power of my country and all the blood of my countrymen."[50]

Unfortunately, MacArthur's pledge of the "full resources" of the United States to defend Australia and defeat the Japanese was in opposition to official policy in Washington. He had still to battle the "Europe first" policy agreed to by Roosevelt and Churchill. What they did not count on was that MacArthur was not about to fight a defensive holding action against the Japanese while U.S. resources were shipped across the Atlantic. In the coming months, he would use every communication, whether written or in meetings with visiting Americans, to request more men, more ammunition, more ships, and more planes to fight an aggressive war.

With little on hand with which to fight, MacArthur wanted and needed everything. Perhaps more than anything, he wanted pilots and aircraft, both fighters and bombers. Despite being an infantry officer, he recognized the value of airpower. As early as 1931, he told the secretary of war: "The next war is certain to be one of maneuver and movement. . . . The nation that does not command the air will face deadly odds."[51]

He was also badly in need of trained and experienced officers. While serving as Army Chief of Staff, he had tried to explain the importance of such officers to a cost-cutting Congress. "An army can live on short rations, it can be insufficiently clothed and housed, it can even be poorly armed and equipped, but in action it is doomed to destruction without the trained and adequate leadership of officers. An efficient and sufficient corps of officers means the difference between victory and defeat."[52]

Over the next few months, he would begin the process of requesting that specific officers he had known and respected be transferred to his new command.

———————

After his grand reception in Canberra, MacArthur returned to Melbourne, where his staff had set up a headquarters. He was a great believer in the study of maps, so a map room was quickly established. Over the next few years, every senior officer arriving in the theater was required to spend time studying the maps. William Manchester wrote that MacArthur spent long evening hours in the map room "mastering the intricacies of the continent's twenty-nine hundred mile eastern coastline, which lay naked to invasion all spring." He learned all he could about the "beaches, bays, inlets, and tides of the oceanic islands between him and the Philippines."[53]

This knowledge, and his appreciation of rivers and seas as highways over which to transport his troops, would contribute to the eighty-seven amphibious landings his forces would successfully make in the coming years. The military correspondent for the *Baltimore Sun* would later describe them as "ingenious and dazzling thrusts which never stopped until Japan was defeated."[54]

Meanwhile, Washington debated the fate and very existence of MacArthur's new command. The Anglo-American Combined Chiefs of Staff, created in January, had agreed that the Pacific would fall primarily under

American jurisdiction. Now it became a battle among Americans over what role the Army and Navy would play in fighting Japan.

The new chief of naval operations, Admiral Ernest King, decided that the war in the Pacific should be the Navy's to fight. He based his claim on the expectation that most of the action would be across vast stretches of ocean, but he was also likely influenced by the embarrassment the Navy suffered at Pearl Harbor. The sailors wanted their revenge. Dwight Eisenhower, chief planner for the Army, had his own description of King's plan for fighting the war: "The Navy wants to take all the islands in the Pacific, have them held by Army troops, to become bases for Army pursuit and bombers." King even used the term "garrison troops" to describe the Army's role. Frustrated by having to deal with the notoriously abrasive and argumentative admiral, Eisenhower wrote in his diary entry for March 10, 1942, "One thing that might help win this war is to get someone to shoot King. He's the antithesis of cooperation, a deliberately rude person, which means he's a mental bully."[55]

Throughout the war, King would be MacArthur's greatest nemesis, the two men doing battle on almost every important issue. The first was who was going to be in command of the Pacific War. As far as King and his admirals were concerned, it should be a Navy man. They disliked Army officers in general, and especially MacArthur after he complained about the Navy offering no support to his troops trapped on Bataan. The Navy, meaning King's men, never forgave MacArthur for this. As Secretary of War Stimson described their attitude toward MacArthur, "The extraordinary brilliance of that officer [MacArthur] is not always matched by his tact, but the Navy's astonishing bitterness against him seemed childish."[56]

The Air Force chief, General Henry "Hap" Arnold, said, "It was impossible not to get the impression that the Navy was determined to carry on the campaign in that theater, and determined to do it with as little help from the Army as possible."[57]

It is ironic that two rivals whose decisions would so greatly shape Allied strategy in the Pacific War were in many ways similar. Both were products of a nineteenth-century education—MacArthur was born in January 1880,

King in November 1878. According to a naval officer who studied the personalities of the two men, each "was confident to the point of arrogance, tenacious to the point of obstinacy, and possessed practical intelligence bordering on genius. These three traits, mixed with a good deal of vanity, a keen sense of honor, and driving ambition, allowed both men to dominate those around them throughout their lives." King was the more fortunate of these two "dominant personalities," from a standpoint of the major decisions of the war. He sat on the war councils in Washington and could use the force of his personality to get his way, while MacArthur had to operate at a distance of nearly ten thousand miles.[58]

While MacArthur struggled with the question of how to create an army of sufficient size and strength to achieve his goal of liberating the Philippines, the Joint Chiefs of Staff had their own difficulties. The questions of how to organize the Pacific War, and who would be in charge, brought many factions into a conflict that took them several weeks in the middle of March to resolve. Many observers expected the result would be a unity of command under one commander in chief for all forces in the Pacific, similar to what later occurred in Europe. The obvious choice for the post was the most senior officer in the Pacific, and the one with the most experience fighting the Japanese, General Douglas MacArthur.

Chief of Staff General Marshall, the man in charge of organizing the war for the United States, made his feelings on the subject of a unified command known in late December 1941. On Christmas Day, he told a meeting of the British and American chiefs of staff, "I am convinced that there must be one man in command of the entire theater—air, ground, and ships. Human frailties are such that there would be emphatic unwillingness to place portions of troops under another service. If we make a plan for unified command now, it will solve nine-tenths of our troubles."[59]

The Navy would not agree. Admiral King took the position that since the Pacific War would be primarily a naval war, the supreme commander should be a Navy officer. The thought of turning over control of his precious aircraft carriers to MacArthur, or any other Army officer, was anathema.[60]

The Army's position, as explained by one historian, was "dead set against relinquishing the entire Pacific area to the Navy, and, in any event, no naval officer outranked General MacArthur or enjoyed anywhere near his prestige and popularity."[61]

Caught between these two powerful forces, the Joint Chiefs finally reached a compromise that went against all established military doctrine. They divided the Pacific theater into two separate theaters with two separate commanders. While many agreed on the importance of a unity of command, they also agreed that it was not practical. They gave the Army what became known the South West Pacific Area (SWPA), and the Navy the entire rest of the Pacific, excluding along the coast of South and Central America; it was designated the Pacific Ocean Areas (POA).

The SWPA included Australia, the Philippines, New Guinea, the Solomons, the Bismarck Archipelago (New Britain and New Ireland), Borneo, and all the Netherlands Indies, excluding the island of Sumatra. When Washington asked its allies—the Australians, New Zealanders, Dutch, and British—to approve the arrangement, the only serious objection came from New Zealand, which resisted separation from her sister British Dominion. It wanted to be more closely tied to the strategic planning of Australia, and wanted to have the territories of New Caledonia and the Fijis included. King argued that the defense of New Zealand was primarily a naval issue, whereas the defense of Australia was primarily a land-air problem. Not wanting to waste time arguing over this, New Zealand accepted the arrangement.[62]

On March 31, 1942, President Roosevelt signed the directive establishing the two theaters of war in the Pacific and appointed MacArthur, as expected, supreme commander of the South West Pacific Area. Two weeks earlier, Prime Minister Curtin had cabled both Roosevelt and Churchill, telling them "the Commonwealth Government desires to nominate him as Supreme Commander of the Allied Forces in this theater."[63]

MacArthur quickly changed his title to commander in chief, explaining why in a letter to Australian minister for defence coordination Frederick Shedden: "I can find no precedent anywhere for the actual title of Supreme Commander and its use for general and colloquial designation was not in my opinion intended to be the actual formal title to be assumed by the individual selected to command." Besides, he thought "the title to be somewhat tinged with military egotism."[64]

Admiral Chester W. Nimitz, who had been made commander in chief of the U.S. Pacific Fleet ten days after Pearl Harbor, was now appointed commander in chief of the Pacific Ocean Areas. The Navy divided its theater into three subtheaters—the South, Central, and North Pacific Areas. Nimitz retained direct control of the Central and North. The South, adjoining MacArthur's theater and covering his lines of communications to the United States, was assigned to Vice Admiral Robert L. Ghormley, who reported to Nimitz. The more aggressive Vice Admiral William "Bull" Halsey would later replace Ghormley.

MacArthur was cheered when Halsey took command in the South Pacific Area in October 1942. Although he did not personally know Halsey at the time, the latter's reputation was such that MacArthur ranked him with such bellicose American naval heroes as John Paul Jones, David Farragut, and George Dewey. MacArthur felt the Navy had abandoned him and his army on Bataan, and he held many naval leaders in low regard, yet Halsey was one major exception. The general never wavered in his admiration and support of Halsey. When, during the invasion of the Philippines in October 1944, Halsey allowed his fleet to be lured away from protecting MacArthur's invasion forces by a Japanese trick, he came under severe criticism—yet not from MacArthur. During dinner with members of his staff, MacArthur listened as several officers accused Halsey of "abandoning us." When he had enough of the criticism, MacArthur slammed his fist on the table and roared, "That's enough! Leave the Bull alone. He's still a fighting admiral in my book."[65]

The absence of a unified command for the entire Pacific War carried with it the possibility of conflict between the commanders. Resolving competing claims for troops, supplies, and priorities rested on the theater commanders themselves, with no local, overall single authority to make these decisions. Despite the Army-Navy rivalry, most of these potential conflicts were settled by the personalities involved, especially

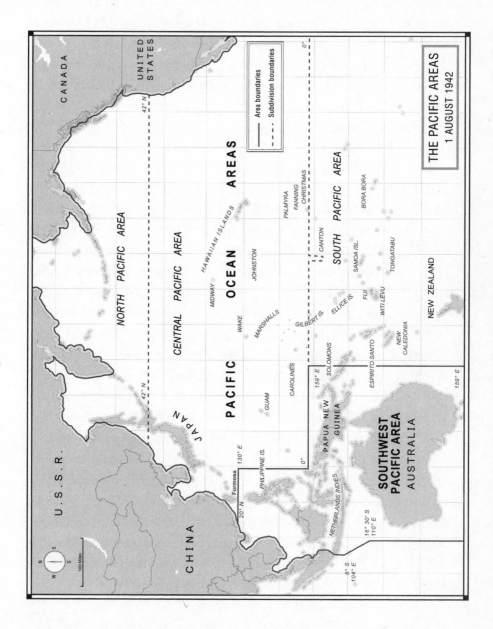

THE PACIFIC AREAS
1 AUGUST 1942

Area boundaries
Subdivision boundaries

when it was between MacArthur and Halsey. Only at the level of the Joint Chiefs in Washington did a unified command exist. This placed on the chiefs a decision-making burden that otherwise would have been handled by the commander in a unified theater command.

Nevertheless, to the surprise of many military strategists, the two-theater approach proved successful. Each served as the pincers of an envelopment of the Japanese. MacArthur's forces were the left pincer, striking north through New Guinea and its adjacent islands, while Nimitz's fleets were the right pincer, pushing north through the central Pacific.

MacArthur received a taste of what was in store for him when he learned that before he left Corregidor eight U.S. Army transports, escorted by Navy destroyers, had landed over twenty-five thousand American soldiers in Melbourne. Known only as Task Force 6814, the highly secret shipment of men and matériel became the new Americal Division. It included two infantry regiments, a tank battalion, several field and coastal artillery regiments, quartermaster companies, a radar intelligence company, a military police platoon, and even an Army postal unit. The ships arrived at Melbourne on February 27, and the troops disbursed to five major billeting areas. Most of the Australian population in the area thought these were the first of a massive American army sent to defend their homeland. They were sorely disappointed when, on March 6, most of the troops and their equipment were reembarked on the transports and sailed away. Their secret destination was the French island of New Caledonia, located in the Navy's South Pacific Area. Left behind in Australia were four thousand Americans, comprising two engineer regiments, a signals company, a weather detachment, a reconnaissance squadron, and a hospital staff. When a third infantry regiment landed at New Caledonia a few weeks later, the cigar-shaped island, 250 miles long and 20 to 30 miles wide at its widest point, had more American ground combat troops than did all of Australia.[66]

As MacArthur worked on plans to defend Australia, the fate of his army on Bataan and Corregidor was never far from his thoughts. Japanese reinforcements were arriving in the Philippines from Singapore as they prepared for a final crushing blow against the cornered and isolated Filipino and American troops.

Before leaving Corregidor, MacArthur had anticipated the possibility that General Wainwright would eventually run out of food and ammunition for his forces. He would have no alternative but to surrender. In anticipation of this, MacArthur divided the command of all Allied forces in the Philippines into four separate groups. Wainwright commanded the troops on Luzon, while three other American generals commanded troops in other parts of the Philippines. This way, MacArthur believed that even after the fall of Bataan, the other three commands would be able to continue at least a guerrilla war against the Japanese. Wainwright would be able to surrender only the troops under his command, leaving the other commands free to continue fighting until MacArthur returned with what he expected would be a large American force. Japan would not be able to station enough troops throughout the many islands making up the Commonwealth to control all areas if Allied forces continued fighting. All four generals reported to MacArthur directly. Unfortunately, he failed to tell anyone in Washington why he did this.

With MacArthur now in Australia, Marshall and the War Department decided they could not run the war in the Philippines by long-distance radio. President Roosevelt, at Marshall's urging, promoted Wainwright to lieutenant general and gave him command of a new headquarters called U.S. Forces in the Philippines (USFIP). Now Wainwright no longer reported to MacArthur, but directly to the War Department, and all American and Filipino troops in the Commonwealth were under his command.[67]

Despite the fact that he was no longer in command of the troops in the Philippines, MacArthur kept up a steady stream of communications with Wainwright and Washington. He offered several ideas for a breakout from Bataan so that the survivors could make their way to the mountains of Luzon and wage a large-scale guerrilla war. At one point, MacArthur claimed he was prepared to slip back onto Corregidor and lead such a breakout himself. Marshall rejected the idea.[68]

In the end, Wainwright surrendered his forces to the Japanese on May 6, 1942. He at first attempted to yield only the troops on the fortified islands in Manila Bay, claiming the others were under a different commander who reported directly to MacArthur. The Japanese commander, Lieutenant General Masaharu Homma, refused to accept the surrender. Homma told the American he had seen a copy of the order from Washington placing him in charge all American forces in the Commonwealth. Faced with the possibility his now substantially disarmed troops would be massacred, Wainwright finally agreed to surrender all Allied forces in the Philippines. Several groups refused, slipping away into the mountainous countryside or onto small remote islands from where they kept up guerrilla warfare until MacArthur returned in late 1944. MacArthur would manage to remain in touch with many of these groups, including sending supplies and intelligence to them over the coming years.

On March 18, 1942, MacArthur received definitive word from Marshall that his theater of war was to remain a minor part of the "global war" until Germany and Italy were defeated. Marshall explained that men and equipment for MacArthur's theater were limited "by shortages in shipping, which is of the utmost seriousness, and by critical situations elsewhere." All the Army chief could promise at this time were five air groups and two infantry divisions that were already en route to Australia. MacArthur pleaded for "one carrier, no matter how small," but none was forthcoming.[69]

The two American National Guard infantry divisions that Marshall promised finally did arrive—the 41st Infantry Division on April 6 and the 32nd Infantry Division on May 14. Originally intended for shipment to Europe, these troops had received no training in jungle warfare, and began drilling soon after their arrival. Of much more value to MacArthur was the arrival of two Australian divisions, most of whom had combat experience in North Africa and the Middle East. Elements of the 6th and 7th Divisions had begun arriving in Australia in mid-March, following their near brush with Burma. Deployed since 1940, they were given brief leaves to visit families. In addition, the Australian government had called up militia and other reserve-type units for training.

The directive MacArthur received from the Joint Chiefs establishing his command stated, among other items, that he was to "hold key military regions of Australia as bases for future offensive operations against Japan. Protect land, sea, and air communications within the South West Pacific Area and its close approaches." It all sounded very defense oriented, but the sentence on which the offense-oriented general hung his hat was "Prepare to take the offensive."[70]

MacArthur, anxious to get on with the task of stopping the Japanese and driving them back to their home islands, quickly ignored the purely defensive nature of his instructions and, as one biographer describes his actions, "proceeded to operate as if he had full authorization for a major counteroffensive to recapture the Philippines."[71]

On March 23, the fifty-seven-year-old commander of the Australian ground forces in the Middle East, the short and stocky General Thomas Blamey, returned to Australia to assume the post of commander in chief of the Australian Army. Blamey, who had served with distinction in the First World War, was known to be a hard-drinking and controversial officer who got the job done. When reporters questioned Prime Minister Curtin about Blamey's reputation and his selection, Curtin told them, "I appointed a military commander, not a Sunday school teacher."

MacArthur appointed Blamey as Commander of Allied Land Forces, U.S. Lieutenant General George Brett as Commander of Allied Air Forces, and U.S. Vice Admiral Herbert Leary as Commander of Allied Naval Forces in the SWPA. Marshall told MacArthur to be sure to include Allied officers, meaning Australian and Dutch, as members of his senior staff. The general ignored this advice, appointing only Americans to senior staff positions. Many of them were the officers who had escaped from Corregidor with him. Allied officers were included as members of subordinate staffs.

MacArthur kept up a steady drumbeat of requests for more men and equipment. At the time, his air force consisted of no more than fifty serviceable aircraft of all types, and his navy included five cruisers, eight destroyers, twenty submarines, and seven small auxiliary craft. No large warships fell under MacArthur's command, such as aircraft carriers, battleships, or heavy cruisers. The small force became known as "MacArthur's Navy."[72]

As far as Admiral King was concerned, MacArthur would never have any ships larger than those he inherited when he arrived in Australia. This was clear in a memo written by King's assistant chief of staff, Rear Admiral Richard Kelly Turner, on March 19. Turner warned that the general would probably "use his naval forces in the wrong manner, since he has shown clear unfamiliarity with proper naval and air functions."[73]

The general's pleas and demands to Washington went mostly unheeded. The president was determined on what he described in a memorandum to Harry Hopkins, General Marshall, and Admiral King on July 16 as "the immediate objective of U.S. ground forces fighting against Germans in 1942." In the same document, he expressed this belief: "Defeat of Germany [in 1942 or 1943] means the defeat of Japan, probably without firing a shot or losing a life."[74]

The White House had been pressing the British for Operation Sledgehammer, a U.S.-inspired plan for an autumn 1942 Allied landing in northern France. The goal was to relieve the pressure on the Red Army battling the Germans west of the Donets, where the Soviets had lost 250,000 men. Churchill and the British Service Chiefs were dragging their feet on the operation, which they considered had little chance of success. They wanted it canceled and replaced by an invasion of French North Africa, code-named Gymnast. Part of the American problem with the British strategy was that on May 30, according to one biographer, the president told Soviet foreign minister Vyacheslav Molotov "to tell Stalin to expect the formation of a second front in 1942, a premature pledge he would later have occasion to regret."[75]

When British field marshal Sir John Dill informed Marshall on July 8 that the British would not proceed with Sledgehammer, the American general was not above using MacArthur's needs as a threat. "Marshall implied that he would rather reinforce MacArthur's offensive, which at least was directed at a real enemy, rather than Gymnast," which was directed against the Vichy French in North Africa, not the Germans.[76]

Despite Marshall's threat, it is difficult to tell whether the president ever seriously considered redeploying troops to Australia at this time. It might have been a political ploy to indicate he supported the hugely popular MacArthur, or he may have truly wanted to give MacArthur what he needed. If the latter was correct, then his feelings about the general had come a long way since 1934, when he told his economic adviser Rexford Tugwell that MacArthur was "one of the two most dangerous men in America." (The other was Louisiana Democratic senator Huey Long.)[77]

By the end of April, with one American infantry division in Australia, another arriving shortly, and most Australian units returning from North Africa, there were four regular divisions at various bases around the country. In addition, seven divisions of the Civilian Military Forces, a militia with limited training and experience, had been activated. Available airpower consisted of three American bombardment groups (one light, one medium, one heavy) and three fighter groups. The Royal Australian Air Force had about 150 planes. Unfortunately, many of the aircraft of both nations were in need of extensive repairs or waiting for the arrival of spare parts.

Although MacArthur considered his forces—ground, naval, or air—inadequate for his mission, he quickly moved ahead with plans to gain air superiority over at least a portion of New Guinea, for it was there that he intended to defend Australia and take the offensive against the Japanese.[78]

CHAPTER 5

To Port Moresby by Sea

Off the northeast coast of Queensland, Australia, is the Coral Sea. Covering a surface area of 1.85 million square miles, its average depth is 7,854 feet, although at its deepest point it plunges to 29,990 feet. In addition to the abundance of living coral, which gives the sea its name, the sea's marine life is rich with manta rays, tuna, barracudas, whales, turtles, and a variety of sharks, including some proven man-eaters.

The southeast coast of New Guinea forms part of the Coral Sea's northern edge. Also bordering the expanse are the Solomon Islands, the Santa Cruz Islands, and the Louisiade Archipelago. Beyond the last is the Solomon Sea. To the east are a series of islands, including New Caledonia and New Hebrides. The Coral Sea's southern rim reaches to the Tasman Sea and New Zealand. The western border with Queensland includes the sixteen-hundred-mile-long Great Barrier Reef, the world's largest coral reef. Two and a half times the size of Texas, the Coral Sea is so vast, and has so few navigational hazards, that huge fleets of warships can sail through it without seeing one another. This is precisely what happened in May 1942, when Japanese forces attempted to use the sea as a gateway to invade Port Moresby on the southwest coast of New Guinea.

The war plan the Japanese developed in November 1941 included the invasion and occupation of New Britain, with the intent to use Rabaul as a defense perimeter to assure the security of their South Pacific base at Truk. The Japanese knew that if Rabaul remained in Australian hands, it would make Truk vulnerable to air attack.

Following the successful occupations of New Britain and New Ireland, the planners at Imperial General Headquarters had decided the perimeter should be extended farther to include Port Moresby. They had two reasons for this. The first was to isolate Australia from the United States. Planners recognized that Australia could serve as the Allied base for counteroffensive operations against Japanese positions, especially in the resource-rich Dutch East Indies, where most of the world's rubber supply existed. The area also held huge quantities of oil, which could fuel Japanese bombers flying out of airfields at Port Moresby to threaten cities in northeastern Australia. The second reason was that Rabaul was within bombing range of Port Moresby; if the Allies expanded the airfields there, they would be able to attack Rabaul almost at will.[1]

As we have seen, Allied aircraft had already conducted several successful bombing raids on Rabaul and on the Japanese beachheads at Lae and Salamaua from Port Moresby. To assure the security of these sites, Japanese strategists insisted that Port Moresby had to be captured.[2]

The first step to taking control of Port Moresby was to soften up what defenses the Allies had in place. On February 3, eight Type 97 flying boat bombers of the Yokohama Air Corps left Rabaul and bombed Port Moresby between one thirty and two a.m. While the raid caused only minor damage and resulted in a single death, the population was so terrified that the Japanese would soon be invading that it began fleeing the town. One journalist reported, "The road from Moresby to Porebada village is black with a long line of refugees heading out of town and heading with such speed that a path of dust hangs constantly over the road."[3] The next night a second raid by five flying boats did additional damage. Tension mounted in the town as more raids were expected.[4]

Bomber raids on Port Moresby would continue on an irregular basis over the next few weeks. The garrison there, which was small and composed almost exclusively of Australian reserve forces, having learned what happened when Australian troops withdrew from Rabaul with only minimal supplies, moved food and ammunition out of town to a nearby gorge that they expected could be easily defended for a prolonged time against a larger force. This would be their fallback position if the Japanese successfully invaded the town.[5]

The bombing raids on Port Moresby were a sideshow and holding action, intended to keep the Allies from building up the town's defenses until the Imperial General Headquarters could sort out a dispute between the army and navy over the next step in what had been until now a surprisingly successful campaign to expand the empire southward. From early on, the navy wanted to invade Australia. The army opposed this, taking the position that the Imperial Army lacked enough troops to occupy the entire continent. In the words of Army Chief of Staff General Hajime Sugiyama, "If we take only part of Australia, it could lead to a war of attrition and escalate into total war."[6]

In December 1941 the Imperial Navy General Staff had insisted on the occupation of strategically important locales in northern and northeastern Australia. The army countered that what was needed was to strengthen the defensive perimeter against the growing Allied threat in Australia by capturing Port Moresby, the Solomon Islands (mainly Tulagi), and several other islands along the route between North America, Hawaii, and Australia. The army's approach was to isolate Australia and force it to withdraw from the war and take a neutral position. The ease with which Rabaul fell and the bombing raids on Darwin convinced army leaders that Australia had little with which to defend itself. Better to let Australia withdraw from the war and give the Army, which was already stretched thin, time to consolidate its territorial victories.

A member of the Navy Ministry, Captain Ishikawa Shingo, explained the navy's position: "There will be no security for the Greater East Asia Co-Prosperity Sphere unless we make Australia the main target in stage two of our basic war plan and annihilate it as a base for the American counteroffensive."[7]

The officers who headed the planning section of each service made clear their differing views concerning Australia. The Army's Major General Tanaka: "Blinded by victory, our onslaught in the Pacific is getting dangerous. We must realize our limits in the Pacific offensive." The Navy's Captain Tomioka: "War operations' first stage had gone according to schedule . . . As we were moving to stage two, what I worried about most, was Australia."[8]

The generals had a powerful ally in Admiral Isoroku Yamamoto, commander in chief of the Combined Fleet, the operational arm of the Imperial Navy. Yamamoto, the man who had led the attack on Pearl Harbor, was concerned about the continued existence of the American aircraft carriers he had missed on December 7. He wanted to focus Japan's efforts eastward, to Midway and Hawaii, hoping to capture both U.S. possessions in the near future and lure the American fleet into a final "decisive battle" that would destroy it.

Yamamoto's opposition was important, for he controlled most of Japan's warships. He refused to release any of his vessels for use in the South Pacific except for the capture of Port Moresby and Tulagi in the Solomons. He considered plans to invade New Caledonia, Samoa, and Fiji as "folly" because these islands would be too difficult to defend once occupied. In addition, their use for cutting supply lines with America would be limited since Yamamoto fully expected the U.S. Navy to find other routes to Australia. He was also adamantly opposed an attempt to invade Australia. The admiral considered such a venture a waste of manpower that would not contribute to ending the war before the industrial might of the United States began producing ships and planes that would rapidly outpace Japan's manufacturing ability.[9]

The debate over invading Australia continued through February and March. At one conference an army officer, Colonel Takushiro Hattori, ridiculed Navy captain Tomioka's planned use of five army divisions to invade the vast continent: the army simply did not have enough troops for such a task. Hattori claimed that the main body of the Combined Fleet plus a dozen army divisions would be required for any chance of success. When the naval officer pressed further, Colonel Hattori picked up a cup and said, "The tea in this cup represents our total strength." He then spilled the tea on the floor. "You see it goes just so far. If your plan is approved, I will resign."[10]

Of great importance, Prime Minister Hideki Tojo, also an army general, agreed with the army position concerning Australia.

Finally, on March 13, an Imperial Liaison Conference presented the emperor with a plan titled "Fundamental Outline of Recommendations for Future War Leadership." Although the option of invading Australia still existed, it had been relegated to a far back burner. Serious consideration to such an invasion ended with the emperor's approval of this document.[11]

While these discussions were taking place, the U.S. Navy and Army were preparing a joint operation that would shake the Japanese military, especially the Navy, to its very core. A carrier task force commanded by Admiral Halsey was sailing across the Pacific with a plan to attack the Japanese Home Islands. Aboard the carrier *Hornet* were sixteen Army B-25 Mitchell bombers. The crews for these land-based aircraft, led by Lieutenant Colonel James Doolittle, had spent three weeks at an Army Air Force base learning how to take their four-engine medium bombers off from runways just 450 feet long, instead of the usual 1,200 to 1,500 feet the aircraft required.

On April 1, cranes at the Naval Air Station Alameda in California loaded the sixteen bombers onto the *Hornet*'s deck, and the carrier left the following day to meet Halsey's task force north of Hawaii. The task force included the carrier *Enterprise*, whose fighters and scout planes provided air cover for the operation since the *Hornet*'s aircraft were stored below to make room for the Army bombers. On April 17, the task force's oilers refueled the two carriers and four cruisers and withdrew to the east, along with the task force destroyers. The carriers and cruisers dashed west into enemy waters at twenty knots, intending to get within 450 miles of Tokyo before launching the bombers.

Still eight hundred miles east of Tokyo, several Japanese patrol boats on picket duty sighted the American ships. Cruiser gunfire sank the patrol boats, but not before they sent warning broadcasts to Tokyo. Japanese officials decided they had time to react to this incursion, since the enemy ships were well beyond the range for carrier-based aircraft. They did not count on the longer-range Mitchells reaching their targets. At about noon on April 18, the raiders bombed military and industrial sites in Tokyo, Yokohama, and four other cities. The surprise was so complete that they faced only minor opposition from antiaircraft and enemy fighters. The bombers shot down six defending fighters.

Although the raid did not inflict extensive physical damage, it had a huge impact. In the United States, public and military morale received a much-needed lift. In Japan, officials bemoaned the Navy's inability to protect the Home Islands from an attack that might have killed the emperor himself. Perhaps hardest hit by the raid was Yamamoto, who saw himself as the protector of the nation and the emperor. He was now more determined than ever to confront the American fleet in a final battle, expecting his forces to win. He insisted more than previously that the only way the Combined Fleet could protect Japan from future raids was by capturing the island of Midway and using it as a launching pad for the capture of the Hawaiian Islands. He intended to drive whatever was left of the U.S. fleet out of the central Pacific.

Both the naval staff and the army staff opposed Yamamoto's plan for an attack on Midway. A primary objection of both was that the mission would take place without the support of land-based aircraft, something that had played a significant role in all operations other than the attack on Pearl Harbor. Both staffs finally gave in when Yamamoto threatened to resign. The navy agreed to support his assault on Midway, but only after the Port Moresby operation. Yamamoto acquiesced. The army agreed because Midway would require at most one regiment of army troops.[12]

The planned capture of Port Moresby, originally scheduled for late May, was now moved up several weeks. The advanced date would give the ships loaned to the Port Moresby operation by the Combined Fleet time to resupply and return to the fleet, making them available on the date set for Yamamoto's "decisive battle" at Midway, June 5.

Operation MO—the code name for the Port Moresby invasion—had three primary objectives. First was the invasion and occupation of Tulagi, an island in the southern Solomons across a narrow strait from Guadalcanal. Tulagi had a harbor ideally suited as a seaplane base, from which planes could help defend Rabaul from attack. Second was the establishment of seaplane bases at several of the tiny islands and reefs comprising the Deboyne Islands, off the east coast of New Guinea. Flying boats at these two locations would be responsible for patrolling deep into the Coral Sea, watching for enemy ships. Third was the invasion and capture of the primary target, Port Moresby.

Although Port Moresby had been bombed in February, the Allies first became aware of Japanese plans to capture the town on April 24. U.S. Navy code breakers reported that the Combined Fleet had ended its operations in the Indian Ocean, and was heading back to the Pacific. They learned that five large carriers would return to Japan for refitting, but two would be available for action in the South Pacific. At about the same time, a decoded message sent by the port director at Truk reported that four heavy cruisers only recently arrived at the base had departed, and were heading in a southerly direction.[13]

Meanwhile, British code breakers in Ceylon learned that two aircraft carriers from Vice Admiral Nagumo's First Carrier Striking Force had been detached for participation in something the enemy was calling Operation MO. They were the carriers *Shokaku* and *Zuikaku*.[14]

A third carrier, not yet identified by the code breakers but assigned the name "Ryukaku," soon joined the Fourth Fleet at Rabaul. The code breakers considered its transfer to the Fourth Fleet as "ominous." *Ryukaku* was later identified as the converted light carrier *Shoho*. She had the capacity to be home to one-third the number of aircraft on the big attack carriers.

The Americans soon realized that the Japanese were planning something big in the southwest Pacific, but as yet did not know what. Then a breakthrough occurred when a code breaker named Finnegan uncovered a reference to what appeared to be a new organization, the "MO Covering Force." The commander of Cruiser Division Six was in charge of this force. Digging further, Finnegan discovered a reference to "MO Occupation Force."[15]

Without realizing it, Allied air forces were giving additional urgency to Japanese plans for Port Moresby. Attacks against Rabaul and Lae from Port Moresby had increased, along with their destructive power. Following one raid on Rabaul by B-26 bombers that had probably refueled at Port Moresby, the commander of the 8th Base Force wrote in his diary: "Suffered a severe raid from four English [sic] aircraft in the morning. At Vunakanau, 30 casualties from the 7th and 8th Establishment Squads, with one dead at the airfield under a torrent of exploding torpedoes. Conspicuous signs of defeat in the air."[16]

Allied reconnaissance flights soon began reporting an increase in both Japanese warships in the area of Rabaul and cargo ships capable of carrying army troops in Rabaul's Simpson Harbor. Cruisers and destroyers from Truk steamed south, and it was clear to anyone reading reconnaissance reports that the Imperial Japanese Navy was planning a major operation. The obvious target was Port Moresby.

General MacArthur was fully aware that the enemy was likely planning to invade Port Moresby, and in late April he ordered antiaircraft reinforcements rushed to the town. Yet current aircraft facilities there were of limited value. Constant Japanese raids and inadequate facilities made it suitable for fighters, but the big bombers the Army was receiving required more than Port Moresby could offer. For more than a stopover for fuel, Allied bombers were based predominately at Townsville, some seven hundred miles to the south. For added protection, MacArthur ordered the expansion of the Townsville Airdrome and the construction of additional aircraft facilities farther up on Australia's Cape York Peninsula, closer to New Guinea.[17]

Allied bombing attacks on Rabaul were also stepped up, as were raids on Lae and other Japanese positions. Commanders in Port Moresby and along the northeast Australian coast received orders to be on the alert for possible enemy landings. MacArthur loaned two heavy cruisers, one light cruiser, and two destroyers, under the command of Rear Admiral J. G. Crace of the Royal Navy, to the Pacific Fleet as it prepared for what many expected to be a major naval confrontation. Intelligence decrypts predicted the coming battle, but not exactly where it would occur. The Imperial Navy then took its first step toward invading Port Moresby. Operation MO was under way.

A powerful war fleet departed Truk and headed south toward the Coral Sea on May 1. This was the "MO Carrier Striking Force" under Vice Admiral Takeo Takagi. Its assignment was to provide long-range cover for the entire operation across the wide expanse of the Coral Sea. The force's primary objective was to seek and destroy Allied warships that might attempt to interfere with the landings. It consisted of the two 29,800-ton fleet aircraft carriers *Shokaku* and *Zuikaku*, each with a capacity of seventy-two aircraft, including eighteen "Zero" long-range fighters, twenty-seven "Val" dive-bombers, and twenty-seven "Kate" torpedo bombers. Accompanying these two powerful ships were two heavy cruisers, six destroyers, and an oiler for refueling.

The primary fleet in the overall operation was the "MO Invasion Force" commanded by Rear Admiral Katsuo Abe. It included six army and five navy transport ships carrying five thousand troops of General Horii's South Seas Detachment and approximately five hundred troops from the Naval Landing Forces. Also included were one minelayer, six minesweepers, several oilers, and a repair vessel. Six destroyers and one light cruiser commanded by Rear Admiral Sadamichi Kajioka provided close-in support. Wider protection for the transports was assigned to Rear Admiral Aritomo Goto, who commanded the converted light carrier *Shoho* with eighteen aircraft on board, as well as four cruisers and one destroyer. Seven submarines under the control of Captain Noboru Ishizaki were to engage in wide-ranging patrols and report sightings of enemy ships.

Not heading directly toward Port Moresby were two additional groups of ships. These made up the Tulagi Invasion Group of Rear Admiral Kiyohide Shima and consisted of two minelayers, two destroyers, five minesweepers, two subchasers, and a transport carrying four hundred troops from the 3rd Kure Special Naval Landing Force, and a construction detachment. It sailed under the protection of Rear Admiral Kuninori Marumo's Close Cover Force of two light cruisers and one seaplane tender with twelve aircraft. Army aircraft provided extra cover from Rabaul and Truk.

The overall commander of Operation MO was Vice Admiral Shigeyoshi Inoue, commander of the Fourth Fleet based at Rabaul. Inoue, whose flagship, the light cruiser *Kashima*, would remain anchored at Rabaul during the coming battle, was under the mistaken impression that a Japanese submarine had sunk the carrier USS *Lexington* in January. This was a widespread belief among high-ranking navy officers, although some were skeptical of the reported sinking. One of those critics was Vice Admiral Matome Ugaki, chief of staff of the Combined Fleet. The entry in his personal diary for January 15, 1942, reads, "The imperial headquarters announced last night that USS *Lexington* was considered sunk, with detailed descriptions of the situation under which submarine I-8 sighted and torpedoed her the other day. This morning's papers took it up with banners." Then a bit cynically, Ugaki added, "I hope this sunken ship never appears in the paper or on the sea in the future. The navy is not supposed to lie."[18]

The admiral was correct: the navy was not supposed to lie, especially about such an important event as the alleged sinking of an American aircraft carrier. Yet it did not matter whether it was a lie or a mistaken report. The fact was the I-8 had fired several torpedoes at the U.S. carrier *Saratoga*, which managed to return to Pearl Harbor for repairs. This and so many other reports of Allied sinkings left unconfirmed but believed was the result of *senshoubyou*, a term tied closely to what Japanese officers would later call the "victory disease." Victory in the war's initial months had come so far ahead of schedule, and at such little cost, that faith in the "Japanese spirit" obscured their ability to judge events realistically.

Added to this was the belief by many high-ranking navy officers that the Doolittle raid had been supported by two or three carriers that had to return to Hawaii for restocking, leaving the South Pacific with possibly only one U.S. carrier, the *Yorktown*, thus giving their three MO Operation carriers air superiority over any enemy fleet.

Just as the German navy had failed to deal in any realistic manner with the possibility that Allied code breakers might be reading its messages, the Japanese refused to believe it was possible that their secret communications were understood by the enemy. Nevertheless, they were—at least enough so that messages were partially decoded when combined with the new practice of radio-traffic analysis, which tracked heavy radio relays to and from ships and identified their locations. This was how the U.S. Office of Naval Intelligence was able to determine enemy intentions.[19]

What the Japanese certainly did not expect was to run head-on into three Allied Task Forces containing two fleet aircraft carriers. The main Allied group, which was already in the Coral Sea, was Task Force 17, under Rear Admiral Frank Jack Fletcher. TF 17 was centered on the USS *Yorktown* and included five cruisers (*Astoria, Chester, New Orleans, Minneapolis,* and *Portland*) as well as five destroyers (*Farragut, Dewey, Aylwin, Monaghan,* and *Phelps*). A second force, Task Group 17.5, under Rear Admiral Aubrey Fitch, had rushed down from Pearl Harbor to join TF 17. It contained the carrier *Lexington* and four destroyers, *Anderson, Hammann, Morris,* and *Russell.* Coming from the south was Admiral Crace's TF 44 with its three cruisers and two destroyers. Two oilers and two destroyers of the Refueling Group supported them. Search groups were composed of the seaplane tender *Tangier* with twelve aircraft, eleven submarines of the Eastern Australian Submarine Group, and several dozen U.S. Army land-based bombers from Australia and New Guinea.

As Admiral Takagi's Carrier Striking Force made its way down the eastern side of the Solomon Islands, well beyond the range of MacArthur's bombers from Australia and New Guinea, the two American carrier task forces met in the southern end of the Coral Sea for joint refueling operations shortly after six a.m. on May 1. The *Yorktown* ships completed their refueling the following afternoon, and Fletcher decided to head north into the center of the Coral Sea and send planes out to search for enemy ships. Fitch was to follow him the next day, as were ships from Crace's force that also arrived at the rendezvous.

The day before the Americans met, the Tulagi Invasion Group of Admiral Shima left Rabaul and sailed down the western side of the

Solomons, heading toward Tulagi. Admiral Marumo's Tulagi Covering Force joined it. An Australian Coastwatcher on the Solomon island of Bougainville provided the first news that the Japanese were in motion on May 2, reporting a large force of enemy ships sailing south toward Tulagi. A second, similar dispatch was made later the same day by another Coastwatcher on New Georgia. Both Coastwatchers transmitted their sightings to headquarters at Port Moresby, from where the information was relayed to what everyone assumed was the destination of the enemy ships: Tulagi, near the southern end of the Solomons. From Tulagi, seaplanes would be able to provide protection for the left flank of the Port Moresby invasion forces.[20]

Australian forces at Tulagi were unsurprised by the news. They realized the constant bombing by Japanese aircraft to which they had recently been subjected was to soften up their defenses. What the Japanese did not know was that those defenses were practically nonexistent. The twenty-four commandos of the 2/1st Independent Company, commanded by Captain A. L. Goode, and the twenty-five members of the RAAF 11 Squadron, commanded by Flight Officer R. B. Peagam, were armed with only three Vickers machine guns and one Bren light machine gun—this to fight off an invasion and protect their four Catalina maritime patrol aircraft. Most of nearby islands' nonnative population, which consisted mostly of Australian and British planters and their families, had evacuated on February 8 aboard the Burns, Philp & Co. passenger cargo steamer S.S. *Morinda.*

After receiving news of the approaching enemy ships from the Coastwatchers on May 2, Goode and Peagam ordered the destruction of all equipment they would have to leave behind at Tulagi and instituted their prearranged evacuation plan. Early the following morning, the Australian soldiers and aviators departed aboard two small vessels just ahead of the first Japanese landing parties, which landed unopposed.[21]

Meanwhile, with Admiral Fletcher's task force over five hundred miles away, several of MacArthur's bombers sighted the Japanese ships at Tulagi and reported them to Townsville. Word was sent to Fletcher, who immediately rushed his force north. Because Allied ships were operating in radio silence to avoid giving their presence away to the enemy, the remaining ships knew nothing of the Tulagi invasion or that Fletcher was rushing to attack the invasion force.[22]

Japanese construction crews immediately went to work building a seaplane base, joining the four hundred members of the Naval Landing Force who arrived aboard the transport *Azumasan Maru*. Machine guns and four antiaircraft guns were positioned around the port, although few Japanese expected their unopposed landing to be interrupted. Six seaplanes arrived and tied up in the harbor. Shortly before noon on May 3, with Tulagi secured, Admiral Goto's Covering Group began to withdraw from the area to join the Port Moresby invasion forces.

Following a restful night, Tulagi echoed with the sounds of construction crews busily erecting facilities required by the seaplanes as well as barracks for the naval troops. The harbor was soon bathed in warm sunlight and filled with warships, under a clear sky, with only a few clouds floating by. One hundred miles to the southwest, the *Yorktown* was launching twelve torpedo planes and twenty-eight dive-bombers. Shortly before nine a.m., the sounds of the first group of thirteen American dive-bombers, led by Lieutenant Commander William O. Burch, shattered the peaceful morning. They raced down to strike the enemy ships, including two destroyers moored together and the minesweepers and minelayers, all at anchor.

As Burch's flight headed back to the *Yorktown*, the twelve torpedo planes of Lieutenant Commander Joe Taylor attacked the destroyers and two of the minesweepers. Following them was a second wave of dive-bombers, led by Lieutenant W. C. Short, whose planes dropped fifteen 1,000-pound bombs.

Each flight returned to the *Yorktown*, refueled, rearmed, and headed back to Tulagi. In all, *Yorktown* launched three strikes against the Japanese forces at Tulagi on May 4. By the end of the day, the jubilant pilots were celebrating what for many had been their first combat missions. Because of their inexperience at ship identification, they erroneously reported sinking seven vessels (two destroyers, a freighter, and four gunboats). They also claimed the beaching of a light cruiser and causing damage to another destroyer, a freighter, and a seaplane tender."[23]

The reality was, in the words of Admiral Nimitz, "certainly disappointing in terms of ammunition expended to results obtained." At a cost of twenty-two torpedoes, seventy-six 1,000-pound bombs, and about 83,000 rounds of machine-gun bullets, the U.S. Navy had succeeded in sinking one destroyer, three minesweepers, four patrol boats, and five seaplanes. Several other ships were damaged, but all of these survived to fight another day. Japanese losses included eighty-seven dead and thirty-six seriously injured. The Americans lost three aircraft, but they recovered the even more valuable pilots.[24] In response to the inadequate results, Nimitz called for "the necessity for target practice at every opportunity."[25]

In spite of the moderate damage caused by the attacks on Tulagi, Japanese admirals were stunned by the sudden appearance of American carrier aircraft. One historian of the Imperial Navy reports, "The shock was felt throughout all of MO Operation's units, but particularly by the Carrier Strike Force."[26]

Admiral Takagi now understood that he was dealing with at least one, and possibly two American fleet carriers. Admiral Fletcher meanwhile would soon learn that he was facing two and possibly three Japanese carriers.

———

With the last of her planes recovered from the Tulagi raids, *Yorktown* headed south to rendezvous with *Lexington* and Crace's cruiser force. When Admiral Takagi, who had been refueling his ships about 350 miles north of Tulagi, learned of the attacks, he immediately stopped the process and rushed south. His search planes failed to find the enemy carriers.

The next two days were filled with erroneous reports and confusion on both sides. Task Force patrol planes spent May 6 searching for the enemy but failed to find anything; the Japanese Carrier Force was just beyond their range. Shortly before noon, Takagi received a report that a flying boat out of Tulagi had spotted the American fleet over three hundred miles south of his position, beyond the range of his own aircraft. Having recommenced his refueling, Takagi decided to take no immediate action other than sending his two carriers, along with several destroyers, south toward the enemy's last known position. The remainder of his force would join them after completing the refueling.

Several times during that same day, MacArthur's B-17s attacked the ships heading toward Port Moresby, including the covering group of Admiral Goto. When the Army flyers reported the presence of a carrier (the light carrier *Shoho*), Fletcher was convinced that the main Japanese attack force was protecting the invasion transports. He did not know that two fleet carriers were racing toward him at that very moment. At around eight p.m. the two carrier fleets came to within seventy miles of each other without either being aware of the other. Frustration ruled across the Coral Sea.

On May 7 Admiral Takagi, worried that the enemy carrier force he was expecting might slip behind him, sent two groups of planes south to search. At 7:22 a.m. a plane from the *Shokaku* reported sighting several enemy ships 160 miles south of the Japanese carriers. Takagi, along with Rear Admiral Chuichi Hara, the tactical commander of the carriers, waited impatiently for further details. Twenty minutes later the same aircraft signaled the presence of one carrier, one cruiser, and three destroyers. When a second plane, sent to confirm the report, agreed with the first, the Japanese admirals were ecstatic. They immediately ordered all available aircraft on both carriers into the air to attack what they convinced themselves was the enemy's main carrier task force.[27]

Beginning at eight a.m., seventy-eight aircraft swept from the flight decks of the *Shokaku* and *Zuikaku*. They included twenty-four Type 97 Kate torpedo bombers, eighteen Zero fighters, and thirty-six Type 99 dive-bombers (known as "Vals" to the Allies). The massive armada headed south. The admirals waited for the report of the destruction of the American carrier fleet.

Meanwhile, a floatplane from one of Rear Admiral Goto's heavy cruisers, the *Furutaka*, reported at 8:20 sighting an enemy fleet northwest of the Japanese carriers. The floatplane reported one battleship, one *Saratoga*-class carrier, two heavy cruisers, and seven destroyers eighty-two miles from Rossel Island, off the southern tip of New Guinea. When a second floatplane from the *Kinugasa*, another of Goto's cruisers, confirmed the sighting at 8:30, it caused great confusion and consternation for the admirals. Could there be two American carrier fleets in the Coral Sea, or was one of the reports in error?[28]

Members of the headquarters staff of the Fourth Fleet at Rabaul were not confused. They had heard the reports of the two floatplanes that the enemy fleet was south of Rossel Island and determined that both planes had sighted the same ships moving west. They were optimistic when they learned the *Shokaku* and *Zuikaku* of the Carrier Striking Force had launched all available attack aircraft. What they did not know was that the aircraft from the two carriers were heading south instead of north. The staff was unaware of the earlier reports from the carrier search planes.[29]

Since their planes were already en route to the first sightings, Takagi and Hara decided to stick to their original plan. Yet the sightings were grossly mistaken. Instead of one carrier, one cruiser, and three destroyers, the two planes from the *Shokaku* had discovered one-half of the American Fueling Group code-named Task Group 17.6. Parked at what was considered a safe location and waiting to be called to refuel the ships of the task force were the fleet oiler *Neosho* and her escort, the destroyer *Sims*.

Five minutes after ten that morning, lookouts aboard the *Neosho* reported the approach of fifteen planes. Both American ships were at battle stations and on high alert after one of the two patrol bombers that earlier reported their presence had dropped a single bomb that splashed about one hundred yards off the starboard of the *Sims*. These new planes did not attack, but simply flew over the two ships, well out of range of their guns. Twenty-three minutes later a second flight of seven aircraft also passed overhead without attacking. When the planes seemed to be within range, both ships opened fire with their antiaircraft guns, with no success. Sailors aboard the oiler and destroyer were unaware that the Japanese pilots were not interested in them, but were searching for the aircraft carrier and cruiser they had been launched to sink. A third pass by bombers resulted in the release of three bombs. Neither ship, both maneuvering radically, was hit.[30]

At eleven fifteen, Lieutenant Commander Kakuichi Takahashi, commander of the *Shokaku* Air Group, realized the original sighting reports were incorrect. He instructed all aircraft, except for the thirty-six dive-bombers, to return to their carriers. In ten minutes, with the other planes out of the way, four dive-bombers attacked the *Sims*, which, despite radical maneuvering, received three direct hits by 551-pound bombs. Two exploded in the engine room and caused the ship to buckle. She began to sink almost immediately when a third internal explosion blew the vessel ten to fifteen feet out of the water. She crashed back into the sea and immediately plunged to the bottom. Only fifteen of her 192-member crew survived.

The fleet oiler endured special treatment from the dive-bomber pilots, who were probably angry and frustrated over not finding an aircraft carrier to target. They must have assumed that the wide-bodied ship, known to the sailors of the fleet she serviced as "the Fat Lady," was the one mistaken for a carrier. Thirty-two dive-bombers attacked the *Neosho* from all directions nonstop for more than seventeen minutes. As the ship maneuvered to avoid the bombs, her gunners fired relentlessly at the attackers, bringing three down. Unfortunately, one of those crashed directly into *Neosho*'s gun enclosure number four, killing all members of the gun crew. By the time the planes departed, they had scored at least seven direct hits on the oiler. Adding to the damage and the suffering of the surviving crew, two boilers exploded. The *Neosho* listed to starboard by thirty degrees and was adrift, without power. Frantic efforts by crew members kept the remains of the vessel afloat for the next four days until a destroyer arrived to take off the survivors. Of the *Neosho*'s complement of 304 men, fewer than 120 survived. Gunfire from the rescuing destroyer sent the gallant ship to the bottom, with many of her crew entombed within.

Meanwhile, by the time the Japanese attackers had returned to the carriers, it was too late in the evening to respond to the second sighting to the north. The flight was short at least six planes, three shot down by *Neosho*, one brought down by *Sims*, and several that crashed when trying to land. It was a high cost to pay for sinking one oiler and one destroyer.

The two Japanese admirals could not have made a worse decision when they continued their attacks southward on May 7. The ships sighted by the two floatplanes were actually Task Force 17.

As the Japanese aircraft had raced south to attack the *Neosho* and *Sims*, a Douglas Dauntless scout-bomber patrolling off the *Yorktown* reported sighting an enemy fleet between 175 and 200 miles northwest of TF 17. The coded message received by the *Yorktown* was that the fleet consisted of four heavy cruisers and two aircraft carriers. Although an error in decoding this message would later be corrected, Admiral Fletcher, believing his scout plane had found the main enemy fleet, immediately responded by ordering all available aircraft into action.

As ninety-three aircraft sped off the flights decks of *Yorktown* and *Lexington*—including twenty-two Douglas Devastator torpedo bombers, fifty-three Dauntless dive-bombers, and eighteen Grumman Wildcat fighters as escorts—Fletcher received another sighting report. This one arrived via MacArthur's headquarters.[31]

Three Army B-17s had flown out of Port Moresby just after dawn on a search-and-bomb mission. Commanded by Captain Maurice C. Horgan, a Texan who would be awarded the Silver Star later in the year, the B-17s reported visual contact with an enemy fleet thirty miles south of the sighting by the scout-bomber. At this stage in the war, errors in ship recognition by pilots of all nations and services were common, as seen with the sightings of the *Neosho* and *Sims*. U.S. Army pilots had until this time very little training in identifying ships at sea, or in bombing these moving targets. Therefore, it is surprising that, of all the reports that day, the report from these three B-17s was among the most accurate. Horgan claimed to have seen a fleet of more than two dozen vessels, including an aircraft carrier, at least ten transports, and sixteen other warships only thirty miles from the original erroneous target.[32] What Horgan saw was the MO Cover Group/Main Body Support Force of Rear Admiral Goto, which included the light carrier *Shoho*, and Rear Admiral Kajioka's MO Invasion Group carrying the invasion troops.

Admiral Fletcher decided to turn his attacking aircraft toward the position where the Army pilots had reported seeing an aircraft carrier. This decision was prompted by the return of the Dauntless scout pilot who, after landing on *Yorktown*, was able to correct his original report that he had seen aircraft carriers. His actual report was that he had seen only "two heavy cruisers and two destroyers." Even that corrected report was wrong, for he had actually seen Admiral Marumo's Support Group, which was composed of two old light cruisers and two seaplane tenders as well as three small gunboats.[33]

In the meantime, Japanese floatplanes searching for the American fleet located the two-carrier task force 140 miles from Admiral Goto's ships and reported its position to Rabaul. The position was soon broadcast to every Imperial Japanese Navy ship in the Coral and Solomon Seas. Even Fletcher became aware that the enemy had located him. With American carrier aircraft approaching, Goto ordered the *Shoho* to launch its nine torpedo bombers to attack the American carriers, then ordered a fighter combat air patrol above the carrier and her escorting ships. Around her were Goto's four cruisers, arranged in a diamond pattern between three and five thousand yards off each corner of the carrier. Unlike American defense plans, Japanese policy was for the cruisers to be able to achieve independent maneuvering and provide information on incoming enemy aircraft to the carrier, not antiaircraft support.[34]

Only three Zeros were flying combat air patrol above the *Shoho* when the American planes arrived. Thirteen dive-bombers swept down on the target and released their ordnance. The captain of the little carrier managed to avoid them all and launch three more Zeros. One near miss blew five planes waiting to launch off the carrier's deck into the water. Then, in what can only be described as gross overkill, a total of ninety-three dive-bombers and torpedo bombers pounded the ship from every direction, with the exception of two dive-bombers that went after the other Japanese ships. *Shoho* burst into flames when two 1,000-pound bombs smashed into her. Two torpedoes crippled her ability to maneuver. Twenty-one minutes after the attack had begun, the carrier's crew received orders to abandon the burning mass. Five minutes later, she noisily slipped below the surface, taking 631 sailors, pilots, and flight crew members with her. No other Japanese ship received serious damage, and all steamed away under their own power.[35]

During the battle, fifteen of the *Shoho*'s twenty-one aircraft were lost. As for the American forces, all but three aircraft returned to their carriers.[36]

As the American planes were rearmed and refueled in preparation for a second attack, Admiral Fletcher learned that the aircraft carrier his pilots had sunk was a light carrier, not one of the two fleet carriers he sought. He decided to stop the second attack: the cruisers and destroyers were not his top priority, the fleet carriers were. He was concerned that his aircraft would be unavailable should one of his searchers find the big carriers. In addition, the weather was turning bad, and if it continued to worsen, the returning pilots might have trouble finding *Yorktown* and *Lexington*. He would wait until the next day.[37]

Learning of the sinking of the *Shoho* on May 7, Vice Admiral Inoue, overall commander of the entire MO Operation, ordered the transports to retreat north, out of potential danger. Perhaps stunned by the ferocity of the American attacks on his light carrier, Admiral Goto ordered his ships to flee north. He did not even bother to pick up survivors until several hours later, when he sent the destroyer *Sazanami* back to the scene. She was able to rescue some two hundred members of the *Shoho* crew, including her captain.[38]

Soon after, Inoue received a report from a floatplane that an enemy fleet that included one battleship, two heavy cruisers, and three destroyers was nearing the southern end of the Jomard Passage, which separates New Guinea from the Louisiade Archipelago. It would be the obvious route for Japanese ships sailing from the Solomon Sea into the Coral Sea heading to Port Moresby. As usual, the sighting report was in error. What the floatplane crew had seen was the Cruiser Support Group commanded by Rear Admiral John Crace of the Royal Navy. Crace, whose force included two Australian cruisers, one American cruiser, and three American destroyers, was tasked with guarding the exit of the passage and preventing enemy transports from getting through. With no air cover and within range of several land-based enemy airfields, including those at Rabaul and Lae, Crace was a bit apprehensive about this assignment.

The MO Invasion Force was near the northern entrance of the Jomard Passage, waiting for orders to proceed. Inoue, needing to clear the way if MO ships were to get to Port Moresby, quickly ordered bombers from Rabaul to attack the Allied ships. At two thirty that afternoon, May 7, twelve Japanese Mitsubishi Type 1 land-based torpedo bombers attacked Crace's ships. The strike was expected, as the crews of all six vessels were aware that twin-engine Japanese bombers had been shadowing them for several hours. By skillfully maneuvering, all torpedoes were avoided. Gunfire from the destroyers *Farragut* and *Wake* brought down two of the enemy planes, and three more fell from the sky before the Japanese departed. A few minutes later, twenty high-altitude bombers dropped their loads on the American and Australian ships, but did no damage to any of them.[39]

When these bombers returned to Rabaul, however, they reported they had sunk a battleship, and seriously damaged another as well as a heavy cruiser, which they considered sunk.[40]

Admiral Crace, unable to communicate with the Task Force 17 commander because the latter was adamant about maintaining radio silence, decided to move his ships south toward Port Moresby. From there he would still be able to keep watch on the Jomard Passage but might also maneuver beyond the range of Rabaul's bombers should they decide to return. From a nearby base, a Japanese floatplane that was shadowing the cruisers reported their movement south. The Carrier Striking Force heard the floatplane's report at three p.m. and incorrectly assumed it was trailing the American aircraft carriers. Within fifteen minutes, Admiral Hara launched eight bombers to search an area two hundred nautical miles to his west to pinpoint the enemy's position. When he had heard nothing of value by four fifteen, the impetuous admiral launched a second flight. This time he sent attack aircraft, including twelve dive-bombers and fifteen torpedo bombers, to join the search. Their instructions were to expand the search area by an additional eighty miles westward. The original eight planes returned and reported they had seen no enemy ships.

By coincidence, Admiral Fletcher's two-carrier task force was just over two hundred miles west of the Japanese force. At 5:47, radar operators aboard *Yorktown* picked up the enemy planes of the second group, and launched eleven Wildcat fighters to intercept what appeared to be a flight of incoming enemy aircraft. The Japanese pilots still did not know the Americans were there waiting for them. Shocked by the sudden attack from an enemy they had not seen, the Japanese reacted poorly. Nine of their number were shot down and one was seriously damaged (it later crashed). The Americans lost three planes in the fight.

After scattering from the attacking Wildcats, the Japanese pilots lost track of their position and became disoriented. Deciding to break off contact with the Americans, they jettisoned their torpedoes and bombs for the return trip to their carriers. At seven p.m., as darkness closed in, six of them mistook *Yorktown* for their own carrier and attempted to land. Antiaircraft fire from the carrier escorts quickly turned them away. When the Wildcats finally did locate their own ships, eleven of them crashed attempting the night landing. It was a costly mistake for a carrier force that was losing pilots and aircraft daily.[41]

During the night of May 7–8, the two enemy carrier forces steamed within one hundred miles of each other. Admirals Fletcher and Takagi considered attempting a night attack once they each knew the enemy's location, but both men decided to wait until dawn.[42]

Pilots on all four carriers attended briefing sessions intended to prepare them for what everyone expected to be a climactic battle the following morning. Typical of these was one led aboard *Yorktown* by Lieutenant John James "Jo-Jo" Powers of Bombing Squadron 5. A native of Brooklyn, New York, and former boxing champion at the Naval Academy, with a broken nose to prove it, Powers told his fellow pilots, "Remember what they did to us at Pearl Harbor. The folks back home are counting on us. As for me, I'm going to get a hit on a Jap carrier tomorrow if I have to lay my bomb right on her flight deck."[43]

As dawn broke over the Coral Sea, *Shokaku* and *Zuikaku* launched seven torpedo bombers to begin the search for the enemy task force. Three long-range flying boats from Tulagi and four bombers from Rabaul joined them. A short time later, *Lexington,* which had drawn search duty that day, launched eighteen dive-bombers to hunt for the Japanese carriers. The striking ability of both fleets was of almost equal size and strength: Takagi's two carriers had 96 operational aircraft, while Fletcher's two carriers mustered 117.

Flying through poor visibility caused by violent squalls and localized rain showers, Lieutenant (j.g.) Joseph G. Smith caught sight of the enemy carriers at about 8:20 and radioed his find back to his carrier. Both fleets found each other almost simultaneously. It became a matter of which side could get its attack aircraft launched first and make the first strike at the enemy. The Japanese won that race, but only barely.[44]

At 9:10, the Japanese carriers began launching their planes, sending toward the American carriers thirty-three dive-bombers and eighteen torpedo planes, along with eighteen fighters for protection. The Americans launched thirty-nine dive-bombers, twenty-one torpedo planes, and fifteen fighters. *Yorktown* launched first, followed by *Lexington* (the latter had a mishap on the flight deck that delayed the launch). Both sides held planes back to fly combat air patrol against enemy planes and antisubmarine patrols. Once all flights had been launched, the two sets of carriers turned toward each other and followed their aircraft toward the enemy to shorten the return flights of their planes.

About halfway between their own carriers and the enemy fleet, several *Yorktown* pilots made visual contact with the Japanese planes speeding in the opposite direction. With neither the fuel nor the instructions to engage enemy aircraft in flight, the Americans continued on their way, hoping their decks would be there when they returned.[45]

At 10:32, the dive-bombers from *Yorktown* arrived over the targets and circled out of sight of the Japanese, waiting for the slower torpedo bombers to catch up. The *Zuikaku* slipped from sight as it sailed into a squall with heavy cloud cover. Finally, at 10:57, both dive-bombers and torpedo bombers attacked *Shokaku* simultaneously, the dive-bombers from high altitude, the torpedo planes from closer to the surface. All the torpedoes were released too far from the target and missed her entirely. Two 1,000-pound bombs from the dive-bombers, including the one dropped by Jo-Jo Powers, smashed into the carrier, inflicting heavy damage to her flight and hangar decks. Antiaircraft fire from the cruisers and destroyers escorting the carriers blasted shock waves in the air, tossing planes around. In the ensuing dogfight, two American dive-bombers and two Zero fighters plunged into the sea.

Thirty minutes after the attack began, aircraft from the *Lexington* arrived. Facing increased resistance from enemy fighters and antiaircraft from the ships, they scored one hit on the disabled and burning carrier and headed back to the *Lexington*, chased most of the way by angry Zero pilots who brought down several of the retreating Americans.[46]

As the sky cleared of enemy planes, Admiral Takagi steered the *Zuikaku* out from under the cloud cover to survey the destruction. It was clear the *Shokaku* had suffered severe damage and would not be able to conduct further operations, even after her fires were extinguished. Luckily, she suffered no damage below the waterline, thanks to the poor performance of the American torpedo planes. She was capable of maintaining speed, but with the loss of 109 crew members and the wounding of an additional 114, she could serve no real purpose. Her aircraft were transferred to *Zuikaku*, and Takagi sent *Shokaku* back to Japan for repairs, escorted by several destroyers. Now the admiral waited for word from the aircraft he had sent to attack the American carriers.[47]

The fact that Japanese pilots were more experienced than their American counterparts at attacking enemy ships was demonstrated at the same time the *Shokaku* was under attack. A few minutes before eleven, radar aboard the American carriers reported a large number of inbound bogeys. Earlier, a Japanese flying boat had been shot down, but this force looked to be much more threatening. Soon, sixty-nine attack planes sent by Admiral Takagi were pushing their way through the outnumbered combat air patrol of Wildcat fighters and dive-bombers. Japanese torpedo planes attacked the *Lexington* from two directions, preventing her from turning away from one spread of underwater missiles without encountering a second from the opposite direction. At the same time, dive-bombers pounced. She began to experience serious damage almost immediately from hits on a ready ammunition box on her port bow and her smoke funnel.

The *Yorktown* was let in for a punishing attack when dive-bombers planted a 750-pound bomb on her flight deck near the base of her island. Several fires were quickly brought under control, and her ability to launch and receive aircraft was not impaired. Thanks to the alertness and fast reactions of her skipper, Captain Elliott Buckmaster, the great ship zigged and zagged in every direction, avoiding incoming torpedoes and bombs. Her escorting ships had difficulty keeping up with her twists and turns, but all remained on station and maintained a lethal barrage of antiair-craft fire that brought down numerous enemy planes.[48]

Pilots returning to *Zuikaku* reported sinking two carriers, one of the *Yorktown* class and a second of the *Saratoga* class. Admiral Inoue, thinking his carrier force had won the battle despite having to send *Shokaku* back to Japan, ordered Takagi to take his ships to Truk for repairs. Because of the increasing intensity of attacks from U.S. Army bombers, Inoue decided to delay the invasion of Port Moresby pending the arrival of another carrier fleet. He did not want to proceed without carrier protection for his invasion force.[49]

Meanwhile, the American task force steamed away from the scene of the battle. Despite a seven-degree list, *Lexington* was moving under her own power, and several officers expected her to be able to reach Pearl Harbor without assistance. The fires were out, and although the damage was severe, it looked as if she had survived the attack. Then, at 12:47 p.m., a spark from a nearby generator ignited fumes from damaged fuel lines. The explosion blew the forward elevator over a foot above the flight deck. Attempts to control the resulting fire proved fruitless, and shortly after five o'clock the "abandon ship" order was given. After nearby ships res-cued more than 2,700 men from the burning behemoth, a destroyer fired five torpedoes into the hulk as flames and black smoke climbed hundreds of feet into the sky. Finally, at 7:52 p.m., the aircraft carrier called "Lady Lex" by her crew rolled over and slipped away.[50]

Who won the Battle of the Coral Sea? Historians have been arguing over the answer ever since the battle took place. The sinking of *Lexington* was a greater loss to the Americans than the loss of *Shoho* to the Japanese. This was obvious. We can arrive at different answers by tallying lost aircraft and lost lives. However, perhaps the most important result of this historic battle was that it averted the invasion of Port Moresby, with all it portended for the safety of Australia and the future of the war. Never again would an enemy fleet attempt to invade that vital port city that would serve as the base of operations for Allied forces fighting on New Guinea.

In addition, one Japanese fleet carrier was out of action for repairs for several months, while the second suffered so many aircraft and pilot losses that she would not rejoin the war until mid-June. Both missed the Battle of Midway, where their presence might have altered the result of that decisive clash.

This was the first time in recorded history that major warships did battle without actually seeing each other. The fleet admirals could not walk out on the bridges of their flagships and see the result of their shelling on enemy ships. Instead, they had to rely on what we now know was the notoriously poor judgment of young aircraft pilots who habitually reported aircraft carriers where there were none; mistook cruisers for battleships, destroyers for cruisers, an oiler for an aircraft carrier; and regularly claimed to sink ships that did not exist or were not sunk. Despite the numerous reports from Japanese pilots of American battleships, not one sailed within several thousand miles of the Coral Sea.

Official U.S. Navy historian Samuel Eliot Morison said of the Battle of the Coral Sea, "It was a tactical victory for the Japanese, but a strategic victory for the United States."[51]

That "strategic victory" completely altered the war for New Guinea. Lieutenant Colonel Shiro Hara, Eighth Area Army staff officer, Operations Section, later in retrospect described it this way: "The loss of the Battle of the Coral Sea affected our strategy in New Guinea to a great extent. After the loss, we realized that our offensive assault against Port Moresby by sea was blocked. This made it obvious that if we were to attack our objective it would have to be made overland via the Owen Stanleys."[52]

As for the citizens of Japan, the Imperial Navy's spokesman, Captain Hideo Hiraide, told them, "A powerful Anglo-American combined fleet was lured into the northern part of the Coral Sea by a feint of a small aircraft carrier of ours, and our naval force speedily entrapped the enemy fleet to finish it off in one fell swoop. This battle clearly shows the faulty nature of the strategy employed by enemy commanders." He then predicted that Britain and the United States would fall "to the position of third-rate sea powers." General MacArthur quickly issued a statement branding Hiraide's claims as "entirely fictional."[53]

Hiraide made another prediction, this one aimed at the people of Australia. "Of all the belligerents, Australia is to be most pitied. The Sixth Continent, considered by many as a paradise, rose against us by banking on the worthless aid of the United States and Britain. This erstwhile paradise is about to be turned into shambles."[54]

Although his Army Air Forces played only a small role in the battle, General MacArthur was so pleased with the outcome that he wrote Admiral Nimitz: "I consider your forces in the recent action were handled with marked skill and fought with admirable courage and tenacity. I am most anxious to perfect air-naval cooperation. . . . Call upon me freely. You can count upon my most complete and active cooperation."[55]

CHAPTER 6

Second Landings in New Guinea

On February 4, 1942, as General MacArthur had remained hunkered down on Corregidor, defying the Japanese invasion, the American submarine *Seadragon* slipped away from the island and headed to Australia. On board were eighteen members of the Navy's code-breaking operation, headed by Lieutenant Rudolph J. Fabian. MacArthur would not leave his fortress for several more weeks, but these naval personnel were deemed so important that they had to be evacuated as quickly as possible. The remaining fifty-seven members of the unit were removed as submarines became available.

Relocated to Melbourne, Fabian's people became the Fleet Radio Unit, Melbourne, or FRUMEL. Beginning in early May, at the general's request, Fabian arrived at MacArthur's office in Melbourne each day to give him an intelligence briefing on whatever they had learned from reading decrypted Japanese naval and diplomatic communications the previous day. MacArthur arranged for Fabian to be picked up at his office by a military car and driven to headquarters to arrive at precisely two p.m. and be shown directly to the general's office without waiting.

The only other person permitted in the room was MacArthur's chief of staff, General Richard K. Sutherland.[1]

Lieutenant Fabian had scored big with the general just prior to the Battle of the Coral Sea. MacArthur, and many others at the time, believed the Japanese ships that engaged in the battle were heading to New Caledonia. When Fabian told him that his people had been reading enemy messages that indicated their true target was Port Moresby, a surprised MacArthur expressed skepticism. The code breaker explained in detail the process FRUMEL had followed when handling secret coded Japanese communications. According to Fabian, so convinced was MacArthur by what he learned that he immediately diverted an army transport ship headed to New Caledonia with troops and sent it instead to Port Moresby.[2]

"MacArthur was so exuberant about our warning him that the Japanese were really going to attack Port Moresby," Fabian reports, that "I had to get my admiral to remind" him about the need for security so that he did not inadvertently reveal his source.[3]

On May 18, Fabian's operation picked up a Japanese communication involving a preliminary discussion of an overland offensive against Port Moresby. The only way the Japanese could accomplish such a mission was by crossing the Owen Stanley Range. This was no easy task, as there were no roads across the mountains; the only available crossing was by way of narrow trails that could not accommodate vehicles and were filled with potentially fatal hazards. The day's intelligence summary explained that translation problems made it difficult to ascertain whether the proposed route was for an invasion or simply to move supplies to Port Moresby after its occupation by Japanese troops. The summary claimed the enemy was definitely planning an overland route for what appeared to be some vital reason.[4]

On the same day, the Pacific Fleet Intelligence Center in Hawaii predicted a Japanese overland offensive against Port Moresby would begin on or about June 15. The point of origin was expected to be the area around Lae and Salamaua.[5]

Before the Japanese began their offensive against Port Moresby, Admiral Yamamoto got what he had been hoping for ever since he had learned that the American aircraft carriers were not at Pearl Harbor the previous December 7: a decisive battle with the U.S. Pacific Fleet. The admiral knew America and its people well, and he understood that a protracted war against such a large and powerful enemy with virtually unlimited resources spelled doom for the Japanese Empire. He needed to cripple the existing American carrier fleet before the United States began building new ships in large numbers.

From June 4 through 7, one month after the Battle of the Coral Sea, the Imperial Japanese Navy clashed head-on with the U.S. Navy near the Midway Atoll, a tiny spot on the globe less than two and a half square miles in size. As its name implies, Midway is located roughly halfway between North America and Asia in the North Pacific Ocean, some thirteen hundred miles west of Pearl Harbor. This was the area that Yamamoto had selected to lure the Americans into a decisive battle through a surprise attack. Unfortunately for more than three thousand of his sailors and aviators, American code breakers had uncovered his plans. But although the U.S. Navy knew the IJN was planning an attack, it was not sure precisely where. All the code breakers knew was that the target had been code-named AF by the Japanese.

This called for some American deception. On May 21, Pearl Harbor wired the Midway garrison commander, via a secure undersea cable linking Hawaii and Midway, instructions to send an emergency radio signal to Pearl complaining of a severe water shortage. The commander immediately radioed a statement that "at the present time we have only enough water for two weeks. Please supply us immediately." The commander of the 14th Naval District at Pearl, Admiral Claude Bloch, kept up the deception when he responded that he was sending a water barge with emergency supplies right away.

The following day, the American intelligence unit at Melbourne listened in as the Japanese radio station on Wake Island reported the plea for water and identified the location making the request as Affirm Fox (AF). An order went out to the attacking fleet to take on additional water supplies. Allied code breakers quickly picked up both signals. They now knew the target for Yamamoto's "decisive battle" was definitely Midway.[6]

Meanwhile, Admiral Yamamoto was doing all he could to determine how many American aircraft carriers in the Pacific were close enough to take part in the defense of Midway. A planned flying boat reconnaissance of Pearl was hampered by three U.S. Navy ships stationed at French Frigate Shoals, some 560 miles northwest of Honolulu. This picket line of two destroyers and a tanker prevented enemy aircraft from approaching Pearl Harbor and effectively blinded the Japanese admiral as to what was happening at the great naval base.[7]

A key question for Yamamoto was what had become of the *Yorktown* after the Battle of the Coral Sea. Her apparent disappearance left many Japanese convinced she had been so seriously damaged that she later sank. In fact, the immense carrier had made it back to Pearl Harbor on May 27 for repairs that were expected to take ninety days. In an incredible display of hard labor and teamwork, some fourteen hundred men worked day and night to repair her so that she sailed from Pearl Harbor ready for combat at nine a.m. on the morning of May 30.[8]

Although thousands of miles away from the scene of the planned action, General MacArthur provided what one naval historian called a "brilliant bit of deception." Both MacArthur and Nimitz were aware that Japanese radio interceptors were eavesdropping on radio communications in SWPA. Deciding to take advantage of this, he recommended to Admiral Nimitz that several shore stations and two or three ships exchange transmissions that indicated a carrier task force was operating in the Coral Sea, far from Midway. Nimitz gave the idea his full approval, and as a result, the seaplane tender *Tangier* and the heavy cruiser *Salt Lake City* steamed across the Coral Sea, exchanging intelligence traffic with each other and shore stations, appearing to eavesdroppers to be part of a carrier-based task force. As expected, Japanese analysts listening in quickly informed Admiral Yamamoto that at least one carrier task force, possibly the vanished *Yorktown,* was still in the Coral Sea, too far to take part in the coming battle at Midway.[9]

According to one Japanese officer, the Naval General Staff believed the reports "constituted powerful evidence that the enemy did not yet suspect our intention, for if he did, he would obviously have called all his scarce remaining carriers back from the Southwest Pacific."[10]

A massive Japanese fleet sailed toward Midway, unsure of what to expect. They had no idea how many American ships would challenge them, and if any were aircraft carriers.

The Imperial force consisted of four fleet aircraft carriers: *Akagi, Soryu, Kaga,* and *Hiryu,* carrying a total of 248 aircraft. Seven battleships, fifty-eight cruisers and destroyers, four floatplane tenders, and one light carrier joined the fleet, as well as tankers, cargo ships, and fifteen transports loaded with five thousand troops. Missing were the two aircraft carriers unable to participate due to damage and losses suffered during the Battle of the Coral Sea.

Admiral Nimitz was fully prepared. Meeting the enemy were three fleet carriers: *Yorktown, Enterprise,* and *Hornet.* Together they were armed with 233 aircraft, but were backed by 127 land-based planes that Nimitz had squeezed onto Midway, including Army B-17 Fortresses and B-26 Marauders. Supporting the carrier forces were twenty-seven cruisers and destroyers, sixteen submarines, and a mix of tankers, tenders, and other auxiliary craft.

The action commenced on June 3, when a scout plane out of Midway reported the appearance of enemy ships. The Battle of Midway was a devastating loss for the Imperial Navy. All four fleet carriers were sunk, as was one cruiser. Just as vital, 228 aircraft were lost, including 121 of Japan's most experienced and virtually irreplaceable pilots. In all, 3,057 men died. The cost to the Americans was the loss of *Yorktown* and one destroyer, as well as fewer than 150 aircraft. Three hundred forty Americans perished in Yamamoto's "decisive battle." America's losses, however, were replaceable; the Japanese would struggle until the end of the war, attempting to replace the carriers, aircraft, and pilots lost at Midway.

As a diversion that he hoped would draw U.S. ships away from the

Midway area, Yamamoto had sent a small force to Alaskan waters to capture two mostly uninhabited Aleutian Islands, Kiska and Attu. The total force invading both islands consisted of two light carriers, three heavy cruisers, two light cruisers, twelve destroyers, one seaplane tender, and eight transport ships carrying 1,550 troops. Unfortunately for the admiral, American code breakers had determined by late May that the attack in the north was little more than a feint, so other than sending five cruisers, thirteen destroyers, six submarines, and assorted auxiliary craft, Admiral Nimitz all but ignored the Alaskan invasion for the time being.[11]

In an incredible spin, the Imperial Navy's chief spokesman, Captain Hideo Hiraide, issued a statement for public consumption describing the attacks on Midway and the Aleutian Islands as "effective blows dealt against the American continent, and at one stroke extending Japan's defensive waters 2,500 nautical miles eastward." He then boasted of sinking two U.S. aircraft carriers, and said American claims of sinking two Imperial carriers and badly damaging two others was "propagandizing."[12]

In a follow-up statement, Hiraide told the Japanese people, who would remain in the dark concerning Imperial defeats throughout the war, "The enormous success in the Aleutians had been possible by the diversion at Midway."[13]

Japan's leading commentator on military matters, Masanori Ito, described the "victory" at Midway in this way: "The brilliant war results obtained are beyond all imagination."[14] Writing about the battle after the war, however, Ito remarked, "So great was Japan's defeat in this one battle that the resourceful and skillful enemy must have been supported by the wrath of an avenging god."[15]

There was a bit more honesty among high-ranking officers, especially in the army. Lieutenant General Shinichi Tanaka, chief of the Operations Bureau, reacted to the defeat by exclaiming, "We have lost supremacy in the Pacific through this unforeseen great defeat." The army chief of staff, General Hajime Sugiyama, agreed. The answer, he declared, was to "choose a method outside of the Pacific region to lay low the enemy."[16]

Stunned by the defeat at Midway, the Imperial Navy was at first worried that the American fleet might plan a counterattack in home waters. On June 11 the planned invasions of New Caledonia, Fiji, and Samoa, as part of Operation FS, originally set for July, were postponed. Cancellation came two months later. The troops earmarked for these invasions received orders to stand down and await further orders.

On June 7, a meeting of the operations staffs of both the army and navy agreed that "research will be immediately undertaken to find out if Port Moresby can be invaded by the overland route."[17] Five days later, army headquarters instructed Lieutenant General Harukichi Hyakutake, commanding general of the recently formed 17th Army at Rabaul, to cooperate with the navy in devising a plan for the capture of Port Moresby by means of an overland route from the east coast of New Guinea. Recognizing the limitations of the facilities at Lae and Salamaua as jumping-off points for such an advance, headquarters ordered Hyakutake to send elements of his army to occupy another location farther down the coast near where the Mambare River empties into the Solomon Sea. He was also instructed to look for additional places to locate air bases. Earlier reconnaissance surveys had already identified the airfield near Buna, some sixty miles south of the Mambare River, as being capable of expansion into a major base.

With the loss of four carriers and many of their aircraft at Midway, the importance of Port Moresby to the Japanese for gaining air supremacy over the Coral Sea increased. The two airfields located there could be expanded for use by Japanese land-based planes over a large portion of the sea. Controlling the airspace over the Coral Sea would allow Japanese forces to sever the communications and supply connections between Australia and the United States and permit reinstatement of Operation FS. The seizure of Lae and Salamaua, already accomplished in March 1942, were initial steps in reaching the objective of occupying Port Moresby.

Meanwhile, Port Moresby was the target of a steady bombing campaign by the Navy's 24th and 25th Air Flotillas. In May alone, 403 planes took part in twenty individual raids. Yet MacArthur and Australian general Blamey kept up a steady flow of supplies and men to replace losses quickly. Enhanced antiaircraft defenses soon forced the Japanese planes to stop low-level bombing and attack from twenty thousand feet, reducing effectiveness.

Based on previous aerial photography, the Japanese were convinced there was a direct route from Buna across the mountains to Port Moresby. General Horii was ordered on July 1 to send a small force from his South Seas Detachment, now part of the 17th Army, to Buna with instructions to investigate roads in the area for the needed over-land route to the opposite coast. The troops Horii selected for this assignment had not yet left when revised orders from Imperial General Headquarters arrived on July 11. The new orders stated, "The 17th Army, in cooperation with the Navy, shall at the opportune time capture and secure Port Moresby, and mop up eastern New Guinea."[18]

By coincidence, four days later, on July 15, General MacArthur issued his plan for developing Buna into an Allied base from which his aircraft could attack Lae, Salamaua, and Rabaul. He planned to send one Australian infantry division and a unit of American Army engineers overland from Port Moresby to "seize an area suitable for operations of all types of aircraft and secure a disembarkation point pending arrival of sea parties."[19]

MacArthur began moving everything he needed in Australia closer to New Guinea, including his own headquarters, which he transferred from Melbourne to Brisbane. The American 32nd Division moved from Adelaide to Brisbane and the 41st Division from Melbourne to Rockhampton, near the Coral Sea coast. Engineers were building airfield facilities along the northeast coast of Australia, closer to New Guinea. Since MacArthur considered Port Moresby too vulnerable to enemy attack to expand Air Force facilities there, he moved existing ones up to Australia's York Peninsula, which juts out like a finger pointing at New Guinea.

During June, MacArthur also sent American engineers to work on a new airfield at Milne Bay, on the southern end of New Guinea. A machine-gun platoon, several antiaircraft batteries, and a platoon from the 101st

U.S. Coast Artillery Battalion joined them. Their primary job was to construct and protect an airfield capable of handling heavy bombers at a place called Gili Gili at the northern end of Milne Bay. This base was to secure the southern end of the Owen Stanley Range and reduce the possibility of Japanese forces enveloping Port Moresby. Anxious to protect this site, MacArthur and Blamey sent Australian brigadier John Field to Milne Bay with elements of his 7th Brigade, which included combat infantrymen, engineers, antiaircraft batteries, and a battery from an antitank regiment. All forces located at Milne Bay, named "Milne Force," American and Australian, were commanded by Brigadier Field, who reported directly to General Blamey. As soon as the airfield was ready for them on July 20, a squadron of Australian fighters arrived to take up air reconnaissance and combat patrols in the area.[20]

MacArthur's plan was to have a force of 3,200 men at Buna by early August to build airfields to accommodate fighters and bombers as a complement to the airfield at Milne Bay.

Meanwhile, MacArthur and Blamey had not forgotten about Lae and Salamaua. The enemy was flying an increasing number of sorties from these two airfields against Port Moresby, and even occasionally against targets on the Australian mainland. Unable to send a substantial force against the two Japanese bases, the Allied generals had decided early on to instead use what the Australians called Independent Companies to harass the Japanese and prevent them from enlarging the area they controlled. An Independent Company was a type of special forces unit whose members were trained in irregular warfare tactics.

The remnants of the small Australian forces that had abandoned Lae and Salamaua had regrouped at several locations in the nearby mountains and valleys from which they kept watch on Japanese activities. Over the weeks, occasional clashes had arisen between Japanese soldiers patrolling the perimeters of their bases and these men, who were mostly members of the New Guinea Volunteer Rifles. In many cases, members of local tribes acted as scouts and spies to aid the NGVR.

In mid-March, an NGVR patrol slipped inside Salamaua to assess the enemy's strength and intentions, then quickly withdrew following a brief firefight. Japanese units pursued the patrol as far as the swollen Francisco River but were unable to find a crossing. They rectified this by forcing local tribesmen to build a bridge that allowed them to continue their pursuit until they found an NGVR munitions and food storage dump, which they blew up before returning across the river.[21]

In April, General Blamey sent one of the Independent Companies, the 2/5th, to Port Moresby in preparation for the reinforcement of the NGVR in the area of the Markham Valley, some 250 miles north-northeast of Port Moresby. The valley runs west from Lae into the gold-producing areas around Wau.

During the third week of April, a meeting at Port Moresby determined what actions the Allies should take against the two Japanese bases. Time was a factor, as it appeared the enemy was rapidly expanding both bases and improving the runways. In attendance were General George Alan Vasey, deputy chief of the Australian General Staff and close confidant of General Blamey, and American general George Brett, commander of Allied Air Forces for SWPA. One important result of the meeting was the decision to form a large guerrilla outfit called Kanga Force, which would absorb the NGVR units and the other Australians in the area around the Japanese bases. Added to the NGVR were two independent companies, a mortar platoon, and an antitank battery. Kanga Force's primary jobs were to expand reconnaissance of the Japanese and, whenever feasible, conduct small-scale raids.

On May 1, General MacArthur told Blamey that he hoped the time was near to take "a limited offensive" against Lae and Salamaua and possibly even retake their airfields. When Blamey explained the difficulty of moving men and material into the area, MacArthur requested that General Brett provide aircraft to move the Kanga Force. Throughout May, June, and July, the men of Kanga Force harassed the Japanese and prevented them from expanding the areas under their control.

Meanwhile, in Washington, plans were under discussion to take advantage of the defeat of the Japanese fleet at Midway. MacArthur had made known his view that a powerful thrust should be made through New Guinea and the Solomon Islands with the ultimate target being Rabaul. Since all the objectives discussed fell within the South West Pacific Area, it made sense to MacArthur and most Army officers in Washington that the SWPA commander in chief be in command of the operation. However, the Navy, in the person of Admiral King, the chief of naval operations, objected.

The Joint Chiefs set down three tasks required to meet their ultimate objective of "seizing and occupying the New Britain–New Ireland–New Guinea area":

a. Task One: Seizure and occupation of the Santa Cruz Islands, Tulagi, and adjacent positions (all part of the Solomons).

b. Task Two: Seizure and occupation of the remainder of the Solomon Islands, and of Lae, Salamaua, and the northeast coast of New Guinea.

c. Task Three: Seizure and occupation of Rabaul and adjacent positions in the New Guinea–New Ireland area.[22]

The Navy's objection to MacArthur's being in charge of the entire operation was that the first task, at least, was almost entirely amphibious in nature. Therefore, Task One was assigned to Vice Admiral Ghormley, commander of the South Pacific Area. SWPA was to provide him with whatever naval and air support it could from its skimpy resources. At Admiral King's urging, the Joint Chiefs excluded MacArthur from command of Task One by moving the border between the South Pacific Area and SWPA slightly to the west. The new border bisected the Solomons, placing the lower half, including Tulagi, in the South Pacific Area.[23]

MacArthur was to command the two remaining tasks. Both Ghormley and MacArthur urged that the target date of August 1 for Task One be moved back since neither command had the resources considered desirable for success. The Joint Chiefs turned them down. MacArthur biographer D. Clayton James suggests that the general accepted the plan as devised, probably because he "realized that, though the directive was not altogether to his liking, it represented the first significant departure from the basic Anglo-American strategic policy of merely containing the Japanese until the defeat of the Germans was assured."[24]

In anticipation of Task Two, on July 15 MacArthur directed Brigadier General Robert H. Van Volkenburgh, the designated commander for what would become "Buna Force," to begin making preparations for the movement of troops and material to Buna. Van Volkenburgh was the commanding general of the 40th Artillery Brigade at Port Moresby, and tasked with control of the forces while they were moving to Buna. Once there, an Australian brigadier would take command.[25]

The plan was to move the force to Buna in four groups, with air cover provided from Milne Bay and Port Moresby. The first group consisted of four Australian infantry companies and a small party of American engineers. These men were supposed to leave Port Moresby on July 31 and cross the mountains on the Kokoda Track in what was expected to take ten days, arriving on or about August 10. Their first task on arrival was to secure the area and prepare for the following groups. The second group, approximately 250 men—including additional engineers, radar and communications specialists, port maintenance personnel, and a .50-caliber antiaircraft battery—was scheduled to arrive by two small ships on August 11.

The third group would also come by ship. It would include an Australian infantry brigade, along with the brigadier who was to take command, an RAAF radar and communications detachment, and the ground crews to support two pursuit squadrons. Americans would be among the support personnel. Two weeks later a company of engineers and additional ground support personnel, all American, were planned to arrive by sea from Townsville.[26]

The key to accomplishing the plan successfully was to get to Buna and prepare the airfield for fighters before the enemy realized the Allies were there. Surprise was paramount.

As everyone was preparing for the move to Buna, MacArthur ordered a reconnaissance party to determine whether a long-neglected emergency landing strip near Buna could serve as the basis for a military airfield. If not, the party was to find a location where the Allies could build one.

On July 10 a Catalina flying boat took six officers from Port Moresby to the coast near Buna Village. On board were Lieutenant Colonel Bernard L. Robinson, the ranking American engineer officer at Port Moresby, as well as Lieutenant Colonel Boyd D. Wagner, a fighter group commander; Colonel Yoder, a second American pilot; and three Australians who were familiar with the Buna area. They quickly determined that the existing airstrip was useless for military purposes, but found that a grassy plain fifteen miles south, near a place called Dobodura, was an entirely different story. Here was a large, flat area with good drainage and an excellent supply of gravel, stone, and timber for construction. A large indigenous population could supply a cooperative workforce. Robinson reported that there was ample room for dispersing aircraft and building a runway seven thousand feet long and three hundred feet wide. It was an all-weather site with good direction in the prevailing winds.[27]

Colonel Robinson believed it possible to build "a number of runways" at the Dobodura site. Robinson did not realize how correct he was when he wrote his report, for by the time the war in New Guinea ended, the U.S. Army had constructed fifteen airfields and interconnecting runways in the Dobodura area. One remains in operation today as a regional airport.[28]

––––––––––

Reports began arriving at MacArthur's headquarters indicating the Japanese were up to something. Air reconnaissance flights over Rabaul reported that on July 17 twenty-four vessels, including several large warships, were anchored in the city's harbor. Also spotted was a group of what appeared to be trawlers or fishing boats filled with troops apparently hidden in a bay along the north coast of New Britain near the village of Talasea.[29]

Added to this were intelligence reports of increased enemy radio traffic referencing an overland route to Port Moresby. One decrypted Japanese message indicated quite clearly that their army planned to land near Buna on July 21, with the intention of crossing the Owen Stanley Range and attacking Port Moresby.[30]

When General Van Volkenburgh, who was at Port Moresby, learned on the eighteenth of the reconnaissance reports concerning the ships at Rabaul, he immediately contacted his assistant commander, Lieutenant Colonel David Larr, in Townsville. The two agreed that the enemy activity could only mean a Japanese invasion along the coast of New Guinea, and the most logical place for such a landing was Buna. They had not yet learned of the decrypted radio transmissions. Colonel Larr telephoned MacArthur's chief of staff, General Sutherland, and proposed that the departure of the first group of troops to Buna begin immediately. He was concerned that if they allowed the schedule to stand, the troops would arrive at Buna too late. Sutherland, who likely had not seen the decrypted radio signal, turned Larr down. He indicated he might be able to speed up the schedule a little, but to Larr's request that they use flying boats to move the first group to Buna immediately, the response was no. Sutherland had to keep in mind that the occupation of Buna was the second task assigned by the chiefs of staff, so he had to wait at least until Admiral Ghormley's invasion of Tulagi, the first task, was under way.[31]

As events transpired, Sutherland's refusal to speed up the movement of Australian troops to Buna probably saved their lives. The few troops available would have been overwhelmed when the two thousand Japanese soldiers swept ashore.

When General MacArthur learned of the transports full of Japanese soldiers, he informed General Brett. Concerned about poor morale and exhaustion among his aircrews—as well as the worn condition of their planes, especially the B-17s—Brett sent a single Hudson from Port Moresby to fly over Talasea and along the northern New Britain coast to confirm the earlier sightings of warships and transports. The Hudson's crew found nothing.

Meanwhile, the Japanese, convinced of the existence of a route from Buna to Port Moresby, decided that the theoretical road could accommodate motor vehicles. The basis for this was an account penned by an English explorer, discovered by Japanese officers in occupied Manila, of his time spent on the northern coast of New Guinea. The explorer reported learning of a road from the coast across the mountains to Port Moresby. Though he failed to describe the road in any detail—in part because he had not seen it and was only recording something told to him—the Japanese military planners took the story as completely accurate and planned their assault based on its misinformation.[32]

Two Japanese reconnaissance flights from the 25th Air Flotilla, on June 27 and June 30, reported finding a "road passable by motor transport between Buna and Kokoda," which is located a little less than halfway to Port Moresby in the upper reaches of the mountain range. The pilots claimed to spot a ten-foot-wide road that wound from Buna for about three miles, then narrowed to about three feet for another six miles. After that, jungle canopy hid the road from view. For some unaccountable reason, the pilots' report clearly stated, "There is a road passable by motor transport between Buna and Kokoda. There is a bridge over the Kumusi River passable by motor transport to the east of Papki. This road is in flat terrain devoid of ravines." It went on to state there were large portions of the road beyond Kokoda "that are passable by motor transport and areas where difficulties would arise." It then summed up the final leg of the trip with the claim that the way west from Kokoda "is judged to be passable by motor transport that proceeds to Port Moresby."[33]

The pilots were lucky that they did not have to travel this "road." Commenting on these reports after the war, the U.S. Army noted, "Actually, the Buna-Moresby road was nothing but a native trail which alternately ran through jungle swamps and over precipitous mountains. Throughout the entire campaign the use of vehicular transport was out of the question."[34]

Based on the faulty reconnaissance report, a Japanese convoy weighed anchor at Rabaul on July 20 and headed west toward New Guinea. On board two high-speed army transports were two thousand soldiers commanded by Colonel Yosuke Yokoyama, including engineers, infantry, and mountain artillery troops consolidated into the Yokoyama advance party. A third transport carried three hundred men from a Special Naval Landing Force, and eight hundred men of a Naval Construction Unit. These army and navy troops were an advance party whose assignment was to establish the beachhead near Buna, then proceed as quickly as possible toward Kokoda prior to the arrival of the main force. This advance party was to determine the best overland route, repair roads as needed, and stockpile ordnance along the way for use by the follow-up units.[35]

A B-17 reported briefly seeing the ships north of Rabaul heading west, but lost them in bad weather. Allied aircraft searched as best they could, but were limited by a heavy mist that reduced visibility to virtually zero. The transports and their warship escorts were briefly seen about ninety miles east of Salamaua. Later that afternoon they were sighted again, this time forty miles from Buna. Several bombers attacked the ships, but with no reportable results. Visibility remained the main problem, and likely accounted for the absence of air cover for the convoy. At six p.m., the warships engaged in a brief shelling of Buna and nearby Gona.

Early on the morning of July 21, army troops landed at a place called Basabua, a short distance from Buna Village, while the naval troops arrived at Gona. By the time Allied bombers found the invading forces, most of the landing parties were already ashore. Troops wasted little time in unloading supplies and weapons, including an antiaircraft gun, and hiding them in the nearby jungle, out of sight of enemy pilots. Over the next few days B-17s, B-26s, and P-39s attacked the landing zones, but with limited results. One transport and one destroyer suffered damage, but all the ships were able to withdraw in relative safety. On July 26, more troops went ashore from a destroyer, followed three days later by troops from two transports, a light cruiser, and a destroyer. On July 30, Allied bombers sank an empty transport, and the next day turned back a second convoy.[36]

Colonel Yokoyama sent a reconnaissance party up the first "road" he saw, and the die was cast. In a bit of irony, the first opposition the Japanese encountered was not from Australian troops but rather native New Guinean soldiers of the Papuan Infantry Battalion. The PIB ambushed the reconnaissance party, but was soon driven back by overwhelming firepower. By the end of August, 13,500 Japanese troops had landed in the Buna/Gona area.[37]

The Japanese were on their way to Port Moresby—or so they thought.

CHAPTER 7

Death Along the Kokoda Track

Kokoda lies about fifty miles from Buna, and slightly more than one hundred miles northeast of Port Moresby. The village is situated in the Yodda Valley in the northern foothills of the Owen Stanley Range, about twelve hundred feet above sea level. In 1942, it was home to a small native population, a rubber plantation, and a government post, but its greatest value was the small airfield nearby. This was the only such field in the Papuan portion of New Guinea between Port Moresby and the northeastern coast. According to Australian military historian Peter Williams, the Kokoda airfield was central New Guinea's "most important feature. Whichever army held the [air]strip could fly in reinforcements and supplies while denying the same to the enemy. In the long run the army that held the Kokoda strip was best placed to win the mountain campaign." To Allied leaders, it quickly became obvious that the Japanese intended to use that airstrip to supply the troops they planned to send across the mountains.[1]

The official Australian history of the war describes the link that connects Port Moresby, through Kokoda, to the Buna-Gona northeastern coast as "a primitive foot track" used primarily by "barefoot natives, or occasionally a missionary, a patrolling officer of the [Papuan] Administration, or some other wandering European."[2]

The history then takes three densely packed pages to describe the full length of the narrow, mud-filled trail as it winds through jungles and across rushing streams and rivers, up the sides of mountains to heights of seven thousand feet and down again in almost vertical descents. The trail clings to the sides of crevices, moves along the edges of narrow precipices that fall away hundreds, sometimes thousands, of feet to crashing rivers below. So narrow is it in many places that two men cannot pass each other without one stepping off the path into the jungle to allow the other to go by.

The U.S. Army's official history claims that "the Japanese could scarcely have chosen a more dismal place in which to conduct a campaign. It often rains as high as 150, 200 and even 300 inches per year, and during the rainy season, daily falls of eight or ten inches are not uncommon. The terrain, as varied as it is difficult, is a military nightmare. Towering saw-toothed mountains, densely covered by mountain forest and rain forest, alternate with flat malarial, coastal areas made up of matted jungle, reeking swamp, and broad patches of knife-edged kunai grass four to seven feet high. The heat and humidity in the coastal areas are well-nigh unbearable, and in the mountains there is biting cold at altitudes over 5,000 feet." Along the banks of the numerous streams and turbulent rivers that drain down from the mountains, "the fringes of the forest become interwoven from ground to treetop level with vines and creepers to form an almost solid mat of vegetation which has to be cut by the machete or the bolo before progress is possible. The vegetation in the mountains is almost luxuriant; leeches abound everywhere; and the trees are often so overgrown with creepers and moss that the sunlight can scarcely filter through to the muddy tracks below."[3]

The hot and humid zones below the mountains were home to a wide variety of animals: crocodiles, snakes, lizards, anteaters, tree kangaroos, wallabies, butterflies with twelve-inch wingspans, and more than six hundred species of birds, including the five-foot-tall cassowary, known to kill a man with a single swipe of one of its daggerlike clawed feet.

Well-practiced Japanese troops and laborers began building headquarters facilities on July 22 at the Buna-Gona landing sites, installing antiaircraft guns and constructing fortified bunkers, as well as improving
and expanding the airfield that American officers had found unsuitable
for military use. A wharf was run out into the water to speed the offload-
ing of supplies and reinforcements, all while Allied aircraft relentlessly
bombed both beachheads.

While all this work was under way, Colonel Yosuke Yokoyama, commander of the advance party, sent Lieutenant Colonel Hatsuo Tsukamoto,
a martinet and heavy sake drinker widely disliked by his men, inland in
search of the road to Kokoda. Tsukamoto's party comprised an infantry
battalion, a signal unit, and a company from the 15th Independent Engineers. In all, about nine hundred men loaded into trucks and followed
tracks that led them inland. After a few miles, the troops abandoned the
trucks when the road narrowed to a footpath. By nightfall, they had
reached the native village at Soputa, seven miles from the coast. Other
than a few skirmishes with Papuan Infantry Battalion troops, the march
had been uneventful but exhausting: some of the soldiers must have had
premonitions of what faced them in the coming weeks as they slipped and
fell into the thick, stinking mud that served as their "road." The Transport
Battalion followed Tsukamoto's men and quickly cleared a track to Soputa
for vehicles.[4]

The following day the troops made it to Awala, about twenty-five
miles inland, where they again encountered PIB troops and some Australian militiamen. The outnumbered defenders had to fall back after
inflicting as much damage to the invaders as they could. Colonel Tsukamoto pressed on toward Kokoda, following his instructions "to push
on night and day to the line of the mountain range."[5]

The Papuan Infantry Battalion was one of two military units composed
of local Papuan natives. The other was the Royal Papuan Constabulary,
an armed police force that worked in conjunction with the PIB, with some
members actually moving back and forth between the two units. About

eight hundred men from both forces fought against the Japanese during the war. All privates and most noncommissioned officers were Papuan, while the officers and some NCOs were Australian, except for the PIB's commanding officer, Major William Watson, a New Zealander. A well-known rugby player, Watson had toured the United States and Canada in the pre–World War I years. During that war, he fought at Gallipoli and on the western front. When World War II broke out, he rejoined the Australian forces. Because he had lived for several years in New Guinea, working as a plantation manager, gold prospector, and trader, he was familiar with the local dialects. This led to his posting to the PIB.

The previous month, even before the enemy invasion of Buna and Gona, General MacArthur had informed General Blamey that there was "evidence that the Japanese are displaying interest in the development of a route from Buna on the north coast of southern New Guinea through Kokoda to Port Moresby. From studies made at this headquarters it appears that minor forces may attempt to utilize this route"[6] MacArthur then added, "Whatever the Japanese plan may be, it is of vital importance that the route from Kokoda westward be controlled by Allied forces, particularly the Kokoda area."[7]

Blamey passed this on to Major General Basil Morris, commander of the New Guinea Force at Port Moresby. The fifty-three-year-old Morris, a decorated artillery officer in the First World War, had served in the Middle East since December 1939, before his appointment to head the Military District in New Guinea. When the civilian government at Port Moresby was withdrawn after the first Japanese bombings, Morris became head of the Australia New Guinea Administrative Unit, the military government of New Guinea.

General Morris already had three hundred men of the PIB and about 130 men of Company B of the 39th Australian Infantry Battalion in the Kokoda area. The company commander was Captain Samuel V. Templeton, a man in his mid-forties who had served in the Royal Navy during the Great War. These were the first elements that Morris had charged with the responsibility to defend Kokoda if the Japanese approached. It had taken Templeton's infantry troops eight difficult days of marching to reach Kokoda from Port Moresby, a distance of just over one hundred miles.[8]

When MacArthur learned such a small force had been sent to defend Kokoda, he discussed his concerns with Blamey, who instructed Morris to send additional troops to protect what they knew was going to be a vital link in the coming battle for the Kokoda Track. Morris quickly ordered the rest of the 39th Battalion to Kokoda. With only one small transport plane available that was able to land at the Kokoda airstrip, he had the battalion commander, Lieutenant Colonel William T. Owen, flown in ahead of the rest of his troops on July 24. As a major back in January, Owen had led his company in defending the beach near Mount Vulcan during the invasion of Rabaul. By July 26, the plane had made two more flights, but was able to bring in only thirty soldiers. The rest had to make the arduous trek on foot.

Meanwhile, Templeton led two platoons in support of the men at Awala, who kept ambushing the advancing Japanese and fighting an almost continual rearguard action. Overwhelmed by the number of Japanese, and their superior firepower, the Australians and Papuans fought a series of gallant but losing skirmishes. When Templeton learned that Colonel Owen was flying into Kokoda, he placed Major Watson of the PIB in charge of the Awala defense and rushed back to the airfield to advise Owen of the situation. About four o'clock that afternoon, July 23, increasing numbers of Japanese swept up the road toward Awala. To the defenders, it was clear that this was not just a simple reconnaissance patrol, but rather a large number of professional soldiers who brought with them, in addition to machetes for cutting through the jungle, heavy machine guns, mortars, and even a field artillery piece.[9]

During the night of July 22, before the big enemy advance, Sergeant Katue, one of the first men to join the PIB in 1940, slipped through the Japanese lines. He traveled "for a distance of several miles and returned to his headquarters with valuable information of the enemy strength and disposition, thereby enabling his unit to take up a strategic position and greatly retard the enemy advance."[10]

On July 27, perhaps buoyed by the speed his advance party was making toward Kokoda, Colonel Yokoyama sent a report to 17th Army headquarters claiming that the engineers could repair the road to Kokoda, thus making it possible for additional troops to reach Kokoda in a four-day march. From there, he claimed, they could reach Port Moresby in an additional eight days. In its delusions that all things were possible, the Japanese official history of the war comments that the 17th Army staff "was overjoyed with this report."[11]

When Templeton arrived back at Kokoda field, he learned that a radio message had reported that as many as two thousand Japanese had landed at Buna. He sent the men at Awala a signal to fight a rear-guard action only and to begin their return to Kokoda. When Colonel Owen's plane arrived on the evening of July 24, Templeton briefed him on the situation, and the colonel sent a radio message to Port Moresby asking that reinforcements be flown in immediately. By now, the Australians and Papuans had withdrawn to a village called Oivi, a two-hour march from Kokoda. Templeton went to Oivi to resume his command. The first flight from Port Moresby arrived on the twenty-sixth, with Lieutenant Douglas McClean and fourteen members of his D Company platoon aboard. Owen ordered him to rush down the track to support the men fighting at Oivi. A second flight brought the fifteen remaining members of McClean's platoon under Sergeant E. J. Morrison.[12]

When it became obvious the Japanese planned to surround them, Templeton started up the track toward Kokoda to warn McClean before he and his men stumbled into the enemy force. Templeton was never seen again, presumed killed by an enemy patrol.[13] In fact, Templeton was wounded and taken prisoner. After a period of intense interrogation, a Japanese officer killed him. This was a fate Templeton shared with all Australians and Papuans who fell into Japanese hands: none who were captured by the Japanese survived the war.[14]

The Japanese troops attacking Oivi were the 1st Company of the 1/144th Regiment, under the command of First Lieutenant Yukio Ogawa. His men were seasoned jungle fighters who had participated in the invasions of Guam and Rabaul, as well as in the combat across New Britain that followed. One of the Australian officers present in New Britain recalled that their "movement in the bush had to be seen to be believed, because they'd just vanish! Their field craft and movement was magnificent."[15]

At nightfall on the twenty-sixth, the Australian officers held a conference at which they determined the enemy had nearly surrounded their positions at Oivi, and if they were to survive, they must find a way out of the village quickly. Daybreak was sure to bring a concentrated Japanese attack from all directions. They agreed that they met the requirement set down in an order from Colonel Owen the day before that Oivi would be held "at all costs unless surrounded."[16]

When word spread about finding a way out, Lance Corporal Sanopa of the Royal Papuan Constabulary, on temporary assignment with the PIB, offered to escort them to safety by way of a little-used trail he was sure the enemy had not found. At ten p.m., the Australians and Papuans slipped away from the encircling Japanese and began a difficult and dangerous slog along a nearby creek in the pitch-black of night. Each man held on to the bayonet scabbard or webbing straps of the man in front of him, who was nearly invisible in the darkness, so that he would not become separated. By dawn, the party had reached the safety of a track south of Kokoda. While they rested and ate their emergency rations, the men could hear explosions and firing in the distance as the Japanese attacked the now-empty village they had deserted during the night. It had been a narrow escape.[17]

Meanwhile, when Owen learned that enemy troops had surrounded Oivi, and that his own soldiers there were attempting an escape, he decided the fifty or so men he had at Kokoda would not survive a Japanese attack. Owen had secretly observed the slaughter of more than 130 prisoners by Japanese soldiers at the Tol Plantation on New Britain, and he was likely concerned that any of his men who fell into enemy hands would suffer a similar fate.[18]

Owen had his men bury extra supplies, such as grenades and ammunition they were unable to carry, at a nearby plantation for later use. He then led them five miles southwest to Deniki, where he met Watson's force from Oivi and a platoon that had been on its way there. Deniki was on the main track to Port Moresby, and any reinforcements sent from there would have to pass through the village.

After spending a cold, cheerless night camped on a windy hilltop overlooking the track, with a spectacular view of Kokoda, Owen received startling news: a scouting party reported the Japanese had not occupied Kokoda. Owen knew the only way he could receive reinforcements quickly was by air, so he decided that if the enemy was not going to occupy Kokoda, he would.

Shortly after ten a.m. on July 28, the Australians and Papuans returned down the hill and reoccupied the plateau on which the Kokoda airstrip was located. At eleven thirty, following a brief reconnaissance of the surrounding area to ensure he had not walked into a trap, Owen radioed Port Moresby: "Re-occupied Kokoda. Fly in reinforcements, including two platoons and four detachments of mortars. [Aero-]Drome opened."[19]

Owen expected that the enemy, which he knew was to the north at Oivi, would come along the track from that direction. He positioned his men in a horseshoe-shaped line around the edge of the plateau, facing north. When the Japanese came, they would have to fight uphill. Tense, tired, and hungry, the defenders remained at their posts for the entire day on the twenty-eighth.

Meanwhile, the Japanese advance had halted at Oivi as the men of Lieutenant Ogawa's company rested and awaited reinforcements that were strung out along the track from Buna. Several hundred soldiers had brought bicycles, a much-used means of transport by the Imperial Army throughout China and in the Malay fighting leading to the capture of Singapore. Yet the muddy trails of New Guinea proved too much for them, and by the time the troops reached Oivi, abandoned bicycles littered the jungle and bush alongside the track.

When Lieutenant Ogawa arrived at Kokoda and learned of the Australian deployment, he positioned his men in a reverse horseshoe, enabling them to attack from the front and sides simultaneously. He also sent a small party on a circuitous route leading to the rear of the Australians.

At some point during that day, two U.S. Army Air Force Douglas transports appeared overhead and circled the airfield. On board were at least thirty Australian troops, mostly from Captain M. L. Bidstrup's D Company, the remainder of whom were waiting at the field near Port Moresby for the plane to return for them. Bidstrup later complained about the American pilots: "The Yanks wouldn't put us down, because they reckoned there were Japs around. I could see our own troops on the ground at Kokoda. And I asked them [the American pilots] to hang around; those people were clearing the barricades on the strip. No they wouldn't, they went back."[20]

Just after nightfall, the Japanese began lobbing mortar shells into the Australian lines. This continued through most of the night. Then, at two-thirty on the morning of the twenty-ninth, Ogawa's two hundred men commenced their charge up the incline to the plateau. Shafts of moonlight occasionally broke the thin gray mist covering the area. This, coupled with the shouting and chanting the Japanese had developed in night attacks in China, gave the entire scene a ghostly feel that left the defenders spooked.[21]

The intense fighting lasted more than an hour as the defenders' machine guns and grenades cut down enemy soldiers clawing their way up the hill. Although at a topographic disadvantage, the Japanese persisted, seemingly unconcerned about taking heavy casualties. One casualty was Lieutenant Ogawa himself.

A short time later, Lieutenant Colonel Owen, who had been moving around the perimeter, encouraging his men, was shot as he lobbed a hand grenade. A half hour earlier, Lieutenant A. G. Garland, a young militia officer and platoon leader, had reproached Owen for exposing himself to the enemy. "Sir, I think you're taking an unnecessary risk walking around amongst the troops like that." Owen responded, "Well, I've got to do it." He was a strong believer in leading from the front.[22]

A doctor who had accompanied the troops from Deniki examined Owen's wound. A bullet had struck him just above the right eyebrow, penetrating his skull and brain. The doctor, Captain Geoffrey Vernon, understood that with such a severe wound the colonel had only a few minutes to live. He was unconscious, so Vernon made him as comfortable as he could.

Despite heavy losses, the Japanese continued pushing their way up toward the plateau. Shells from several large mortars located out of rifle range across the nearby Mambare River rained down on the defenders almost unceasingly. As the Japanese attempted to break through the defensive line, the fighting degenerated into hand-to-hand combat in several places. Each breakthrough resulted in the Australians and Papuans pulling back a little, until Major Watson, now in charge, decided the battle had been lost and ordered everyone to withdraw toward Deniki. The walking wounded were the first to leave, followed by most of the men in small groups. The remainder, fighting a rear-guard action against the attackers, were last to depart.

Among the stragglers was Captain Vernon, who moistened the dying Owen's lips and wiped dirt from his face before withdrawing. Vernon described the scene in his diary: "The mist had grown very dense, but the moonlight allowed me to see where I was going. Thick white streams of vapour stole between the rubber trees, and changed the whole scene into a weird combination of light and shadow. The mist was greatly to our advantage; our own line of retreat remained perfectly plain, but it must have slowed down the enemy's advance considerably, another chance factor that helped save the Kokoda force."[23]

This first battle for Kokoda cost the Allied side seven dead, including Colonel Owen, and five wounded. The Japanese reported twenty killed or wounded, including Lieutenant Ogawa. For reasons of their own, both sides reported the clash with a lack of honesty. Despite a message sent by the retreating Australians from Deniki that Owen had been killed, Templeton was missing, and Kokoda had been lost, and requesting bombing raids on both the airfield and the track between there and Oivi, an Allied communiqué failed to mention the loss of the vital airfield. It said simply: "Kokoda—Allied and enemy forward elements engaged in skirmishes in this area." A Japanese report claimed the retreating Australians had "left forty dead" when they fled Kokoda. Another maintained: "In the Kokoda area, our advance force has been engaged in battle with 1,200 Australians, and has suffered unexpectedly heavy casualties."[24]

All was relatively quiet during the next week, aside from an occasional clash of reconnaissance patrols. Both sides rested their troops and moved up supplies and reinforcements. Bombing attacks kept the Kokoda airfield out of service for the victors, so supplies, especially food, were slow to reach the men there. Meals were reduced to two a day. An Allied bomber made the situation worse when it destroyed a hut filled with potatoes on August 2. With the arrival of more troops, Colonel Tsukamoto decided Kokoda was safe from ground attack and vulnerable only to enemy aircraft. He sent most of his men fit for combat down several jungle tracks in search of a way to surround and isolate the enemy at Deniki.[25]

A company from the 15th Independent Engineer Regiment that had landed with the Yokoyama advance party began clearing the track between Oivi and Kokoda. Other engineers worked on building bridges across streams and rivers from the coast to Oivi, or repairing existing ones that retreating Australian or Papuan forces had damaged or destroyed. In all, some seventeen bridges required their attention.[26]

On the same day the bomber blew up the potato storage building, a Japanese patrol had its first encounter with an American weapon recently issued to some of the troops arriving at Deniki from Port Moresby: the Thompson submachine gun. Nine Japanese died in that confrontation, and five days later another eight were killed and five wounded. Total Australian casualties were one man wounded.

The Thompson was widely popular with the men who received them. Raymond Paull, an Australian war correspondent and historian, wrote that the weapon, called "an American gangster's gun" by some senior officers, "encouraged them [the young Australian soldiers with limited combat experience] to adopt aggressive tactics against the enemy."[27] Its one drawback was an incompatibility with the jungle environment, requiring it to need constant cleaning to avoid jamming. Later in 1942, the Australian-made Owen Gun superseded it. A similar weapon invented by twenty-four-year-old Evelyn Owen from Wollongong, New South Wales, in 1939, the Owen Gun better withstood the mud and humidity of the New Guinea jungle, and was soon favored by many Australians and Americans alike. Australian soldiers called it the "digger's darling"—*digger* being a slang military term used by both Australians and New Zealanders to describe soldiers who have been in combat. The Owen Gun would continue to be used by the Australian Army through the Vietnam War.

On August 4 a new commanding officer arrived at Deniki: Major Alan Cameron, a veteran of the fighting on New Britain following the fall of Rabaul, and at Salamaua when the enemy landed there in March. Cameron was promised reinforcements, contingent on his driving the Japanese out of Kokoda so that the airstrip could be used for that purpose. Having a reputation as an able officer, he immediately began planning his assault.

Between six thirty and eight a.m. on August 8, three companies set out from Deniki on three separate missions. A Company, guided by Lance Corporal Sanopa, moved along a little-used track to circle around to attack the Japanese occupying the airstrip and the buildings still standing. If successful, it was to hold on until other companies arrived. D Company embarked along a track heading northeast to set up an ambush along the main track from Buna to Kokoda in order to stop additional enemy troops from moving toward Kokoda. C Company went along the track leading directly from Deniki to Kokoda for a frontal attack.

When the men of A Company, commanded by Captain Noel Symington, arrived at the airfield, they saw a small number of Japanese soldiers who turned out to be engineers. These Japanese fled when the Australians opened fire. Symington stationed his one hundred men in the best defensive positions available for what he expected would surely be a concentrated enemy attack to retake the airfield.

D Company, under Captain M. L. Bidstrup, set up its ambush, which was at first successful. Soon, however, they came under intense fire from both directions on the track as the Japanese troops who had already passed the ambush place earlier heard the shooting and turned back. The fighting lasted all day and into the night. When Bidstrup realized he could not reach Kokoda, and that his company would soon be surrounded and greatly outnumbered, he withdrew back toward Deniki. It took the men of D Company two days to reach their starting point, pursued by screaming Japanese most of the way.

A Japanese ambush by the 2nd Company of the 1st Battalion/144th Regiment caught C Company by surprise as it crossed a gully that left it in the open. Among the first killed was the company commander, Captain A. C. Dean. The Australians, pinned down all day, were unable to break through to reach Kokoda. Finally, after nightfall, they withdrew. The Japanese chased them back to Cameron's camp at Deniki, where they kept up intensive fire until the pursuers eventually turned back toward Kokoda.

That evening Colonel Tsukamoto learned, to his great surprise, that Australian troops had occupied Kokoda. Under the impression that just one enemy platoon held the airfield, he sent his weakest company, along with a platoon from the machine gun company and the battalion gun, to dislodge them.

Early the next morning, Lance Corporal Sanopa reported to Cameron that A Company had occupied Kokoda with little resistance and was waiting for the reinforcements that General Morris had promised once the airfield was in Australian hands. The major called Morris on a newly installed telephone and learned that new troops could not be sent until the following day. By then, Cameron warned Morris, it might be too late.

About the same time that Sanopa was reporting to Cameron, the Japanese launched a daylong series of assaults on Symington's A Company at the airfield. The battle raged as rain poured down relentlessly. An Allied supply plane circled the field but left when the pilot saw the large number of Japanese. He did not even bother dropping supplies to the Australian defenders, who by then had exhausted their meager food rations and were running low on ammunition.

Seeing his mostly young and inexperienced troopers suffering from fatigue and hunger, and having heard nothing from Cameron, Symington ordered a withdrawal at seven p.m. on August 9. He knew there was no way his small force could stop what appeared to be a great many enemy soldiers. The men of A Company picked up their wounded comrades and kept the enemy at bay until they reached the relative safety of a small village on August 12. The villagers roasted sweet potatoes for the famished troops. A patrol of PIB soldiers met them and took the badly mauled company on a track around Deniki to a place further south called Isurava, where there was an Australian camp with medical personnel and food.

Meanwhile, the men at Deniki could look down on Kokoda and see it was again in enemy hands. On August 12, as A Company circled around them, they witnessed large numbers of heavily armed Japanese troops moving off the plateau and heading their way. The evenly matched opposing forces prepared for battle. Cameron had approximately 450 Australians and Papuans defending a large perimeter. Colonel Tsukamoto launched his attack with a similar number of soldiers. The advantage was with the attackers, who could pick where along the perimeter they would strike, like a spear driving through a body.

The following morning the Japanese attacked in concentration against the position held by E Company. Despite numerous casualties, the Australians held the line for the entire day, yet it became clear they could not hold out much longer with just small arms against the Japanese, who had several mortars, machine guns, and the battalion gun. The shells rained down on the defenders all day and night, even when the infantry fighting had ceased.

On August 14, Tsukamoto began the day with a heavy bombardment from his big gun and mortars. Cameron, seeing the futility of his position, ordered a withdrawal to Isurava. The Australians fled in a hurry, leaving behind a huge quantity of ammunition and equipment, including blankets, tools, and food.[28]

The previous day, August 13, a Japanese convoy arrived at Basabua, near Buna, with three thousand members of two Naval Construction Units along with construction equipment, vehicles, and supplies for the army troops making their way up the Kokoda Track. The convoy had initially left Rabaul on August 6, but returned the next day because of the American invasion of Guadalcanal in the Solomons. An Allied amphibious fleet commanded by Rear Admiral Richard K. Turner landed sixteen thousand troops, most from the American 1st Marine Division, on Guadalcanal, Tulagi, and Florida Island. They met with only light opposition at first. The Japanese Naval Construction Units waited at Rabaul for possible redeployment to the Solomons in response.

A more powerful response to the Allied invasion came from Vice Admiral Gunichi Mikawa, who rushed his task force, comprising one destroyer, two light cruisers, and five heavy cruisers, south from the Bismarcks. Just after midnight on August 9, Mikawa launched a surprise attack on the Allied fleet under British rear admiral Victor Crutchley, consisting of eight cruisers and fifteen destroyers, covering the Marine landings. In this First Battle of Savo Island, the Japanese scored a decisive victory over the surprised Allied force, sinking four cruisers, resulting in over a thousand deaths. Mikawa's task force suffered only moderate damage to three cruisers, with fifty-eight killed. To the surprise of many, Mikawa withdrew without actually attacking the transports that were still putting ashore men and supplies. The admiral and his staff decided that with daylight only a few hours away, and no air cover of their own, they risked attack from American carrier aircraft that they believed were in the neighborhood. Mikawa drew the ire of Admiral Yamamoto for failing to destroy the troop transports as he had ordered. However, true to form in the way the Japanese handled a lost opportunity, Yamamoto did not criticize Mikawa; instead, he sent him an official message of praise for his actions.[29]

Acknowledging the victory of Mikawa's task force, the Imperial Navy convoy carrying the Naval Construction Units left Rabaul during the night of August 12, heading once again for Basabua. Despite attacks from Allied aircraft, the convoy reached its destination the next day and completed unloading the three thousand men, the vehicles, and seventy tons of supplies the following morning. On August 18, a more important convoy arrived. On board the three transports that sailed under warship protection was the main strength of the South Seas Force. This included the Headquarters Detachment under General Horii; two battalions of the 144th Infantry Regiment; two companies of the 55th Mountain Artillery; and various detachments from the 47th Field Anti-Aircraft Battalion, the 55th Cavalry, an antitank gun section, a medical unit, a water purification unit, seven hundred natives from New Britain to work as carriers or laborers, and 170 horses. Most of these forces headed for Kokoda.[30]

Meanwhile, fighting continued on and around Guadalcanal and would influence events in New Guinea for months to come as Imperial planners kept changing priorities between the two islands. Both were vital to Japanese plans of conquest and defense, but Tokyo did not have enough troops available to fight successfully on both fronts simultaneously. One example of distraction from New Guinea was the assignment of forty-nine-year-old Colonel Kiyonao Ichiki, commander of the 28th Regiment, to lead what was called the First Echelon of the Ichiki Detachment to capture Henderson Field, the airfield still under construction by the Americans on Guadalcanal. Driving the Allies out of Henderson was especially important because control of the field, once it was completed, would give the Allies a large base from which to launch land-based bombers against Imperial Navy ships in the Solomons area. Ichiki, considered by many a superb infantry tactician, was an interesting selection for this mission. As a company commander in China, he had provoked the Marco Polo Bridge Incident, which many historians date as the beginning of World War II. Ichiki's instructions were to capture Henderson Field if it was lightly defended, or to wait for the arrival of the Second Echelon.[31]

The Ichiki Detachment, with Colonel Ichiki leading the way, landed on Guadalcanal from six destroyers on August 19, meeting with no opposition. Ichiki left 125 troops to guard the landing site and set off toward the airfield with 791 men, seeking an "opportunity for immortal fame." Each soldier carried 250 rounds of ammunition and seven days' food supply. A strong believer in night attacks, Ichiki planned a nighttime frontal assault against whatever force guarded Henderson. Unknown to him, the U.S. Marines were aware of the landing and had set a trap for the overconfident Ichiki. The fighting that ensued annihilated almost his entire detachment and he committed suicide. Fifteen of the invaders became prisoners. The Marines suffered thirty-five killed and seventy-five wounded.[32]

On August 21, two battalions of the Japanese 41st Infantry Regiment landed at Basabua (the third battalion remained in reserve at Rabaul). These tough, experienced troops had fought the British and Indian armies in Malaya. The regiment's commanding officer, Colonel Kiyomi Yazawa, had a reputation as an aggressive leader and a strict taskmaster. September 2 saw the arrival of logistical and support units, including three hundred horses, and several hundred additional laborers from as far away as Korea and Formosa.[33]

Over 13,000 Japanese troops now occupied the coast, and another 3,555 were strung out along the track leading to Kokoda and beyond.

The small airfield near Buna was quickly prepared for the arrival of several Zero fighters. A dummy airfield, intended to deceive Allied aircrews into attacking it instead of the real airfield, was also completed. The Imperial Army was now positioned to meet the requirements for success outlined by Army Chief of Staff General Sugiyama Hajime in July: "We must hold the fronts in eastern New Guinea and Rabaul to the end. If they fall, not only will the Pacific Ocean be in peril, but it will allow the western advance of MacArthur's counterattack through New Guinea and herald the fall of our dominion in the southeast area."[34]

That counterattack weighed heavily on the mind of the Allied commander in chief, General MacArthur. Also disturbing him was the lack of an aggressive air campaign against the convoys steaming from Rabaul to the east coast of New Guinea. Allied planes had inflicted minor damage on some enemy ships, while others were not attacked at all. MacArthur had never been happy with SWPA Air Force chief General George Brett ever since Brett had sent decrepit aircraft to rescue him from Mindanao. Matters had not improved when he discovered that Brett had suspended air operations for July 18 and 19, despite MacArthur's having informed him that Japanese troop transports were off the New Britain coast and headed toward New Guinea. These were the first troops that landed at Buna and Gona. Brett's explanation was that his crews were exhausted and suffering from low morale. By the time he sent aircraft in search of the enemy convoy, weather conditions caused bad visibility. When his aircraft finally did locate the ships, they were already unloading their cargoes. Several bombing runs proved disappointing.[35]

That there was bad blood between MacArthur and Brett was clear to almost everyone. When Lieutenant Colonel Samuel E. Anderson, an officer sent to SWPA to survey Air Force needs, returned to Washington, Chief of Staff General Marshall had asked him whether he thought Brett should be relieved. Anderson's response was a definite yes, and he explained, "As long as General MacArthur and General Brett are the commanders in the Southwest Pacific, there is going to be no cooperation between ground and air, and I don't think you are going to relieve General MacArthur."[36]

A widespread feeling persisted both in Washington and at MacArthur's headquarters that Brett was not being aggressive enough and was relying too much on the Australians. In addition, he had evidently formed a close relationship with the Australian political party out of power (it was rumored the party had offered him overall command if they won the next election). He had integrated crews and staffs, so that an American bomber pilot would often have an Australian copilot next to him in the cockpit. This was an arrangement that neither Marshall and nor U.S. Air Force chief Lieutenant General Henry "Hap" Arnold thought was effective. Arnold maintained, "The Australians have been operating our combat units in accordance with their doctrines and no attempt has been made on our part to regain control." According to Major General Robert C. Richardson, whom Marshall had sent to SWPA to investigate conditions, resentment also existed "throughout the entire command from top to bottom," over American pilots receiving their mission instructions from Australians.[37]

When Marshall and Arnold offered MacArthur several possible replacements for Brett, MacArthur made clear that he wanted someone with actual combat experience. Everyone was surprised when he gave an unqualified yes to the suggestion that Major General George C. Kenney replace Brett. Although Kenney had flown forty-seven missions against the Germans in World War I and had shot down two enemy planes, MacArthur, when he was chief of staff, had had to suppress Kenney's campaigning for an air force independent of the Army.[38]

Probably no one was more surprised than Arnold, who had responded to the suggestion of Kenney by one of his staff by wondering how MacArthur would "get along with sharp, gruff, and forceful George Kenney if he couldn't take smooth and capable George Brett."[39]

Before leaving for Australia, General Kenney spent several days in briefings concerning SWPA and its place in the war plan. What he learned was that "no one is really interested in the Pacific, particularly the SWPA." Despite this, his admiration for MacArthur and his enthusiasm for the new assignment were undiminished.[40]

The fifty-three-year-old major general who arrived at MacArthur's headquarters on July 30 looked like anything but the dashing airman who was going to take over command of all Allied air forces in SWPA. At five feet five and a half inches tall, Kenney was a bit on the bulky side. He had closely cropped, graying hair, and his blue eyes appeared to take in everything. His most distinguishing feature was a jagged line across the right side of his chin, the result of an aircraft accident. Journalist Clare Boothe Luce described him as "a bright, hard, scar-faced little bulldog of a man."[41]

Kenney spent his first hour with MacArthur listening to him vent about the shortcomings of the Air Force in general and the SWPA Air Force in particular. He later said MacArthur looked "a little depressed . . . tired, drawn, and nervous." As far as MacArthur was concerned, Brett's aircrews had done nothing right, and were little more than "an inefficient rabble of boulevard shock troops whose contribution to the war effort was practically nil."[42]

Some of this may have been MacArthur's response to the deficiencies of his air force at a time when he knew airpower over New Guinea was what would spell the difference between victory and defeat. Some might have been his way of testing how Kenney would react to such pressure, as Kenney himself suspected.[43]

When MacArthur paused to take a breath, Kenney stood and told him he "knew how to run an air force as well as or better than anyone else." He would be loyal to MacArthur, something the commander in chief suspected Brett wasn't, and he would "produce results."[44]

Impressed by his new air commander, MacArthur put his arm around Kenney's shoulders and told him, "George, I think we are going to get along together alright."[45]

The two then sat for over another hour discussing the war. Despite his isolation from the fighting in Europe, MacArthur demonstrated his understanding of events there. He told Kenney that the opinion then common among officials in Washington that Hitler would soon force Russia out of the war was wrong. Although the Germans were better soldiers than those fighting for Stalin, he believed Hitler had already overextended himself by failing to provide his forces with adequate road and rail communications. The Russian winter and the overwhelming Russian numbers would bleed the German army white.[46]

His meeting with MacArthur completed, Kenney departed on a survey of air force facilities in Australia and New Guinea. What he discovered was that "I had about 150 American and 70 Australian aircraft, scattered from Darwin to Port Moresby and back to Mareeba and Townsville, with which to dispute the air with the Jap. He probably had at least five times that number facing me and could get plenty more in a matter of a few days by flying them in from the homeland. I issued orders that no more airplanes were to be salvaged [for parts]. We would rebuild them, even if we had nothing left but a tail wheel to start with."[47]

Satisfied he had a competent man who would sweep the "dead wood" from the SWPA Air Force, MacArthur returned his attention to New Guinea. He had earlier ordered the Australian 7th Division to New Guinea, one battalion to Milne Bay, the other to Port Moresby. These were experienced combat troops led by a highly regarded combat commander, forty-seven-year-old Major General Arthur S. Allen. Allen had fought in World War I, led the 7th Division against Vichy forces in Syria and Lebanon, and commanded a brigade at Tobruk against the Germans before being called home to defend Australia.

Soon hundreds of Australians—some inexperienced militia, others combat veterans—made the slow, grueling climb toward Isurava to support the troops attempting to stop the Japanese advance. The 2/27th Battalion from General Allen's 7th Division was among the first to leave the Port Moresby area. Commanded by Lieutenant Colonel Arthur Key— a thirty-six-year-old former assistant sales manager from Victoria who had served in Libya, Crete, and Greece—517 men and 24 officers began their trek to the battle area on the morning of August 16. By late afternoon, they reached Uberi, a village thirty-two miles from the capital. Dragged down by nearly constant rainfall and mud that sucked the boots off some men, each soldier carried a seventy-pound load.

The following day was especially challenging, as the troops had to climb the "golden stairs." These "stairs" consisted of several thousand pieces of logs that had been jammed into the muddy mountainside and held in place by wooden pegs. Behind each log, which was set at irregular heights, the "step" filled with putrid mud and filthy water that caused the climbers' feet to slip. Overloaded and exhausted, the men slipped and fell off the steps and crashed into one another. Many were reduced to making the climb on their hands and knees as the rain pounded down on them and the stairs spilled over with rapidly running, yellowish, stinking water. The first section rose some 1,300 feet in less than two miles, dropped 1,600 feet, and rose again over 2,200 feet in two and a half miles. Some companies took twelve hours to complete the total nine-mile trek up and down.[48]

By the time they reached their destination, many soldiers were in no shape to fight the Japanese. Twenty-seven-year-old Captain Philip E. Rhoden described the conditions of his men: "Gradually men dropped out utterly exhausted—just couldn't go on. You'd come to a group of men and say, 'Come on! We must go on.' But it was physically impossible to move. Many were lying down and had been sick . . . some ate, others lay and were sick, and others just lay. Some tried to eat and couldn't."[49] In addition to fatigue, the men were beginning to show signs typical of New Guinea: dysentery, fever, open wounds caused by the ripping of the undergrowth. Japanese survivors later referred to the Kokoda Track as "the path of infinite sorrow."

Matters were not much better on the other side. With the arrival of General Horii, Japanese troop morale was at its highest level despite the fact that the more progress they made in pushing the Australians back, the more tenuous was their line of communication and supply from the coast. The more than 3,500 men posted from Deniki and Kokoda to the front line facing Isurava required roughly three tons of food and supplies daily. Trucks and other wheeled vehicles moved them about twenty miles from the coast along the slippery and still-dangerous log road built by the Japanese engineers, often subject to Allied air attacks. From this point, they were unloaded onto the heads of native carriers, including some who had been brought from New Britain and as far away as Korea for this backbreaking duty.

As they marched, carriers suffered terribly, from the mud and unbearable humidity of the lower altitudes, to the freezing cold of the higher levels. Horii estimated that he would require 4,600 carriers tramping along the track to keep his men fully supplied for combat. A major problem was that as the trek stretched out to a twenty-one-day round trip, the carriers consumed an increasing amount of their load simply to keep up their strength. There was also the constant problem of carriers falling ill, tumbling to their deaths over cliffs, and desertion. The latter increased as the days dragged on and the men became increasingly homesick for families and villages.

For the Japanese soldiers at the tip of the spear, driving a group of Australians from their position became doubly important because the retreating forces often left behind food supplies they could not take with them. Some units virtually existed on these supplies. When the Australians realized how hungry their opponents were, they started leaving behind purposely contaminated food. Eating these tainted foods, large numbers of Imperial soldiers were put out of action by disabling gastric ailments, such as amoebic dysentery and severe diarrhea. This was on top of the malaria that had begun spreading like wildfire among the undernourished troops.[50]

When uncontaminated food was discovered following an Australian retreat, chaos often erupted among the normally well-disciplined soldiers as they scrambled to scoop up as much as they could carry. A Japanese war correspondent accompanying the troops described a scene in one village when a hut containing piles of untouched goods was found: "Here in the Papuan mountains the standard of living was higher than in Japan! I thought I saw something of the appalling power of Anglo-American civilization that Japan had so recklessly challenged."[51]

General Horii took personal command of the troops facing Isurava and commenced his advance during the night of August 25. The village was situated in a flat clearing with creeks running on either side. Horii's plan was to feint a frontal attack to draw Australian fire while units circled around to attack the enemy flanks and force their way to the Australians' rear to prevent their withdrawal. The Japanese commander was not aware that the Australians had been reinforced by powerful elements of the regular army. Both sides were now almost evenly matched in size: when the battle for Isurava began, the Japanese strength was 2,130 men, facing an Allied force of 2,292.[52]

The Australians' determined resistance forced the failure of Horii's envelopment plan. Yet with the arrival of Japanese heavy guns, the situation was altered. By August 30 eight guns were blasting shells into the Allied lines, including several 75mm mountain artillery cannons. The Australians continued fighting, but it was a fighting withdrawal day after day. General MacArthur, who some historians have charged with being too critical of Australian troops, received daily reports of the action in the mountains of Papua. On September 10, he let his true feelings be known when he issued a communiqué describing the Australian and Papuan forces as "fighting tenaciously and gallantly under conditions of extraordinary hardship and difficulty."[53]

By September 10 the Australians had fallen back to a high point known as Ioribaiwa Ridge, some twenty-five miles from Port Moresby and within sight of the Papuan Gulf on the south side of New Guinea. Relentless attacks by Japanese patrols made inroads on the defenses and prompted the current Australian commander, Brigadier Kenneth Eather, to request permission from Port Moresby on September 15 to withdraw to the nearby Imita Ridge, the last major natural obstacle on the Kokoda Track before Port Moresby. Eather believed he could establish a truly defensible position there, shorten his supply line, and take advantage of the artillery that was slowly moving up from the capital. Major General Allen approved of Eather's plan, but warned, "There won't be any withdrawal from the Imita position, Ken. You'll die there if necessary."[54]

At eleven the following morning, the Australians began their final withdrawal. The departure from Ioribaiwa left the ridge to the surprised Japanese. When it was clear their enemy had gone, Japanese troops poured onto Ioribaiwa Ridge, impatient to see what food the Australians had abandoned.[55] Little that was edible had been left—the Australians and their carriers had taken nearly everything with them. The Japanese were on the brink of starvation.[56]

A Japanese correspondent described the scene when the troops arrived at the Ioribaiwa Ridge: "We gazed over the Gulf of Papua from the peak of the last main ridge we had fought to ascend. 'I can see the ocean! The sea of Port Moresby!' Later that evening we stood on the peak and saw the lights of Port Moresby. We could just make out the searchlights shining over the airfield at Seven Mile to the north of the city."[57]

Their objective was so near, yet remained out of reach.

Events transpired in both camps to halt the Japanese attempt to capture Port Moresby. General MacArthur, recognizing that Horii had stretched his forces to their limit, on October 3 ordered the 16th Infantry Brigade of the 6th Australian Division to Port Moresby so the 25th Brigade, which was in reserve there, could be sent to Imita Ridge and support the forces preparing an offensive against the Japanese.

The commander in chief then decided that American troops, with little jungle training and no combat experience, should be sent across the mountains using a different route to cover the right flank of the Australians, and possibly even cut General Horii off from his supply line. MacArthur selected the 126th Infantry Regiment of the 32nd Division for this task. On October 2, before they left, MacArthur visited them and, according to General Kenney, found the men eager to join the Aussies in fighting the Japanese.[58]

Nine hundred Americans participated in a forty-two-day trek across the mountains without ever seeing one Japanese soldier. To their amazement, they stumbled on a party of thirty-five Australian soldiers who had been isolated by the speedy Japanese advance against Isurava. Their shredded uniforms and gaunt appearance made them appear ghostlike.[59]

Meanwhile, attacks and counterattacks by the Japanese on Ioribaiwa and the Australians on Imita failed to dislodge either army. General Horii established his headquarters in a valley behind Ioribaiwa Ridge and issued an order proclaiming that the final advance on Port Moresby would begin on September 20. He had to know this was untrue because his intelligence officer had reported that nearly twenty thousand Allied troops were in the capital. Besides, his starving men were in no shape for a large-scale attack. He must have issued this order as a way to lift his soldiers' morale with the hope that they would soon be in a town full of food. His own supplies from the coast were now nonexistent.

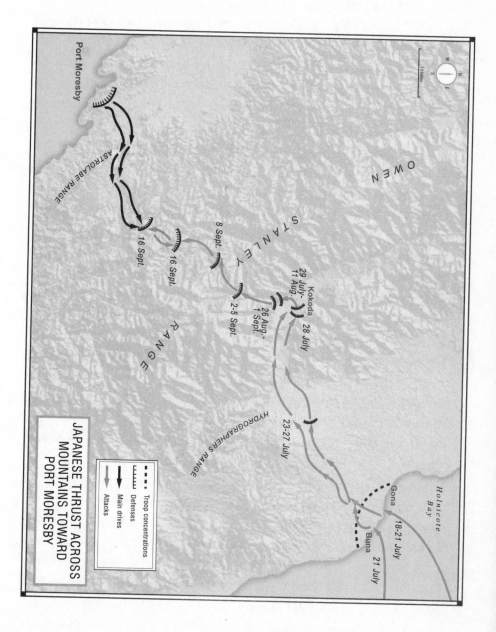

JAPANESE THRUST ACROSS
MOUNTAINS TOWARD
PORT MORESBY

Troop concentrations
Defenses
Attacks
Main drives

Port Moresby

ASTROLABE RANGE

16 Sept.

16 Sept.

8 Sept.

2-5 Sept.

26 Aug.-
1 Sept.

29 July-
11 Aug.
Kokoda

28 July

23-27 July

HYDROGRAPHERS RANGE

OWEN

STANLEY

RANGE

N
W   E
S

10 Miles

Holnicote
Bay

Gona   18-21 July

Buna   21 July

Men and matériel were being diverted to Guadalcanal, where the U.S. Marines were making great headway.[60]

On September 24 Horii received a telegram from General Hitoshi Imamura at Rabaul with orders to "stop attacking Port Moresby and wait for further instructions at present position." A second telegram later that evening instructed him to "withdraw from present position to some point in the Owen Stanley Range, which you may consider best for strategic purposes."[61]

Horii contemplated disobeying these orders but soon realized that doing so would only increase the suffering of his men, with little chance of success. On September 28 the Japanese began their own fighting withdrawal that would eventually bring them back to where they had begun: the opposite coast.

As the Australians advanced, they came across the bodies of two soldiers from the 21st Brigade who had been captured by the Japanese. One was beheaded, while the other had received several bayonet stabs while tied to a tree. Members of a local tribe, the Orokaivas, told the Aussies the enemy had destroyed much of the tribe's food supplies, bayoneted and shot several of their men, and raped their women, even abducting some.[62]

The Japanese soldiers who survived the withdrawal to arrive at Buna were small in number. Some reports put the figure as low as 500, others at a perhaps more realistic 1,500. Estimates place the number of Imperial troops who had perished in the fight for the Kokoda Track at as high as 6,500. Allied losses were slightly over 600.

General Tomitaro Horii, commander of all Imperial troops on the Kokoda Track, was not among the survivors. Attempting to cross a rapidly flowing river to escape the Australians, the general, along with several of his staff, drowned when their raft capsized.

A Japanese correspondent who watched the returning survivors described their condition: "Their uniforms were soiled with blood and mud and sweat, and torn to pieces. There were infantrymen without rifles, men walking on bare feet, men wearing blankets or straw rice bags instead of uniforms, men reduced to skin and bones plodding along with the help of a stick, men grasping and crawling on the ground."[63]

CHAPTER 8

First Defeat at Milne Bay

While the fighting along the Kokoda Track was under way, General MacArthur turned his attention to what he believed was another route the enemy was considering in its attempt to secure Port Moresby. He told his staff he was concerned that a Japanese force of at least division size, supported by land- and carrier-based aircraft, would try to reach the capital by coming around the eastern end of the island.[1]

Naval historian Samuel Eliot Morison described New Guinea as "shaped like a prehistoric monster, half bird and half reptile."[2] A long tail splits in two parts that project into the Coral Sea, and between them lies Milne Bay, named for a nineteenth-century British admiral. More than twenty-two miles long and averaging over ten miles wide, the bay is dominated by the heavily wooded Stirling Mountain Range, which reaches almost to the water's edge on all three sides. A narrow strip of mangrove swamp stretching back from the water is covered with wildly growing brush, except for occasional patches of coconut trees planted in orderly rows by Australian plantation owners. Never more than a few hundred yards from the water's edge, a twelve-foot-wide trail circles the closed end of the bay beginning at an old outpost known as K.B. Mission and ending on the opposite shore at the village of Gili Gili, ten miles away.[3]

A survey party, headed by an American engineering officer, traveled to Milne Bay in a Catalina flying boat on June 8, 1942, to determine the suitability of the site for construction of an airfield large enough to accommodate both pursuit aircraft and heavy bombers. MacArthur had in mind using such an air base to attack the enemy at both Buna and Rabaul. What the survey party discovered was a coconut plantation and factory complex used by Lever Brothers before the war. The grounds were large enough to accommodate at least three airfields, in addition to the small field already located there. A number of buildings connected by a small network of roads could be made useful by Allied forces, as well as several small jetties reaching into the bay that had been used by cargo vessels over the years.

A few months later, following the arrival of Allied troops and war correspondents, an Australian newspaper described Milne Bay as a virtual tropical paradise. "The water is deep and clear of reef. There are coconut plantations along the bay."[4] Not mentioned was that this soggy paradise received two hundred inches of rain each year, and the malaria rate among the Allied troops stationed there would soon reach four hundred per thousand per year.[5]

One Australian soldier, Leading Aircraftman Harold Pyke, would describe Milne Bay differently: "Even without the war, Milne Bay would have been a hell hole—it was a terrible place. The sun hardly ever shined and it rained all the time. It was stinking hot and bog holes everywhere and it was very marshy, boggy country. Even without the Japanese, it would have been hard to live there. It was a disease-ridden place—it was terrible."[6]

On June 22, MacArthur's headquarters issued orders for the occupation of Gili Gili, and three days later two cargo ships, escorted by a pair of small Australian warships, entered the bay. On board the Dutch-owned *Karsik* were two companies and a machine-gun platoon from 55th Infantry Battalion of the Australian 14th Infantry Brigade. There was also an antiaircraft battery with eight Bofors 40mm guns, and a platoon from the U.S. Coast Artillery Battalion with eight .5-inch machine guns and two

3.7-inch antiaircraft guns. Aboard the second Dutch ship, *Bontekoe*, was a company from the 46th Engineers of the U.S. Army Corps of Engineers. The latter arrived with air base construction equipment. The engineers immediately began construction of the new base, while the combat units set up defense perimeters in case of enemy attack.

Early in July the 7th Australian Infantry Brigade, considered one of the best trained of the militia units, arrived in several waves. The units were the 9th, 25th and 61st Infantry Battalions from Queensland. Forty-three-year-old Brigadier John Field, recently returned from the fighting in North Africa and the Middle East, commanded these troops. Until the arrival of a second brigade, Field was the only man at Milne Bay with combat experience in this war. He was quickly assigned as commanding officer of a new entity, Milne Force, which included not only his 7th Brigade but all naval, land, and air forces in or arriving at the Milne Bay area. Considered a reliable and able soldier by his contemporaries, Field had been commissioned as an officer in the militia in 1923; he held a degree in mechanical engineering and was a member of the engineering faculty at the University of Tasmania. His engineering knowledge and experience were just what Milne Bay needed.[7]

By the end of July, as construction moved along rapidly, elements of the 75 and 76 Squadrons of the RAAF landed at the nearly completed No. 1 Airstrip. They were flying American-made P-40 fighters.[8] Built by the Curtiss-Wright Corporation of Buffalo, New York, the P-40 was known to American pilots as the Warhawk and to the Australians as the Kittyhawk. It was the main fighter–ground attack aircraft used by the RAAF during the war. Australian pilots generally liked piloting the P-40. One Australian double ace, Nicky Barr, said of the single-engine, single-seat craft, "It was quite capable of getting you out of trouble more often than not. It was a real warhorse."[9]

While American engineers concentrated on building the three airstrips MacArthur wanted, as well as new wharves, Australian sappers and infantrymen went to work hacking out minimally passable roads, strengthening or replacing many of the seventeen lightly built bridges in the area, constructing living quarters, and, under Field's expert guidance, building well-camouflaged dispersal areas for a minimum of thirty-two fighters. The camouflage worked so well that when Japanese reconnaissance aircraft flew over the area, they failed to see many of the Allied aircraft parked on the ground.

Meanwhile in Rabaul, Lieutenant General Harukichi Hyakutake of the 17th Army was busy working on a plan to flank Port Moresby from the southeast. He selected the tiny island of Samarai, just a few miles into the sea from the opening of Milne Bay, as the ideal location for a seaplane base. The island, less than one square mile in size, had once been a busy trading post and stopover for ships sailing between Australia and East Asia. What the Japanese general did not know was that in January 1942, the Australian government, fearing the Japanese would use the island as a base to invade Australia, ordered its population evacuated and destroyed all its buildings and wharves. This made the island virtually uninhabitable without major construction projects, which the U.S. Navy Seabees would undertake in July 1943.[10]

Reconnaissance flights over Samarai revealed that the island could offer support only for floatplanes, and that it was not large enough for an airfield. What was needed if General Hyakutake was going to be able to provide air cover for an invasion of Port Moresby was a location for land-based aircraft, both fighters and bombers. Still smarting from the losses at Midway, the Imperial Japanese Navy's Eighth Fleet decided to proceed with an amphibious assault inside Milne Bay. Special Naval Landing Force troops were to be deployed because the army, now bogged down on the Kokoda Track and Guadalcanal, could not participate.

Increased Japanese reconnaissance flights over Milne Bay revealed that there were about thirty enemy fighters stationed at the completed airstrip, and that work was under way on two additional landing fields. There was little time to waste. Without troops of his own available, Hyakutake asked Vice Admiral Mikawa to proceed quickly with plans to capture Milne Bay. Japanese photo interpreters scanning pre-invasion photographs of Milne Bay underestimated the number of Allied troops protecting the airfields. This was in part due to the camouflage efforts of Brigadier Field. Intelligence officers of the 17th Army staff concluded that because the base was so new it did not yet have a large garrison for defense.[11]

While the Japanese planned their attack, the Allied forces in Milne Bay increased in numbers and strength. A second Australian infantry brigade had arrived by August 21, the 4,500 members of the 18th Infantry Brigade, under the command of forty-nine-year-old Brigadier George Wootten. This brigade and its commander had fought with great distinction against the Italians in Libya and against the Germans at Tobruk. MacArthur once said of Wootten that he was "the best soldier in the Australian army who had it in him to reach the highest position."[12]

Soon after, the arrival of several American and Australian antiaircraft batteries increased the overall strength of the Allied land forces at Milne Bay to nearly eight thousand Australians and almost fourteen hundred Americans, as well as another six hundred members of the RAAF. A new overall commander soon arrived in the person of Australian Major General Cyril Clowes, a fifty-year-old veteran of the fight against the Germans in the Middle East and a graduate of the Australian Royal Military College, Duntroon. All three senior officers at Milne Bay had distinguished themselves in the First World War.

General Clowes, an experienced combat officer, conducted a quick survey of the men and territory under his command and immediately set about preparing a defense should the Japanese decide to assault Milne Bay. He assigned the inexperienced militia troops of the 7th Brigade the first line of defense. Units guarded key locations against either seaborne or airborne attack. The veteran 18th Brigade was held in reserve so that it could respond quickly wherever the enemy landed.[13]

Clowes sent several patrols into the mountains to guard the overland trails from the north coast along Goodenough Bay, and to guard along the south coast. He had no idea yet whether the enemy was coming, and if so, from which direction.

Airstrip No. 1, located at the center of the Lever Brothers plantation, was as fully operational as was possible to construct it in the rain-drenched mud. By the time Clowes arrived, the two squadrons of Kittyhawks and a few Hudson bombers were using it. Meanwhile, the

Americans of the 46th Engineers were busy laying out No. 2 Strip, about four miles farther inland. The 43rd Engineers worked on No. 3 Strip that was northeast and close to the shore. Yet No. 1 Strip was a mess. Constant rain turned the terrain into fast-flowing rivulets of muddy water that washed across or seeped up through the open mesh of the steel mats the engineers had laid out on what passed for a runway. Planes regularly slid off the mats. Damaged beyond repair, some of them suffered the indignity of being cannibalized for spare parts. With no time or extra labor for rebuilding the field, each day bulldozers scraped the mats, dumping the mud on either side of the airstrip.[14]

During the last week of August, American code breakers uncovered the fact that enemy submarines had formed a picket line across the entrance to Milne Bay, a typical Japanese preinvasion tactic. General MacArthur met with General Kenney, his recently appointed air chief, to discuss countermeasures, including increased air patrols over likely sea routes from Rabaul to Milne Bay.[15]

The Japanese invasion of Milne Bay was to be a pincer movement. The main landing was to take place inside the bay at a place called Rabi, some three miles east of Gili Gili along the north coast. From there the invaders were to attack along the coast directly into the Allied base. This force was composed of 612 members of the Kure 5th Special Naval Landing Force (SNLF), 197 men from the Sasebo 5th SNLF, and 362 men from the 16th Naval Pioneer Unit. The second force, which was coming down along the northern coast from Buna, was made up of 353 men from the Sasebo 5th SNLF. This group would move in barges during nighttime hours; its orders were to land at Taupota in Goodenough Bay, directly north of Milne Bay, and march overland less than ten miles to attack the Allies from the rear. In all, 1,524 Japanese would strike what they believed were a few Australian militia companies. In reality, they faced ten thousand men, over half of whom were combat veterans.[16]

―――――――――

On August 23 and 24, aircraft from the Japanese 25th Air Flotilla conducted several bombing raids that appeared to be targeting No. 1 Strip, between Gili Gili and Rabi. General Kenney, interpreting these raids as a prelude to an invasion, decided to reduce the enemy's air cover before the action even began. He sent eight B-17s with incendiary bombs to attack the Rabaul airdromes, and a squadron of P-39 Bell Airacobra fighters to attack the Japanese fighter base at Buna. Ten enemy fighters were put out of commission during the strike. Kenney's goal, as he reported, was to "keep the Jap air force whittled down so that it couldn't support their landing operation."[17] He succeeded.

The Japanese main invasion force, under Rear Admiral Mitsuharu Matsuyama, commander of the 18th Cruiser Division, departed from Rabaul at seven a.m. on August 24 and headed south through St. George Channel. Troops were packed aboard two transports, *Nankai Maru* and *Kinai Maru,* which were escorted by two light cruisers, *Tenryu* and *Tatsuta,* as well as the destroyers *Tanikaze, Urakaze,* and *Hamakaze.* For additional protection, two submarine chasers joined the convoy, *CH-22* and *CH-24.*[18]

The Imperial Japanese Navy had sixty-three of these purpose-built subchasers. At 167 feet long, they were half the length of the three destroyers. Not especially fast, they had a maximum speed of eighteen miles per hour, roughly half that of the U.S. Navy PT boats. They carried a crew of sixty-eight, and in addition to three antiaircraft guns, each was armed with thirty-six depth charges and special depth-charge launchers. To fulfill their primary mission, each subchaser was equipped with active sonar.[19]

In less than two hours, an RAAF Hudson patrol plane spotted the convoy as it rounded the Trobriand Islands in the Solomon Sea. A short time later, three Australian Coastwatchers stationed on the islands confirmed the sighting. It was obvious the fleet was destined for Milne Bay.

At the same time the convoy left Rabaul, seven large motorized barges departed from Buna and headed along the coast toward Taupota, where several Australian Coastwatchers quickly spotted them. The invasion plan called for the convoy's landing to take place during the late evening, but the barges made excellent time. Arriving too early, Commander Torashigue Tsukioka decided to land nearby to allow his men to eat a meal and rest. He selected a small offshore location called Goodenough Island.

As word of the approaching Japanese forces passed through the Allied communications chain, fighters and bombers took flight unless, as was the case at Milne Bay, the driving rain and thick cloud cover were so bad that visibility was almost nil. Although some minor attacks were made on the Rabaul convoy, inclement weather hindered the B-17 pilots whom General Kenney had sent from airfields in Queensland, along with Kittyhawk pilots from Port Moresby.

Finally, at midday the clouds over Milne Bay lifted enough so that ten Kittyhawks of 76 Squadron took off after the troops on Good-enough Island. By three p.m., twelve more Kittyhawks and an available Hudson lifted off from No. 1 Strip to attack the main convoy. Again, only minor damage resulted from that attack, but when the ten Kitty-hawks arrived over Goodenough Island, they found clear skies and saw the seven barges pulled up on the beach. As Kittyhawks came in low with guns blazing, the naval troops ran for the tree line for cover. The raid killed eight Japanese and destroyed all seven barges, along with the communications equipment, food, arms, and ammunition they contained. The entire force was stranded, and without the ability to communicate, the troops were completely isolated. RAAF Pilot Officer John Petter, who took part in the attack, described it as a "massacre."[20]

Named for a nineteenth-century British commodore, Goodenough is an oval island measuring thirteen miles wide and twenty-one miles long. At its center rises the eight-thousand-foot Mount Vineuo. The island's five-mile-wide coastal belt is covered with swamps and grass-lands, while the interior and western edges contain jungle and rain forest. Unbeknownst to the stranded Japanese, also on the island was a small American group operating a fighter-control station to provide advance warning to Milne Bay of approaching enemy aircraft. Ships and planes traveling between Buna and Milne Bay had to pass Good-enough, making it a valuable watch station. Outnumbered and out-gunned, the Americans quickly destroyed their radio equipment and left before the Japanese discovered them.

Imperial Headquarters knew nothing of the fate of the SNLF troops until one of them found a canoe and paddled his way back to Buna, arriving there on September 9. The following day, two destroyers left Buna to pick up the survivors. A flight of five B-17s sighted the two ships and succeeded in sinking one, *Yayoi*. Survivors from the destroyer managed to make their way to nearby Normanby Island, where they, too, were stranded. Two destroyers later rescued them.

Several times during September, messages and food supplies were dropped to the Japanese on Goodenough, but all attempts to rescue them were driven off by Allied aircraft. Meanwhile, the men subsisted on limited rations and coconut milk, and struggled with an outbreak of malaria. On October 3, an IJN submarine arrived carrying a forty-six-foot waterproof landing barge along with a cargo of food, ammunition, and a wireless radio. The barge managed to take about fifty wounded and sick men aboard and transported them to Buna. Ten days later, the submarine returned and off-loaded additional supplies, but when a Hudson patrol bomber dropped a flare over it, the captain took his boat down and rushed away.[21]

On October 1, General MacArthur issued new orders that sealed the fate of the SNLF troops on Goodenough. "Occupy and hold Goodenough Island and the north coast of Southeastern New Guinea south of Cape Nelson in such force as to deny these areas to the Japanese forces."[22] On October 22, two destroyers put ashore more than six hundred Australian soldiers from the 18th Infantry Brigade at two locations on Goodenough Island. In the fighting that ensued, thirteen Australians and at least thirty-nine SNLF sailors were killed. The exact number of Japanese dead could not be determined because they buried many of the bodies. During a lull in the fighting on the night of the twenty-fourth, two landing craft took 261 Japanese off the island to safety.[23]

The fate of the main Japanese invasion force was even worse than that of the troops who landed at Goodenough Island, due in large part to their lack of knowledge concerning the strength of their enemy. Lieutenant Chikanori Moji, paymaster of the 5th Kure Special Naval Landing Force, later wrote that during a meeting of the officers prior to leaving Rabaul, the commanding officer, Commander Masajiro Hayashi, who was also overall commander of all invasion forces, "said that nothing was known yet about the enemy situation in the relevant area. When I glanced at him, I saw in his eyes, as he said this that he seemed near tears. He had been unable to recce the area by air, nor could any special aerial photographs be taken . . . enemy strength was not known."[24]

At 9:50 p.m. on August 25, with the entire fleet inside Milne Bay, the Japanese invasion forces, including two light tanks, began going ashore. They faced no opposition. As they unloaded their equipment, somebody realized they were in the wrong place. Perhaps due to bad navigating or inaccurate charts, they had arrived not at Rabi but several miles to the east, at a village called Waga Waga, putting them farther away from their target, No. 3 Airstrip.

As reports from reconnaissance patrols poured into his headquarters at Gili Gili, General Clowes, the Australian commander on the scene, decided to wait. He knew several enemy ships had arrived in the bay but had no idea how many troops they had brought, or where or when they would be landed. He assumed that after daylight he would have a better opportunity to assess the situation accurately.

A brief firefight erupted in the dark when an Australian patrol in a small vessel accidentally ran into the invaders. The two-masted ketch, more commonly called a lugger, was named *Bronzewing*, and had once been owned by Tasmanian-born actor Errol Flynn.[25] Eleven Australians died in the encounter.[26]

Cloud cover the next day prevented high-level bombers from locating the enemy ships, although one was lucky enough to find a hole in the low clouds and managed to drop at least one, possibly two bombs on the one Japanese transport still at the landing site. The attack did considerable damage to the ship and much of the supplies it carried. The remainder of the enemy fleet had withdrawn from the area to avoid attack.[27]

The clouds did little to hinder the Kittyhawks from No. 1 Airstrip. The entire morning of the twenty-sixth, they bombed and strafed the landing zone. In the process, they destroyed virtually all the powered barges the Japanese troops intended to use to move along the coast. The only option left to them was to follow the muddy coastal tracks through swamps and across numerous streams and flooded areas toward Gili Gili.

Fleeing inland from the air attacks for the cover offered by the jungle, the invaders dragged whatever supplies and equipment they could rescue from the Kittyhawks' strafing of the beaches. The two light tanks survived the assaults and soon led about a thousand men along the track toward their target. Some of the navy soldiers, with a reputation for extreme cruelty even among regular army forces, spread out and attacked several small villages in the area.

Battling torrential rains, mud so thick it pulled the boots off their feet, and keeping weary eyes to the sky for enemy planes, the Japanese trudged westward toward their objective, their tanks in the lead. Just before they reached K.B. Mission, an abandoned Christian missionary station, they were ambushed by a company from the 61st Australian Battalion, known as the Queensland Cameron Highlanders. This was the first combat for these militia soldiers, but despite their inexperience, they fought the veteran Japanese to a standstill, and after several hours forced them to withdraw.

After reorganizing, the Japanese renewed the battle, which continued sporadically all day. Additional troops arrived to support the Australians, but they had nothing large enough to combat the two tanks, which fired shells into their positions. Brigadier Field eventually ordered a withdrawal of about one mile to the Gama River, where a new defensive line was established. They were soon reinforced by the combat-experienced 2/10 Battalion from the 7th Division.

At eight p.m. on August 27, the Japanese launched a powerful attack at the Gama River line. Their two tanks led the way, with large bright headlights exposing the Australians while the attackers remained behind in the darkness. Over the next few hours, the Australians repelled four frontal assaults but suffered heavy casualties. By two a.m., the exhausted Australian troops were forced across the river. When the Japanese persisted in their pursuit along with the two tanks, the Australians continued to fall back in disorder until they reached the No. 3 Airstrip, which was still under construction.

The retreating Australians moved through the defense line that had been established on the west side of the incomplete airfield by the

61st and 25th Infantry Battalions, as well as the American 709th Anti-Aircraft Battery and two companies from the U.S. 43rd Engineers. Only partially graded, the one-hundred-yard-wide runway, which ran east to west, provided an ideal defensive position that the enemy would find difficult to cross, offering the defenders a clear killing field. While the runway's eastern end was buried in deep mud that made the area almost impassible, the western end reached nearly to the water's edge. The Japanese had no option other than a frontal attack across the strip.

The two Australian battalions held most of the line. The American antiaircraft battery, with its .50-caliber machine guns, provided support at the eastern end, and the American engineers joined Australian mortar crews in the center with their .50-caliber and 37mm guns at just the spot where the coastal track crossed the runway.[28]

At dawn on the twenty-eighth, the Japanese launched their attack as aggressively as possible but found crossing the runway a deadly and fruitless venture. They were swiftly driven back. Unknown to the defenders, who kept a sharp eye out for the tanks, the two-tracked vehicles had bogged down and their three-man crews abandoned them in nearly waist-deep mud. They were no longer a factor in the fighting. Over the next two days, the naval troops continued to attack the defense line without success and with growing loss of life.

Frustrated by what he saw as scanty reports from General Clowes, and perhaps sensing that Clowes had not yet committed all his forces to the fight, General MacArthur told General Blamey to instruct Clowes "at once to clear the north shore of Milne Bay without delay" and submit daily progress reports.[29]

During the night of the twenty-ninth, a Japanese fleet of destroyers and patrol boats entered Milne Bay. On board were nearly eight hundred men from two SNLF units led by Commander Minoru Yano, a gung ho officer anxious for a glorious victory. The troops and the supplies they brought with them were unloaded near K.B. Mission while the escorts shelled the Allied positions. As the senior commander on the scene, Yano took overall command of the operation. Although Yano wanted to attack the Allies immediately, Hayashi prevailed on him to give his men a rest before they resumed combat. Low on ammunition and subsisting on limited rations, Yano's men, along with the Allied troops, were exhausted from the laborious fighting in the mud. Adding to everyone's discomfort, malaria was beginning to sweep through both sides.[30]

Unknown to the Japanese, General Clowes had finally swung into action. While the enemy rested, several American half-tracked armored vehicles mounting heavy guns arrived just behind the Allied lines. Additional machine guns and mortar crews also arrived to bolster the defense. When Yano ordered his attack across the airstrip before dawn on August 31, in what would be the climactic battle of the fight for Milne Bay, the surprised Japanese met fierce resistance. As tracers lighted their positions, the machine guns cut them down. After three such attacks across open ground, Japanese bodies littered the airstrip.[31]

Finally, a bugle sounded retreat and the Japanese attempted a fighting withdrawal. Allied forces rushed across the runway, trying their best not to trip over the dozens of dead Japanese soldiers, and began pushing the dispirited and shocked enemy back. Some retreated along the coast the way they had come, while others scattered into the jungle for safety. Daylight was even worse, for it revealed many of them to the Kittyhawks that filled the skies and strafed the fleeing enemy.

Over the next few days, as they retreated beyond their original landing zone, Commander Hayashi died and Yano was seriously wounded. Rabaul had no accurate picture of what was happening at Milne Bay until Admiral Mikawa received a message from Yano on September 2: "We have reached the worst possible situation. We will together calmly defend our position to the death. We pray for absolute victory for the empire and for long-lasting fortune in battle for you all."[32]

The following morning the commander of the 4th Destroyer Squadron was ordered to enter Milne Bay and "endeavor to contact the naval landing units, whatever the circumstances, and if at all possible, evacuate them."[33] The Japanese were giving up the fight and wanted to get whatever troops still surviving out of Milne Bay. On September 5, destroyers evacuated about thirteen hundred men, including Yano.

Japanese losses totaled nearly 750 dead, scattered around the battle sites. While a small number of Japanese who missed the evacuation survived for some time, they all either eventually perished at the hands of pursuing Australians or from revenge-seeking native villagers, or simply vanished in the jungle.

Allied losses were 167 Australians and 14 Americans. In addition, 59 Papuans, mostly women who had been bayoneted by Japanese troops, usually after being raped, died.

Although the battle for Milne Bay lasted only a few days, it had wide-ranging and long-lasting effects. In his book *Defeat into Victory,* British field marshal Sir William Slim claimed he used the action, which he described as "the Japanese first undoubted defeat on land," as a "morale raiser" among his own troops fighting in Burma.

Australian newspapers hailed the victory as a "turning point." Virtually everyone cheered the performance of the militia members who stood their ground against experienced combat veterans. Strategically, it essentially put an end to Japanese efforts to capture Port Moresby, and allowed MacArthur to focus his mind and his forces on driving the enemy completely out of New Guinea.

Despite this focus, MacArthur always kept an eye and an ear open for what was going on in the rest of the war. He demonstrated this when he discussed with a British intelligence officer recent flights by Prime Minister Winston Churchill to Washington, Moscow, Cairo, and Gibraltar. "If disposal of all the Allied decorations were today placed by providence in my hands, my first act would be to award the Victoria Cross to Winston Churchill. No one of those who wear it deserves it more than he. A flight of 10,000 miles through hostile and foreign skies may be the duty of young pilots, but for a statesman burdened with the world's cares, it is an act of inspiring gallantry and valor."[34]

This was a generous comment about the man MacArthur knew was responsible for convincing President Roosevelt that Germany had to be defeated first, and that that was where most American resources must be expended. The war against Japan would wait until victory over Germany was achieved.

CHAPTER 9

"Take Buna, or Not Come Back Alive"

As fighting raged along the Kokoda Track and at Milne Bay, Japanese engineers at the Buna-Gona beachheads constructed virtually impregnable defenses. The high water table precluded deep bunkers, so instead they constructed hundreds of ground-level bunkers from steel plates, forty-four-gallon drums packed with sand, and thick tree trunks. Steel plates or three layers of eighteen-inch-thick coconut logs provided overhead protection. The bunkers were then covered with several inches of soil in which fast-growing tropical vegetation was planted—so well were they camouflaged that many were invisible up until a few feet away. Each contained several machine guns that provided supporting fire to each other, catching the enemy in a deadly cross fire. Some bunkers served only as shelters during an air attack or artillery barrage; crawl tunnels connected them to nearby machine-gun positions. When the artillery or bombing halted, soldiers would crawl to the machine-gun positions on each side of the bunker and prepare to resist infantry attack.

Covered with dense jungle and decaying swamps, the coastal plain over which the coming battle for Buna and Gona would be fought stretched inland to the foothills of the Owen Stanleys. Along the coast and a half mile southeast of Buna Village was Buna Mission, also called Buna Government Station. This had been the seat of local government as administered by the Australians. Before the arrival of the Imperial troops, three government officers lived here. It was also home to between one hundred and two hundred native villagers.

What made this otherwise near-worthless stretch of coast valuable to both sides was found less than a mile and a half south of Buna Mission: In a large expanse of kunai grass was the Buna Airfield. Japanese engineers had been busy expanding its 800-yard-long runway to over 1,300 yards, and widening it from 60 yards to 90 yards. South of the airfield, the engineers built a dummy airstrip where some Allied pilots were tricked into attacking mock aircraft parked along the decoy strip.

Once in control of Milne Bay, MacArthur set his sights on the powerful enemy bases at Buna and Gona. On September 6, one day after the Japanese evacuation of Milne Bay, MacArthur cabled General Marshall, explaining the importance of the U.S. Navy winning control of the sea-lanes between northern Australia and Papua. MacArthur still had no ships under his helm other than the few small vessels he had lent to the Navy for the Guadalcanal operation. Despite the victory at Milne Bay, he believed the situation remained precarious with the enemy in control of the north coast of New Guinea. "If New Guinea goes," he told Marshal, "the result will be disastrous."[1]

MacArthur emphasized his belief about the consequences of a potential Japanese victory in New Guinea during a September 25 visit by Army Air Force commanding general Hap Arnold. With a bit of hyperbole, he told Arnold that if New Guinea fell, the Japanese would rule the Pacific for the next hundred years. MacArthur then praised General Kenney's performance since taking over air operations in SWPA, telling Arnold, who was the first member of the Joint Chiefs to visit the theater, that he would "not exchange Air Force units for any others."[2]

General Arnold, who kept a diary throughout the war, wrote that his meeting with MacArthur gave him "the impression of a brilliant mind—obsessed by a plan he can't carry out—frustrated."[3] On his return to Washington, Arnold suggested to the Joint Chiefs that the entire Pacific be placed under MacArthur's command.[4]

MacArthur's frustration was a product of several factors that were hampering his plans to push the enemy out of New Guinea and then out of his beloved Philippines: delays in receiving large numbers of American troops, lack of support for his operations by the Navy, and Washington's emphasis on the war against the Germans.

A major problem for MacArthur in planning action against the enemy bases along the north coast of New Guinea was the shortage of ships. At the time, what was beginning to be called "MacArthur's Navy" consisted of five cruisers, eight destroyers, twenty submarines, and seven smaller vessels. MacArthur had earlier requested the assignment of two aircraft carriers to the SWPA naval commander, but was turned down. This was a tough pill to swallow for the man Samuel Eliot Morison described as "perhaps the most enthusiastic advocate of carrier-based air outside the Navy." It was clear to Morison that in the worldwide Allied strategy, the southwest Pacific led the list of "have nots," and "won't gets."[5]

During MacArthur's preparations for the Buna-Gona assault, two talented men joined the MacArthur circle. On September 11, "MacArthur's Navy" was given a new commander when Vice Admiral Arthur "Chips" Carpender replaced Vice Admiral Herbert F. Leary, who was reassigned as commander of battleships, Pacific Fleet. It is possible that MacArthur, who was behind the change in naval commanders, had learned of Leary's resistance to lending two of his new B-17s to General Brett to rescue MacArthur's party from Mindanao and bring it to Australia. MacArthur was not one to forget or forgive such a slight.

The second addition resulted from the growth of the U.S. Army in SWPA, which had grown to 110,000 American soldiers in-theater. Although most were engineering or supply troops, there were two National Guard combat infantry divisions, the 32nd and the 41st. A corps commander was now required to direct all Army operations. MacArthur tapped Major General Robert L. Eichelberger for the position. Like MacArthur, Eichelberger was a former superintendent of

West Point who had missed action in Europe during the First World War, instead spending two years in Siberia with the American Expeditionary Force in support of the Allied intervention in the Russian Civil War. Among several decorations he received there were the Distinguished Service Cross for bravery, and, ironically, the Order of the Rising Sun from America's then ally, the Imperial Japanese government. MacArthur considered Eichelberger "a commander of the first order, fearless in battle, and especially popular with the Australians."[6]

With the Japanese retreating along the Kokoda Track across the mountains to Buna, and the Australians hot on their tail, MacArthur was anxious to get some American infantry into the fight. While he wanted to use his troops to attack the enemy's beachhead facilities along the coast, his biggest handicap was an absence of amphibious craft that could get his soldiers ashore safely. With an eye on the fighting on Guadalcanal, where the enemy was heavily committed, MacArthur issued an operation order on October 1, stating, "In the absence of secure lines of communication on the north coast of New Guinea we still are unable to maintain large forces there." As a result, if Allied troops arrived in large numbers, planners had to have a contingency plan for the rapid withdrawal of such forces if the enemy overwhelmed them.[7]

General Kenney suggested that he fly troops to the small landing strip Australian engineers had built at the deserted Wanigela Mission, halfway along the coast between Buna and Milne Bay. Kenney claimed he could keep troops supplied by airdrop and then by landing his transports on a newly expanded airfield. During the first week of October, American Douglas C-47 Dakotas flew the Australian 2/10th Battalion of the 18th Brigade to Wanigela. American antiaircraft guns and their crews, as well as U.S. Army Engineers, joined them. Tasked with expanding the airfield in order to accommodate heavy bombers and fighters, the engineers accomplished their mission in a couple of weeks without the enemy's knowledge, distracted as they were by the assaulting Australians sweeping down from the mountains.

On October 14, Kenney's planes flew the 2nd and 3rd Battalions of the 128th Infantry Regiment of the 32nd U.S. Infantry Division and the Australian 2/6th Independent Company to Wanigela, where they awaited orders to move northwest along the coast to attack the Japanese at Buna. A plan soon developed to move some of these troops along a coastal trail to Pongani, about thirty miles from Buna. Air reconnaissance claimed it was free of Japanese troops. An attempt by Australian and American forces was made to reach Pongani, but swollen rivers and deep swamps halted all but the lightly encumbered commandos of the 2/6th Independent Company from reaching their destination. The men of the 3rd Battalion had to settle for setting up camp at a place called Guri Guri. The battalion commander, Lieutenant Colonel Kelsie E. Miller, called it "the most filthy, swampy, mosquito infested area" he had seen in New Guinea.[8]

On October 17 a coastal shuttle began operations from Milne Bay to Pongani, which was now the most forward allied base facing Buna. Fishing vessels brought supplies from Milne Bay through a route charted through the numerous coral reefs by several Coastwatchers to Wanigela. There the supplies were off-loaded and put aboard shallow-draft luggers at night to evade Japanese aircraft, to sail to Pongani. Unable to close in more than several hundred yards from the coast without risking striking coral and sinking, the luggers dropped anchors, and American troops, led by Lieutenant Colonel Laurence A. McKenny, quartermaster of the 32nd Division, stripped off their clothes and jumped naked into the sea. The supplies were loaded aboard a mix of small vessels, including canoes, rowboats, and canvas-sided engineer boats. One soldier recalled "waves pounding over their heads" as they pushed the boats through the breakers to the beach. The quartermaster troops "made dozens of exhausting trips without rest each night in order to get the vulnerable trawlers on their way again before daylight."[9]

Construction of an airfield suitable for military use was under way at Pongani when Major General Edwin Forrest Harding, commanding general of the 32nd Division, learned of the existence of a small field only forty-five miles away that could serve as a landing strip. A missionary, Cecil Abel, brought the information to him. The thirty-nine-year-old Abel was a lifelong resident of New Guinea and realized the potential value the field had for the Allies. Harding asked Abel to return to the field and enlist local labor to prepare it for a landing strip. Hand tools dropped by parachute from an Air Force plane enabled the project. The first C-47 landed at "Abel's Field" on October 19.[10]

General MacArthur moved his advance base to Port Moresby on November 6. Four days earlier, he had selected November 15 as the tentative date of attack against Buna. The 32nd Division was ordered to send patrols as far as Oro Bay, fifteen miles southeast of Buna. Meanwhile, the Japanese were holed up in a well-fortified zone that varied from several hundred yards to several miles deep from the coast, and was approximately ten miles long. A promontory called Cape Endaiadere anchored the southeastern end just beyond Buna Village, and its northwestern end was at Gona. In between, the zone encompassed both old and new airstrips, Sanananda Point and Basabua. Occupying the zone were over seven thousand Japanese troops, all of whom had had combat experience. About half had survived the fighting along the Kokoda Track. They all waited for the attack they knew was coming while enemy forces maneuvered around them.[11]

Because it was not possible to bring heavy artillery over the mountain trails, or along the swampy coast, the Allies had no long-distance weapons with which to bombard the enemy fortifications prior to assaulting them. The Japanese, on the other hand, had numerous field artillery pieces well positioned to defend their beachhead.

The American 32nd Division, which had received only minimal training, was entering combat for the first time. The Australians, coming over the mountains, had more experience, but all, including the enemy, suffered terribly from diseases. The Japanese, whose supplies were drastically reduced by General Kenney's air attacks on ships approaching the coast, also suffered from malnutrition. Yet these soldiers were trained and determined to die for their emperor, and despite all handicaps, remained a powerful and deadly force.

No one among the Allied leaders realized how powerful the Japanese forces were. Division commander General Harding thought Buna, where battalions from his 32nd Division were to attack, would be "easy pickings," as only "a shell of sacrifice troops" defended it.[12] MacArthur's intelligence chief, Brigadier General Charles Willoughby, reported his belief that there were only a few thousand starving Japanese clinging to makeshift defenses at the water's edge.[13]

On November 16, the 1st and 3rd battalions from the 128th Infantry Regiment of the 32nd Division moved out in a drenching rain along two tracks toward Buna. Their first contact with the enemy was made about one mile from Buna, close to the dummy airstrip at Cape Endaiadere. Despite noise from the rain and gunfire, the Americans could hear the sounds of trucks moving around behind enemy lines, a clear indication there were forces held in reserve to be sent wherever the Allies attacked. Heavy and well-directed machine-gun fire stopped the Americans in their muddy tracks. Japanese planners had done an excellent job establishing their defensive positions. Visibility in the jungle and swamps was so poor that companies lost sight of each other for hours on end. Even squads from the same company found it hard to keep in contact with one another.

Japanese positions were too well fortified to attack directly with infantry. What was needed was artillery. Yet General Kenney had earlier convinced MacArthur that his aircraft could replace field artillery pieces that were at best difficult, and at worst impossible to transport to the Buna area aboard the small boats that were bringing in men and supplies. Another weapon that might have helped, despite the risk of their being bogged down in the mud, as happened to the Japanese at Milne Bay, were tanks. Not until December 18 would artillery and tanks arrive on the scene.

Air support's arrival added to the confusion. Battle lines were so indistinct, and enemy fortifications so well hidden, that when the A-20s and B-25s of the 3rd Bombardment Group dropped their ordnance from medium and even low altitude, their bombs caused casualties among members of the 3rd Battalion.

The following day, the 2nd Battalion from the U.S. 128th Infantry Regiment attacked the enemy fortifications from the northwest. A battalion from the 126th Infantry Regiment joined it, but was soon diverted north to meet the Australian 16th Brigade of the 7th Division; they headed to Sanananda, while the Australian 7th Division's 25th Brigade set out for Gona.

On the night of November 17, Japanese reinforcements arrived aboard six destroyers, bringing over a thousand fresh troops, including a battalion from the 229th Infantry Regiment that had fought in China, Hong Kong, and Java. These soldiers proved to be among the best fighting force the enemy had at Buna-Gona. Most of these men went directly to the Buna area.[14]

The days dragged on with little progress. The 7th Division took more than two hundred casualties in the first three days. American units lost contact with one another, and everyone was suffering from the hundred-degree daytime heat and the nightly rainstorms. Exhaustion and disease were taking more men out of the line than combat.

New Yorker writer E. J. Kahn Jr., who served in the 32nd Division during its time in New Guinea, left this description of the soldiers of the division fighting at Buna: "They were gaunt and thin, with deep black circles under their sunken eyes. They were covered with tropical sores and had straggly beards. Few of them wore socks or underwear. Often the soles had been sucked off their shoes by the tenacious, stinking mud. Many of them fought for days with fevers and didn't know it. During one comparative lull, an inquisitive medical officer with a thermometer inspected some hundred men, and everybody involved was surprised to find that sixty of them were running temperatures of from two to three degrees above normal. Malaria, dengue fever, dysentery, and in a few cases, typhus hit man after man."[15]

The situation for the Japanese was much the same, with the exception that they had the protection of well-planned and well-constructed fortified bunkers. Food was always the issue, especially as Allied warplanes were doing their best to sink ships attempting to resupply the bases. Some Japanese, cut off from most resupply efforts even within their defense zone, were soon forced to exist on a half-pint of rice a day. For some, the desperate hunger overcame normal inhibitions. One machine gunner wrote in his diary, found after the fighting had ceased:

"Our food is completely gone. We are eating tree bark and grass. In other units, there are men eating the flesh of dead Australians. There is nothing to eat." Yet they continued to fight on ferociously as long as they could fire their weapons. There was no thought of surrender.[16]

The Americans had entered the field of action only lightly armed. The heaviest weapons they carried for the attack on Buna were light machine guns. Coastal trawlers were supposed to bring .50-caliber machine guns and 81mm mortars, ammunition, rations, and other supplies.[17] Yet Japanese Zeros relentlessly attacked the trawlers, sending several of them and their cargoes to the bottom of the sea. Attacks were especially prevalent in the evenings, when American fighter escorts had to fly back over the mountains to Port Moresby before dark, leaving the skies and the fate of the trawlers to the enemy. In one instance, the 32nd Division's commander, Major General Harding, was aboard a trawler when it came under attack. It was part of a four-vessel convoy loaded with ammunition and other supplies for the division. Harding was having dinner with the trawler's captain shortly after the fighter escort had departed when he heard the sounds of approaching aircraft. Eighteen Zeros swept in out of the evening sky, guns blazing. All four vessels were set aflame, and the men who survived the initial explosions of gasoline tanks or ammunition cases jumped overboard and swam for shore. Harding was among them. Rowboats and life rafts pushed out from the nearby shore to rescue all they could. In addition to fifty-two killed, one hundred men were wounded, many with serious bullet wounds. Also lost were several tons of rations, artillery shells, two twenty-five-pounders, and the 128th's heavy weapons.[18]

Several times Japanese supply and reinforcement convoys attempted to approach the beachheads. Most often American planes drove them off, but on a few occasions they were able to put fresh troops as well as limited rations and ammunition ashore. On November 24, several destroyers landed at least five hundred fresh soldiers. Several hundred more, who had fought along the Kokoda Track and returned to the shore several miles to the north, soon arrived by small boats at Gona.

At Japanese army headquarters in Rabaul, officers continued to hatch unrealistic plans for reinforcing the Buna-Gona area despite their inability to control the skies over the nearby seas. Finally, Imperial Headquarters in Tokyo recognized the futility of continuing the fight. Whereas a telegram to Rabaul dated November 16 had stated, "It is essential for the execution of future operations that the Buna area be secured. Our strategy position in the seas will be fundamentally shaken if this area is lost," a December 12 telegram changed the picture entirely: "Great importance must be placed on securing the northeastern end of New Guinea. Buna will not be reinforced, but should eventually be evacuated."[19]

Meanwhile, with all Allied troops—Australian and American—bogged down before the fortified Japanese positions, General Blamey met with MacArthur on the afternoon of November 25 to discuss additional troops to put in the line. The conference took place at MacArthur's headquarters in Port Moresby, called Government House because it had been the residence of the civilian territorial governor before the war. Also present were General Kenney and Lieutenant General Edmund Herring, commanding general of the Australian I Corps, which included the 7th Division and all the Australian troops fighting at Buna-Gona. Herring also commanded the American forces at the scene.

MacArthur suggested that the American 41st Infantry Division that had been training at Rockhampton, Australia, be sent to the Buna-Gona front to support the troops there. Blamey disagreed; he said he would rather have the Australian 21st Brigade, because he had confidence in their fighting ability. Both Australian generals said they did not think much of the fighting qualities of the 32nd, and even less of the division's leadership. It was, as Kenney reported, "a bitter pill for General MacArthur to swallow." He ordered Kenney to fly in the Australian 21st Brigade, as Blamey requested.[20]

Two American officers MacArthur sent to investigate the condition of the 32nd Division reinforced the comments of the two Australian generals. Lieutenant Colonel David Larr, of the operations staff, returned to Port Moresby with a negative assessment of the fighting ability of the troops and reported that Harding had located his command post at Embogo, some thirteen miles from the front. MacArthur's chief of staff, Major General Richard K. Sutherland, visited the front and reported that the soldiers lacked the will to fight and lacked aggressive leadership. All this reinforced rumors that had been drifting back to Port Moresby of American soldiers throwing down their weapons and fleeing from the Japanese. Sutherland recommended Harding's removal from command.[21]

A few days later Blamey informed the Australian chief of the general staff, Lieutenant General Northcott, of conditions at the front and his plan to use the 21st Brigade. He then told Northcott of MacArthur's offer to call up the 41st Infantry Division. "The Americans say the other division which they left in Australia is a much better one than the one they have here, but since they chose this as number one, I believe their view to be merely wishful thinking. I feel quite sure in my own mind that the American forces, which have been expanded even more rapidly than our own were in the first years of the war, will not attain any high standard of training or war spirit for very many months to come." He then bemoaned the fact that the Australian 9th Division, which was still in the Middle East, had been replaced by two American divisions whose "fighting qualities are so low, I do not think they are a very considerable contribution to the defense of Australia."[22]

Although MacArthur was not privy to Blamey's report, he would have been apoplectic had he heard American soldiers described in such disparaging terms. So too would another American military giant: Eddie Rickenbacker, who was visiting the general at the front. The famed World War I ace was on a secret mission to meet with MacArthur on behalf of Secretary of War Stimson. On the journey from Pearl Harbor, Rickenbacker's B-17 had crashed in the Pacific, and he and several crew members spent twenty-four days lost at sea in three small life rafts. They had no food but for a few fish and a seagull they killed, and no water other than what they could collect from the occasional rainfall. Rickenbacker carried a message from Stimson he was to deliver personally to MacArthur. To this day, it is unknown what the message contained, because neither man ever revealed it. Some historians suggest that Stimson told MacArthur to stop publicly complaining about not receiving enough men and supplies to fight the war. Others believe he came to tell MacArthur about the pending landings on North Africa, information Marshall would not have trusted to radio communications.[23]

Despite having once been antagonists during their careers, the two old soldiers hit it off surprisingly well. In one conversation, MacArthur made a confession that surprised Rickenbacker. "You know, Eddie, I probably did the American Air Forces more harm than any man living when I was chief of staff by refusing to believe in the future of the airplane as a weapon of war. I am now doing everything I can to make amends for that great mistake."[24]

Eddie Rickenbacker described MacArthur's living arrangements as "not luxurious. His headquarters consisted of a frame shack and an outhouse. MacArthur was interested not in comfort but in winning a war." He went on to describe Port Moresby as a "hellhole," and a "bombed-out ruin of a city in the center of a cloud of swirling red dust."[25]

November 29 was a sunny, quiet Sunday at Rockhampton, Queensland, where General Eichelberger was overseeing the jungle training of the 41st Infantry Division. Unexpectedly, Eichelberger received a message from General Chamberlin, chief of the operations staff, to gather up a small staff and await orders to fly to Port Moresby. Allowed to bring a small staff, Eichelberger sent a messenger to retrieve his chief of staff, Brigadier General Clovis E. Byers, who was swimming at a beach thirty miles away. At midnight, he received orders that two C-47 planes were being sent for him and his men. They were to take off at dawn.

Upon arrival at Port Moresby, Eichelberger and Byers were told they would spend the night at MacArthur's headquarters. Driven to Government House, they were taken directly to the screened veranda on which

MacArthur kept a desk. In addition to the commander in chief, Generals Sutherland and Kenney were waiting for them.

Without preliminaries, MacArthur, pacing up and down the veranda as he spoke, told Eichelberger, "Bob, I'm putting you in command at Buna. Relieve Harding. I am sending you in, Bob, and I want you to remove all officers who won't fight. Relieve regimental and battalion commanders; if necessary, put sergeants in charge of battalions and corporals in charge of companies—anyone who will fight. Time is of the essence; the Japs may land reinforcements any night."

With increased emphasis, he added, "Bob, I want you to take Buna, or not come back alive; and that goes for your chief of staff too. Do you understand?" Eichelberger responded, "Yes, sir." He intended to leave first thing in the morning.[26]

At breakfast with Eichelberger the following morning, MacArthur amended his statement of the night before: "Now, Bob, I have no illusions about your personal courage, but remember that you are no use to me dead."[27]

After breakfast, Eichelberger flew from Port Moresby to a small airfield a few miles from the front that was under expansion and entered a radically different world. "My staff and I landed at eleven a.m. on December 1. Forty minutes from Moresby—but when the stink of the swamp hit our nostrils, we knew that we, like the troops of the 32nd Division, were prisoners of geography. And like them we would never get out unless we fought our way out."[28]

Some writers have taken Eichelberger to task for unkind remarks he made concerning some of the officers and men of the division soon after his arrival at the front. Perhaps as a mea culpa for those comments, in his own memoir of the war he went to great lengths to identify the root causes of the problems faced by the division, beginning with the lack of adequate training. "A great deal has been said and whispered about the 32nd Division, and much of it makes no sense. The 32nd, which failed at Buna, was the same 32nd that won the victory there. No one else did."[29]

Eichelberger found an army in disarray and in need of aggressive direction. The troops were in deplorable condition. Many had long, dirty beards, their uniforms were in rags, and they were ill fed. When he visited the soldiers facing Buna Village he found them in need of food, vitamins, and cigarettes. Those closest to the Japanese positions had gone without food since the day before, and when some did arrive, it was only two tins of C rations per man.

Eichelberger knew that as corps commander, he did not have to relieve Harding just because MacArthur had told him to; such a command change was up to his own judgment. Yet based on what he witnessed at the front and reports from his own staff, he concluded that Harding had to go, as did his regimental commanders. After relieving Harding, Eichelberger put the division's artillery commander, Brigadier General Albert W. Waldron, who had a much-deserved reputation for ingenuity and bravery, in command of the entire division.[30]

An early attempt by Eichelberger to smash the enemy fortifications ended badly. As a result, he allowed all troops two weeks to rest and replenish their strength. The airfield that engineers had been expanding at Dobodura was finally ready to receive large aircraft, such as C-47s, on December 3. Supplies began pouring in, including rations that allowed the troops their first hot meal in days, if not weeks in some cases. Uniforms and boots arrived, as did artillery, and up the coast from Milne Bay came vessels large enough to carry the badly needed tanks. The situation began to turn around perhaps in part because Eichelberger was able to get better cooperation and support from both the American and nearby Australian units.

When the fighting resumed, Eichelberger did something that Harding had probably never thought of doing: he spent a lot of time at or near the front. He made a point of wearing his three silver stars, even though it increased the danger of enemy fire. Eichelberger exposed himself to risk so that his troops would know their commander was with them.[31]

Fresh troops, nutritious rations, artillery, tanks, Bren gun carriers, and a renewed aggressive attitude among the American commanders made the difference. On December 8, the Australians took Gona Village, counting 650 dead Japanese as they swept through the village.[32]

Six days later, troops from the 32nd Division occupied Buna Village. Four days after that, Japanese warships landed thirteen hundred reinforcements, but by then the die had been cast. On Christmas night a Japanese submarine managed to elude patrolling PT boats and put ashore a quantity of rations and ammunition for the troops holding out at Buna Mission. Before it departed, the boat fired a few shells at the American forces facing the mission. That was the last time supplies got through to the Japanese.[33]

After days of bloody and ferocious fighting, the 32nd Division, aided by the Australian 18th Brigade, and especially by tanks from the Australian 2/6th Armored Regiment, captured the Japanese positions at Buna Mission on January 2, 1943.[34]

The last holdout of any consequence was Sanananda Village, which was perhaps the best-fortified and -supplied of all the Japanese coastal locations. On January 12, Major General Kensaku Oda sent an urgent appeal to the Eighteenth Army headquarters in Rabaul: "Starvation is taking many lives, and it is weakening our already extended lines. We are doomed." He begged that reinforcements arrive "at once."[35]

The next day Lieutenant General Hatazo Adachi, the recently appointed commander in chief of the Eighteenth Army in Rabaul, ordered all remaining troops evacuated. Those who could not be reached by small boats and barges were instructed to make their way up the coast to the nearest Japanese base. Estimates of the number of Japanese who were evacuated or managed to work their way up the coast to safety range from 800 to 1,000. Of the more than 7,000 Japanese who fought at Buna-Gona, roughly 6,000 died there. Fewer than 200 surrendered. American losses were approximately 1,000 killed, while the Australians lost 1,300. Over half the Allied troops who fought there suffered at least one, sometimes two of the debilitating diseases associated with the jungle and swamp-infested territory. Looking back on the casualties resulting from combat and the environment, General Eichelberger wrote that they were a "high purchase price for the inhospitable jungle."[36]

The commander in chief acknowledged what the American and Australian troops had been up against at Buna-Gona when he told the

Australian war minister, Frederick Shedden, "Of the nine campaigns I have fought, I have not seen one where conditions were more punishing of the soldier than this one."[37]

MacArthur was shocked at the cost in lives in taking Buna. Determined never again to make a direct assault on an enemy position, he implemented a new policy, which he explained at a staff conference, of bypassing enemy strongholds and using the Air Force to help isolate them so they could not be resupplied. He told General Kenney, "You incapacitate them!" Let the Japanese sit in their jungle fortifications and wait. "The jungle," he said with great flare, "starvation. They're my allies." That was the way he would conduct the rest of the war. Large, powerful enemy formations would be isolated and left to wither. There would be no more Bunas.[38]

Part Two

1943

CHAPTER 10

Sailing the Bismarck Sea

As congratulations poured into MacArthur's headquarters over the Buna-Gona victory, the SWPA commander in chief was hard at work planning his future strategy for dealing with the Japanese. MacArthur knew that in order to avoid future battles like Buna, he would need to control the sea—and, just as important, the air over the sea—to prevent reinforcements and supplies from reaching large, isolated enemy forces along the New Guinea coast.

To accomplish this, he badly needed a navy capable of landing troops on an assault beach in a timely and safe manner. MacArthur and Blamey both had attempted to convince Vice Admiral Arthur Carpender, commander of Allied naval forces, to supply destroyers to escort the luggers and trawlers that brought men and matériel up the coast from Milne Bay. The admiral refused, believing the shallow, reef-ridden waters south of Buna would endanger his vessels. He was also concerned the ships would be easy targets for enemy aircraft due to an absence of reliable charts reducing their ability to maneuver.[1]

Several attempts by MacArthur to have large warships assigned to his theater, including aircraft carriers, had met with resistance from Admiral King. As a result, the battle for Buna-Gona had been fought without assistance from the Navy, other than a squadron of motor torpedo patrol boats based at Milne Bay. MacArthur, who had been impressed by the vessels during his evacuation of Bataan, had pressured Admiral Carpender to force the Navy to send these four PT boats, along with a PT boat tender to service them.[2] These powerful wooden boats were heavily armed, but their fuel consumption limited their range to less than two hundred miles without a means to refuel. Though they played havoc with Japanese attempts to sneak troop barges and supply submarines onto the beachheads, providing a valuable service, they were not the navy MacArthur needed. If he could not have large warships, then he wanted amphibians such as landing craft to get his troops to shore for future assaults.

Samuel Eliot Morison claimed, "If the Southwest Pacific command had been blessed with an amphibious force of shoal-draft beaching craft supported by carriers, cruisers and destroyers, the Japanese garrisons on that coast could have been cleaned up in a week. Carrier air strikes against enemy airfields on New Britain would have kept Japanese flyers grounded, and combat air patrol would have intercepted many who broke through."[3]

Supporting this view is a report made to the War Department by a Naval officer from Washington who visited the Buna front in December. He wrote that there was "every reason to believe that Buna could have been taken during November if one of our units could have put a minimum of one combat team afloat."[4]

For months, MacArthur had beaten the drum for the establishment of an amphibious force in his theater to facilitate troop landings. He also wanted an experienced amphibious officer assigned to his naval force who could build and command an amphibious fleet. In addition, he told Marshall and King he wanted Marines trained in amphibious landings. King promised him the 1st Marine Division as soon as Army troops relieved them on Guadalcanal. The 5th Marine Regiment began arriving in early December. Over 75 percent of the division had suffered from malaria while on Guadalcanal, and on their arrival at a camp outside

Brisbane, they discovered the site infested with the same malaria-bearing mosquito that had caused them so much misery. Although they were quickly relocated to a site near Melbourne, hundreds of the men were reinfected and the number of new cases mounted. With more than 7,500 men incapacitated by malaria, and a rehabilitation period of as long as six months, the Marines would not be fully ready for combat for close to a year.

Admiral King finally did agree to assign an amphibious officer to MacArthur's naval forces. On December 15, 1942, King ordered Rear Admiral Daniel E. Barbey to the South West Pacific Area. A 1912 Naval Academy graduate, Barbey was a leading expert in amphibious warfare. His interest began when he saw photographs of landing craft with hinged bows that the Japanese had used while assaulting the northern Chinese port city of Tianjin in July 1937. After immersing himself in the subject and gaining a reputation as an authority, Barbey was assigned to update the Navy's official manual on amphibious landings, which had last been revised in 1918. Barbey's revision became the "bible" of amphibious warfare, used by the Navy throughout the war.[5]

In May 1942 King had created the Amphibious Warfare Section within the Navy Department and appointed Barbey to command it. In this role, he was responsible for coordinating amphibious warfare training programs and overseeing the design and construction of landing ships and landing craft. Within months the construction budget grew to a billion dollars. The main difference between a "landing ship" and a "landing craft" was the size of the vessel. Anything over two hundred feet long was a "ship," while anything of lesser length was a "craft." The best known of the ships was the LST, or landing ship, tank, which their crews often referred to as "long, slow, targets" due to their bulky size and slow speed. Best known among the smaller vessels was the LCI, or landing craft, infantry; and LCT, landing craft, tank. Many of these vessels were designed by Higgins Industries of New Orleans, and became widely known as "Higgins boats." Barbey not only oversaw the design and construction of these vessels but also participated in testing many of them. Rear Admiral Barbey was exactly the man MacArthur needed.

With MacArthur in New Guinea when Barbey arrived in Australia on January 8, 1943, he met first with Admiral Carpender, who described his own strained relationship with MacArthur over the Navy's lack of support during the Buna-Gona campaign. Carpender remained adamant about not sending any of his ships into the area until General Kenney had better control of the skies and better charts were developed.

Next, Barbey met with the operations officer, Brigadier General Stephen J. Chamberlin, who outlined MacArthur's timetable for moving up the New Guinea coast to Lae, then across the Vitiaz Strait, a narrow waterway between New Britain and New Guinea, and invading New Britain. He told Barbey that MacArthur "expects you and your amphibious force" to take an active role in maintaining the schedule. At that moment, Barbey's amphibious force was composed of himself, one other officer, and one ship, the attack transport *Henry T. Allen*, which was in such poor shape that Barbey dared not send it into a combat zone.[6]

When he returned to Australia, MacArthur met with Barbey, describing in detail his plans for driving the Japanese out of New Guinea and then out of the Philippines. Using a map on his office wall to highlight where the coming campaigns would take place, MacArthur turned to Barbey and said, "Your job is to develop an amphibious force that can carry my troops in those campaigns."[7]

On February 8, General Adachi, commanding the Eighteenth Army at Rabaul, issued orders for the assembly and evacuation by barges of all remaining Imperial troops in the Buna-Gona area to Lae and Salamaua. The South Seas Force—which had invaded Guam, Rabaul, and New Guinea, almost making it to Port Moresby—had been so devastated that it was dissolved as a unique formation. Only 1,951 survivors remained of the 7,383 troops originally assigned to the South Seas Force when it arrived at New Guinea.[8]

When Imperial General Headquarters recognized the possibility that Buna-Gona might be lost to the Allies, it had begun issuing orders for the movement of additional troops from Rabaul to Lae and Salamaua, and the establishment of new bases on New Guinea's northern coast. Lieutenant General Imamura, Eighth Area Army commander, received instructions to occupy a number of sites even farther north than Lae. Making use of recently arrived units of the 5th Division, he sent one infantry battalion to Wewak, 382 miles northwest of Lae, another to Madang, halfway between Lae and Wewak, and the 31st Road Construction Unit to Tuluvu at the western end of New Britain. Another infantry battalion was shipped from Kavieng to Finschhafen, about one hundred miles northeast from Lae on the Huon Peninsula. Construction of air bases began at all locations as soon as the troops and their equipment landed. The convoys carrying these troops suffered some losses from air and submarine attacks, but for the most part the majority made it to their destinations.

In early January a reinforced infantry regiment from the 51st Division that had arrived from China in December reported to the Eighteenth Army. The regiment was attached to the newly named the Okabe Detachment, commanded by Major General Toru Okabe. General Okabe quickly received orders to leave Rabaul to bolster the defenses at Lae and Salamaua. Meanwhile, General Adachi was ordered to "secure important areas to the west of Lae and Salamaua." The most important of these areas was Wau, currently held by the Allies. Both Okabe and his commander, Adachi, were confident they would succeed.[9]

Code breakers had informed MacArthur that Japanese radio traffic indicated the movement of large numbers of troops from China, the Philippines, and the Japanese Home Islands into the South West Pacific Area. They also told him a convoy of troopships would soon leave Rabaul, heading to Lae. Allied planners determined that these troops were intended for an assault on Wau. MacArthur instructed Kenney to attack the convoy before it departed from Rabaul, and to fly in men and supplies in support of the Australians holding the area around the airfield at Wau.[10]

General Kenney ordered his bomber commander, Brigadier General Kenneth Walker, to increase reconnaissance of Rabaul and prepare a full-scale attack on shipping located in its busy harbor. Reconnaissance reported that since late December the number of ships at the powerful base had increased substantially. Photoreconnaissance revealed the presence of ninety-one ships, including twenty-one warships. They estimated that merchant shipping totaled 300,000 tons.[11]

General Blamey was concerned about losing Wau to the enemy, so he decided to reinforce the area's defenses. On January 4 he requested that Kenney fly the 17th Infantry Brigade, stationed at Milne Bay, to Wau. Commanded by forty-three-year-old Brigadier Murray Moten, a former bank officer, the brigade had fought in North Africa and Greece prior to its return to Australia and transfer to New Guinea. Blamey instructed Moten to assume command of all forces in the Wau area.[12]

The Wau airfield was deep in a valley 3,300 feet above sea level. Surrounded by mountains, no roads led to it, just native foot trails. The landing strip was 3,600 feet long, with a width starting at 450 feet at its northeast end, where aircraft came in, and narrowing to 250 feet at the southwest end. Landings were made on a ten-degree uphill gradient, and takeoffs downhill because of the nearby mountains. Little more than a grass strip, it suffered from drainage problems. During the rainiest season, mud was as deep as eight inches, making landings and takeoffs problematic at best.

Wau had once been the center of a great gold-mining boom, whose miners included Errol Flynn. All supplies then had come in by aircraft, including the heavy equipment used in the mining operations, and even the pool table in the hotel. Now soldiers, rations, and military supplies were heading into Wau.

As with the airfield at Kokoda, the one at Wau, despite its dangers, was valuable to both sides. For the Allies it offered a base from which to attack enemy forces along the coast and in the Bismarck Sea. For the Japanese it offered a place from which to attack enemy concentrations throughout New Guinea, especially Port Moresby, less than 150 miles to the southeast. During the fight along the Kokoda Track and at the Buna-Gona beachheads, neither side paid a great deal of attention to Wau. The Allies occupied it in March 1942, and aside from the occasional supply flight, it had sat nearly forgotten, except by the men stationed there, the members of the Kanga Force.

The Kanga Force was a composite formation consisting of men from the New Guinea Volunteer Rifles (NGVR), and troops from the 1st and 2/5th Independent Militia Companies. During the months of March and April they had conducted reconnaissance missions on the enemy forces at Salamaua and Lae. In May 1942, General MacArthur ordered Major Norman Fleay, the force's twenty-four-year-old commanding officer, to start harassing raids at Lae and Salamaua. Fleay, who was promoted to lieutenant colonel in June, had served in the Middle East in 1941, where he was wounded, before returning to Australia. MacArthur wanted the Kanga Force to destroy enemy facilities and even possibly capture one of the airfields that Japanese fighter planes were using. At the time, only a small number of Imperial Navy troops defended both bases.[13]

In one attack launched during the early-morning hours of June 29, seventy-one Australians from 2/5th and the NGVR assaulted the Japanese at the airfield near Salamaua. Of the two hundred fifty defenders, the Australians reportedly killed one hundred, suffering only three men wounded. Although they failed to occupy the airfield, they did destroy several buildings and an important nearby bridge. Japanese aircraft raced along at treetop level, strafing and bombing various foot trails in their frantic search for the attackers. Over the next few days an additional two hundred Japanese troops arrived from Lae, where two thousand troops were stationed, to reinforce the garrison.[14]

Because an Allied airpower buildup at Wau would make the Japanese positions at Lae and Salamaua untenable, General Imamura, commander in chief of the Eighth Area Army, was determined to drive out the Australians. His biggest problem in achieving this was that he had only 3,500 troops at both locations, and many were ill and insufficiently supplied. They just were not strong enough to push the Australians out of Wau.[15]

The Okabe Detachment, preparing to leave Rabaul for Lae, numbered more than five thousand men. They included three infantry battalions of the 102nd Infantry Regiment, the 2nd Battalion of the 14th Artillery Regiment, the 3rd Company of the 51st Engineer Regiment, and the 3rd Company of the 51st Transport Regiment. It would attempt to drive out the Australian defenders and capture the increasingly vital airfield at Wau.[16]

On January 5, General Walker sent six B-17s and six B-24s against the shipping targets at Rabaul. Results were minimal, with only one Army transport sunk, but two attackers were lost to enemy fighters, including a B-17 in which Walker himself was a passenger. Kenney had ordered the general not to go on missions, but he disobeyed and was never seen again.[17]

At noon that same day, the convoy carrying the Okabe Detachment left Rabaul for Lae. It comprised five transports, escorted by five destroyers, and above it flew a large protective cover of fighters. Several of the transports were armed with antiaircraft guns. The five destroyers were from two different squadrons and sailed under the command of Captain Masayuki Kitamura. Because the transports had an average speed of only eight knots per hour, the 466-mile trip would take fifty hours.

At ten thirty the following morning, when the convoy was less than halfway to its destination, searching RAAF Catalinas located it. Over the next two days Allied bombers attacked the ships while dozens of Allied fighters tangled with dozens of Japanese fighters in prolonged dogfights. One transport, *Nichiryu Maru*, sank in flames, taking with her a large quantity of medical supplies and equipment. Destroyers rescued fewer than eight hundred of the twelve hundred soldiers aboard.[18] During the early afternoon on January 7, a second transport, *Myoko Maru*, was so badly damaged that its crew beached her some nine miles east of Lae. No casualties were reported, although several Army crew members did suffer wounds. The next day a flight of Curtiss P-40 Warhawks, each equipped with a single three-hundred-pound bomb, attacked the *Myoko Maru*. One direct hit dropped down the transport's stack and destroyed her engine. She remained on the beach for the next fifteen years as scavengers and salvagers hauled away anything of value.

Late in the day, the remaining three transports dropped their anchors less than a mile from shore and rapidly transferred troops, equipment, and supplies into motorized barges that ran back and forth between the ships and the beach. Once ashore, soldiers moved a half mile inland and set up camp under the protective cover of the jungle canopy.[19]

After completion of the landing of about four thousand troops and their supplies, the three transports and their destroyer escorts left during the night and sped, as fast as the empty transports could, back toward Rabaul, harassed by Allied planes during most of the return trip. Also harassed by bombing and strafing were the soldiers who had been landed. For several days, the beach and nearby jungle were targeted by Allied planes flying out of Port Moresby, Milne Bay, and airfields in Australia. Large quantities of supplies waiting for removal under cover were destroyed, including an ammunition dump.[20]

Over the next week, General Okabe moved almost his entire force down the coast to Salamaua using motorized barges. With a garrison now numbering about 6,500 troops, Salamaua was no longer a target for the small harassing patrols from Kanga Force. As he prepared to launch his attack on Wau, Okabe selected Colonel Yasuhei Maruoka, commander of the 102nd Infantry Regiment, for this task. Maruoka took half the men of two full battalions and one partial battalion (it had suffered losses during the Allied attacks) and headed toward Wau on January 16. The second half of the force followed the next day. Because so many of their supplies had been destroyed in the air attacks, each man carried only enough food for fourteen days.[21]

Although Wau was only thirty miles away, neither Maruoka nor any of the 2,500 to 3,000 men he led had any idea what the countryside they were entering was like. What's more, they had neither reliable intelligence on the location or size of Australian forces between Salamaua and Wau nor a clear-cut route to take them there. At times, due to fear of ambushes by roving Australian patrols, they were forced to leave a long-established foot trail called the Black Cat Track and cut their own path. There was also the danger of attack from Allied aircraft searching for them. Every open stretch of terrain left them vulnerable to such strikes.[22]

As the Japanese made their way toward Wau over the next two weeks, fighting both Australian patrols and the jungle, Allied aircraft brought reinforcements into Wau. Elements of the 17th Brigade began arriving by Dakotas on January 14. This ferrying of troops from Port Moresby kept up each day that the weather cooperated. They brought in 535 men and

28 officers, well rested and ready to fight. Until victory was declared at Buna on January 23, fewer than a dozen Dakotas were available for this duty. The number quickly doubled when troop flights to the Buna front stopped, and with the arrival of new Dakotas from the United States.[23]

On January 27, Maruoka's forces reached a ridge overlooking the Wau airfield and Wau village. His men were exhausted from struggling through muddy trails and almost continual fighting with relentless Australians, but more than anything else, the soldiers were hungry—they had not eaten in days and were beginning to show signs of starvation. In their weakened condition, the Japanese troops were quickly driven back by Wau's growing number of defenders, who now had twenty-five-pound artillery pieces that had been flown in and assembled by their crews.

In the early-morning hours of February 1, Colonel Maruoka finally concluded that he was never going to capture the airfield. Over the previous three days, he had watched as 130 transport planes landed at Wau, bringing in about a thousand fresh troops, as well as field artillery pieces, heavy machine guns, and mortars. He was now outgunned and outnumbered.[24]

Maruoka began moving his troops back in preparation for a complete withdrawal, which Eighteenth Army headquarters in Rabaul finally ordered on February 13. The withdrawal began the next day. By then the troops were in extremely bad shape. They had suffered in battle and from lack of food. Estimates of numbers lost to combat and starvation reach as high as twelve hundred men. Over 70 percent of the survivors suffered from malnutrition, malaria, dysentery, and other diseases that left them unfit for combat duty.[25]

Yet the Okabe Detachment's failure to capture Wau did not lessen the airfield's value. Another attempt had to be made to drive the Allies from that airfield. What's more, now that Japanese forces had been driven from the Papua section of New Guinea, Eighth Area Army commander General Imamura recognized the importance of strengthening their position in northern New Guinea, including the territory once controlled by the Dutch.

He had already begun doing so in January. On the nineteenth,

13,700 men from the 20th Division arrived at Wewak, having come directly from Pusan, Korea. The entire 41st Division, previously stationed at Tsingtao, China, would join them in the coming weeks, bringing the total number of troops at Wewak close to 25,000. Additional troops, especially units specializing in road building and airfield construction, landed at Madang and other locations farther up the coast. Imamura's plan was to build a 135-mile-long coastal road linking all these places with Lae and Salamaua so that the movement of troops and supplies would not have to rely on small vessels prone to attack by Allied planes, submarines, and PT boats. He also wanted airfields that would accommodate a large number of fighters. His final goal was to ship 100,000 troops into New Guinea.

Convoys to New Guinea were vulnerable to attack by the increasing number of Allied aircraft, and to the low-level bombing of ships that General Kenney had instituted for his pilots and crews. Both sides recognized that one of the most important keys to victory was control of the air. Convoy schedules relied more on weather reports than on any other form of intelligence. It was safest to sail when the skies filled with storm clouds, and when heavy winds kept Allied aircraft grounded.

Once masters of the air over the Bismarck and Solomon Seas, the Imperial Navy and Army air forces were now losing more planes than could be quickly replaced. Even more important was the loss of experienced pilots, whose replacements soon turned out to be recruits with limited training and few actual flight hours. This change in dominance of the skies was not lost on many of the officers, especially air force officers, at Rabaul. One, FPO First Class Hisashi Igarashi, a pilot with Air Group 705, wrote in his diary, "Just several months ago we had the mastery, but to our regret we retreated enormously and the situation reversed. Yet, looking at the reality of the front, I am really irritated."[26]

General Imamura realized he must reinforce the garrison at Lae, which was to serve as the anchor for Japanese control of central and northern New Guinea. With the loss of both Buna and Guadalcanal, and the consequent danger to the entire Solomons chain, Imamura knew that Imperial Headquarters viewed New Guinea as the valuable right flank protecting Japan's entire southern empire. Considering this, he decided to transfer the headquarters of the Eighteenth Army, along with its commanding officer, General Adachi, to Lae. He also ordered plans to ship the 51st Division, less the men sent earlier with the Okabe Detachment, to Lae.

Imperial Headquarters urged Imamura to send these Lae reinforcements in May, but after consulting with his staff, the general refused to wait—a delay would simply give the Allies more time to increase the number of aircraft they could commit to attacking his convoy. Imamura's staff estimated the convoy to Lae had no better than a fifty-fifty chance of success whenever it was sent. Based on current Allied strength, they estimated a ten-ship convoy would suffer losses of four transports and thirty to forty aircraft. Despite these horrendous assessments, Imamura's chief of staff, Lieutenant General Yoshihara Kane, later noted his commander had "no alternative" but to send the division to Lae if he was to keep that vital location out of Allied hands. There was also the possibility, however remote, that once established, the division might be able to march on Wau and capture the airfield.[27]

On February 14, Imamura issued his order for the deployment of the 51st Division and the Eighteenth Army headquarters to Lae. The actual date of departure would depend on reports from meteorologists at Rabaul.

Preparatory to the sailing of the convoy, plans were made to launch attacks on enemy airfields to reduce the danger from that quarter. Photoreconnaissance flights overflew Port Moresby, Milne Bay, and Buna. The commanding officer of the 6th Air Division, Lieutenant General Giichi Itabana, learned there were ninety-seven bombers and eighty-one fighters at the Allied bases. Photos of Port Moresby in particular convinced him the town was too heavily defended and the aircraft at the airfield too widely dispersed for a quick, successful raid. Plans for airfield attacks proceeded anyway, but bad weather grounded the Japanese air fleet.[28]

On February 19, MacArthur received a report from the radio interception and translation operation at Melbourne that the Japanese were planning a major convoy to New Guinea soon. The information was based primarily on radio traffic in and out of Rabaul and on ship movements. MacArthur met with General Kenney on the twenty-fifth to review what they knew. In his opinion, MacArthur said, the enemy was going to reinforce the troops at Lae. Kenney tended to agree that it seemed the logical place for a large troop insertion. MacArthur also expressed the opinion that the convoy would be at least twice the size of the one that brought the Okabe Detachment to Lae.[29]

The next day Kenney ordered as many aircraft as possible to congregate at the airfield near Buna. He wanted to reduce the possibility that any of his planes would be unable to participate in the attack on the convoy. MacArthur had made it clear to his air chief that he wanted the reinforcing troops stopped before they reached New Guinea. Kenney met with his second in command of the Fifth Air Force, Brigadier General Ennis Whitehead, to lay out the tactics they would use for the attack on the convoy. Most important, they wanted to locate the convoy as soon as possible after it steamed from Rabaul.

Their goal was to begin attacking the ships day and night with heavy bombers until the convoy steamed within range of the commerce-destroying B-25s. Once they reached this point, the heavy four-engine B-17s would drop their bombs from eight to ten thousand feet just seconds before the B-25s pounced. Flying in at two hundred feet and at speeds between 200 and 250 mph, the B-25s would attack, using a new "skip bombing" tactic many of the pilots had been practicing. Behind them would be Douglas A-20 light bomber/intruders with all guns blazing. Then it would be the turn of the Bristol Beaufighters from the RAAF 30 Squadron, speeding in at mast level with their four 20mm nose cannons and six wing-mounted 7.7mm machine guns suppressing enemy fire by strafing the warships' antiaircraft guns, bridges, and crews. Meanwhile, every P-38 they could put aloft would provide air cover against Japanese fighters.

Skip bombing had been developed because of the ineffectiveness of high-altitude bombing against moving targets such as ships. In the early part of the war, Army pilots had very little, if any, training in bombing ships at sea, and less than 1 percent of their bombs hit the targets. American major Paul Gunn had modified several B-25 Mitchells at Townsville by removing the bombardier and replacing him with four .50-caliber machine guns. This gave the plane added protection as it swept in on an enemy ship at what would normally be considered a dangerously low level and released its bomb with a four- to five-second delay fuse at a distance of sixty to one hundred feet from the ship. The plane would then lift up over the vessel as the bomb "skipped" across the surface of the water and slammed into the side of the ship. It was said this method improved target hits to 72 percent.

Kenney and Whitehead then turned to the all-important question of where they would find the convoy. As Kenney described, they "went over all the information at hand and tried to guess how we would run the convoy if we were Japs. We plotted all the courses of all Jap ship movements reported for the past four months between Rabaul and Lae, checking both the route around the north coast of New Britain and the one around the south. The courses followed regular grooves. The weather forecaster still insisted that during the first three or four days of March the weather would be very bad on the north coast and quite good along the south coast." That settled it. They would focus on searching for the convoy in the Bismarck Sea, off the north coast of New Britain, where the enemy was expected to take advantage of the inclement weather.[30]

When Kenney explained his plan for attacking the convoy to MacArthur, the commander in chief smiled and said, "I think the Japs are in for a lot of trouble."[31]

At Rabaul, the meteorologists were telling General Imamura virtually the same thing: good weather on the south coast, bad weather on the north coast. Just as Kenney and Whitehead had predicted, Imamura decided to use the route through the Bismarck Sea.

During the night of February 28 the convoy steamed out of Rabaul, headed around Crater Peninsula and entered the storm-tossed Bismarck Sea. Eight transports packed with six thousand soldiers, plus their equipment and supplies, sailed toward Lae, escorted by eight destroyers under the command of Rear Admiral Masatomi Kimura. Aboard the destroyers were an additional 958 soldiers. One hundred army and navy fighters assigned to local air groups were to take turns flying cover if the weather cleared. An additional eighteen fighters from the carrier *Zuiho*, stationed at Truk, were to offer added protection. Lieutenant General Hatazo Ada-chi, commander of the Eighteenth Army, was aboard the destroyer *Toki-tsukaze*, while the commanding officer of the 51st Division, Lieutenant General Hidemitsu Nakano, was on board the *Yukikaze*. Admiral Kimura's flag flew from the *Shirayuki*. The convoy traveled at the speed of the slow-est transport, seven knots per hour, an agonizingly slow pace for the destroyers, which had top speeds of thirty-five and thirty-eight knots.

All went well with the convoy—except possibly for the soldiers packed inside the tossing and plunging transports—until four p.m. on March 1, when a sudden clearing of the thick clouds above revealed the presence of a B-24 Liberator from the 321st Bomb Squadron/90th Bomb Group. Nicknamed "the Jolly Rogers," the group's aircraft each had a distinctive skull and crossbones painted on the outside of the vertical stabilizers mounted on its tail. Soaring above the convoy was a plane with the name MISS DEEDS painted on its nose, piloted by twenty-five-year-old Lieutenant Walter E. Higgins. After taking off from Ward's Strip at Port Moresby at noon, Higgins had patrolled along the south coast of New Britain before moving north over the island to get away from a developing storm. He had been circling around to return south when his navigator, Lieutenant George Sellmer, caught sight of the ships. It was pure luck on their part that the clouds had briefly opened, and unlucky for the convoy.[32]

Higgins was not about to launch a single-plane attack on the convoy. He had already attempted that once before. On January 5, during the same operation in which General Walker's B-17 was lost, Higgins had attacked the convoy carrying the Okabe Detachment to Lae. When flak from an escorting destroyer crippled his aircraft, Higgins was forced to ditch the plane near a small island off the southern coast of New Britain. Two members of his crew perished as the plane's belly caved in on impact. A search plane rescued the survivors the following day. Most likely, because of that incident, an order had gone out to all pilots in the group not to attempt a single-plane attack on convoys. Higgins obeyed the order, instead radioing the position of the convoy, which was sixty miles off the coast near Cape Hollman.[33]

After receiving Higgins's report at Port Moresby, a flight of seven B-17s that Kenney and Whitehead had standing by was immediately dispatched to the area. Unfortunately, the weather had turned back to rainstorms and clouds, and night darkness set in, so the heavy bombers never found the convoy.

One destroyer in the convoy intercepted Higgins's report, and the information was radioed to Rabaul and to the convoy commander, Admiral Kimura. The admiral informed General Adachi, aboard *Toki-tsukaze*, who passed the word to his army officers aboard the transports. Kimura did not appear to be too concerned about the sighting—after all, he had expected they would be found eventually. Perhaps the bad weather would keep up until they reached Lae. As a precaution, he issued more rigid security and blackout orders.

The same inclement weather that protected the convoy was grounding Japanese aircraft was well, and thus protecting the Allied airfields that Vice Admiral Gunichi Mikawa, commander of the South East Area Fleet headquartered in Rabaul, had promised to attack while the convoy sailed.

At daybreak on March 2, with the weather beginning to clear, several B-24 Liberators took to the skies in search of the convoy. Meanwhile, a flight of six RAAF A-20 Bostons (the Australian version of the Douglas A-20 Havoc light bomber and intruder fighter) attacked the airfield at Lae in an effort to prevent aircraft stationed there from coming to the aid of the convoy once the assault was under way.[34]

At 8:15, a Liberator from the 320th Squadron reported finding the enemy ships about thirty miles north of Cape Gloucester and heading toward the Vitiaz Strait. The plane continued shadowing the convoy until 10:15, when the first eight B-17s from the 63rd Squadron/43rd Bomb Group arrived to begin the attack. Trailing the B-17s were three Imperial Navy fighters that were quickly jumped by P-38 Lightnings from the 39th Fighter Squadron. All three were shot down.

Once over the target, the B-17s dropped their thousand-pound demolition bombs from five thousand feet. In a matter of minutes, one transport, *Kyokusei Maru*, was hit five times, exploded, and quickly sank with twelve hundred soldiers aboard. A second transport had fires burning amidships and appeared to be settling in the water. When the bombers withdrew, two of the destroyers began picking up survivors from the sunken transport; Admiral Kimura ordered the destroyers to then proceed at high speed to Lae and discharge the survivors, as they were too overcrowded to engage the enemy, and return immediately to the convoy. They sped away, taking 950 soldiers to Lae.[35]

Meanwhile, the transports kept advancing at slow speed toward the Vitiaz Strait. The day was ending as eleven B-17s arrived and dropped their bomb loads. The crews claimed two direct hits and one ship sunk. So many burning and sinking ships were reported that it was obvious many were citing the same vessel from different angles. As the bombers struck, Zeros and Lightnings tangled in wild confusion. Two B-24s from the 321st Squadron entered the scene and bombed a destroyer and transport without visible results.[36]

At nightfall, with one transport sunk and two seriously but not fatally damaged, the surviving convoy entered the strait. Admiral Kimura ordered the ships to circle for several hours so that they would enter Lae early the next morning. This turned out to be a horrendous decision. Had he proceeded directly to Lae, the ships would have arrived in time to discharge their troops before enemy aircraft began attacking again. One historian described this decision as having "doomed the Lae convoy."[37]

To ensure the Allies did not lose the convoy, several RAAF Catalinas remained overhead during most of the night, occasionally dropping a flare and even a bomb among the circling vessels just to keep everyone aboard anxious about what was coming next. Sometime during the night a Catalina pilot, Flight Lieutenant Terry Duigan, received an unusual radio message from Port Moresby stating that he should remain shadowing the convoy so that he could guide a flight of RAAF Beaufort torpedo bombers to their targets. The message was so strange and discordant with what Duigan knew of the attack plan that he decided to ignore it. In a masterly bit of deception, Port Moresby was stating that the first aircraft in the coming attack would be torpedo bombers—a false transmission intended for Japanese radio operators the Allies expected to be listening in on their radio traffic. As it turned out, the ship captains reacted accordingly.[38]

Before dawn, a B-17 relieved the last Catalina over the convoy. Although reconnaissance reports were confused and differed considerably, it appears that several ships joined the convoy during the night, and at least one unknown vessel departed from it. Anxious to get a crack at the Japanese, eight RAAF Beaufort bombers had flown out of Milne Bay at four a.m. in search of the enemy ships. Rain, thick clouds, and heavy winds hampered visibility, so only two Beauforts arrived at the target. They both attacked, but with no recordable result.[39]

Shortly after dawn on March 3, over ninety aircraft took off from the airfields around Port Moresby. Aircraft from Milne Bay and Dobodura, near Buna, soon joined them. As the convoy received its two destroyers back from their survivor run to Lae, well over one hundred Allied aircraft were assembling over Cape Ward Hunt, southeast of Lae. Every pilot knew the mission and his place in it. Nearly all of these aircraft were tasked to attack the convoy with an important exception: Twenty-two RAAF A-20 Bostons from 22 Squadron were to conduct raids on the fighter airfield at Lae, suppressing the base's ability to defend the convoy.[40]

The attack began a few minutes before ten a.m. From the start, it went off mostly as Kenney had explained to MacArthur. Thirteen B-17s from the 403rd Bomb Group struck the convoy from between seven and nine thousand feet. As expected, many of the forty Zeros assigned to protect the convoy immediately went after the big bombers. Just as quickly, a group of P-38 Lightnings from among the sixteen Kenney had sent into the battle attacked the Zeros. B-25 Mitchell medium bombers at a lower altitude soon joined the B-17s. While the bombers dropped their loads, several of which made direct hits on ships, their machine gunners joined the mayhem of the dogfights in the sky around them.

While many of the crews aboard the ships were looking skyward at the action, their attention was suddenly drawn to the arrival of thirteen Beaufighters from 30 Squadron. The fighters sped toward their targets at between one hundred and two hundred feet above the sea's surface. This was to give the Japanese captains the impression that they were Beaufort torpedo planes (both craft had similar nose configurations). The ship captains fell for the deception, and many turned their vessels to face the enemy planes. That was the best defensive move against a torpedo attack, giving the enemy the narrowest target. Instead, the fighters found just the target they actually wanted as they raked the ships from bow to stern with their four 20mm nose cannons and six wing-mounted machine guns, killing and wounding many of the antiaircraft gun crews aboard the destroyers and transports.

Then came the twelve B-25 Mitchells, whose crews had been practicing skip bombing. With the ships facing the Beaufighters, the skip bombers attacked from their sides at just above sea level. Firing their cannons and machine guns as they approached, they released their fused bombs at the last second to skip along the water's surface and slam into the hull of the targeted ship. Behind them flew twelve A-20 Havoc light bombers, attacking from a lower level than the other bombers.

On the surface, ships were exploding and burning. Some quickly settled in the water, yet others, with their engines and steering seriously damaged, swung back and forth. At least one destroyer slammed into another, and both burned together.

Sometime during the attack, an event occurred that changed forever the face of the air war over New Guinea. One B-17, the *Double Trouble*, piloted by Lieutenant Woodrow W. Moore, collided with a Zero. Both planes immediately burst into flames and began to fall apart and tumble into the sea. Seven members of the bomber's crew managed to get out and release their parachutes. In full view of nearby bombers and fighter crews, several Zeros broke off from combating enemy planes and machine-gunned the seven men hanging from their chutes, killing all of them as they floated helplessly down.

As the attackers ran low on fuel and ammunition, they returned to their bases to restock. At three p.m. the attack was resumed, but by then few target ships remained afloat, and most of them were burning furiously.

That night, word of the machine-gunning of men hanging from parachutes spread from aircrew to aircrew and air base to air base. Revenge was on everyone's mind. Many of the aircrews had heard the horror stories of Japanese torturing prisoners and even cannibalizing the remains of Australian soldiers along the Kokoda Track and during the fighting at Buna-Gona. Some had heard of the massacres inflicted on civilian populations in Chinese cities, but these seemed distant and almost impossible to comprehend. Now they had witnessed the enemy at his worst. Moreover, it was seven of their own, even if they did not know a single member of the crew of the *Double Trouble*—regardless, they were all a part of the aviators' brotherhood.

Several heavy and medium bombers returned to the scene later in the evening, accompanied by several Lightnings for cover. They found one destroyer still afloat, busily picking up survivors from the water. The *Asashio* had on board an estimated five hundred men plucked from the sea when Allied bombers swept down and almost completely obliterated it with bombs. The ship became a burning, blackened hulk that eventually turned on its side and sank. Few on board could have survived.[41]

As darkness fell, no peace came for the Japanese in lifeboats, on rafts, or clinging to wreckage in the sea. Late that night, eight PT boats arrived to sink whatever was still afloat and pick up a few prisoners for interrogation. They fired torpedoes at two burning ships, attacked a submarine that had surfaced to take on survivors, and machine-gunned enemy soldiers on rafts and lifeboats.[42]

Over the next few days, Allied aircraft and PT boats continued to search for survivors of the convoy. Hundreds of enemy soldiers were killed as Americans and Australians took revenge for the murder of the *Double Trouble*'s crew. Some Japanese were picked up by their own destroyers and submarines, while others managed to drift to shore. The lucky ones landed on Japanese beaches, while the unlucky ones had the misfortune to come ashore in Allied territory, where they faced death or prison. The rationale for the bloodbath that took place following the Battle of the Bismarck Sea was that any of the Japanese who survived would be returned to duty and have to be killed by American or Australian soldiers in combat.

Of the 6,900 soldiers sent to Lae on the convoy, fewer than 1,200 made it to their destination. For the most part, they arrived ill equipped for combat duty as they had lost everything on the sunken ships. Japanese records indicate about 2,700 troops were rescued. The rest, about 3,000 soldiers and sailors, died. Among those rescued were General Adachi and Admiral Kimura, who both returned to Rabaul. In the future, troop transfers from Rabaul to New Guinea would be made using submarines and barges. There would be no more convoys. All the transports in the Lae convoy were lost, as were four of the escorting destroyers, as well as twenty of the fighters sent to cover the convoy.

Allied losses were infinitesimal by comparison. Thirteen aircrew members died, ten in combat and three in accidents. One B-17 was lost in combat, as were three P-38 Lightnings. Two additional planes were lost in accidents.[43]

Controversy erupted in the aftermath of the battle. General Kenney, perhaps due to his excitement over such a great victory, accepted the reports of his aircrews that as many as twenty-two ships had been sunk. He gave this figure to MacArthur, who used it in a press release. MacArthur later amended the number when he received more accurate reports that put the size of the original convoy at eighteen ships.

On hearing the news of the great victory from Kenney, MacArthur sent his air chief a message to be shared with his airmen: "Please extend to all ranks my gratitude and felicitations on the magnificent victory which has been achieved. It cannot fail to go down in history as one of the most complete and annihilating combats of all time. My pride and satisfaction in you all is boundless."[44]

CHAPTER 11

Assault on Salamaua

As commander in chief of the South West Pacific Area, General MacArthur was, by directive of the Joint Chiefs, "not eligible to command directly any national force."[1] Therefore, the troops of each Allied country—American, Australian, Dutch, Papuan—required a commanding officer or officers who reported directly to the commander in chief.

MacArthur's leadership style allowed his commanders to plan and execute assigned missions as they saw fit. He rarely interfered in an ongoing operation.[2] As such, he needed officers in whom he had complete confidence, trusting their ability to carry out missions with both speed and limited loss of life.

One officer that MacArthur trusted implicitly was Admiral Barbey. In Australia since January, assembling MacArthur's naval landing force, Barbey soon had his efforts officially designated as the Seventh Amphibious Force of the U.S. Navy. It was later strengthened by the addition of the 2nd Engineer Special Brigade of the U.S. Army. Originally organized by the Army Corps of Engineers, members of the ESB were combination soldier-seamen who specialized in amphibious invasion landings.[3]

To school his men in how to land on hostile shores under fire, Barbey instituted a four-week-long training program for all combat teams. By mid-March, his Amphibious Force collected four old destroyers that were converted to troop transports, six LSTs, and a little over two dozen assorted landing crafts. The admiral was going to need every vessel he could get his hands on if he was going to be able to deliver MacArthur's troops to the beaches of New Guinea.[4]

Following Barbey's example, the peculiarities of tropical and jungle warfare were taught to naval, ground, and air units throughout MacArthur's command. Troops were instructed in steps to avoid jungle diseases such as malaria, in dealing with mud and lack of mobility in New Guinea's terrain, and in how to cope with the inability to see an enemy who may be lurking nearby. The Imperial Japanese Army had been training and fighting in jungle terrain for several years, while the U.S. Army's training was based on a 1941 field manual that devoted less than three pages to jungle combat. America had been preparing for another war in Europe, not for combat in the rain forests of New Guinea.[5]

The Japanese General Staff, in response to lost battles along the Buna-Gona beachheads and on Guadalcanal, redrew their line of defense, which would now run from the northern Solomons, through New Britain, and across the northern part of New Guinea. Key frontier posts were Lae and Salamaua. "New Guinea especially," their report read, "was the strategic point on the right flank of the defensive line, and if it should fall into the hands of the enemy . . . it would be a case of giving the enemy the best possible route to penetrate into the Philippines and any part of the South Co-Prosperity Sphere. This would be a great menace to the foundation of our general defense system. The strategic value of the Lae and Salamaua areas in the present stage of the operation was of immense importance."[6]

It was as if the authors of this report were reading General MacArthur's mind: he too saw the northern coast of New Guinea as his direct route to the Philippines.

A directive from Tokyo instructed Eighth Area Army commander

Imamura to increase his efforts to strengthen the bases at Lae and Salamaua. He needed to extend Japanese control over New Guinea beyond Papua, which the Allies now controlled. He was also to increase construction of roads and airfields, reinforce troops throughout occupied New Guinea, and stockpile supplies for the expected Allied offensive. Among these defensive measures, the Imperial Navy air arm received orders to "wage aerial annihilation operations in concert with the Army."[7]

Unfortunately for MacArthur, Allied military leaders took a view of the war in New Guinea different from that of their Japanese counterparts. On January 19, 1943, the Combined Chiefs of Staff developed six recommendations for the remainder of the year. The first was concerned with defeating the U-boats; the second was assistance to Russia; the third was operations in the European theater; the fourth focused on offensive action in the Mediterranean. The fifth stated, "In order to insure that these operations and preparations are not prejudiced by the necessity to divert forces to retrieve an adverse situation elsewhere, adequate forces shall be allocated to the Pacific and Far Eastern Theaters." The final recommendation dealt with the Pacific and Far East. It said, "Operations in these theaters shall continue with the forces allocated, with the object of maintaining pressure on Japan, retaining the initiative and attaining a position of readiness for the full scale offensive against Japan by the United Nations as soon as Germany is defeated. These operations must be kept within such limits as will not, in the opinion of the Combined Chiefs of Staff, jeopardize the capacity of the United Nations to take advantage of any favorable opportunity that may present itself for the decisive defeat of Germany in 1943."[8]

The Combined Chiefs made it clear that SWPA, and the Pacific in general, remained a backwater of the war to which only limited resources would be provided. It remained a Germany-first war as far as Washington and London were concerned.

Yet despite the Combined Chiefs' policy regarding the Pacific, American forces in SWPA continued to increase, although at a pace that tested MacArthur's patience. Under him was I Corps, consisting of the 32nd

Infantry Division, the 41st Infantry Division, the 1st Marine Division, the 503rd Parachute Infantry Regiment, the 158th Infantry Regiment, the 98th Field Artillery (Pack) Battalion, the 40th and 41st Antiaircraft Brigades, and the 2nd Engineers Special Brigade. Due to arrive were the 24th Infantry Division and the 1st Cavalry Division.[9]

All of these U.S. Army units reported to Australian general Thomas Blamey, as did fifteen Australian divisions. Yet MacArthur, who felt that American soldiers should serve under American commanders, decided to divide the land forces into two distinct armies based on their nationalities. Blamey would remain as commander of all land forces in title, but MacArthur would create an entirely separate force under an American commander. All U.S. Army ground forces would report to this new officer, who would report to MacArthur, not Blamey. Such a structure would give MacArthur the overarching organization he needed to ensure a unified effort in his drive up the New Guinea coast toward his ultimate goal of the Philippines.

MacArthur's opinion had quite possibly moved closer to that of Hap Arnold, who, following his visit to Papua in September 1942, wrote in his diary, "General Blamey has no idea of attacking unless he is forced into it."[10] MacArthur may also have been reacting to protests from American officers, who complained that the Australians were attempting to control command arrangements by promoting Australian officers one grade higher than the Americans with whom they dealt.[11]

MacArthur did not reveal to the Australian government his plans to remove American forces from under Blamey's control, yet he laid the groundwork for doing so in a conversation with Defense Secretary Frederick Shedden. Asked about Blamey's performance during the Buna-Gona campaign, MacArthur described him "as a good, courageous commander in the field, but not a very sound tactician." He added that Blamey did "not command the fullest support of all in the Australian Army and that he had political ambitions." He recommended that Blamey be made commander of the Home Defence Forces in Australia, and be replaced by the commander of the 9th Division, Lieutenant General Sir Leslie Morshead, just returning from North Africa.[12]

Under the terms of his directive, MacArthur should have consulted both the American and Australian governments about this change in command structure. Although he did not, the Australians took a benign view of this reduction of their general's authority. As described by Australian historian David Dexter, "the new arrangement was probably the only one that, in the circumstances that had developed, would have been politically acceptable in Washington. . . . There were practical and psychological obstacles in the way of leaving an Australian commander in control of the Allied land forces in the field now that they included a substantial American contingent; and the Americans evidently considered that, if separate roles could be found for the Australian and the American Armies, difficulties inseparable from the coordination of forces possessing differing organization and doctrines could be avoided."[13]

Once again, MacArthur knew exactly the man he wanted for a job. On January 11 he sent a message to General Marshall explaining his need and identifying the officer he sought: "Experience indicates the necessity for a tactical organization of an American Army. In the absence of such an echelon, the burden has been carried by GHQ. I recommend the U.S. Third Army under [Lieutenant] General Krueger, which would provide an able commander and an efficient operating organization. I am especially anxious to have Krueger because of my long and intimate association with him."[14]

Two days later, Walter Krueger received a surprising radiogram while inspecting troops at Camp Carson, Colorado. "I have just recommended to Chief of Staff that you and the Third Army Headquarters be transferred to this area," wrote MacArthur. "I am particularly anxious to have you with me at this critical time."[15]

MacArthur's request for the sixty-two-year-old general surprised many people, including Marshall. Born in West Prussia in 1881, Krueger immigrated to the United States with his mother after his father died. He never completed high school, and unlike so many of his contemporaries, did not attend West Point or earn a college degree. Enlisting as a private during the Spanish-American War, he served in Cuba and the Philippines, then journeyed to France as a staff officer during World

War I. Following the war, he earned a reputation for his skill in planning and especially training, which led to several posts as a training officer of increasingly larger forces until May 1941, when he was promoted to lieutenant general and commanding officer of the Third Army, then in training for the expected war in Europe. His reputation grew when he twice defeated the Second Army in combat maneuvers, proving the value of various doctrines he had been teaching.

What surprised Marshall about MacArthur's request was that Krueger had no real combat experience. Marshall did not think of Krueger as a combat commander, but rather as a highly valuable trainer of soldiers who would go into combat. Yet Marshall knew he could not deny MacArthur's request—and, besides, he did not know what else to do with Krueger.[16]

The appeal from the SWPA commander also amazed Krueger, who had resigned himself to the likelihood that there would be no combat role for him in this war. He wondered about MacArthur's comment concerning their "long and intimate association." True, Krueger had once worked in the War Plans Division of the Army Chief of Staff's office when MacArthur was the chief, but that was a decade ago. He told a friend that MacArthur having "remembered me well and favorably enough to ask for my services in SWPA was as remarkable as it was flattering."[17]

The War Department approved MacArthur's request for Krueger, but not for the Third Army Headquarters staff. It seemed there were not enough American troops in the theater to qualify as an army. As a result, Krueger could take only a limited number of staff with him.

Krueger arrived in Brisbane on February 8, 1943, to a warm welcome from MacArthur. He was surprised that his command of the Sixth Army, to which the War Department had assigned him, was changed by MacArthur to command of something called the Alamo Force. He soon learned that all units in the Sixth Army had been transferred to this Alamo Force. The reason for this bit of deception by MacArthur became clear when Krueger realized that, as a regular army, the Sixth would have to report to the Australian general in charge of Allied Land Forces, but as a task force, Alamo Force could report directly to MacArthur. General Blamey might not have been fooled by this ruse, but he never said anything to MacArthur about it.

MacArthur, who now had the men he wanted commanding his land, air, and amphibious forces, could not be more pleased with his decision concerning Krueger. He later wrote that Krueger "became to the Sixth Army what George Kenney was to the Fifth Air Force. History has not given him due credit for his greatness."[18]

If the destruction of a Japanese convoy in the Bismarck Sea brought one message home to the Imperial General Staff in Tokyo, it was that the Allies were clearly dominating the skies over New Guinea. This was an unacceptable situation for a military that relied heavily on airpower. Japanese warships rarely engaged in combat unless they could be sure of the protective cover offered not only by the aircraft from their own carriers but also by land-based bombers and fighters. On land, Japanese army advances always included engineers to build forward airfields as quickly as possible.

One consequence of the Bismarck Sea fiasco was the development of Operation I-GO—sustained concentrated air attacks on Allied air forces in the Solomons and New Guinea. The goal was to drive enemy planes from the skies over those islands.[19]

Admiral Yamamoto, who made the fateful decision to take personal command of the navy's part of I-GO, divided the operation into two phases. The first focused on the Solomons, especially Guadalcanal. The second phase targeted sites on New Guinea. Yamamoto flew to Rabaul to be near the action, and he transferred 150 aircraft from the 3rd Fleet carriers *Zuikaku, Junyo, Hiyo,* and *Zuiho,* at Truk to Rabaul, where they joined the planes of the 11th Air Fleet commanded by Vice Admiral Jinichi Kusaka. Yamamoto had over 350 carrier- and land-based aircraft for his operation, including 72 twin-engine bombers.[20]

When the first phase of attacks on Guadalcanal were complete on April 7, Yamamoto's pilots claimed a great victory in the Solomons, including the sinking of ten transports, a cruiser, and a destroyer, and the shooting down of thirty-six enemy planes at the cost of twelve Japanese planes. In truth, they had sent only one American destroyer—the *Aaron Ward*—one New Zealand corvette, and an American tanker to

In March 1942, General Douglas MacArthur, along with his wife, Jean, and their son, was smuggled out of the Philippines to Australia. The general took command of a nascent army unprepared to fight the Japanese. Vowing to liberate his beloved Philippines, MacArthur soon set out to conquer New Guinea, the first step in defeating his enemy. Husband and wife are seen here in Brisbane, Australia, in 1944.

MacArthur is greeted by General Sir Thomas Blamey, Commander of Allied Land Forces, near Port Moresby.

Australian troops train on an obstacle course in Canungra during the early months of the war.

Rabaul, once a cosmopolitan town before the surrounding volcanoes destroyed much of it, became Japan's most important base near New Guinea after they seized New Britain in 1942. The harbor is seen here packed with Japanese ships during an Allied air attack.

Papuan constabulary troops stand at attention before Australian officers.

Left: General George C. Kenney, MacArthur's trusted air chief throughout much of the New Guinea campaign. Journalist Clare Boothe Luce described Kenney as "a bright, hard, scar-faced little bulldog of a man."

Right: Robert L. Eichelberger, the American general tasked with taking Buna from the Japanese. MacArthur considered Eichelberger "a commander of the first order, fearless in battle, and especially popular with the Australians."

An American antiaircraft battery searches the sky for Japanese planes at Port Moresby, New Guinea.

Major General Edwin Forrest Harding, commander of the 32nd Division. A frontline general, he was nearly killed prior to Buna, but performed poorly during the battle and was relieved of his command.

Top: Australian troops trudge through thick mud along the Kokoda Track on the way to Buna.

Middle: An Australian mortar team fires at a tree line infested with Japanese snipers in the area of Gona.

Bottom: Papuan natives carry a wounded American soldier from the front line near Buna Mission.

Japanese dead litter the beach at Buna.

Specially designed landing craft, known as "Higgins boats," proved vital for the campaign's numerous amphibious operations. Higgins boats are seen here under assembly at a military plant in Cairns, Australia.

An Imperial Navy warship under attack during the Battle of the Bismark Sea, a disastrous setback for the Japanese.

Australian soldiers fire a mountain gun on Japanese positions during the assault on Salamaua.

Parachute bombs descend on two Japanese fighter planes during an attack at Dagua airdrome. Every plane at Dagua was destroyed in the Wewak raids of August 1943.

MacArthur visits with troopers of the 503rd Parachute Infantry Regiment before their drop on the Nadzab airfield.

Paratroopers of the 503rd prepare for their first combat drop of the war.

Left: A 503rd paratrooper wields a Thompson submachine gun while guarding the Nadzab airstrip.

Right: Lieutenant General Walter Krueger (*second from left*) confers with 41st Division officers on Aitape. Brigadier General Jens Doe (*second from right*) looks on.

An Australian soldier carries a wounded comrade back to a dressing station in the wake of a dawn attack on the Japanese-held village of Sattelberg.

Jeeps haul troops of the 32nd Division to the airstrip at Saidor.

LVTs line up, loaded with troops, preparing to embark for the invasion at Arawe.

Alamo Scouts, members of MacArthur's own elite reconnaissance units, land on the rocky shore of tiny Kwokeboh Island in Tanahmerah Bay.

MacArthur meets with Lieutenant General Walter Krueger, the commander of Sixth Army, on Goodenough Island. The German-born Krueger had no real combat experience when he arrived in the Pacific, but he quickly proved himself an essential leader in MacArthur's campaign to seize New Guinea.

Five American generals hold a conference on Goodenough Island: *(left to right)* Kenney, Brigadier General Stephen J. Chamberlain, Krueger, MacArthur, and General George Marshall.

A Marine captain displays a plaster model of Cape Gloucester to MacArthur prior to the invasion. Major General William H. Rupertus, commander of the 1st Marine Division, looks on in the background.

Marines of the 5th Regiment lug weapons and ammunition during the fight on Cape Gloucester.

Left: Two M-3 Stuart light tanks roll beneath a coconut grove on Los Negros.

Right: MacArthur, accompanied by Vice Admiral Thomas Kinkaid and soldiers of the First Cavalry Division, surveys Japanese dead on Los Negros.

Troops unload ammunition from a conveyor belt set up off an LVT at Tanahmerah Bay.

Top: MacArthur congratulates General Frederick A. Irving at Tanahmerah Bay, surrounded by soldiers of the 24th Division, as Admiral Daniel E. Barbey looks on.

Middle: Troops crawl down cargo nets into landing craft bound for Wakde Island.

Bottom: Paratroopers of the 503rd descend on the dangerous drop zone near the Kimiri airstrip on Noemfoor Island.

Soldiers of the 167th Infantry Regiment, 31st Division, eat a meal under the Pacific sky while sailing for Morotai.

MacArthur poses with the fighting men of the 31st Division on Morotai.

the bottom of the sea. Seven American fighters were downed at a cost to the Japanese of thirty-nine aircraft.[21]

The second phase of attacks against targets on New Guinea began on April 11. First hit was the small port at Oro Bay, fifteen miles southeast of Buna, where several small ships were unloading supplies for the airfield at Dobodura. Twenty-two "Val" dive-bombers and seventy-two Zero fighters swept in a few minutes before twelve thirty p.m. One merchant ship sank, a second was so seriously damaged that its crew drove her up on the beach to prevent her from sinking, and an Australian minesweeper received light damage. Fifty fighters that scrambled from Dobodura assaulted the Japanese, downing six of the attackers at no cost to them.[22]

The following day it was Port Moresby's turn. In what was the largest Japanese air raid so far in the entire theater, forty-three Mitsubishi medium bombers flew over the Owen Stanley Range, escorted by 131 Zeros. Several aircraft were damaged while still on the ground, and at least five attackers were shot down.[23]

Two days later, the formations attacked Milne Bay. Advance warning allowed several ships in the harbor to escape out of the bay, resulting in only one Dutch cargo ship lost, and several other small vessels damaged. Seven enemy and three Allied planes were shot down.[24] Once again Japanese pilots greatly exaggerated their success, reporting 175 Allied planes downed, and the sinking of one cruiser, two destroyers and twenty-five transports.

The emperor sent Yamamoto his heartfelt congratulations on what everyone, including the admiral, believed was a highly successful operation. The message, forwarded through the naval general staff, read, "Please convey my satisfaction to the Commander in Chief, Combined Fleet, and tell him to enlarge the war result more than ever."[25]

Evidently so taken with this lofty recognition, Yamamoto was prepared to believe the reports of his returning pilots concerning how much damage they had inflicted on the Allies. In his heart, he likely knew better, but, wanting the operation to be a great success, he did not question his pilots' claims, and concluded I-GO on April 16. Despite the urging from some of his staff for additional raids, he returned the carrier planes back to Truk. He then decided to pay a personal morale-boosting visit to his successful pilots.

The Japanese still had no idea that American code breakers had for some time been listening to their transmissions. As soon as Yamamoto's itinerary was distributed among Japanese insiders, the U.S. Navy learned of it. Admiral Halsey asked Admiral Nimitz for approval to carry out what was essentially an assassination. Although there is no paper trail—probably for good reason—Nimitz most likely asked Navy Secretary Knox for his approval. Knox is believed to have put the issue to the president, who discussed it with several close advisers. Everyone gave support. Nimitz sent Halsey an "execute" order, along with the comment, "Good luck and good hunting."[26]

True to his schedule, at eight a.m. on April 18, Admiral Yamamoto and several members of his staff climbed aboard a "Betty" bomber at one of Rabaul's airfields. A second bomber contained his chief of staff, Admiral Ugaki, and more high-ranking officers. The two aircraft lifted off and headed south, quickly joined by six Zero fighters as escorts. Waiting for them off the coast of Bougainville near their destination of Buin were sixteen U.S. Army P-38s. Halsey had specifically selected P-38s for this mission because, with added drop fuel tanks, the fighters could manage both the long range and the potentially long wait for Yamamoto's arrival.

The 494-mile flight from Guadalcanal took the P-38 Lightnings of the 399th Fighter Squadron a few minutes shy of three hours. Yamamoto's plane was scheduled to land at ten a.m., and the admiral had a reputation for being a stickler about being on time. The Americans were flying close to the water to reduce visibility when suddenly the two bombers approached and prepared to land at the nearby airfield. In the ensuing action, Yamamoto's plane was decimated and hurtled down into the jungle. Japanese search teams later discovered his body. The second bomber crashed into the sea, and Admiral Ugaki, although injured, managed to swim to the nearby beach. The Zeros put up an impressive defense of their admiral, successfully destroying one Lightning, but with both bombers down, the P-38s turned and raced away.

The Americans kept quiet about the attack for fear of revealing how they had obtained Yamamoto's itinerary. Not until May 21—when Tokyo acknowledged that the great admiral, "while directing general strategy on the front-line in April of this year, engaged in combat with the enemy and met gallant death in a war plane"—could the Allies be sure they had actually gotten him.[27]

Meanwhile, Australian forces from Wau kept increasing pressure on the Japanese troops at Salamaua. MacArthur's next major objective was Lae, now a powerful enemy base, but first he had to deal with Salamaua. He also had to carry out a directive from the Chiefs of Staff to invade and occupy two islands in the Coral Sea. The directive was part of an operation code-named Cartwheel.

This operation was the outgrowth of a plan developed by MacArthur to isolate the enemy's primary base in the South Pacific, Rabaul. His strategy, he explained, was "massive strokes against only main strategic objectives, utilizing surprise air-ground striking power supported and assisted by the fleet. This is the very opposite of what is termed 'island hopping' which is the gradual pushing back of the enemy by direct frontal pressure with the consequent heavy casualties which will certainly be involved." MacArthur was going to bypass strong enemy concentrations and invade places where airfields were lightly defended, or where the rapid building of a new airfield was possible. As he had decided after Buna-Gona, the general wanted no more costly fighting. He intended to isolate these strongpoints and let them "wither away." Perhaps thinking of the massed frontal attacks of the last war that cost so many lives, he added, "Wars are never won in the past."[28]

MacArthur's plan went through several alterations but was finalized at his first face-to-face meeting with Admiral Halsey. Halsey and his staff arrived in Brisbane on April 15, 1943, and the two men spent three days discussing strategy and making plans. As commander of the South Pacific Area, Halsey was in the unenviable position of having two masters. On one hand, he was subordinate to Admiral Nimitz, who controlled his manpower and ships. On the other, he was subordinate to General MacArthur, who dictated his strategy.[29]

Halsey had what is best described as the typical Navy officer's attitude toward MacArthur, who was widely known to bad-mouth the Navy over its failure to support his defense of the Philippines. Halsey's feelings about the quarrelsome general prior to their meeting were conveyed to Nimitz in February: "I refuse to get into a controversy with him or any other self-advertising son of a bitch."[30]

The two strong-minded leaders had clashed several times in recent months over the loan of forces to each other: ships from Halsey and B-17s from MacArthur. Yet the general had evidently decided to put that behind them. MacArthur welcomed Halsey like a returning hero. Standing at the wharf as Halsey's PB2Y taxied to a stop, he vigorously shook the admiral's hand and turned on the famous MacArthur charm.[31]

The explosions and fireworks many expected never happened. The pair, which one newspaper a month later described as "kindred souls," established a bond that lasted for the remainder of the war. Describing this first meeting, Halsey wrote, "Five minutes after I reported, I felt as if we were lifelong friends. I have seldom seen a man who makes a quicker, stronger, more favorable impression."

As for MacArthur, he found the admiral "blunt, outspoken, dynamic, and a battle commander of the highest order."[32] He described Halsey in his memoirs as being "of the same aggressive type as John Paul Jones, David Farragut, and George Dewey. His one thought was to close with the enemy and fight him to the death. No name rates higher in the annals of our country's naval history."[33]

The final plan on which these two men agreed called for thirteen separate operations within the overall Cartwheel. In the next eight months, forces from both commands were to advance in stages toward the ultimate goal, which was now the much more realistic isolation of Rabaul, rather than its capture. Rabaul, with its 100,000 infantrymen, five airfields, hundreds of planes, and dozens of warships, was virtually impregnable. Thus, MacArthur's forces were to capture Woodlark and Kiriwina Islands in the Coral Sea, then move up the New Guinea coast and capture Salamaua,

Lae, Finschhafen, and Madang, before finally invading Cape Gloucester on the western end of New Britain. Halsey's forces would battle up the Solomons, capturing the Shortlands, Buin, and Bougainville.

———————

After the Okabe Detachment was driven from the Wau area, Allied cargo planes delivered several thousand troops and tons of supplies and equipment into the small airfield. On April 23 the Kanga Force ceased to exist as an independent unit and was absorbed in the newly arrived Australian 3rd Division. The commanding officer was Major General Stanley Savige, who as commander of the 17th Brigade had fought across North Africa, in Greece, and in Syria. In New Guinea, Savige's assigned tasks were to maintain security of the Wau area and continue developing the region as a base for planned operations against Lae and Salamaua.[34]

Over the next few months, Australian troops kept up a series of attacks on Japanese positions leading to Salamaua. Both Blamey and MacArthur were considering an attack on Salamaua as a feint to draw off enemy troops from their primary target, Lae, although it is believed Savige was not aware of this. With orders not to attack Salamaua directly, Savige established forward bases as close to enemy positions as possible and continued a campaign of harassing the Japanese.[35]

Salamaua was located on an isthmus about twenty-two miles from Lae. The surrounding country was full of high mountains, with numerous steep ridges interspersed by deep gullies filled with knife-edged kunai grass. The ridges varied from eight hundred to three thousand feet in height, forcing Australian units to constantly advance up and down them. The Japanese had taken advantage of the terrain to create well-fortified positions. Sheltered in coconut-log pillboxes reinforced with mud, they made extensive use of their heavy machine guns, which could easily trap approaching Allied soldiers in their cross fire. Deep trenches and tunnels allowed the defenders to move safely from one position to another.[36]

About six thousand Australian troops occupied the Wau area, and General Kenney saw to it that they were regularly supplied, and in some cases relieved and reinforced, through frequent flights of DC-3 transports escorted by fighters. The official Australian history of the campaign describes the importance of these flights to an area with no roads and only ancient foot trails: "Possession by the Allies of the DC-3 transport aircraft was thus a big factor in enabling the Australians to hold their positions in the forward area against the Japanese who had more accessible bases at Lae and Salamaua."[37]

Although the Japanese bases may have appeared "more accessible," they were not what Japanese commanders would have wished for. The Bismarck Sea debacle had all but eliminated the use of convoys to move troops and supplies from Rabaul. Now the Japanese were forced to rely on submarines to transport food and provisions to the 2,500 naval and 7,500 army troops in the Lae-Salamaua area. Many of these men had fought at Buna-Gona and were, in the words of a Japanese general, "sick and exhausted." The defeat of the Okabe Detachment added considerably to the number of sick and wounded.

Despite the hardships they faced, the Japanese were determined to defend Salamaua. Lieutenant General Hidemitsu Nakano, commander of the 51st Division, had survived the Bismarck Sea disaster and managed to land at Lae. He immediately moved to Salamaua, where he assumed command of all Imperial troops in the area.[38] Nakano would prove to be a determined adversary to Allied forces attempting to seize the area. "Holding Salamaua is the Division's responsibility," he stated in an order distributed to his troops. "This position is our last defense line, and we will withdraw no further. If we are unable to hold, we will die fighting. I will burn our Divisional flag and even the patients will rise to fight in close combat. No one will be taken prisoner."[39]

Fortunately for his men, Imperial General Headquarters ordered Nakano not to make a suicidal last stand. If he could not repel the enemy advance, he was to withdraw to Lae.

———

While the fighting on the Salamaua front continued to rage in a dozen locations, General MacArthur and Admiral Halsey prepared for their first steps in Operation Cartwheel. Halsey was to land troops on New

Georgia in the Solomons and capture an enemy airfield located at the village of Munda. Only 175 miles from Henderson Field, the American airstrip on Guadalcanal, the Japanese airfield at Munda had several cleverly concealed runways and was "a thorn in my side," according to Halsey. Almost daily air strikes had produced minimal results, and the admiral knew the only way he was going to eliminate the threat from Munda was to land troops on the island and drive the enemy off New Georgia.[40]

Meanwhile, MacArthur's troops were to make amphibious landings on and capture two islands one hundred miles from the New Guinea coast called Woodlark and Kiriwina, which offered the possibility of building airfields to house short-range fighters to escort heavy bombers heading to Rabaul. MacArthur assigned command of the invasion troops to General Krueger, while Admiral Barbey was responsible for getting them there and putting them ashore.

On June 20 Krueger set up his headquarters at Milne Bay. Barbey arrived the same day and raised his flag on the USS *Rigel* at anchor in the bay. MacArthur, who always exhibited a need to be close to the action, soon joined them.

Between June 23 and 30, the Seventh Amphibious Force under the command of Admiral Barbey made its first amphibious landings in hostile territory when it put American forces ashore on Woodlark and Kiriwina Islands. Most ranking officers knew from reconnaissance missions that no enemy soldiers defended either island, yet the troops were not informed of this so as to get some realistic practice landing on enemy-occupied beaches.

Krueger had learned from General Kenney that the Fifth Air Force would not be capable of providing fighter protection to his troops being convoyed to the islands because planes from his nearest airfield would not have enough fuel to linger over the ships. Krueger therefore decided the landings would be made at night. As it turned out, the Japanese were either completely ignorant of the landings or had decided to ignore them in favor of attacking Halsey's landing parties at New Georgia.[41]

At a few minutes after midnight on June 23, six landing craft put ashore on Woodlark two hundred men of the 112th Cavalry Regiment, commanded by Major D. M. McMains. Although there were no Japanese on the island, McMains's men were nearly fired on by a native guerrilla force led by an Australian Coastwatcher who had not been told of the landing. After forming his men in a skirmish line, the Coastwatcher heard the incoming troops speaking English with an American accent and soon joined them.[42]

The following day troops from 158th Infantry Regimental Combat Team, along with a company from the 59th Combat Engineers, landed on Kiriwina. Units from the 112th Cavalry, the 12th Marine Defense Battalion, and 134th Field Artillery Battalion landed at Woodlark.

The engineers quickly set about building an airfield on each island. By July 14, C-47 cargo planes were able to land on Woodlark's 5,200-foot runway, and in less than ten days the airfield was home to P-47 Thunderbolts. Hampered by heavy rains and the need to build a three-hundred-yard-long coral causeway across the reef surrounding the island, the airfield on Kiriwina was not completed until the end of July. Its five-thousand-foot runway welcomed RAAF Spitfire fighters on August 18. P-40 Kittyhawks soon joined them. On both islands, antiaircraft and anti-invasion defenses were put in place, yet other than two minor bombing raids and several surveillance flights, the Japanese paid little attention to the Allied invasions and occupations of the two islands. As the war moved farther up the New Guinea coast, the utility of these two airfields gradually declined, although they continued providing fighter protection to bombers heading to Rabaul.[43]

At about the same time the missions on Woodlark and Kiriwina were taking place, another set of amphibious landings were under way up the coast of New Guinea at Nassau Bay, ten miles south of Salamaua. Nassau Bay was an important target for MacArthur, who was anxious to support the troops facing Salamaua and to find a better way to provide the food and matériel they needed. Flights into Wau were fine, but the cargo then had to be carried, usually by hired local villagers, across jungle-cloaked mountains, ridges, and rivers to soldiers at the front. Opening up a beachhead at a locale such as Nassau Bay would speed up the process and enable the Allies to pour more combat troops and equipment into the fight.

To add to the enemy's potential confusion, the Nassau Bay landings were scheduled for June 30, the same day as the landings at Woodlark, Kiriwina, and New Georgia were to take place. The operation would also deceive the enemy into believing that MacArthur's target was Salamaua because he was massing so much firepower there, when his real goal was Lae itself. He hoped to draw off Japanese troops from Lae toward Salamaua.[44]

This time the Navy played no role. Instead, the landings were conducted by a U.S. Army force known as the "Seahorse Soldiers," a name derived from an oval uniform patch they wore bearing a red seahorse bordered in blue. Officially designated the 2nd Engineer Special Brigade, it was one of several units, known as ESBs, that were developed by the Army Corps of Engineers when the Navy proved unable to provide "shore-to-shore" amphibious landing support to the Army.

On the night of June 28, a reconnaissance platoon from the 162nd Infantry Regiment installed navigation lights on offshore islands along the route leading to Nassau Bay. With the operation to unfold under the cover of darkness, the pilots of the invasion boats needed all the help they could get finding the correct beach. The reinforced 1st Battalion of the 162nd Regimental Combat Team of the United States 41st Infantry Division, called the MacKechnie Force after its commander, Colonel Archibald MacKechnie, formed the main body of the troops for the landings. Once ashore, they would link up with the Australian 3rd Division and come under the control of Major General Stanley Savige, commander of all Allied forces facing Salamaua.

Company D of the Australian 2/6th Infantry Battalion was to create a diversion, drawing Japanese attention away from the landing zone. A platoon from that company arrived at the beach prior to the landing and set up guide lights to bring the landing craft in safely. Company A of the Papuan Infantry Battalion stealthily moved to Cape Dinga on the southern flank of the landing zone. There were about 150 Japanese, both infantry and naval guard, at Cape Dinga. The PIB troops were to guard against enemy infiltration during the landings.

The invasion force consisted of twenty-nine LCVPs (landing craft, vehicles, personnel), one LCM (landing craft, mechanized) and two Japanese motorized barges that had been captured by PT-boat crews.

On board were 1,090 troops and several artillery pieces, as well as ESB troops for operating the vessels. Accompanying them were four PT boats, three of which carried seventy men each while the fourth kept its decks cleared for action and patrolled ahead and to seaward of the convoy, which moved in three waves. The convoy began heading toward their destination at six thirty p.m. The weather could hardly have been worse. Rain and high winds rocked the vessels, and the sea grew rougher as the night wore on. Visibility was extremely poor.

The speedy PT boats had difficulty throttling down their engines to allow the slow-moving and heavily loaded Higgins boats to keep up. Soon the third wave lost sight of its PT boat guide and continued on its own. PT-68, the patrol craft carrying no troops, lost sight of the entire convoy and just kept scouting for enemy vessels.

The first wave, guided with great difficulty by PT-142, overshot Nassau Bay by three miles. It took Lieutenant Commander Barry Atkins some time to herd eleven boats and a Japanese barge back to Nassau Bay. They arrived simultaneously with the second wave of twelve boats led by PT-143. Alarmed by the arrival of these boats in the dark, the boats of the first wave scattered and had to be rounded up again. While all this was going on, PT-120 arrived with its charge of seven Higgins boats and a Japanese barge. It became a regular traffic jam as the boats were tossed around in the rough seas. The three PT boats stood by while all the landing craft hit the beach. Then came a radio signal that all the boats had broached in the ten- to twelve-foot pounding surf and could not get off the beach. PT-143 and PT-120, still carrying their complement of seventy men each, returned to their port of origin, Morobe. PT-142 remained to patrol the area throughout the night. Luckily for all involved, the landing was unopposed.[45]

To the Japanese soldiers and sailors at Cape Dinga, the roaring engines of the landing craft sounded like so many tanks that they reported a large invasion was in progress and quickly fled the area.[46]

Over the next few days PT and Higgins boats landed additional troops, and by July 8 the entire regiment was at Nassau Bay. This unit of the American 41st Division quickly linked up with the Australians who were fighting their way toward Salamaua. Among the soldiers of the 41st Division who landed at Nassau Bay was the son of former President Theodore Roosevelt, Lieutenant Colonel Archibald Roosevelt. "Archie," as everyone knew him, was the commanding officer of the 2nd Battalion, 162nd Infantry. He had served as an infantry captain in France during the Great War, receiving a severe shrapnel wound in his right knee that put him in a Paris hospital for four months. Awarded the Croix de Guerre by the French government, he was later discharged from the Army with full disability.[47]

Archie was forty-eight years old when he pestered his cousin, FDR, to allow him to reenlist in the Army. "There may come many places and many times," he wrote to Franklin, "where you would like to have the son of a former President and someone with your name to share the dangers of soldiers or sailors in some tough spot. . . . I would be perfect for such a job. . . . You would not be throwing away [someone] who was useful elsewhere." Archie also reached out to George Marshall, under whom he had served in France. Knowing Archie wanted frontline service, Marshall sent him to MacArthur. When MacArthur learned Archie wanted not a staff position but combat, he assigned him to the 41st Division and sent him to New Guinea.[48]

A month after landing at Nassau Bay, Archie's once-injured knee was shattered again, this time by a Japanese hand grenade. A stint in an Australian hospital was followed by a desk assignment. Informed there would be no more combat roles for him, Archie returned to the United States in late 1944. Almost immediately, he began lobbying FDR and Marshall for a new assignment. Struck down by a relapse of malaria he had acquired in the jungle, he was again hospitalized. President Roosevelt and Marshall were trying to determine what they were going to do with the persistent Archie when on April 12, 1945, the president suddenly died from a stroke. That ended the issue for Archie, who remains to this day the only American soldier to receive 100 percent disability from injuries received in both world wars.[49]

The number of Allied soldiers pushing in on Salamaua increased rapidly both through airlifts to Wau and additional landings at Nassau

Bay. Landing craft were able to bring in a large number of artillery pieces and ammunition. Japanese forces, who were gradually pushed back toward Salamaua, had no idea that the attacks on their defenses were a diversion to pull troops from the much-better-situated Lae. MacArthur, with little interest in Salamaua, assaulted it only as means to "siphon off enemy strength from his Lae defenses and lure his troops and supplies southward to be cut to pieces on the Salamaua front."[50]

The deception worked. Major General Ryoichi Shoge, the Japanese commander in Lae, sent troops south to protect Salamaua, thinning his defensive line around Lae. Yet it was a curious decision for the general. The almost senseless defense of Salamaua is "difficult to understand," notes one historian. The town had been all but destroyed by Allied air raids, as had the air base and port facilities. Salamaua was of little strategic value, while Lae was vitally important if Imperial forces were to hold on to the Huon Peninsula. For MacArthur, Lae served as the gateway to this vital territory. Beyond Lae were numerous flatlands that could provide excellent terrain for airfields. Valleys around the Markham and Ramu Rivers offered good routes to the Japanese stronghold up the coast at Madang. The harbor at Lae could be quickly improved and expanded to be useful to Allied shipping.[51]

Ever since the Battle of the Bismarck Sea, General Kenney's Allied Air Forces had conducted regular bombing raids on a wide range of Japanese targets, including Rabaul, Kavieng on New Ireland, Salamaua, Lae, and Madang, where General Adachi had his Eighteenth Army headquarters. Yet the one base Kenney could not hit was Wewak. Located up the coast, approximately 316 miles from Lae, it was beyond reach of all Allied planes except the B-17. The few raids made against Wewak had to be done at night due to the impossibility of fighter protection, and the results of bombing under darkness were negligible. Kenney was itching to get his B-25s and fighters closer.

Wewak had been a late occupation for the Imperial forces; Lae was invaded and occupied in March 1942, whereas Wewak was not taken until December of that year. The Japanese wasted little time in transforming the Wewak area into a major air base and port facility to receive shipments of supplies and troops. Toward the end of July, the Japanese Fourth Air Army transferred there from Java along with two hundred aircraft. By the time Kenney was able to raid Wewak in August, it had four airfields in operation and contained the highest concentration of Imperial Army troops anywhere in New Guinea.

Reconnaissance flights over Wewak proved difficult, as air defense patrols were constant. Several planes sent to photograph the area failed to return. Those that survived reported widespread activity across the entire region, with a great number of fighters parked alongside the airfields and several small ships usually steaming in or out of the harbor.

Frustrated by his inability to provide fighter protection to the heavy bombers he wanted to send against Wewak, Kenney was determined to build an airfield closer to the enemy's huge base. During the first week of June, he sent a ground reconnaissance party from Wau toward a village about forty miles to the north, well within territory controlled by the enemy. He had heard that there was an old abandoned airstrip near the village. The party found that the small airstrip, which had been used years earlier by gold miners, was now overgrown with kunai grass and limited by the surrounding terrain to only twelve hundred feet in length, unsuitable for fighters. It was also subject to flooding during the rainy season. Four miles farther north, near the village of Tsili-Tsili, they discovered a site that looked ideal for an airfield, with two landing strips of seven thousand feet each. There also appeared to be plenty of space for parking additional aircraft.[52]

When Kenney informed MacArthur of his plan to build an airfield behind enemy lines, the commander in chief was surprised and delighted. "How are you going to protect it from Jap ground forces?" MacArthur asked. Kenney explained that Australian general Edmund Herring promised to loan him one thousand Australian soldiers and some machine guns to guard the trails leading to the site. "Good, good," said a grinning MacArthur. Then he asked, "Say, George, have you told my staff about this?" When Kenney responded that he had not, the commander told him, "Don't tell them yet. I don't want them scared to death."[53]

The 871st Airborne Engineers flew into Tsili-Tsili and worked around the clock building the airstrip. Kenney changed the name to Marilinan, because Tsili-Tsili (pronounced "silly silly") "might have suggested to some people that it was descriptive of our scheme of getting a forward airdrome."[54] The new airfield became active with the arrival of the first group of fighters on July 26.

Late in the afternoon of August 16, a photoreconnaissance plane flew over the four airfields associated with Wewak and photographed 225 Japanese bombers and fighters on the ground. At dawn the following morning, forty-one B-24 Liberators and twelve B-17 Fortresses attacked the Wewak airfields. They found the enemy planes on the ground, lined up with their engines warming. They had obviously planned an attack on an Allied base that day. A few hours later, thirty-three B-25 Mitchells escorted by eighty-three P-38s came in at treetop level and strafed all the airfields. Three more raids took place over the next three days. The effect on the Japanese was devastating. More than one hundred Japanese planes were destroyed, as well as a large quantity of fuel. Many of the aircraft had their crews on board waiting to take off when they were hit and exploded into flames. Allied losses amounted to ten aircraft.[55]

For the Japanese 51st Division, the loss of air support as a result of the Wewak raids made their situation at Salamaua even more perilous.[56]

Commenting on the Wewak bombing raids, General MacArthur said, "It was a crippling blow at an opportune moment. Nothing is so helpless as an airplane on the ground. In war, surprise is decisive."[57]

MacArthur had issued orders that Salamaua not be taken until the attack on Lae had begun. Therefore, Australian and American forces maintained a tight ring around most of the devastated town, but held back from capturing it. The Japanese were deceived into thinking Salamaua was MacArthur's objective, so while they were watching Salamaua and slipping additional troops into the area—further weakening Lae's defenses—Allied forces prepared for the true objective, Lae.[58]

CHAPTER 12

Pincers Around Lae

Although located on the island of New Britain, Rabaul had been the capital of all New Guinea until 1937, when it was partially buried under volcanic ash. Before settling on Port Moresby, the Australian government considered making Lae, the second-largest town on the main island, the new capital. With a well-developed port on the Huon Gulf near the mouth of the Markham River, Lae had grown up during the gold rush of the 1920s and 1930s, serving as a supply depot for the thousands of miners and prospectors working in the nearby mountains and valleys.[1]

Japanese troops first landed at Lae in March 1942 and worked tirelessly to build a well-fortified base that, when fully garrisoned, the Allies would find extremely difficult to penetrate. MacArthur's deceptive attacks on Salamaua, however, fooled General Adachi. He bled off troops from the more important base at Lae and sent them south in numbers that were more or less easily devoured by the Australians and Americans. By the time of the Allied invasion in early September, Lae's defense relied on fewer than ten thousand combat and noncombat solidiers—too small a force to withstand MacArthur's powerful drive against the base from three directions at once, with nearly thirty thousand troops.

———

While the forces around Salamaua were in a holding action, generals MacArthur and Blamey devised a two-pronged pincer attack on Lae. The Australian 9th Division was to be brought up the coast from Milne Bay aboard ships of Admiral Barbey's amphibious force, set to assault the beaches near Lae, while the Australian 7th Division would move along a road running through the Owen Stanley Range toward Nadzab, twenty miles northwest of Lae. There, a small airport, idle for more than one year, offered the opportunity, once improved and expanded, to locate fighters and bombers even closer to the enemy.

The importance of Nadzab lay not just in its airfield but also in its location in the Markham Valley, nestled between two vitally important waterways, the Markham and Ramu Rivers. The Markham runs for 110 miles southeast from its source in the mountains to Lae on the Huon Gulf. The Ramu flows northwest for nearly four hundred miles before emptying near the Hansa Bay between Madang and Wewak, two future targets for the Allies. These rivers form the huge Markham Valley, which divides the Huon Peninsula from the rest of New Guinea and offered the Allies a route to the big Japanese bases at Madang and Wewak.

Despite the planning, the 7th Division's role in the mission was soon forced to change. When MacArthur learned that their road through the Owen Stanleys—a route being hacked by Allied troops through thick jungle, across rivers, and up and down mountains—was proceeding too slowly to meet his timetable, he turned to an idea suggested by the Air Force's General Whitehead: parachute troops.

Never before had Allied paratroopers made a combat jump into enemy-held territory in the Pacific. The previous year another airborne unit, the 1st Marine Parachute Battalion, fought at Guadalcanal, but as infantry, with no tactical jumps.

Allied intelligence believed Nadzab to be only lightly defended, as the Japanese saw no real strategic value in the airfield. Following a brief bombing raid, American paratroopers were to land, drive out any survivors, and begin work on the airfield so that C-47 transports could touch down the next day with construction equipment and reinforcements. When the airfield was ready, the Australian 7th Division would be airlifted in to begin its march toward the rear of Lae.[2]

To provide the Navy a role in the operation, Admiral Carpender instructed Captain Jesse H. Carter to take four of his destroyers from Milne Bay and sweep the Huon Gulf, telling him, "There is good reason to believe that the enemy is moving both supplies and troops from Finschhafen [further up the coast] to Salamaua." He ordered Carter to bombard Finschhafen, and that all "targets of opportunity are to be destroyed."[3]

For ten minutes during the night of August 22–23, Carter's destroyers fired at various targets as they steamed back and forth along the coast at Finschhafen. Although they achieved complete surprise and encountered no opposition, the results were negligible. Yet the attacks demonstrated that American warships could maneuver along the New Guinea coast, provided they made judicious use of their sonar to avoid unchartered coral reefs.[4]

As planners moved forward with the operation, Blamey made it clear that he wanted to transport all nine thousand soldiers of the Australian 9th Division to the landing beaches at Lae. Since the landing craft of the ESBs could deliver only a single brigade—fewer than three thousand men along with their supplies—it soon became apparent that Admiral Barbey's Seventh Amphibious Force, with its larger ships, would take control of the landings. The 2nd Engineer Special Brigade, who had been training with the 9th, was placed under Barbey's command.

Admiral Barbey and Major General G. F. Wootten, commanding officer of the 9th Division, met to work out plans. Both agreed the best approach was during darkness just before dawn, so that the troops could go ashore with some light behind them to see where they were going. General Kenney, who was to provide air cover for the invasion, argued for the landings to take place an hour or so later so that his pilots could fly in daylight. Failing to reach an agreement, Barbey and

Kenney took the dispute to MacArthur, who came down on Barbey's side. The landing ships and craft would sail under cover of night, mostly without air cover, and put the troops ashore at first light.[5]

On December 2, 1942—forty-three days after leaving San Francisco aboard a Dutch cargo ship converted to a troop transport—the 503rd Parachute Infantry Regiment (PIR) landed at Cairns, in Queensland, Australia. Its arrival tactically altered the face of the war in New Guinea. A massive, jungle-covered land with virtually no roads, the island was sprinkled with small, mostly unused airfields, reachable only by air. Many of the fields in enemy territory, like the one at Nadzab, were defended by small but determined detachments of Japanese soldiers. Unable to use the fields themselves, the enemy had placed numerous obstacles across the landing strips and installed machine guns and other heavy weapons nearby that would destroy any plane attempting to land. The fastest way to seize these important targets was to drop in troops from above.

The 503rd PIR was formed from several independent parachute battalions in February 1942 at Fort Benning, Georgia. The following month the troopers moved to Fort Bragg, North Carolina, for intensive unit jump training. Most of the men expected to be shipped to England to join several independent parachute battalions that were preparing to drop into Vichy French territory in North Africa. To their surprise, their commanding officer, Lieutenant Colonel Kenneth H. Kinsler, ordered the regiment aboard a California-bound train. There, they boarded the Dutch freighter *Poelau Laut* shortly after midnight on October 20 and the next morning slipped through the fog of San Francisco Bay and headed south. During their first nine months in Australia, the regiment trained and participated in exhibition jumps before military and civilian audiences. General MacArthur attended at least one of these jumps.

Colonel Kinsler, anxious to give his troopers the best possible chance to succeed, met with Brigadier Ivan N. Dougherty, commander of the Australian 21st Infantry Brigade. Dougherty had been highly praised for his leadership when his battalion defended against a German paratroop attack on Heraklion, Crete, in 1940.[6] Although the Germans were ultimately successful, the initial drop had cost so many paratroopers' lives that Hitler canceled all future plans for massed jumps. Kinsler sought to avoid whatever mistakes the Germans had made and avoid high casualties.

After nearly a year and a half of intense combat training, the entire regiment was finally prepared for its first combat jump. On August 20, 1943, the 2nd Battalion of the 503rd flew into Port Moresby. Two days later the 1st and 3rd Battalions arrived aboard an Australian ship.

Within days, the regiment was joined by thirty-three Australian soldiers from the 2/4th Field Artillery of the 7th Division, who brought along two twenty-five-pounder short field artillery pieces that they had dismantled and prepared for the drop into Nadzab. None of the Australians had ever jumped previously and were in fact unaware they were going to until they joined the American paratroopers. With the attack quickly approaching, the artillerymen received instructions on how to jump, land, and roll once on the ground. They participated in one practice jump in the Port Moresby area, during which three men were injured.[7]

While the American paratroopers and the Australian artillerymen, soon to be dubbed "paragunners," prepared for their mission, the Australian 9th Division began embarking into Admiral Barbey's ships and landing craft at Milne Bay on September 1. The next day, with the landing firmly scheduled for September 4, Barbey and General Wootten went aboard the U.S. destroyer *Conyngham*, which was to serve as the fleet's flagship, and headed up the coast toward Buna, were they would stop for fuel and to pick up additional members of the 9th Division. Trailing behind the makeshift flagship was one of the strangest fleets the world had ever seen: seven destroyers, four destroyer-transports, thirteen LSTs, twenty LCIs, fourteen LCTs, and an assortment of tugs, oilers, tenders, and other small vessels. Partway up the coast they were joined by fifty Higgins boats from the 2nd Engineers Special Brigade carrying supplies and ammunition. Once at the beachhead, the engineers would come under General Wootten's command, and were to act as the shore party, quickly moving supplies inland and constructing passable roads for follow-on troops and vehicles. All told, Barbey reported that this "hodge-podge"[8] of "156 miscellaneous ships and craft" carried "about 17,000 troops and 12,000 tons of supplies."[9]

Conditions aboard the vessels varied, depending on the craft. Crowded and uncomfortable, and with no means to provide hot meals, the landing craft—the LCIs and LCTs—made a stopover at Buna so that the men aboard could go ashore, get exercise, and enjoy a hot meal before continuing the journey. Soldiers on board the destroyer-transports and the LSTs found the voyage more comfortable, and the larger ships had the luxury of cooking facilities and cooks. They remained aboard during the Buna stop.

When cooks aboard the destroyer-transport *Gilmer* caught sight of the unappetizing bully beef rations issued to Australian soldiers, American sailors told them to "dump the whole damn lot over side" and distributed roast beef and other delicacies to their allies, as well as American cigarettes. One recipient wrote, "A more generous, friendly, goddam crew it would be hard to find."[10]

To keep the enemy's response to the fleet heading their way to a minimum, General Kenney ordered bombing runs against the airfields at Wewak, or what was left of them after the massive attacks of mid-August. Sixteen B-25s swept down on Wewak during the morning of September 2, but found few targets at the airfields. The Japanese had moved their surviving aircraft farther up the coast, out of range of American bombers. The Americans did find a number of newly arrived cargo ships and smaller vessels loaded with supplies for the Wewak garrison. Each anchored ship had one or two barrage balloons aloft at between five hundred and a thousand feet for protection. In the ensuing attack, at least one ship sank and several others were set afire. Twenty to thirty Imperial Navy Zero fighters, evidently serving as air cover for the supply ships, attacked the bombers, but were driven off by the twenty-eight P-38s escorting the bombers. The American pilots claimed ten enemy fighters downed at a cost of three B-25s and one P-38.[11]

On September 3, as Admiral Barbey's jumbled fleet approached its destination off the Huon Peninsula, General Kenney's fighters and bombers gave the enemy at Lae a final blow with eighty-four tons of bombs directed primarily at the Japanese defensive gun positions. Thirty-five thousand rounds of machine-gun fire followed from strafers attempting to kill anything remaining alive at the base.[12]

Ever fearful of the several hundred warplanes stationed at Rabaul and the additional airfields in New Britain, the U.S. destroyer *Reid* had installed up-to-date radar equipment and taken on a fighter-director team. Because of the limitations of Allied radar at the time, she positioned herself fifty miles off the New Guinea coast as an early-warning system against Japanese aircraft approaching from Rabaul. By extending their radar reach, Allied commanders could be notified much sooner of planes approaching from the east and north. "It was not," as Admiral Barbey described it, "a very pleasant assignment for the *Reid*, all alone and in the path of any Japanese bombers. But there was always the possibility she would not be bothered, as one destroyer might not be considered worthy of a concentrated plane attack when there was bigger game ahead."[13]

Before sunrise on D-Day, September 4, the fleet's flagship, the *Conyngham*, with Barbey and Wootten aboard, sped ahead of the convoy to identify the two beaches on which the Australians were to land. Designated Red Beach and Yellow Beach, they were a few miles apart, about sixteen miles east of Lae. The flagship served as the reference point so that the various vessels of the fleet could find their appropriate location for the landings. Consisting of firm black sand, each beach was about four hundred yards long and twenty yards wide. Behind each were mangrove swamps. A small number of trails led from the beaches inland through the swamps.

At eighteen minutes after six, just as the sun was making its appearance out over the Huon Gulf, the five destroyers of Captain Carter's squadron stationed themselves two and a half miles out in the gulf and opened fire. The preinvasion bombardment lasted ten minutes, targeting the tree line behind the beaches in an attempt to destroy any enemy defensive positions that might be there, and to knock Japanese lookouts and snipers from their perches at the tops of coconut trees (the Allies had learned this was a favorite tactic of their enemy).[14]

When the guns fell silent, motorized rubber boats from the destroyer-transports sped toward the shore, packed with Australian soldiers who strained their eyes looking into the dark jungle ahead, seeking enemy troops. Eight boats rushed at Red Beach, while eight went to Yellow Beach. Red Beach was the goal of troops from the 20th Australian Infantry Brigade, and Yellow Beach was the goal of troops from the 26th Australian Infantry Brigade.

Within fifteen minutes, the big, ungainly LCIs pushed their bows onto the black sand beaches and dropped the ramps on each side. Troops rushed down and ran toward the tree line. No opposition was encountered on Red Beach; the few lookouts who had tied themselves to the tops of coconut trees had been felled by the destroyer bombardment, and the infantry finished off any survivors. On Yellow Beach a small group of Japanese soldiers manning a machine-gun position evidently realized the size of the invading force and were seen fleeing into the swamp.[15]

Opposition to the landing finally made its appearance a few minutes after seven, when six Zero fighters approached the beaches from the direction of the still-functioning airfield at Lae. They raced across the landing zones at low altitude, each firing their two 7.7mm light machine guns and two 20mm wing cannons to great effect. A number of Australian soldiers were wounded or killed as they scattered into the tree line for cover. Three Betty bombers followed, dropping loads from about twelve hundred feet. One LCI received a direct hit through her main deck, and near misses that badly damaged her hull and bracketed another. Both vessels managed through the skill and courage of their commanders to put their troops ashore before they had to be abandoned. The attack killed two dozen Australians and Americans, and wounded twenty-eight others.[16]

Meanwhile, the landing craft continued to put Australian soldiers on the beaches. Slightly over a thousand members of the 532nd U.S. Engineer Special Brigade soon joined them, quickly taking control of the beach and directing infantry. The engineers brought along a variety of tractors, road graders, power-driven saws to cut down trees, and wire mesh to lay down temporary roads into the interior. Joined by Australian engineers, they pushed through the jungle with their mesh and log roads.

The arrival at Red Beach of six LSTs, the largest landing vessels in the fleet, drew everyone's attention. The 328-foot-long ships each carried four hundred soldiers, thirty-five vehicles, and eighty tons of bulk stores. The historian of the 2nd ESB described the scene: "As these ponderous hulks drove to the beach even the longshoremen working frantically in their unloading of the smaller craft stopped to view these monsters as they magically opened their bows and dropped immense ramps slowly to the edge of the surf. Ton after ton of equipment was unloaded and, interspersed with the vehicles and matériel, companies of infantry filed out while artillerymen rode guns drawn by tractors."[17]

By ten thirty a.m., over eight thousand Australian and one thousand American soldiers were ashore, as were fifteen hundred tons of supplies. General Wootten established his headquarters in a coconut grove about one mile inland. So excited was he about the successful landing, and brimming with confidence in his troops, he told Barbey that his men would be in Lae in less than two weeks.[18]

At about two p.m., patrols from each beachhead met inland at an unnamed river designated Suez by the planners. Soon, almost the entire Australian force was pushing its way through mangrove swamps and jungle undergrowth westward toward Lae, some sixteen miles away. Enemy opposition was sporadic. The most dangerous came from hidden pillboxes and machine-gun emplacements on opposite riverbanks. Swiftly moving rivers were bridged where possible. In other instances boats manned by the ESB ferried troops across, often under enemy fire. The move west was relentless as the now-outnumbered and outgunned enemy slowly withdrew before the massive invasion force. More landing craft arrived at the beaches. Their cargoes were quickly unloaded and sent along the newly created roads to keep the infantry and artillerymen supplied and fed.[19]

The following day, the men of the 503rd PIR awoke at three a.m at their Port Moresby bivouac. After a hastily eaten breakfast of pancakes soaked in syrup and gallons of coffee, they loaded into eighty-two trucks, each bearing a number that corresponded to a number on a C-47 transport plane. Driven to two nearby airfields, each truck was pulled alongside the aircraft with the corresponding number and twenty-two paratroopers and supply bundles were loaded into each C-47.[20]

As the troopers made their way from the trucks to the planes, many were surprised to see their commander in chief arrive, accompanied by General Kenney. MacArthur spoke briefly to Colonel Kinsler about his mission, and as Kenney described, "walked along the line of airplanes greeting the troops and stopping occasionally to chat with some of them and wish them luck. They all seemed glad to see him and somehow had found out that he would be watching the 'jump.'"[21]

At 8:25 a.m., the transports began moving out onto the runways. Within fifteen minutes all eighty-two C-47s were airborne, soon joined by three B-17s. The first one carried MacArthur, the second Kenney, and the third General Vasey, commander of the Australian 7th Division. Several days before, when MacArthur learned Kenney intended to observe the drop over Nadzab, he attempted to talk Kenney out of it. As Kenney later explained, he told MacArthur he had always obeyed his order to stay out of combat, but this was too important for him to miss. He closed his argument with "they were my kids and I was going to see them do their stuff."

"The General listened to my tirade," Kenney recalled, "and finally said, 'You're right, George, we'll both go. They're my kids too.'"

Kenney protested that it did not make sense to risk the life of the commanding general of the entire theater by "having some five-dollar-a-month Jap aviator shoot a hole through you."

MacArthur responded that he was "not worried about getting shot. Honestly, the only thing that disturbs me is the possibility that when we hit rough air over the mountains my stomach might get upset. I'd hate to get sick and disgrace myself in front of the kids."

MacArthur's mind was made up, so Kenney arranged for what he called a "brass hat" flight of the three B-17s to fly above the C-47s and observe the parachute troops drop into Nadzab.[22]

The plan of attack was straightforward. The 1st Battalion of the PIR, commanded by Lieutenant Colonel John W. Britten, was to drop directly onto the landing strip, capture it from any surviving Japanese, and prepare it for Allied planes to land. The 2nd Battalion, commanded by Lieutenant Colonel George M. Jones, was to drop close to a village called Gabsonkek, across a trail leading from the northwest. Its assignment was to prevent enemy troops from entering the airfield area from that direction. Lieutenant Colonel John J. Tolson's 3rd Battalion was to drop east of the airfield, take control of the village of Gabmatzung, and guard against enemy infiltrators from that direction.

Once the paratroopers of the 503rd were airborne and heading toward the mountains, five more transports left Port Moresby and headed for Tsili-Tsili. On board were the Australian paragunners, with their dismantled and bundled guns. One hour after arriving at Tsili-Tsili, they reboarded the aircraft and took off for the ten-minute flight to Nadzab.

Across the Owen Stanley Range, fighters and bombers from eight different airfields in New Guinea and Australia joined the C-47s. By the time the armada reached the target zone, it consisted of more than three hundred aircraft. The first to the scene were six squadrons of Mitchell B-25s flying at one thousand feet, strafing the entire area around the field with their .50-caliber machine guns and then dropping sixty fragmentation bombs equipped with parachutes from each plane. Immediately after them came six Douglas A-20 Havoc light bombers that laid smoke over the area to hide the men who would be hanging virtually helpless as they descended to the ground.

Then came the C-47s, flying in three columns, one for each battalion. Fighter cover was at a thousand feet above the transports on each side of the columns, as well as a group at seven thousand feet and yet another at between fifteen and twenty thousand feet. Pulling up the rear were twenty-four B-24s and five B-17s. As the armada approached Nadzab, these B-24s and B-17s left the flight and headed toward a place called Heath's Plantation for a bombing mission. Halfway between Nadzab and Lae, Heath's housed a large force of enemy troops.[23]

As the armada made its way to Nadzab, it flew directly over an Allied force of Australians and Papuans commanded by Lieutenant Colonel J. T. Lang heading to the same target along jungle trails. Its assignment was to meet with the American paratroopers once they had control of the airfield and help them clear the landing strip for the arrival of transports carrying the 7th Division.

Thirty minutes from the target, the crew chiefs on each C-47 opened the jump doors. The door on one plane jammed in the wind and blocked the exit, forcing it to return to Port Moresby, the paratroopers greatly disappointed that they had missed the first American combat jump in the Pacific war.[24]

As they approached the airfield, the C-47s dropped to a level of four hundred feet. At 10:22, the green light inside each plane lit and the paratroopers began jumping out. Above them, General MacArthur was thrilled as he watched more than fifteen hundred parachutes carrying "my boys" and their supplies smoothly descend. "One plane after another poured out its stream of dropping men over the target field," MacArthur described. "Everything went like clockwork."[25] Four and a half minutes after the first man jumped, the entire regiment, less the twenty-two men aboard the plane with the defective door, was on the ground.

The drop was not without its costs. Two men were killed when their chutes failed to open, and a third died when he landed in a tall tree and released his harness, only to fall to the ground. Thirty-three others suffered injuries ranging from broken bones to minor cuts and bruises. That evening when Colonel Lang's column arrived, medical personnel with the field ambulance reset broken bones and patched up other injuries. There was no opposition, as the Japanese stationed at Nadzab had been ordered earlier to withdraw.

The Americans had believed that kunai grass about four feet high covered the drop zone around the airstrip; it must have looked that way in photos taken from reconnaissance planes. Yet the grass, with its razor-sharp edges, was actually closer to ten feet high. Luckily, the paratroopers had been issued machetes to cut their way through the tough grass. It took several hours of men shouting to each other and slashing away at the grass before many of the companies were assembled, by which time the men were completely exhausted by the effort in hundred-degree heat, weighed down with weapons and other equipment. One soldier described the base of the grass as "impossible to walk over . . . kind of like deep snow when you're trying to walk on it in the winter."[26]

One hour after the Americans jumped, the planes with the Australian gunners and their two dismantled artillery pieces arrived. It was only the second drop for these courageous men who, as members of a field artillery unit, never expected to have to jump out of an airplane six hundred feet above the ground. All landed safely, but it took them several hours to locate the parts so that they could assemble one gun.

That evening, Colonel Lang's Australian and Papuan soldiers, who had arrived overland with engineering equipment, cleared the field of obstacles such as bushes and fallen trees while paratroopers stood guard around the entire perimeter. Early the next morning two C-47s landed. The men unloaded two bulldozers, twelve portable flamethrowers, and elements of the American 871st Airborne Engineer Battalion. The flamethrowers were employed to burn away grass. Unfortunately, the fire got out of control and consumed many of the parachutes the men had left where they landed, as well as some supplies, before it finally burned itself out.[27]

When the B-17s of the "brass hat" flight returned to Port Moresby on September 5, MacArthur told all three crews gathered around him, "Gentlemen, that was as fine an example of discipline and training as I have ever witnessed." Kenney learned from the officer who piloted MacArthur's B-17 that one of its engines had failed during the first fifteen minutes of the flight. The pilot sent an officer to tell MacArthur about the engine and his recommendation that they return to the airfield. The commander in chief responded that he had been on a B-17 with General Kenney when one engine quit, and he knew the bomber could fly as well on three engines as four. There was no turning back.[28]

Unperturbed, MacArthur then radioed his wife, Jean, in Brisbane describing the operation as "a honey."[29]

––––––––––––

On September 6, C-47s began landing at Nadzab and unloading infantry troops. All day long, in General Kenney's words, "we ferried troops of [General] Vasey's 7th Division from Marilinan [Tsili-Tsili] to Nadzab, while twenty-four heavy bombers plastered Lae with 82 tons of 1,000-pounders and forty-eight B-25s dropped 61 tons of bombs and fired 75,000 rounds of ammunition in support of Wootten's advancing troops of the 9th Division."[30]

By September 10, the entire Australian 7th Division had been airlifted into Nadzab and elements had started their trek east along the Markham River toward Lae. They battled pockets of Japanese defenders but steadily drove them back. The enemy forces at Lae were bombed relentlessly, shelled from the ships offshore, while pincers of infantry troops pressed in on them from the east and the west. On September 14, soldiers from the 7th Division reached the outskirts of Lae.[31] To the south, American and Australian forces were hammering Imperial Army and Navy troops at Salamaua.

Meanwhile, the Japanese commander at Lae radioed Rabaul with a frantic call for help. General Imamura responded by sending eighty-one planes to attack the Allied landing zones. At first delayed by fog across New Britain, the planes were spotted by radar on board the destroyer *Reid*. They flew in three large groups and included twelve Betty bombers, eight Val dive-bombers, and sixty-one Zero fighters. To counter these invaders, the fighter direction staff aboard *Reid* called out forty P-38s and twenty P-47s. These included fighters from the 80th Fighter Squadron flying cover along the routes being used by Seventh Amphibious ships and craft traveling back and forth between the two Lae beachheads and Buna with supplies. The destroyer also called out planes that were on "standby" at Dobodura airfield near Buna. As the fighters engaged in running dogfights, a few of the enemy's bombers and dive-bombers managed get through and attack several landing ships returning to Buna, causing several dozen casualties.[32]

On September 8, as four American destroyers bombarded Lae from offshore, General Adachi, commanding officer of the Eighteenth Army, headquartered at Madang, radioed General Nakano at Salamaua to withdraw his forces to Lae. Realizing his position was defenseless, Nakano, who had once ordered his men to "die fighting," had already shipped his wounded and his remaining artillery to Lae. Now Imperial forces lingering at Salamaua began to abandon the town and head north. Nearly five thousand men moved to Lae, using seventy-three barges that hugged the shore in an attempt to avoid patrolling Allied aircraft. Six hundred naval troops boarded submarines bound for Rabaul, while a rear guard of about 250 men walked toward Lae.[33]

Fearful of having the 51st Division surrounded at Lae, Imperial Headquarters instructed General Imamura to withdraw all troops from Lae and have them move overland to the north coast of the Huon Peninsula. Tokyo was determined to remain in control of the Ramu Valley and the base at Finschhafen. A regiment from the 20th Division, stationed at Madang, rushed south to Finschhafen to cover the withdrawal of the 51st Division. On September 15, the last Japanese troops left Lae for an extremely difficult overland withdrawal that would be repeated several times in the coming months as Allied forces pushed the Japanese farther north and west across New Guinea.[34]

When Allied commanders realized the enemy had withdrawn for Lae, leaving behind only a small volunteer force to fight a delaying action to buy the fleeing troops time, a battalion from the Australian 29th Brigade circled around the town and pursued and harassed the fleeing enemy up the coast as far as possible.

Meanwhile, on September 11, Australian troops from the 3rd Division, along with the American 162nd Regiment, had taken control of the Salamaua airfield, which they found virtually useless. Two days later, they occupied what remained of the town. When General Herring, commander of the Australian I Corps, arrived by American PT boat on the fourteenth to determine Salamaua's usefulness as a potential air and naval base, he rejected the idea entirely. The high point of the occupation of Salamaua took place on September 16, when a chaplain serving with the New Guinea Volunteer Rifles raised the same Australian flag the NGVR had lowered and taken with them when the Japanese invaded in March 1942.[35]

Salamaua, which war and Japanese occupation had transformed into what members of the 162nd Regiment called "a filthy, rat-ridden, pestilential hole," ceased to exist. Once the scene of a thriving 1930s social life for wealthy Australians living in Lae, with weekend dinner parties at their summer houses and numerous tennis courts, nothing remains of it today.

The campaign for Salamaua cost the Japanese over eight thousand casualties, including nearly three thousand killed. Australian losses were 1,120 wounded and 470 killed. The American 162nd Regiment of the 41st Infantry Division suffered 76 killed and 396 wounded.[36] The Japanese never realized that the battle for Salamaua was a diversion for the Allies' real target, Lae. Fooled by this, General Adachi had transferred too many men to Salamaua, thereby weakening Lae's defenses.

Battling a small but determined opposition, the Australian 25th Infantry Brigade, the part of the 7th Division that had landed at Nadzab, entered Lae on September 15. Later that day, the 24th Infantry Brigade that had landed on the beaches as part of the 9th Division, joined the 25th. The campaign for Lae ended, and remnants of the Japanese 51st Division along with other enemy forces rushed northwest along the coast, seeking safety. Lae would eventually serve MacArthur's forces as Lae Fortress, with both an Australian base and an American base.

The Nadzab landing zone was soon converted into a busy air base, with four all-weather airfields four thousand to seven thousand feet in length. It would serve as the main base for the Allied air forces in New Guinea for the remainder of the war, but it was especially important for the next campaign: the fight for the Huon Peninsula.

CHAPTER 13

War on the Huon Peninsula

The Japanese army that fled from Lae was a shadow of the force that had landed the year before. Sick, wounded, and dispirited, the army and accompanying naval troops had blown up all supplies and weapons they could not carry. Their remaining food stores, already greatly reduced by the Allied blockade of the sea routes, limited each man to a maximum of two weeks' supply. The Imperial soldiers fell into two primary categories: first were the survivors of the 51st Division from Salamaua, all of whom were worn down by nine weeks of almost continuous combat against an enemy growing daily in size and power. Second was what remained of the Lae garrison itself, which had been stripped of most of its combat effectives who had been sent to Salamaua.

These nine thousand men struggling to make their way to safety faced many difficulties. Australian units that had landed at Nadzab were often ahead of the Japanese, laying ambushes for harassing attacks. Allied aircraft bombed and strafed the retreating columns whenever they moved into open country. The most obvious escape routes, especially those through the Markham and Ramu Valleys, could not be used because Allied troops had so completely infiltrated the areas and Allied planes had total control of the airspace over them. Forced to improvise their own path, the Japanese spent days exhausting themselves even further by hacking trails through the dense jungle. When they approached a wide or rapidly moving stream, such as the Busu River, everything came to a halt while engineers felled trees and constructed rough bridges.[1]

The route behind the retreating Japanese was littered with the decaying corpses of men who had succumbed either to wounds or to the malaria and dysentery that swept through their ranks. There was also a long trail of abandoned rifles, packs, and helmets, mostly discarded by men of the 51st Division who had become so disheartened about reaching safety that they could barely gather the strength to continue trudging through the jungle and swamps. Men of the 1st Battalion of the 20th Infantry Division, which had been sent to Salamaua to support the 51st Division, were generally in better shape. They had spent less time fighting the Allies, and their commanding officer, Major Shigetoshi Shintani, threatened to put to death any soldier who abandoned his weapon. As a result, all the soldiers of the 1st Battalion who would reach their destination still carried their weapons.[2]

When their food ran out about September 25, the retreating men raided local villages for anything to eat, even pulling half-grown potatoes from native gardens. Grass and roots quickly became the mainstay of their diet. On that same day, the soldiers began climbing the Saruwaged Range, whose peaks reached thirteen thousand feet. The intense cold at the higher elevations made life for the men, most of whom were wearing tropical uniforms, even more miserable. Those who survived the mountain cold descended into the sweltering heat of the insect-infested jungle and swamps of the valley formed by the Kwarna River.[3]

Troops began arriving at Kiari, on the north coast of the Huon Peninsula, by the second week in October. Most were sent on to a rest camp near Hansa Bay farther up the New Guinea coast, while the small number who appeared fit for service were assigned to units guarding the coast. Of the 9,000 soldiers and sailors who retreated from Lae, barely 6,500 survived.

The Japanese defeats at Salamaua and Lae had an impact on both the Allies and the Imperial government in Tokyo. For the Japanese, the setbacks had wide strategic consequences. The loss of these two linchpins in their defensive line joined two other defeats at the outer edges of the empire. First was the loss of Attu Island in Alaska several months earlier, with the death of the entire 2,900-man garrison (except for 29 taken prisoner), and the Northern Army's decision to evacuate its troops from a second American island, Kiska. Next came defeat at the hands of American and New Zealand troops in the central Solomons. Now, with the loss of the two New Guinea outposts, the Japanese were convinced they were overextended and a new defensive line would have to be drawn.

The Imperial Army and Navy planners soon drafted an agreement developing what they called the "absolute zone of national defense." The perimeter of this zone ran across the western end of New Guinea through the Caroline Islands to the Mariana Islands. This would be where Japan would make her final defense against an enemy increasing daily in numbers and strength who seemed determined to launch an invasion of the Home Islands. The planners anticipated that strongpoints outside the perimeter—such as Madang and Wewak in New Guinea, Rabaul in New Britain, and the northern Solomons—would fight delaying actions to buy time for the empire to build up its forces within the absolute zone for a future counterattack against the Allies.

An Imperial Conference, only the fourth such conference since the start of the war, approved the Army and Navy agreement, with some modifications, on September 30, 1943. One of the modifications, which demonstrates the absence of reality in Japanese planning, reduced the aircraft production requirement from fifty thousand planes in 1944 to forty thousand. In truth, Japanese industry in 1943 was struggling to produce substantially fewer than two thousand planes per month.

The speed with which Lae fell surprised everyone at Allied headquarters. General MacArthur now looked ahead to the capture of the Huon Peninsula. Named for an eighteenth-century French navigator and explorer, the Huon is 6,400 square miles of jungle with three mountain ranges crossing it. The peninsula extends east into the Bismarck Sea like a thick finger pointing directly at New Britain, across the narrow Vitiaz Strait and Dampier Strait. These two straits are separated by several small islands, the largest of which is Rooke Island. Control of the two straits, especially the larger Vitiaz, held strategic value because they blocked access from the Solomon Sea to the Bismarck Sea. The Japanese had commanded the straits since their invasion of Lae and Salamaua, and had effectively blocked MacArthur's plans to move amphibious forces up the New Guinea coast.

To capture the Huon, MacArthur's next target was Finschhafen, a small port on the edge of the finger at the place where the straits were the narrowest. Fifty miles east-northeast of Lae, Finschhafen guarded the western side of the Vitiaz Strait. The original schedule called for invading Finschhafen about a month after Lae fell. Yet when Allied intelligence learned that troops from Japan's 80th Infantry Regiment and the 21st Field Artillery Regiment, both from the 20th Division, were advancing toward Finschhafen to bolster its defenses, MacArthur immediately moved up the date.

In addition to its location, Finschhafen's value lay in its two excellent harbors, one at the port itself and the other a little north at Langemak Bay; both served as bases for the increased barge traffic on which the Imperial Army had come to depend for troops and supplies. In addition, a small airstrip that could accommodate fighters and light bombers was nearby. The primary defense of the area was in the hands of the 1st Shipping Group—twelve hundred troops who were mostly barge operators and mechanics—under the command of Major General Eizo Yamada. To support these largely noncombat troops, General Adachi, commander of the Eighteenth Army, decided to rush the rest of the 20th Division south. These troops, many of whom were exhausted from their efforts to construct a road from Madang to Lae, now had to trek two hundred miles from the construction site at Bogadjim to Finschhafen.[4]

General Yamada realized that his base was the next likely target of the enemy. The arrival within days, mostly by barges, of the additional

four thousand combat troops of the 20th Division gave him the opportunity to prepare his defenses. Anticipating that the Allies would send
most of their troops overland from Lae, Yamada stationed three thousand men in defensive positions south and west of Finschhafen, facing
the trails from Lae. This left slightly more than a thousand soldiers to
defend the town itself. He also sent a small number of men to prepare
defenses along a beach six miles north of Finschhafen, which appeared
to be the only likely place for an amphibious landing.[5]

The day after the first troops of the Australian 9th Division entered Lae,
September 15, 1943, General MacArthur called a conference in Port
Moresby with the intention of moving up the date for invading Finschhafen. In attendance were Australian General Herring, General Kenney,
and Admiral Barbey. MacArthur, mindful of intelligence reports that
large groups of enemy troops were moving toward Finschhafen by barge
and land, asked Herring how quickly troops could be made available for
a landing there, and asked Barbey if he could assemble enough ships
and craft to deliver those troops to the beaches off Finschhafen. Barbey
claimed the ships could be ready in seventy-two hours but expressed
concern about air cover for the convoy and the landing, pointing out
that the target was on the Vitiaz Strait and that enemy bombers were
based at several airfields on New Britain, just sixty miles away.[6]

Kenney was reluctant to offer any guarantees about air cover over
the narrow straits. He had originally opposed additional amphibious
assaults, favoring instead an "interior option." This called for moving
troops up the Markham and Ramu Valleys and the construction of
additional airfields for Kenney's pilots to use in attacking Madang,
Wewak, and other powerful and important enemy air bases in northern
New Guinea. Under pressure from MacArthur, he relented and agreed
to provide air cover for Barbey's convoys and over the landing beaches
as soon as daylight made it possible for his pilots to fly. He pressed once
again, as he had with the Lae landings, for the amphibious assault to
take place after sunrise to give his planes time to reach the beaches

and bomb and strafe them prior to the landing, but Barbey once again held out for what he considered the benefit of surprise in a predawn landing. General Herring said he could have his troops and supplies ready to load on Barbey's ships in four days. That settled it for MacArthur; he decided on a predawn assault to take place on September 22.[7]

On September 21, the soldiers of the 20th Australian Infantry Brigade from the 9th Division, commanded by Brigadier Victor Windeyer, boarded Barbey's landing craft at Lae and were joined by eight LSTs that had been loaded with supplies at Buna. In addition to the landing craft and LSTs, the convoy that was to sail along the coast toward Finschhafen included sixteen LCIs, four destroyer-transports, and ten destroyers as escorts. Five hundred seventy-five men from the 532nd American Engineer Boat and Shore Regiment soon joined the convoy.[8]

On the same day, troops from the 22nd Australian Infantry Battalion marched out of Lae and headed along the coastal road, such as it was, for Finschhafen. Meanwhile, units of the 7th Australian Infantry Division pursued remnants of the Lae garrison up the inland route through the Ramu and Markham Valleys.

The place selected for the amphibious landing was a nine-hundred-yard-long strip of coral and sand that was only thirty feet deep and backed up to sharply rising mountains of the Kreutberg Range. Its north and south boundaries were marked by coral headlands. It was less than seven miles north of Finschhafen. A scouting party consisting of six men from the 532nd EBSR and four New Guineans had rowed ashore in rubber boats launched from two PT boats during the night of September 11 to reconnoiter the area. Recovered during the night of the fourteenth, the party's report did not contribute much to the planning, other than to confirm there were several machine-gun emplacements near the north end of the beach.[9]

It was the habit of U.S. Navy planners to identify a main landing beach as Red Beach. At Lae there was a Red Beach and a Yellow Beach, and advance parties from the 532nd had gone ashore at both beaches and raised colored screens to make it easier for the landing craft to put in at the correct beach. This had caused some confusion about the

Finschhafen landing, since the site there was referred to as Scarlet Beach. An erroneous story persists that the name came from a scarlet flag that a native supposedly raised on a hill at the back of the beach. Brigadier Windeyer, who led the troops ashore, explained in 1947 that the name actually came from General Herring, who suggested it to avoid confusion with Red Beach, which was still in use at Lae. Although the banners marking the beach at Finschhafen would be red, scarlet was the closest color Herring could think of.[10]

The Finschhafen invasion convoy left Lae just after sundown on September 21. As it did, it came under attack from six enemy bombers that were evidently on a bombing mission against Allied ground forces. The surprise sighting of the ships proved too tempting for the Japanese pilots, but they released their bombs too soon, missing the convoy by a quarter of a mile. Unfortunately for the bombers and their fighter escorts, the American destroyer *Reid*, still on picket patrol in the Huon Gulf with a complement of fighter-directors on board, picked up the Japanese flight on its radar and recalled a homebound patrol of American fighters that swept in on the Japanese. The American pilots reported shooting down five of the bombers and several of their escorts.[11]

A few minutes before the landing at Scarlet Beach was to take place, the escorting destroyers bombarded the beach to drive any defenders under cover. At 4:45 a.m. on September 22, the assault began in earnest. As had been experienced at the earlier landings at Nassau Beach and Lae, confusion reigned. Some craft missed the beach entirely, forcing their troops to wade or in some cases swim ashore. Nevertheless, overall the landing was a success.

The few Japanese defending the beach put up fierce but brief resistance. Overwhelmed by the invading force, they soon retired to the jungle-covered mountain to the rear. Meanwhile, the Australian units began moving south toward Finschhafen. Reinforcements arrived at Scarlet Beach over the next few days, and Barbey's ships kept up a steady run of supplies.

Following the successful landings, General Adachi ordered General Yamada to pull in his now-almost-useless southern and western defense line and concentrate on nearby Sattelberg. Situated fifteen miles north of Finschhafen on a 3,200-foot mountain, the town overlooks a large portion of the north coast of the Huon Peninsula, especially the Finsch-hafen sector. Adachi instructed Yamada to hold the town pending the arrival of the 20th Division, which continued struggling through the jungle to support him but was still one hundred miles away. It was expected to arrive about October 10.

Meanwhile, the landing zone came under attack from Japanese aircraft. While bad weather over New Guinea kept most of the Imperial Army's planes grounded, the Navy's 11th Air Fleet from Rabaul attacked Barbey's ships and the beachhead several times over the next few days. Each time, the *Reid* gave early warning of the approaching enemy and Allied fighters generally drove them off with little or no damage to Allied ships.

Following days of heavy fighting across several rivers and through thick jungle and kunai grass, the lead elements of the 20th Australian Brigade entered Finschhafen on October 2 and made contact with the 22nd Australian Infantry Battalion, which had marched up from Lae. Faced with encirclement by an overwhelming force, the Japanese defenders, who were primarily naval base and combat troops, had begun their withdrawal the day before. In less than a week, Allied aircraft were flying into and out of the Finschhafen airfield. This left the primary Japanese force in the area at Sattelberg, especially after the arrival of Lieutenant General Shigeru Kitagiri and three thousand troops from the 20th Division.

Determined to drive enemy forces off Scarlet Beach—where they busily unloaded supplies, several Australian Matilda tanks, and ad-ditional troops—General Adachi ordered bombing raids that were repelled by Allied fighters before they could do much damage. He also attempted to send more troops in by using motorized barges to land on the beach. His spies may have told him that only two companies of Australians, along with some American soldiers who operated the land-ing craft of the 532nd EBSR, defended the beach.

At about four a.m. on October 18, in a driving rain, four barges filled with 155 Japanese soldiers from the 10th Company of 79th Infantry Regiment quietly moved in toward the beach. With their engines muffled in the pitch-black darkness before dawn, they were less than two hundred yards from shore when they were spotted. First to see the approaching landing craft was Brooklyn native Sergeant John Fuina and Corporal Raymond J. Koch of Wabasha, Minnesota, both members of the 532nd. Fuina bolted to his nearby .37mm antitank gun as Koch ran through the area whispering for the Americans and Australians to wake up and man their guns. Unfortunately, the heaviest weapon the Australians had was a Swedish-designed Bofors 40mm antiaircraft gun. Because its primary use was against aircraft, its long barrel could not be lowered enough to fire at the barges.[12]

As the first barge hit the beach, Sergeant Fuina opened fire with his antitank gun, accompanied by several Australians with Bren guns. They disabled the barge, killing several of the enemy. Survivors were pulled aboard the other barges, which quickly moved down the beach, away from the firing. What they did not know when they touched beach sand again and dropped their ramps was that they were clearly in the sights of a .50-caliber heavy machine gun manned by nineteen-year-old Private Nathan Van Noy from Grace, Idaho, and his twenty-nine-year-old loader, Corporal Stephen Popa. Wounded the previous month, the baby-faced Van Noy, called "Junior" by his friends, had insisted on returning to his unit.

Among the first enemy soldiers to leap off the barges were two men equipped with flamethrowers. Too dark to see anything other than muzzle flashes, the soldiers swept the area with their weapons, starting small fires ahead of their advance. It was then that Private Van Noy let loose with his heavy machine gun and cut the two men down. As the Japanese poured out of the barges, they dove to the sand for protection from Van Noy and other Allied soldiers who were firing submachine guns, rifles, and handguns from out of the dark. Several of the enemy attempted to silence the heavy machine gun by lobbing hand grenades in its direction.

From behind the camouflaged machine-gun position, Australians with Bren guns fired over the heads of the two Americans and shouted for them to pull back. Van Noy and Popa ignored their calls until a grenade wounded the latter. Popa, thinking his buddy was right behind him, crawled out of the gun pit they were in, and two Australians pulled him to safety. Van Noy kept firing, continuing to ignore calls to fall back. In front of him, the bodies of enemy soldiers piled up. Then, as Fuina watched in shock, a grenade exploded right inside the pit. The blast ripped Van Noy's leg from his body, yet he kept up a steady stream of fire until suddenly everyone, Allied and Japanese alike, heard the loud click as the machine gun ran out of ammunition. The men behind him continued to call for Van Noy to retreat, but the private simply reloaded and began firing again.

After a while, the shooting slowed as surviving Japanese slipped into the water and swam up the shoreline, pursued by Australian and Papuan soldiers. As the sun rose over the water, the Australians and Americans roamed the beach, finishing off the enemy. When they approached the pit occupied by Van Noy, he was dead. His gun having run out of ammunition again, his finger was still on the trigger of the empty weapon. A rifle bullet to the temple had finally done in Van Noy. He had killed at least half of the thirty-nine Japanese soldiers lying dead on the beach.

For their actions that morning on Scarlet Beach, Private Van Noy was posthumously awarded the Congressional Medal of Honor and Corporal Popa was awarded the Silver Star for gallantry.[13]

Meanwhile, Australian units prepared to attack the Japanese stronghold at Sattelberg. Not one to sit around waiting for the enemy to strike, General Kitagiri launched a series of attacks from Sattelberg against Scarlet Beach. When General Wootten learned through captured Japanese documents that Kitagiri planned a major counterattack, he requested that a reserve brigade be sent to support his exhausted troops. On October 20, American landing ships delivered the Australian 26th Brigade to Scarlet Beach. Over the next five days, Kitagiri attempted to drive the Allies off the beach, but failed. With food supplies running low, he decided to regroup back at Sattelberg to plan further attacks. The action cost the Australians 49 dead, but the number of Japanese killed exceeded 675.[14]

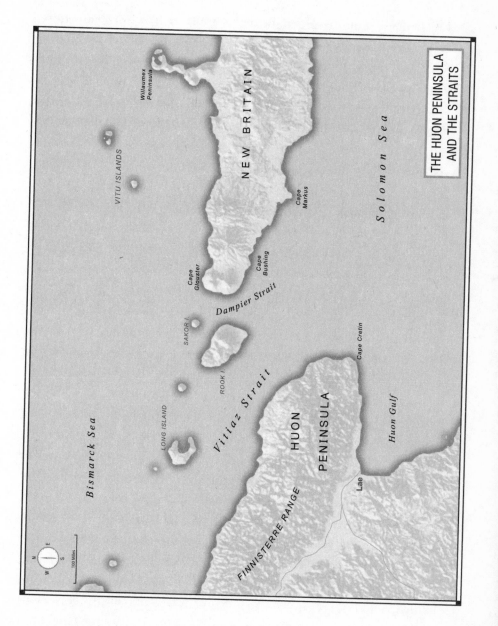

THE HUON PENINSULA
AND THE STRAITS

Bismarck Sea

VITU ISLANDS

Willaumex
Peninsula

NEW BRITAIN

Cape
Markus

Solomon Sea

Cape
Glouster

Cape
Bushing

Dampier Strait

SAKOR I.

ROOK I.

LONG ISLAND

Vitiaz Strait

Cape Cretin

HUON

PENINSULA

Huon Gulf

FINNISTERRE RANGE

Lae

N
W E
S

100 Miles

Located five miles from the coast, Sattelberg had once served as a German mission, but was now estimated to hold close to five thousand Japanese troops. From its perch high above the surrounding countryside, Sattelberg gave its occupiers an excellent view of the entire coast. What's more, it could serve as the base from which to launch future attacks against Allied lines of communications and resupply. The Allies had little choice but to attempt to capture it, despite its obvious strong defensive position. The Japanese there could not simply be bypassed—left alone, they could create a danger to future operations.

Strong defensive positions around Sattelberg were aided by the fact that an attacking force not only had to climb steep hills to reach its target but also had to deal with nature herself. The surrounding hilly countryside consisted of thick woods of tightly packed bamboo and betel nut palm trees. Bulldozers had to clear paths for the Matilda tanks that had recently arrived. Designed to support infantry troops fighting in close proximity to the enemy, the Matilda was slow moving but heavily armored. Its 40mm main gun and 7.92mm Bresa machine guns proved devastating against Japanese pillboxes that dotted the area surrounding Sattelberg.

Another new weapon introduced in New Guinea was the 4.5-inch barrage rocket manned by the American amphibians. Launched from a metal frame that held twelve rocket guides, or sleeves, it could be fired from a vehicle or landing craft or from the ground. Each rocket weighed thirty pounds and had a range of twelve hundred yards. The concussions from the rocket's extremely loud explosions were known to kill men fifty yards away. Commanded by Maryland native Major Charles K. Lane, the rocket team mounted its launchers on a three-quarter-ton weapons carrier that pushed its way through the jungle and up a steep hillside to within range of Sattelberg. From there the team launched its rockets into enemy forces with laudable results. Surprised by this new weapon, the Japanese were at a loss to locate the launcher's position and wasted much of their limited artillery ammunition seeking to silence, without success, the rockets. When the fighting ended, many dead enemy soldiers had no visible wounds, evidently victims of the terrific concussions caused by the exploding rockets.[15]

Following intensive Allied bombing and the relentless push of Australian and American forces on the ground, Sattelberg finally fell on November 26. In one of the final actions of the battle, twenty-nine-year-old Sergeant Tom Derrick, commander of the 3rd Platoon of B Company, Australian 2/48th Battalion, led his men up to the edge of the plateau on which the town is located. Previous attempts by his and other platoons had been turned back by heavy machine-gun fire and the Japanese tactic of rolling live grenades down the hillside. Crawling ahead of his pinned-down platoon, Derrick lobbed grenade after grenade into the Japanese positions while the enemy tried to kill him with their machine guns. After eliminating ten enemy positions, he called his men up. The Australians soon occupied the former Japanese gun posts and settled in for the night. The following day they discovered the enemy had withdrawn from the town under the cover of darkness. For his actions, Sergeant Derrick, who was first to raise the Australian flag over Sattelberg, was award the Victoria Cross, the British Commonwealth's highest honor.[16]

Describing Sattelberg as a "ruin," an Australian war correspondent wrote that "practically every building now is only twisted sheet iron and splintered wood." He claimed that the battle "will always remain a classic example of the skill and 'guts' of the Australian Imperial Forces infantry. They have rarely fought under worse conditions."[17]

Another Australian newspaper wrote that the relationship established during the Finschhafen and Lae campaigns "have provided a fine example of the effectiveness of Australian-American cooperation" between the Australian soldiers and men of the 532nd Engineer Boat and Shore Regiment. "These Yanks have fought and some have died alongside Australians and have done both so gamely as to win the respect and affection of the Diggers."[18]

Finschhafen and Sattelberg proved to be among the early moves to reach two of MacArthur's goals. First, he wanted to take control of the

Vitiaz Strait away from the enemy to enable Allied ships to sail up the New Guinea coast relatively unmolested. A longer-term goal was to develop what he called a "loop of envelopment" around the Japanese Eighteenth Army and its sixty thousand troops stationed around Wewak and Madang, isolating them from reinforcement and resupply. His next step toward the latter goal was to push fifty miles up the coast to the next concentration of enemy forces, Sio. Moving along the coast, he would land forces at locales they could use as temporary bases from which to push the enemy along, and eventually herd them together, much as cowboys round up and herd cattle.

After clearing the Nadzab area of enemy forces, General Vasey's Australian 7th Division pushed its way eastward from the Ramu Valley toward the coast, crushing small units of enemy troops who were not fast enough to get out of the way of the Australians rushing across the mountainous jungles. Meanwhile, General Wootten's 9th Division turned away from Sattelberg and fought running battles along the rugged coast toward Sio. In what one Australian newspaper called a "daring flanking movement," soldiers, supported by Matilda tanks and artillery, cut off a main escape route called the Bong-Wareo Trail by capturing and occupying Pino Hill, an irregular promontory overlooking the trail and the surrounding countryside.

Determined to close the loop around the Japanese fleeing Finschhafen and Sio, General MacArthur instructed General Krueger to put American troops from his Alamo Force, newly renamed as the U.S. Sixth Army, ashore at Saidor, approximately 110 nautical miles from Finschhafen and only 52 nautical miles from Madang. He set January 2 as D-Day for the invasion, which was code-named Michaelmas. MacArthur suggested, and Krueger agreed, that the landing force should come from the U.S. 32nd Division, which had been recuperating from the fighting around Buna. The commander in chief also assigned an engineer boat and shore regiment, two engineer aviation battalions, and an amphibious truck company to the operation. In addition to cutting off the Japanese retreat, a second value of Saidor was a small airfield with potential for expansion.

Krueger selected Brigadier General Clarence A. Martin's 126th Infantry Regimental Combat Team for the task, and Admiral Barbey sent the 532nd Amphibians to put the 7,500 troops ashore. The invasion task force—comprising fifty-five vessels, including six destroyers for shore bombardment, four serving as escorts for the landing craft, and five as a covering force farther out to sea, watching for enemy ships and planes—approached Saidor in darkness. Although Japanese Coast-watchers reported sighting the ships, by the time reconnaissance planes arrived overhead, the combination of darkness and scattered rain showers shielded the entire fleet from the enemy. Admiral Barbey led the way aboard his flagship, the destroyer *Conyngham*. Accompanying him was General Martin and several of his staff officers.[19]

On January 1, forty-eight B-25s and sixty B-24s slammed the intended beachhead and surrounding area with 218 tons of demolition bombs. At 7:05 the following morning, with the rains stopped and the sun slipping above the eastern horizon, the six destroyers bombarded the Saidor beaches with 1,725 five-inch shells. Several LCIs equipped with rocket launchers joined in by firing over six hundred rockets. Once the firing ceased, the landing craft put the men and their supplies and equipment ashore with no opposition worth reporting. By noon, the landing vessels had withdrawn and the riflemen who had hit the beaches were headed inland, seeking Japanese. Later reports claimed that 120 to 150 enemy soldiers in the landing zone who survived the shore bombardment fled as the landing craft roared onto the beach.[20]

Steel matting laid by the 542nd Shore Battalion swiftly covered the landing site at Saidor, allowing vehicles to be quickly unloaded from the large LSTs. The original plan called for the Americans to move south toward Sio, blocking any escape routes the enemy might use. Unfortunately, monsoon rains swamped the troops and their vehicles, delaying their departure long enough that thousands of Japanese managed to make their way north to the next main base at Madang.[21]

Fearing the loss of too much of his dwindling manpower resources, General Adachi boarded a submarine at Madang and made a run past the busy Americans at the Saidor beachhead to Sio during the night of January 7. The sub came under attack by U.S. Navy PT boats hunting for enemy barges, but the submarine skipper managed to dive to safety and brought his valuable passenger into Sio on January 8. Once there, Adachi oversaw the evacuation of several thousand troops of the 20th Division on motorized barges. Thousands more, unable to find a place in the barges, were ordered to make their way north toward Madang as best they could. In all, fourteen thousand bedraggled Japanese troops began slogging through the swamps, jungle, and mountains, urgently trying to gain the relative safety of the Madang stronghold.[22]

During the night of January 10, Japanese submarine *I-177* arrived off Sio to take Adachi and Rear Admiral Kudo Kyuhachi, commander of the 7th Base Unit, along with ten staff officers to Madang. While awaiting the passengers, the submarine came under attack by PT-320 and PT-323, but armored barges fitted with tank gun turrets drove off the Americans. The two PT boats backed out of range just long enough for Adachi and his party to board the sub and flee the area. They arrived at Madang shortly after noon.

The headquarters detachment of the 20th Division withdrew from Sio in such haste that it left behind an incredible gift for the Allies. Unable to carry a large steel trunk containing the division's cryptographic materials, and fearful that the smoke caused by burning such a large quantity of mostly damp paper would draw enemy fighters, the radio operators decided to bury the trunk in a nearby streambed. Before doing so, they tore off the covers of the codebooks and substitution tables to show their superiors they had destroyed the books. Despite their efforts, an Australian trooper sweeping for mines discovered the trunk. When an intelligence officer recognized its contents as codebooks and other related materials, it was quickly flown to the Central Bureau in Brisbane. Once there, code breakers and translators found they had an intact version of the Japanese Army four-digit code. All of a sudden, Allied intelligence officers, thanks to the code breakers and that trunk, could read tens of thousands of Japanese Army communications, including a thirteen-part message outlining decisions concerning New Guinea made at a high-level conference of Imperial Japanese Army and Navy officers.

The impact of the trunk contents would be felt in coming months as MacArthur continued his climb along the New Guinea coast.[23]

In one of the worst episodes of the war in New Guinea for the Japanese, fewer than ten thousand of the fleeing soldiers and sailors ultimately reached Madang. Some arrived as late as the first week of March. Over four thousand perished along the way from ambushes by Allied patrols; bombing and strafing attacks from General Kenney's B-25s flying at tree-top level seeking them; or from hunger, disease, and exhaustion. One of those survivors, Sergeant Eiji Lizuka, remembered seeing many dead and dying soldiers stripped of their uniforms and shoes by passing comrades who desperately needed them. The worst, according to the sergeant, was when canteens containing water were taken from dying troops who would cry out, "Don't take my canteen away from me. I'm still alive."[24]

In September 1949, eight Japanese soldiers who were among the four thousand that never reached Madang were discovered living with a small tribe in an isolated mountainous region some sixty-two miles inland from the coast. The tribe's chief had taken pity on them due to their emaciated condition and allowed them to live in the tribe's village. Taken into custody by local police officers who had learned of their existence, the men were eventually placed aboard a British ship taking released prisoners of war to Japan. They landed at the port of Nagoya on February 13, 1950. One of the former soldiers was quoted as saying, "It's like a dream. I never thought we'd be able to return."[25]

As additional troops and equipment arrived at the Saidor beachhead, Army and Air Force engineers went to work repairing the bombed Saidor airfield. By January 9 they had widened the narrow strip to 250 feet and lengthened it to 2,500 feet. It was now capable of handling heavily loaded transport planes, yet work continued so that by March its length exceeded six thousand feet and its surface was hardened so that rainwater ran off instead of sinking it in mud.[26]

On February 10 American patrols from Saidor made contact with Australian patrols from the 5th Infantry Division, which had relieved the 9th Division after the fall of Sio. Unfortunately, by the time the "loop" closed, most of the enemy forces had escaped the trap and were desperately making their way to Madang.[27]

The successful landing of American troops at Saidor caused the staff of the Japanese Eighth Area Army headquarters at Rabaul to question their original orders to defend Sio by rushing additional troops. Following a heated debate, General Imamura decided it was important to save as many troops as possible to defend against MacArthur's likely next target, Wewak. He ordered General Adachi to have the troops fleeing Sio bypass Saidor and move inland to Madang. Adachi, meanwhile, was convinced Madang was the next Allied target, so he moved troops from Wewak to Madang and pulled in from the surrounding mountains small defensive posts that were unlikely to halt the Australian forces moving overland. Imperial General Headquarters, perhaps dissatisfied with the way the defense of the Huon Peninsula had been conducted, removed Adachi's Eighteenth Army from the Eighth Area Army and transferred it to control by the Second Area Army. This accompanied instructions to Adachi to withdraw from Madang and move his forces to Wewak, Hollandia, and Aitape. As a result, Australian troops entering the once-powerful Japanese stronghold on April 24, 1944, found Madang mostly abandoned except for a small rearguard detachment and a horse-drawn artillery gun. The landings at Saidor and the subsequent attempted envelopment of the Japanese forces in the region had evidently convinced the powers in Tokyo that the Huon Peninsula was lost for the last time.[28]

Time magazine hailed the Allied successes on the Huon Peninsula by calling it "The General's Little Blitz" and declaring that MacArthur "demonstrated in New Guinea that he is a great offensive commander. In less than three weeks he gobbled up most of the Huon Peninsula." It then referenced Chief of Staff General Marshall's comment that "New Guinea had become unhealthy for the Japs."[29]

CHAPTER 14

Invasion Across the Straits

For General MacArthur and Admiral Halsey, Rabaul remained the elusive and most desirable target. Since the Japanese invasion of New Britain in January 1942, Imperial forces had turned the once-sleepy town and surrounding region into the most powerful military base in the South Pacific. It contained one of the best natural harbors in the region in Blanche Bay. When combined with three other nearby harbors, Rabaul was anchorage to dozens of large warships, and its seven wharves could serve a wide variety of vessels. Its seven airfields were home to more than three hundred warplanes of all descriptions. On top of this, more than a hundred thousand troops were stationed in and around the Gazelle Peninsula on which Rabaul was located.

MacArthur and Halsey both realized, as did the Joint Chiefs in Washington, that Rabaul could not be captured by a direct assault. It had to be isolated and worn down. For MacArthur, this meant continuing up New Guinea's northern coast and extending his forces out into the Bismarck Sea, thereby cutting off seaborne supplies and reinforcements to and from Rabaul. For his part, Halsey had to continue his climb through the northern Solomons, pushing enemy forces he could not destroy back toward Rabaul.

When ULTRA intercepts on September 13, 1943, revealed that the Japanese 1st Carrier Division stationed at Truk had moved some of its aircraft to Rabaul to reinforce the land-based 25th and 26th Air Flotillas stationed there, General Kenney decided the time had arrived to launch a massive air raid on the enemy stronghold, focusing on airfields and shipping. Kenney now had three airfields added to his arsenal that made such an attack possible: Lae, Finschhafen, and Nadzab. From these fields, as well as from Woodlark and Kiriwina Islands, long-range twin-engine P-38 Lighting fighters could escort bombers all the way to Rabaul and back.[1]

On October 12, Rabaul was struck by the biggest air raid to date in the Pacific. Seventy B-24 bombers, 117 B-25s, 12 Australian Beaufighters, and 117 P-38s darkened the skies above the airfields and anchorages. Kenney, who ordered the raid after photoreconnaissance showed nearly three hundred planes at Rabaul's airfields, later wrote that he threw in every aircraft he had that was in commission and could reach the target.

First in were the B-25s and Beaufighters, which swept low over the three main airfields, setting dozens of planes ablaze, as well as fuel dumps and bomb and ammunition supplies. The B-24s then pummeled Rabaul Harbor. Kenney reported that his aircrews sank three large ships and forty-three smaller ones, damaged several others, and destroyed a hundred planes on the ground and another twenty-six that had engaged in combat. The Japanese claimed substantially fewer losses. While there remains some dispute over the damage caused by this raid, Japanese officers who were present and interrogated after the war called it one of the most effective attacks on Rabaul.[2]

Anxious to keep the pressure on the enemy stronghold and reduce his own losses during air raids, Kenney had taken the advice of General Whitehead, his deputy, to forgo night bombing raids in favor of daylight attacks. Whitehead had pointed out that Allied aircraft and crew losses had grown to nearly 5 percent of the planes sent on a mission—an intolerable loss for an air force short of planes and receiving only minimal replacements. Whitehead blamed the losses primarily on night missions: a combination of accidents, the enemy's improved use of searchlights, and the performance of their antiaircraft crews. The October 12 raid was one of the first against Rabaul made during daylight hours.[3]

During the rest of October, severe thunderstorms and fog hampered air operations over New Britain and the New Guinea coast for both sides. The Allies did succeed in several devastating attacks against the buildup of aircraft at Wewak, and Japanese dive-bombers and their fighter escorts struck at Finschhafen and Oro Bay. Throughout the air war in New Guinea, weather conditions were always a factor in deciding when planes would fly and what their targets would be. The loss of aircraft and crews to thunderstorms and powerful winds prompted Whitehead to tell Kenney, "Weather is still our greatest enemy."[4]

Whenever weather permitted, Allied bombers and fighters attacked Rabaul. This was part of a plan to cripple the Japanese air forces as much as possible prior to Admiral Halsey's landing of troops at Empress Augusta Bay on the island of Bougainville in the northern Solomons. The plan, worked out between MacArthur and Halsey, was to capture control of this area on the west coast of Bougainville and build an airfield there from which Halsey's aircraft could reach Rabaul. The area around the bay was selected because it was known to be lightly defended, and preliminary investigation suggested that several airfields could be constructed there. Imperial forces had occupied the 3,500-square-mile island since March 1942. It was home to forty thousand soldiers of the 17th Army, but they were concentrated in what army commander Lieutenant General Harukichi Hyakutake considered the strategic locations at the northern and southern ends of the island. The 3rd Marine Division hit the beaches at Cape Torokina inside Empress Augusta Bay on November 1, and quickly drove off the three hundred Japanese stationed there.

The combination of horrific flying conditions, improved enemy anti-aircraft, desperate fighter defenses, and mechanical breakdowns had a serious impact on Kenney's Fifth Air Force. By the end of October, Kenney reported having only about fifty serviceable P-38s available for combat—a severe drop from the 117 that had taken part in the October 12 raid on Rabaul. Kenney's attempts to acquire replacement P-38s and P-38 pilots ran into the higher priority accorded to the European theater. Air chief General Arnold informed Kenney it would be at least two months before he could receive any more of these invaluable fighters.[5]

From the massive naval base at Truk, Admiral Mineichi Koga, who assumed command of the Combined Fleet following Admiral Yamamoto's death, reacted to both the landings at Empress Augusta Bay and the massive air raids on Rabaul by sending reinforcements. He ordered seven heavy cruisers, one light cruiser, four destroyers, and several supply ships from the Second Fleet to Rabaul. As the Imperial Army air service was now virtually nonexistent in the area, he also sent between 250 and 300 aircraft from the 11th Air Fleet, and alerted planes from the 12th Air Fleet in Japan to prepare for transfer to Rabaul. Obviously, the Imperial Navy, which had a long-standing love affair with Rabaul, had decided to defend it at all costs.[6]

The Allies did not know that so many veteran naval fighter pilots had arrived at Rabaul until they suffered what General Whitehead called "a real brawl" on November 2, when General Kenney, seeking another hugely successful raid, sent seventy-five B-25s escorted by fifty-seven P-38s against the town. The Americans, expecting to be challenged by 50 to 60 fighters, were instead overwhelmed by between 125 and 150 of Japan's most experienced and toughest fighter pilots in sleek Zeros. The defenders swept into the oncoming B-25s, immediately sending three down, and then fought a grueling series of dogfights against the outnumbered P-38s. When the battle—which Kenney called the toughest his air force had fought during the course of the war—was over, nine B-25s had been shot down or reported missing, and nine P-38s were lost.[7]

Two days later, an air patrol caught sight of the Japanese fleet heading from Truk to Rabaul when it was roughly one hundred miles north of its destination. When Admiral Halsey learned of the nineteen enemy warships, he decided he had to act quickly. Reaching General MacArthur by radio, he explained that he planned to send Rear Admiral Frederick Sherman's fast carrier force, based around the heavy carrier *Saratoga* and the light carrier *Princeton*, in a surprise attack on the enemy ships. MacArthur agreed to have General Kenney take advantage of Sherman's attacks by staging a raid of his own against Rabaul and its airfields, timed for when the enemy's planes were expected to be racing to defend the approaching Japanese fleet from Sherman's carrier aircraft.

Admiral Sherman's task force, which included two antiaircraft light cruisers and nine destroyers, rushed from its refueling stop south of Guadalcanal to a location 230 miles south of Rabaul and prepared to launch every available airplane at daybreak. At nine a.m. on November 5, the two carriers began sending ninety-seven aircraft aloft. The American planes speeding toward the enemy fleet now at Rabaul included twenty-three Avenger torpedo-bombers, twenty-two Dauntless dive-bombers, and fifty-two Hellcat fighters.[8]

The Navy planes rushed into the Rabaul's Simpson Harbor anchorage area in tight formations that left no room for defending fighters to pick them off. Pilots trained in bombing moving vessels found those tied up or anchored relatively easy targets. Although none of the Japanese warships were sunk, most received some damage. Several, including the heavy cruiser *Maya*, had to be towed out of the area for repairs that took as long as five months. Two other heavy cruisers were out of commission for several months as they returned to Japan for repairs. The light cruisers suffered light to moderate damage, as did several destroyers.[9]

As the U.S. Navy planes sped off to return to their two carriers, most of the Japanese defending aircraft chased after them. This left Rabaul with virtually no air defense as twenty-seven B-24s and sixty-seven P-38s charged in from their bases in New Guinea and bombed and strafed the town, the airfields, and the harbor.[10]

These November 5 raids provoked the Imperial Navy to rethink its commitment to Rabaul. Although the stronghold would remain operational until its forces surrendered in September 1945, it was now no longer considered of great importance. While some warships remained at Rabaul, the surviving heavy cruisers were pulled back to Truk. Yet that great base had its own problems. So many aircraft and pilots had been lost defending Rabaul that Truk was now short of both. This was revealed when Admiral Koga was unable to send his aircraft to help the defenders on Tarawa in the Gilbert Islands when the 2nd U.S. Marine Division assaulted its beaches on November 20, 1943.[11]

It soon became apparent that Rabaul, along with its 100,000 defenders, faced abandonment by the Imperial forces. During December, nearly fifty cargo ships brought in supplies, including food and ammunition, to keep the Japanese soldiers and sailors, and Korean and Indian forced laborers, alive for an extended time. They also unloaded enough ammunition to sustain the base's defenses. Over the coming year, large portions of the troops at Rabaul turned to cultivating extensive gardens to grow food, which would never be shipped in again. Subjected to regular bombing raids from Kenney's Fifth Air Force and Navy and Army air forces in the Solomons, the Japanese waited for what they expected to be a major Allied assault. It never came. Rabaul had been written off as a target of assault at the Quadrant Conference between President Roosevelt and Prime Minister Churchill in Quebec in August 1943. Both leaders concurred with a Joint Chiefs of Staff recommendation that Rabaul be isolated and not assaulted.[12]

———

Much of the news from the Quadrant Conference was disheartening to MacArthur and Prime Minister Curtin, especially the continued de-emphasis on the South West Pacific Area. Yet there was good news in that Allied planners called for "the seizure or neutralization of eastern New Guinea as far west as Wewak and including the Admiralty Islands and the Bismarck Archipelago." They also recommended that the Allies press "along the north coast of New Guinea as far west as Vogelkop, by step-by-step airborne-waterborne advances."[13] While the planners still prioritized the central Pacific, they were not about to stop MacArthur from gaining control of New Guinea and moving ever closer to his ultimate goal, the Philippines.

Meanwhile, on New Guinea, Japanese aircraft were arriving at Wewak.

Having recovered from Kenney's devastating attacks of August 17, the base now went on the offensive. The day following the great Rabaul raid, November 6, aircraft from Wewak struck several Allied airfields, including the one at Nadzab. Caught by surprise, the Americans suffered four P-39 single-engine fighters destroyed and twenty-one damaged on the ground, while the attackers returned to their base with no losses.[14]

Once ashore at Cape Torokina in Empress Augusta Bay on Bougainville, Admiral Halsey's Marines and Army troops pushed out a perimeter protecting an area one mile deep and five miles long to permit Army engineers to begin construction of the first of several airfields. For MacArthur, the next step in isolating Rabaul was to gain complete control over the waterways between New Guinea and the western end of New Britain. This would give him unfettered access to the Bismarck Sea so that he could move along the New Guinea coast, capture outlying islands such as the Admiralties, and tighten the noose around Rabaul.

MacArthur's forces already controlled one of the two straits between the Huon Peninsula and New Britain: Vitiaz Strait, on the western side of Rooke Island, although the island remained in enemy hands. While Vitiaz was the safest for use by larger ships, Dampier Strait, between Rooke Island and the New Britain coast, was convenient for Japanese barge traffic. Since the Allies' control of the air over the Huon Peninsula's coast increased the danger to warships sailing through the Bismarck Sea, small, motorized barges were the favored Japanese method for moving troops and supplies around.

MacArthur wanted to control both straits, as well as to capture limited territory on the western end of New Britain. This would have the added benefit of greatly reducing enemy surface and air attacks on his vessels plying the narrow straits as they moved up the coast. He wanted an airfield from which fighters could protect his shipping, and a base from which PT boats could operate.

General Walter Krueger's Sixth Army was selected to invade New Britain. Headquartered on Goodenough Island, the troops assigned to the invasion were army soldiers of the 32nd Infantry Division, the 126th Regimental Combat Team, and the 112th Cavalry Regiment.

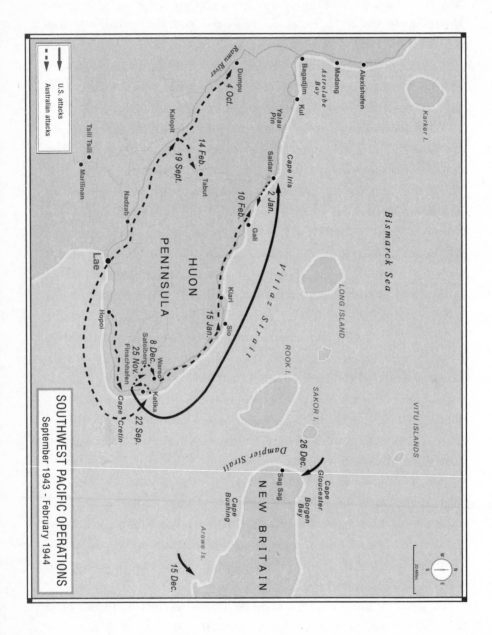

SOUTHWEST PACIFIC OPERATIONS
September 1943 - February 1944

U.S. attacks
Australian attacks

Bismarck Sea

Karker I.

Alexishafen
Madang
Astrolabe Bay
Bagadjim
Kul
Yalau Pin
Cape Iris
Saidar
4 Oct.
Dumpu
Ramu River
14 Feb.
Kalopit
19 Sept.
Tabut
Tsili Tsili
Marilinan
Nadzab
HUON PENINSULA
10 Feb.
2 Jan.
Gali
Klari
15 Jan.
Sio
Vitiaz Strait
LONG ISLAND
Lae
Hopoi
8 Dec.
Wareo
Sateiberg
Finschhafen
25 Nov.
Katika
22 Sep.
Cape Cretin
ROOK I.
SAKOR I.
Dampier Strait
26 Dec.
Cape Gloucester
Borgen Bay
VITU ISLANDS
Sag Sag
Cape Bushing
NEW BRITAIN
15 Dec.
Arawe Is.

20 Miles

N
W   E
S

Krueger's soldiers would be joined by the 1st Marine Division, who had been undergoing rest and recuperation at a base near Melbourne, Australia, after their exhausting campaign on Guadalcanal. Admiral Halsey transferred the Marines from the South Pacific to the South West Pacific Area and placed them at MacArthur's disposal, which pleased him because he needed troops experienced in amphibious operations for the assault on New Britain.

While planning for the New Britain operation was under way, MacArthur learned of the reassignment of Admiral Carpender, who he believed was much too reluctant to commit his small Seventh Fleet force to combat. MacArthur had requested that Carpender be replaced twice during the year, and Admiral King finally agreed, assigning Carpender to command the 9th Naval District headquartered in Illinois. King did not ask the general's opinion of Carpender's replacement. He never lost sight of the fact that the commander of the Seventh Fleet, and simultaneously commander of the Allied Naval Forces SWPA, reported directly to him. King was also very aware that the Seventh Fleet commander operated in MacArthur's theater and commanded what many American newspapers were calling "MacArthur's Navy." When General Marshall learned of King's exclusion of MacArthur from the decision, he contacted the general, discussed the replacement, and gave him the option of disapproving the new man.

MacArthur gladly accepted Vice Admiral Thomas C. Kinkaid as his new naval commander. The grim-faced, forty-five-year-old Kinkaid had earned a reputation as a fighting admiral in several of the Navy's biggest battles to date: the Coral Sea and Midway. What's more, Kinkaid had earned his second Distinguished Service Medal as commander of a carrier task force during the Battle of the Eastern Solomons, when the Imperial Navy tried to prevent the Marine landings on Guadalcanal. A proven warrior, he was just the man MacArthur wanted to command his Navy.[15] Of course, it did no harm that MacArthur's favorite living naval officer, Admiral "Bull" Halsey, accompanied Kinkaid to Brisbane to introduce him personally to MacArthur on November 23. Kinkaid took command of MacArthur's Allied Naval Forces, which included Australian and Dutch units, three days later.

After months of haggling among Army, Navy, Air Force, and Marine planning officers, the final plan called for landing the Marines on Cape Gloucester at the northwestern tip of New Britain, where there was at least one enemy airfield in operation. The site had command of Dampier Strait and Rooke Island. A few days before the Marine landing, the 112th Cavalry Regiment would go ashore at Arawe, sixty miles cross country from Cape Gloucester, as a diversion to draw Japanese troops away from the Marines' landing site. In Allied hands, Arawe's small harbor on the southern coast facing the Solomon Sea could serve as a PT boat base.

MacArthur delayed selecting dates for the two invasions until he felt confident about enemy strength at Arawe. He did not want to send his troops into battle while there remained open questions about Japanese troop movements and strength. Insisting on almost daily reconnaissance flights over the area, he did not want to be responsible for a bloodbath such as the Marines had suffered on Tarawa, where they endured over three thousand casualties in less than seventy-six hours for territory half the size of New York's Central Park.[16]

Because General Krueger was distrustful of the intelligence he received from other sources, including MacArthur's HQ, he formed and trained his own reconnaissance units, known as Alamo Scouts. The men selected for this duty, all volunteers, went through six weeks of training that included using rubber boats to get ashore, scouting enemy positions, and counting enemy forces, as well as survival training, use of various weapons and communications equipment, and navigation techniques.[17]

On December 13, General MacArthur flew to Goodenough Island to visit Krueger and the troopers of the 112th Cavalry Regiment, commanded by Brigadier General Julian W. Cunningham. The commander in chief inspected Cunningham's soldiers and watched as they boarded the vessels that were to transport them to the landing zone at Arawe. At midnight, the fleet departed Goodenough in a heavy rain. In the lead were two high-speed destroyer transports, USS *Humphreys* and USS *Sands*. Following was a landing ship dock, USS *Carter Hall*, loaded with a variety of small landing craft and amphibious tractors and tanks for crawling over the coral surrounding the landing beaches. Joining these three U.S. Navy ships was HMAS *Westralia,* an Australian former armed merchant cruiser that had recently undergone conversion to an LSI. The ships moved up the New Guinea coast to the area off Buna, where ten escort destroyers joined them. They then turned east toward Arawe.[18]

A cluster of small islands around a narrow peninsula jutting into the sea, Arawe possesses a small harbor accessible only by shallow-draft vessels because of coral blocking its entrance. The Japanese used it to support limited barge traffic and maintained a small garrison near the beach. The plan of attack called for each of the two destroyer transports to put ashore small landing parties at two locations prior to the main assault.

The fleet arrived in the area at three thirty a.m. for a scheduled assault at six thirty. A few minutes after five a.m., the *Humphreys* sent 150 men aboard fifteen rubber boats to Pilelo Island, which dominated the harbor entrance and contained a radio transmitter. The small number of enemy troops stationed there quickly withdrew into nearby caves. When they refused to come out, they were killed with hand grenades and flamethrowers.

Fifteen rubber boats from the *Sands* were to land cavalrymen of Troop A at a small beach designated Blue Beach, a few miles east of the harbor. Once ashore, they were to proceed west toward the harbor to block any enemy troops fleeing the main invasion. Unfortunately, the local Japanese commander had learned that a small American reconnaissance party had landed on that same beach the week prior, and surmised from this that Blue Beach was going to be the site of an insertion. He had positioned several heavy machine guns in the woods behind the beach. When the rubber boats, each containing ten men, were about a hundred yards from shore, and clearly visible in the moonlight, the guns opened fire. Riflemen located throughout the wooded area joined in. Twelve of the boats suffered punctures from enemy bullets and quickly sank. The men on board who survived the gunfire swam seaward, seeking rescue.

Less than half the invaders, seventy-one men, survived the aborted landing. The escorting destroyer *Shaw,* meanwhile had opened fire on the gun flashes emanating from the dark woods. A few minutes later, the enemy machine guns fell silent as the Japanese who endured the salvos quickly withdrew. The American survivors were picked up by the *SC-699*, a 110-foot wood-hull subchaser that also claimed credit for shooting down an enemy plane that arrived to attack the invasion force. Admiral Barbey later singled out the small warship's skipper, Lieutenant James W. Foristel, for the performance of his vessel.[19]

The main landing at Arawe took place at a site the Australians called House Fireman Beach. It was preceded by a shore bombardment by the five-inch guns of the destroyers and several bombing and strafing runs by B-25s. The landing of the Army troops was assisted by the inclusion in their force of ten tracked amphibious landing vehicles known as "Buffalos," which were on loan from the Marines and operated by troops from the 1st Marine Tractor Battalion. Opposition to the landing was minor and sporadic, as only two companies of Japanese soldiers occupied the entire area.[20]

Once the landings had given American forces control of the area, including the nearby small Lupin airfield, PT boats quickly moved in and began regular patrols, guarding against a possible Japanese counterattack using troop-carrying barges. Although no barges approached the Arawe beaches, over the next week the PTs fought off several attacks from Japanese dive-bombers and fighters, shooting down five.[21]

Responsibility for the defense of Arawe and the entire western end of New Britain was in the hands of Lieutenant General Yasushi Sakai, commanding officer of the 17th Infantry Division. The division had recently arrived from Shanghai but had lost over twelve hundred men on the voyage as Allied submarines and aircraft struck the convoys in which it sailed. Sakai kept his headquarters at Cape Hoskins, about halfway between Rabaul and Cape Gloucester. He had entrusted command of the direct frontline defense to Major General Iwao Matsuda, a seasoned officer who had commanded an infantry regiment in Manchuria. His men, known as the Matsuda Force, consisted of troops from the 65th Infantry Brigade—some of whom had taken part in the conquest of the Philippines—elements of the 51st Division that had fought in New Guinea, and some artillery and antiaircraft units. Matsuda's headquarters was located five miles east of the airfields at Cape Glouces-ter. Major Masamitsu Komori was in overall command of the immedi-ate Arawe section, but when the invasion took place, he was still traveling overland from Rabaul with some of his troops.

When word of the Arawe invasion reached General Sakai, he sent word to Major Komori to rush troops to the beachheads. Komori ordered the 1st Battalion of the 141st Infantry Regiment, which was at Cape Bush-ing some forty miles east of Arawe along the southern coast, to mount seven barges and race to the scene. During early dawn on December 17, the Japanese barges loaded with troops encountered two American land-ing craft halfway toward their goal. The Higgins boats were manned by a patrol from the 112th Cavalry Regiment that General Cunningham had sent out to watch for just such an approaching enemy force. Outnumbered and outgunned by the heavy barges, the two American boats made a forced landing along the swampy coast and the cavalrymen quickly moved inland. The Japanese did not pursue them; instead, they continued along the coast and landed the next night at the coastal village of Omoi.

The American cavalrymen found their way to a native village where the locals welcomed them and made them at home. With help from the villagers, the soldiers located a trail that would eventually return them to their own lines. The Japanese who landed at Omoi moved out the following morning, December 19. Their orders were to meet Major Komori and the troops he had with him seven miles north along the Pulie River at a place called Didmop. Anxious to launch a counterattack on the Americans, Komori waited impatiently for the 1st Battalion to arrive. When there was still no sign of it by December 24, he decided to attack with the men he had brought with him and those who had retreated from Arawe. It took the troops from the barges eight days to travel the seven miles to reach Didmop. They had wandered around the trackless jungle, continuously getting lost.[22]

Komori's initial attack against the thin defense line guarding the Lupin airfield was successful in driving the Americans back and taking control of the landing field. The six-hundred-yard-long strip had been constructed in 1937, but was totally unusable, as it was overgrown with kunai grass six to eight feet tall and had deep burrows plowed across it in several locations. A Marine Corps historian called it "perhaps the most useless piece of real estate in the whole region."[23]

Major Komori, incorrectly guessing the enemy's objective was the airfield, was determined to hold on to it at all costs. Yet he was unable to beat back the main line of American defense on the other side of the field, even when the lost troops from the 1st Battalion arrived. Over the next few weeks, Komori's force of more than a thousand men fought gallantly defending an airfield the enemy did not want. All General Cunningham wanted was to tie down as many Japanese troops as possible and distract the enemy from the main landings by the U.S. Marines at Cape Gloucester.

————————

While MacArthur was on Goodenough Island, meeting with Alamo Force commander Walter Krueger and Major General William H. Rupertus, commander of the 1st Marine Division, he was visited by George Marshall. Following the Second Cairo Conference of the Combined Chiefs of Staff, Roosevelt, and Churchill, Marshall decided it was time he had a face-to-face meeting with his South West Pacific Area commander.

Marshall left Cairo suddenly, accompanied by General Tom Handy and other members of his staff. The president was not informed of his departure until several hours later. The night before, the two men had privately discussed who would be the supreme commander for the Normandy invasion. Roosevelt, who considered Marshall irreplaceable, knew that his Army chief of staff wanted the post, but the president did not want to lose Marshall from Washington, where he was both extremely popular and influential with the Congress. Knowing Marshall was too proud to ask for the assignment, FDR did what he was famous for: He manipulated the general into allowing the job he wanted so badly to pass to Dwight Eisenhower.[24]

Although we cannot know Marshall's frame of mind at the time, it is not difficult to assume he was unhappy at the way the president had played him. Perhaps this is why he decided to cancel his plans to fly to Italy to visit his favorite stepson, who was fighting north of Naples, and instead flew to New Guinea to spend time with the general that Roosevelt probably disliked above all others. According to his principal biographer, Marshall "wanted to show MacArthur he had not been forgotten."[25]

After landing in Port Moresby, Marshall and his party flew to Goodenough, landing in time for lunch on December 15. Afterward, the two groups—Marshall and his staff, and MacArthur and his commanders who were present, including Generals Kenney and Krueger—discussed the war in Europe. MacArthur then outlined the situation in his own theater and emphasized, according to Kenney, the need for additional planes and pilots to maintain the highest level of air strength for future operations. The next morning there was a briefing on the Arawe landings and a discussion of the plans for the Marine landings at Cape Gloucester the day after Christmas. Marshall departed late the following morning.

It is unfortunate that minutes were not kept of this one and only meeting between MacArthur and Marshall during the entire war. All we know about what transpired comes from memoirs of various participants.

MacArthur later wrote of the meeting that Marshall was extremely open about Admiral King's opposition to naval forces commanded by Army officers and suggested that King viewed the entire Pacific as the Navy's domain. King was, MacArthur quoted Marshall, on a campaign to rid the Navy of the blot caused by the Pearl Harbor attack. Marshall promised to address additional support for Kenney's Fifth Air Force with Air Force chief General Arnold on Marshall's return to Washington.[26]

The Goodenough Island meeting between the two American generals garnered wide attention. The London *Times* wrote that it would increase the apprehension of Japanese leaders, while the Melbourne *Herald* remarked that Marshall's visit was "evidence of the importance attached by the Allied Command" to operations in New Guinea.[27] During a Christmas Eve 1943 broadcast to the nation and the nearly four million Americans serving in the armed forces around the world, President Roosevelt claimed that the meeting would "spell plenty of bad news for the Japs in the not too distant future."[28]

With the successful Arawe landings behind him, it was now time for MacArthur's main event: landing the 1st Marine Division on Cape Gloucester. Beginning on December 15 and running through Christmas Day, the Fifth Air Force pounded the area around the tip of New Britain in what the *Canberra Times* called a "terrific bombardment." General Kenney's planes dropped over four thousand tons of bombs and fired several million rounds of cannon and machine-gun shells on "anything that looked like a target" in reconnaissance photographs.[29]

On December 23, MacArthur was again on Goodenough Island, despite suffering from a severe cold and sore throat. This time it was to wish Major General William H. Rupertus and his 1st Marine Division good luck in their invasion of Cape Gloucester. MacArthur told Rupertus he knew that when the Marines "go into a fight they can be counted upon to do an outstanding job."[30]

D-Day was December 26, 1943. For the Marines, sailors, coast guardsmen, soldiers, and aviators committed to the landings, it was the day after Christmas, but back home on the other side of the International Date Line it was Christmas Day. The invasion plan called for putting more than twelve thousand Marines ashore at two main beaches east of the Cape, along with a smaller number of Army personnel to provide additional firepower.

Admiral Barbey personally commanded Task Force 76, charged with getting the troops safely ashore. The task force included eighty-two troop and equipment landing ships and craft, twenty-three destroyers, four cruisers, forty-three PT boats, two subchasers, eight minesweepers, and ten miscellaneous small craft for patrolling and coastal transport duty. As this vast fleet converged on the Cape Gloucester landing zones, the western end of New Britain was subjected to high-level bombing by five squadrons of B-24s and shelling from destroyers. Once the shelling stopped, B-25s bombed and strafed the beach landing areas.

The enemy had not failed to notice the buildup of Allied warships and landing craft. Lieutenant General Sakai, commander of the 17th Division, with responsibility for the defense of western New Britain, warned that an invasion was imminent. Yet the Japanese expected that the landing of additional Allied forces would occur at Arawe. So on the morning of December 26, as the Marines waded ashore at beaches around Cape Gloucester, two Japanese combat battalions—over a thousand men who had fought in China and the Philippines—were engaged in driving U.S. Army troops from the small, nearly useless airfield near Arawe, miles from the Marine landing zones.

The invasion convoy itself was used as further deception to draw enemy forces away from Cape Gloucester. On December 25, the day before D-Day, the convoy had sailed in daylight toward Arawe. A Japanese coast watcher and a patrolling submarine reported this to Rabaul. Once night fell and the convoy was no longer visible to prying enemy eyes, it turned sharply toward the Vitiaz Strait and Cape Gloucester. Having fallen for the ruse, Rabaul sent aircraft from the Eleventh Air Fleet and the Fourth Air Army to attack the invasion fleet. When the planes arrived over the Arawe area, they of course found no enemy fleet.[31]

The landing at Cape Gloucester met so little opposition that the official Marine Corps history records that "not a shot of any sort greeted the onrushing assault waves."[32]

Over the next few days and weeks, as Marine and Army troops pushed their way through the swampy terrain, fighting would grow in intensity and frequency, but it never reached the level that Allied planners had expected. The Japanese launched several counterattacks, but all were driven off at considerable cost in Japanese lives. The arrival of tanks would soon give the Americans a great advantage in overrunning prepared defenses.

At noon on December 31, General Rupertus raised an American flag at Cape Gloucester airdrome and radioed General Krueger that the airfield was in Allied hands. Krueger passed the good news on to MacArthur, who quickly sent a congratulatory message to the Marine general: "Your gallant division has maintained the immortal record of the Marine Corps and covered itself with glory."[33]

MacArthur was anxious to make full use of these experienced amphibious landing troops while they were still under his control for operations along the New Guinea coast and the Admiralty Islands. He even attempted, without success, to have them permanently transferred to his forces. Lieutenant General Alexander Vandegrift, who was about to be named commandant of the Marine Corps, opposed MacArthur's plans for future deployment of the Marine Division. Once the operation was completed, Vandegrift wasted no time in getting the division out of SWPA. He felt if the Marines spent too much time in New Britain fighting an infantry campaign, they would "no longer be a well-trained amphibious division."[34]

With the Japanese 17th Division decimated by Allied forces and facing complete annihilation, on February 23, 1944, Eighth Area Army commander General Imamura ordered General Sakai to withdraw all his troops and attempt to return to Rabaul. In early May, the 1st Marine Division returned to control of the U.S. Navy and was replaced by the Army's 40th Infantry Division. MacArthur continued his attempts to retain the Marines, but Admiral Nimitz was adamant that he required this experienced amphibious force for his planned assault on the Palau Islands.

Even as the fighting in western New Britain continued, MacArthur was planning his next move in isolating Rabaul.

Part Three

1944

CHAPTER 15

The General and the Admiralties

The envelopment of the enemy bases at Rabaul was MacArthur's paramount concern at the beginning of 1944. A plan prepared by MacArthur's staff in mid-1943 called for an invasion of the Admiralty Islands on April 1, 1944. This would help close the ring around Rabaul and effectively reduce the ability of Eighth Area Army commander General Imamura to communicate with and send supplies and reinforcements to his soldiers battling Allied forces along the New Guinea coast.

The Admiralties are eighteen islands located at the northern reaches of the Bismarck Sea that cover approximately 810 square miles. Situated 360 miles northwest of Rabaul and about 200 miles from the New Guinea coast, the islands are covered in thick tropical rain forests, the product of 154 inches of annual rainfall, extremely high humidity, and average daytime temperatures of around ninety degrees Fahrenheit. When war in Europe began in 1939, the indigenous Melanesian population was thirteen thousand, while fewer than fifty Europeans lived on the islands.

The first Europeans to visit were Dutch explorers in 1616. In 1767, a famed Royal Navy explorer named Captain Philip Carteret rediscovered the islands and gave them the name that remains today. In addition to their geographical location, the islands' chief military value in 1944 was in several large tracts of hard-packed, relatively dry land that could provide the basis for several airstrips. In addition, there was Seeadler Harbor, located on Los Negros, the second largest of the eighteen islands. Protected by a large, curved stretch of land, this anchorage was four miles wide and over fifteen miles long. Reaching a depth of 120 feet, it was large enough to accommodate an entire naval task force.[1]

War had come to the remote Admiralty Islands in April 1942 with the arrival of a Japanese force of three destroyers and six light cruisers escorting three transport ships carrying several hundred troops. The invaders swarmed ashore on Manus Island and quickly began work on a four-thousand-foot runway. At the time, a platoon-sized unit of Australians from an independent company occupied Manus. After several skirmishes, the outnumbered and outgunned Aussies evacuated the island in two small boats.[2]

During the following year, the Japanese built a second airstrip, and the garrison was increased to slightly more than four thousand men. The Imperial invaders brought with them a large number of POWs to work as slave labor. Many of these were Sikh soldiers captured at Singapore.

In Washington, the Joint Chiefs called for dual invasions on April 1, 1944. MacArthur's SWPA forces were to land at the Admiralties simultaneously with Halsey's South Pacific assault at Kavieng on New Ireland. In early and mid-February, pilots on bombing runs over the Admiralties began reporting an absence of antiaircraft fire. General Whitehead, second in command of the Fifth Air Force, decided to try to draw out enemy fire in an attempt to determine the size and strength of Japanese forces on the islands. On February 23, he ordered three B-25s to circle Manus and Los Negros at slow speed and low altitude. On their return, the three crews reported no enemy antiaircraft fire and no sign of Japanese troops anywhere. In fact, the airstrip the enemy had constructed on what was called Momote Plantation was filled with bomb craters, and weeds were growing through cracks in its surface. Buildings nearby appeared abandoned.[3]

Based on this information, MacArthur, seeing no reason for delay, decided to move the invasion of the Admiralties up to February 29. He believed waiting was a waste of time, and that he might be able to move the timetable for the entire war up a few months by occupying the Admiralties sooner rather than later. No one was quite sure what the enemy's strength was, or even if Japanese soldiers remained on the islands, so he decided to launch a "reconnaissance in force." Using this method, he could launch an offensive against Los Negros using a sizable force that would be able to elicit a reaction from any Japanese hidden there, but not too large that it could not be quickly withdrawn if the enemy proved to be of serious strength. On the other hand, should this force succeed in establishing a foothold, it could be quickly reinforced by troops waiting along the New Guinea coast and immediately move to capture the apparently unused airfield at Momote.[4]

General Krueger was charged with leading the invasion. Krueger was unhappy with the new invasion date, which gave him five fewer weeks to prepare. On top of that, a debate raged over the number of enemy soldiers his men would face. The Fifth Air Force intelligence staff was estimating only five hundred Japanese, while the intelligence officers of the 1st Cavalry Division, whose one thousand men were to be the "reconnaissance in force," estimated enemy strength at 4,900 men. Major General Willoughby, MacArthur's intelligence officer, who based his estimate on intercepted enemy radio traffic, claimed between 3,250 and 4,000 troops were stationed there.[5]

Krueger thought it would be too easy for the enemy to fool reconnaissance aircraft, and that the local commander might be crafty enough not to fire on Allied planes and reveal his strength and locations. With this in mind, the general ordered a team of Alamo Scouts to slip onto Los Negros and report back what they found. Lieutenant John R. C. McGowen led the six-man team. A Catalina PBY dropped them and their rubber boats off the coast of Los Negros in the early-morning hours of February 27. Throughout the day, as the Scouts reconnoitered the area, they not only picked up numerous signs that the enemy was dug in and awaiting an invasion—the Americans spotted several machine-gun positions and trenches for use by riflemen—they also came within yards of a Japanese patrol. From their well-pressed uniforms and larger-than-average size, McGowen noted that they were not ordinary troops. He later learned they were the Japanese equivalent of U.S. Marines. The following morning, before evacuation, McGowen radioed that "the area is lousy with Japs."[6]

Unknown to the Americans, however, the Japanese had seen the Scouts landing. Colonel Yoshio Ezaki, commander of the garrison, proved to be a wily adversary. Having earlier ordered his men not to fire at enemy aircraft to give the impression there were no forces on the islands, he now sent out patrols to keep an eye on the six Americans and capture them if possible. McGowen and his men did not realize that the enemy soldiers they had encountered were actually looking for them, and not simply on routine patrol. Nevertheless, Ezaki proved too wily for his own good when he interpreted the landing team as scouts for a larger force coming behind; he transferred troops from the southeastern end of the island to the northwest, where McGowen's team had landed. It was Ezaki's logical conclusion that when the Allies came it would be in large numbers, and that the only area that could accommodate a large fleet and massive numbers of men was Seeadler Harbor. The invasion, when it arrived, would actually be in the southeast, a location named Hyane Harbor.[7]

MacArthur was reluctant to take McGowen's report at face value since the lieutenant had not actually seen a large number of enemy troops. Besides, General Willoughby's intelligence had already estimated that there were at least four thousand Japanese on the islands. Additionally, photographs taken by reconnaissance flights clearly indicated that at the very least the major airstrip in the islands, Momote, was not being used. This reduced the possibility of Japanese aircraft attacking the invasion fleet and troops.[8] Counting on what he saw as "temporary confusion and weakness" in the enemy's absence of effective defense against Allied operations in the air and in the Bismarck Sea, MacArthur's determination to invade did not waver.

MacArthur decided he would accompany the fleet carrying the invasion force so that he could be close enough to the action to make a quick decision whether to send in reinforcements if the 1st Cavalry gained a secure foothold or order an evacuation if things went badly. In an optimistic frame of mind, MacArthur ordered a second force comprising

1,500 combat troops also from the 1st Cavalry Division, along with several hundred men from a naval construction battalion, to stand by at Finschhafen to reinforce the original thousand troops.

MacArthur's order to move up the invasion date caused some confusion among his commanders and serious logistical problems for Krueger. First was the question of the Momote airfield. The invasion was to take place at Hyane Harbor, which was close to the airfield. MacArthur indicated in his order that the reconnaissance force should include a fifty-man unit assigned to rehabilitate the airfield and prepare it for transport planes that would bring in airborne engineers. This left Krueger and his staff wondering whether the "reconnaissance in force" was to be responsible for the airstrip rebuilding, or whether that would fall to a group of follow-on engineers and construction crews.[9]

A more important and urgent concern for Krueger was how he was going to transport a thousand men along with supplies and equipment from Oro Bay on the New Guinea coast to the landing site. The vessels that would normally be assigned to put the forces ashore were LSTs, LCTs, and LCIs. Unfortunately, Admiral Barbey had not expected that they would be required until April 1, so he had sent most of them to various naval yards for repair and overhaul. They were either too far away to arrive in time for the new invasion date, or in varying states of disassembly to be put to immediate use. In addition, many of their crews had been given liberty in Australia.

The only troop-carrying vessels Barbey had available were three APDs (transport destroyers). However, all three combined could deliver only slightly more than 510 troops, about half of the invasion force. The remaining cavalrymen would have to be divided among nine regular destroyers that would do double duty as escorts. Due to the crowded conditions aboard the ships, the men would be limited to only the supplies and equipment they could carry. All else, including heavy weapons and even cooking utensils, would have to follow later, provided the reconnaissance in force was able to establish and hold a beachhead. If it were overwhelmed by an enemy counterattack, the destroyers would be standing by to evacuate as many men as possible and to shell enemy troop positions.

There were several risks associated with this invasion, not the least of which was lack of knowledge concerning how many Japanese troops were on the islands, and what firepower they had. In addition to the open question concerning Japanese defenders, there was the limited timeframe in which the planning, which would normally have required at least another month, took place. In the end, General Krueger, Admiral Barbey, 1st Cavalry Division commander Major General Innis Swift, the reconnaissance in force commander, Brigadier General William Chase, and their staffs managed the feat admirably. Perhaps the greatest risk was MacArthur's decision to use the 1st Cavalry Division. These men had never been in combat before—this was to be their first encounter with the enemy.[10]

The landing presented difficulties of its own. Instead of Seeadler Harbor, the original site for the April 1 invasion, Hyane Harbor had been selected for various reasons, including the potential surprise if the Japanese were waiting for an American invasion in force at Seeadler, and, once ashore, the Americans would be only two hundred yards from their immediate objective, the airfield at Momote. Not actually a harbor, Hyane was more of a fifty-yard-wide beach surrounded by coral reefs that made it impossible for the APDs and other destroyers to get close to shore. Barbey planned to use the four small Higgins boats carried aboard each APD to run the men to shore from not only the APDs but the other destroyers. All this was expected to be done under enemy fire.[11]

The invasion fleet of three APDs and nine destroyers left Oro Bay for the five-hundred-mile trip to Los Negros in the early-morning hours of February 28. Two light cruisers and four destroyers, all to serve as escorts for the troop-carrying destroyers, soon joined them. Aboard the cruiser *Phoenix* was General MacArthur and Vice Admiral Thomas Kinkaid, the new commanding officer of the U.S. Seventh Fleet. General Krueger attempted to dissuade MacArthur from going with the fleet, saying it would be a disaster if anything happened to him. The commander in chief listened to his general's arguments, thanked him for his concern, but then said, "I have to go."[12]

The fleet arrived off Los Negros the following morning, February 29. A combination of steady rain and the greatly reduced airpower available to Japanese commanders for reconnaissance patrols left the fleet undiscovered by the enemy. The weather also reduced the substantial air cover that had been promised by General Kenney.

At 7:43 a.m., Rear Admiral William Fechteler, whom Barbey had designated commander of the invasion fleet, gave the order to commence shore bombardment. A few minutes earlier, three U.S. Army B-24 Liberators swept in over the beach and the airfield and dropped their bombs. Of the forty bombers Kenney had sent to the Admiralties, these three were the only aircraft that managed to find Los Negros in the heavy rains that blanketed the entire region.

With the warship guns booming, the APDs lowered their Higgins boats and filled them with soldiers. The boats then rushed to shore, put the men onto the beach, and turned around to pick up more from the APDs and the destroyers. The troops came ashore in waves. As the guns aboard the ships ceased firing for fear of hitting their own men, each succeeding wave of boats came under increased machine-gun and other heavy-weapons fire from Japanese troops who had fallen back into the nearby jungle to avoid the bombardment and now returned to their prepared defensive positions nearer the beach.

By ten, General Chase's troops had control of the airfield. Yet the general was concerned that his thousand men were too spread out to defend against a concentrated counterattack, so he pulled them back to cover the eastern section of the airfield and called for reinforcements. Intelligence reports he was receiving indicated there might be between two and three thousand enemy soldiers on the other side of the airfield, hidden in the deep jungle. If these were true, then his force could be outnumbered by two or three to one.

At four p.m. General MacArthur and Admiral Kinkaid landed to inspect the front line in a torrential downpour that turned whatever dry ground there was into thick, soupy mud. Wearing a gray trench coat, khaki pants, and his trademark beat-up gold braided officer's cap, the commander in chief rode ashore, standing erect in a landing craft so that he could see what was happening on the beach. *Newsweek* war correspondent Robert Shaplen, who was also in the landing craft, wrote that the scene reminded him of George Washington crossing the Delaware. According to Chase's G-2 officer, Major Julio Chiaramonte, MacArthur "ignored sniper fire" and was "wet, cold, and dirty with mud up to the ears" when he praised Chase and his men for a marvelous performance. He then told Chase to hold the airstrip at any cost, and he would send in the reinforcements.[13]

Accompanied by several nervous officers, including his physician, Colonel Roger Egeberg, MacArthur walked out on the airstrip, despite being able to hear the voices of enemy soldiers in the woods on the other side and the sounds of sporadic gunfire. He wanted to inspect the condition of the landing field personally.[14]

When he came across the corpses of two Japanese soldiers who had been killed only twenty minutes before, he examined the bodies to see if they were officers and had any markings on their uniforms that indicated their units. They did not. Walking away, MacArthur muttered, "That's the way I like to see them."[15]

When MacArthur and Kinkaid returned to the *Phoenix*, the general immediately radioed orders to send in more troops, supplies, and equipment. He told Krueger to take whatever steps he deemed appropriate to exploit Chase's foothold as quickly as possible. Krueger ordered the fifteen hundred cavalrymen waiting at Finschhafen to board boats for the trip to Los Negros.

When word of the Admiralties invasion reached Japanese Eighth Area Army headquarters in Rabaul, General Imamura was not surprised. He had expected the islands would soon be MacArthur's target and had attempted to have reinforcements sent to support the islands' garrison. Throughout December, he had tried to convince Tokyo to send the 66th Infantry Regiment to the Admiralties, to no avail. Finally, following the Allies' successful invasion at Saidor, Tokyo had agreed to send additional troops from Korea. En route, the *Denmark Maru,* packed with nearly three thousand soldiers heading first to Palau in the Caroline Islands and then on to the Admiralties, was attacked and sunk by the American submarine USS *Whale.* At least thirteen hundred of the emperor's soldiers perished with the ship. A distraught Imamura managed to get a few hundred soldiers to the islands during January, but his attempt to transfer a full infantry battalion and a field artillery battalion from Rabaul met with only partial results as another submarine sank a troop transport, killing 350 men. In all, prior to MacArthur's invasion, the Japanese commander succeeded in getting slightly over a thousand troops to the Admiralties.[16]

U.S. cavalrymen searching the area around Momote airfield discovered signs that a large force of enemy troops had occupied the area but had withdrawn under the bombing and withering ship bombardment. They found what appeared to be a headquarters for a battalion-size unit, including a warehouse full of supplies and three large kitchens.[17]

Colonel Ezaki had pulled his men back to allow the Americans to be drawn into what he hoped would be a trap to annihilate them. He had prepared well for the invasion, having received advanced warning when his radio operators intercepted and translated several messages discussing the coming event between American submarines patrolling the area around Los Negros.[18]

Sometime during that first day, Ezaki received orders from General Imamura at Rabaul. Perhaps incensed by the fact he had not been able to get additional troops to the Admiralties, partially the result of the navy's reluctance to provide transports for the dangerous voyage, the general instructed Ezaki to launch a full-scale counterattack against the Americans. Instead, Ezaki did what Japanese Army commanders often did; he attacked the enemy in a piecemeal fashion instead of a massive assault. Had he done as ordered he might have succeeded, since he had nearly four thousand men at his disposal against the one thousand Americans who had landed. Instead of sending them all against the invaders, Ezaki ordered Captain Baba, commander of the 1st Battalion of the 229th Infantry Regiment, whose troops were closest to Hyane Harbor, to "annihilate the enemy." He told Baba his attack was not a delaying action waiting for reinforcements. Ezaki said he was "highly indignant about the enemy's arrogant attitude," and Baba should kill himself if captured.[19]

After dark, the troops of the 1st Battalion moved against the defense perimeter that General Chase had positioned around the eastern end of the airfield. Attacking with machine guns and rifles, the Japanese were able to infiltrate the American line in several places, but were ultimately thrown back at terrible cost in lives. At one point, at least two Imperial soldiers reached Chase's command post and nearly killed or captured him. They themselves were killed by one of Chase's staff officers armed with a submachine gun.

The following morning the bulk of the infiltrators had withdrawn, leaving behind sixty-seven dead and a few stragglers who attempted to hide in the overgrown jungle. Most were hunted down and killed. The night's action had cost the Americans fifteen wounded and seven killed.[20]

During that day, March 1, badly needed supplies arrived, courtesy of the Fifth Air Force. B-25s and B-17s made several runs over the Allied controlled area, dropping ammunition, food, blood plasma, mines, and grenades via parachutes. Chase knew his reinforcements would not arrive until the following day, so he wanted to understand the size of enemy forces in the area and learn what he could of their plans. When his intelligence officer said he suspected at least three thousand Japanese were on Los Negros, Chase was concerned that a concentrated attack would overwhelm his defenses. The enemy outnumbered him three to one, and with his back to the sea, he had no place to retreat. Reconnaissance patrols found numerous bunkers and other fixed positions that had only recently been vacated. There were also clear indications that large groups of Japanese soldiers were nearby, some as close as four hundred yards from the American lines. More important was the discovery of Japanese documents that revealed the locations of concentrations of enemy soldiers. Chase passed this information on to the Navy and Air Force. Allied planes bombed several of these locations, and two destroyers that had been left behind by Admiral Fechteler's invasion fleet bombarded those they could reach.

Late in the afternoon, a group of seventeen Japanese officers and sergeants somehow managed to get within fifty yards of Chase's command post before being discovered. This was truly a suicide mission. After the Americans gunned down several of the men, the remainder, including Captain Baba, killed themselves using swords and hand grenades.[21]

The surviving members of Baba's battalion launched another, better-coordinated attack at five p.m., but faltered and broke up against the determined defense of the American cavalrymen. Small groups of

Japanese soldiers attempted to infiltrate the American lines throughout the night. By daybreak, March 2, they had all withdrawn, leaving behind several hundred dead. One group of about fifty men actually swam out into the harbor wearing life belts in an attempt to get behind the American line. Their discovery cost virtually all of them their lives as the 75mm pack howitzers the cavalry regiment had wrestled ashore swept the swimmers with three hundred rounds.[22]

With reinforcements on the way, General Chase decided to push out his defensive perimeter to include the entire airfield. About five hundred of the men on the approaching ships were members of the Seabees and other construction groups who would immediately go to work repairing and expanding the landing zone. The Americans took control of the airfield without serious opposition. Chase was concerned that his weary men, most of whom had not slept since landing, would soon face a large concentrated enemy assault aimed at driving them into the sea. He was correct.

Colonel Ezaki was gathering his forces for an attack on the invaders on two fronts. He had centered his original defense on Seeadler Harbor because it seemed the obvious place for a large invasion force. As a result, many of his units had to struggle across Manus and Los Negros before they were in place. Although he wanted to attack quickly before Allied reinforcements could arrive, the colonel had little choice but to delay his all-out assault until the night of March 3.[23]

Early on the morning of March 2, Allied relief arrived aboard six LSTs carrying the reinforcement troops. There were also six LCMs loaded with a wide array of heavy equipment, including bulldozers and graders for the Seabees. Two U.S. Navy destroyers, one Australian destroyer, and two American minesweepers escorted them. Aboard the landing craft were the remainder of the 5th Cavalry, the 99th Battalion Field Artillery, and the 40th Seabees. Expecting a quiet landing, the soldiers and sailors were surprised to see American bombers and fighters bombing and strafing close to the beachhead. They came under fire themselves from Japanese mortars and machine guns, and the landing craft had to fight their way to the beach using their 40mm and

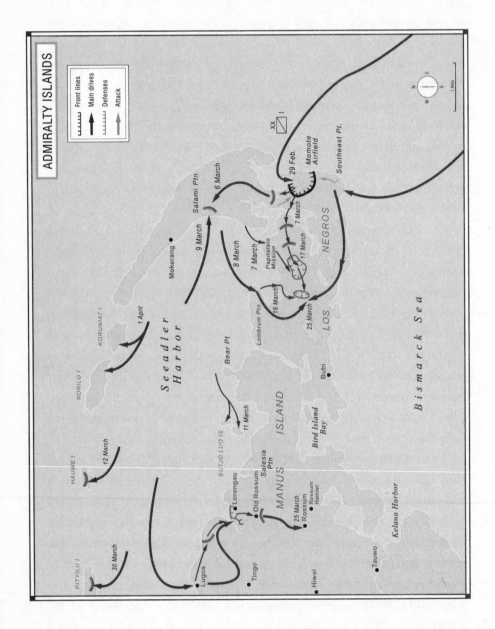

ADMIRALTY ISLANDS

three-inch guns. Several arriving troops also uncovered .50-caliber machine guns they were to bring ashore and opened fire on the enemy.

It took most of the day to unload all the landing craft. With their bulldozers and graders ashore, the Seabees and Army engineers cleared a road from the beach toward the airfield. Meanwhile, several destroyers and the minesweepers sailed around the island and attempted to force their way into Seeadler Harbor. Shore batteries there proved too well hidden for the destroyers to take them out, and the ships withdrew.

There was sporadic fighting around the airfield during the day and that night. Small groups of Japanese soldiers attempted to pierce the defense perimeter, but all failed. The following day most of the landing craft and several destroyers returned to New Guinea, leaving several destroyers to provide bombardment support when needed.

At seven p.m. on March 3, Ezaki's coordinated attack began with troops from an independent regiment sweeping in from north. It quickly broke under intense fire from the destroyers, which received their direction from cavalry soldiers with eyes on the approaching enemy. Well-placed machine-gun nests and rifle fire from men in trenches devastated attacks by two other Japanese columns from different directions. What had started as a stealthy assault soon became a rush with screaming Japanese troops dropping from enemy shells and mines planted during the day. One report of the battle claims Japanese soldiers were able to cut radio communication cables to field artillery and mortar units and redirected their fire.[24]

After dark, several Japanese bombers attacked the destroyers and some shore positions but did little damage. By morning, the Japanese had pulled back, leaving some seven hundred dead for the Americans to count and dispose of. The action cost the Americans sixty-one dead, including nine Seabees who left their equipment to fight alongside the cavalrymen. A disheartened and angry Ezaki ordered a complete withdrawal in an attempt to reorganize his forces.

Over the next few days additional men arrived from the 5th and 7th Cavalry, along with more Seabees and engineers. The Japanese had lost so many men that they were reduced to fighting a defensive war, initiating an attack only occasionally. By March 5, the situation for the defenders had become so grave that Colonel Ezaki signaled Rabaul that he was discontinuing night attacks. He described the Allied artillery shelling as "severe" and admitted his situation was "desperate."[25] On that same day, Allied radio operators picked up a message from someone on the islands to the Eighth Area Army headquarters proclaiming, "The time of our last hour is drawing near. We are striving for our fatherland."[26]

Allied ship bombardment soon silenced Japanese shore batteries around Seeadler Harbor, and more Americans from several different divisions landed there. Localized combat was sometimes furious as the defenders were determined to fight to the death. Such fighting continued over both Los Negros and Manus Islands as the Americans hunted down and killed straggling Japanese. As for the original prime objective, Momote airfield, Australian spotter planes began using it on March 10. Except for a few small areas where minor concentrations of Japanese soldiers, now running low on food and ammunition, continued to hold out, MacArthur's forces controlled the Admiralty Islands by April 3. Of the original Japanese garrison of nearly four thousand men, only seventy-five surrendered. The rest perished.

On May 1, General Krueger declared victory. Cavalry Division commander General Swift gave full credit to the Navy, saying, "They saved our necks." Momote airfield was expanding to over seven thousand feet long as Krueger issued his declaration, and was soon joined by several more airfields, including two on nearby islands. Seeadler Harbor developed into one of the largest naval bases in the Pacific, with facilities to repair all types of warships. With control of the Admiralties, the Allies could isolate both Rabaul and Kavieng, preventing substantial aid from reaching both Japanese bases.

For MacArthur, the victory was a major step toward achieving his goal of securing the entire coast of New Guinea and ultimately driving the Japanese out of the Philippines. The U.S. Army's official historian proclaimed that MacArthur's decision to move quickly against Los Negros with a "reconnaissance in force" had "the very great virtue of hastening victory while reducing the number of dead and wounded." The Navy's historian claimed "the Admiralties' gambit was a brilliant success; MacArthur's decision was justified."[27]

CHAPTER 16

Reckless and Persecution

The speed with which the Admiralties fell surprised just about everyone, except possibly General MacArthur. As the fighting wound down, he was busy altering Allied plans and changing his next objective.

The original plan, approved by the Joint Chiefs, called for MacArthur's forces to move next against the powerful Japanese base at Hansa Bay, located between Madang and Wewak. The Imperial Japanese Army, anticipating MacArthur's strategy, quickly began shipping troops there, resulting in the deployment of more than forty thousand Japanese soldiers in and around Hansa Bay by March 1944. Most were combat troops experienced at preparing well-fortified defenses. The Allies became aware of this buildup when code breakers in Brisbane intercepted a message from General Imamura in Rabaul to Tokyo that described the reinforcements then en route to the Hansa Bay area, including Madang and Wewak. The message also suggested that defenses at Hollandia, much farther up the coast, would also need strengthening.[1]

Meanwhile, Australian forces continued battling their way through the jungle toward Madang. General Adachi, Eighteenth Army commander, decided that the approaching Australians and the American forces now in the Admiralties could easily outflank and trap his troops at Madang. He ordered the war-weary men there to march along the coast to Wewak, 150 miles away. Short of food and harassed by Australian patrols and Allied aircraft, many of these men never reached their destination.[2]

Assaulting Hansa Bay worried at least one member of MacArthur's planning staff, Brigadier General Bonner Fellers. Fellers feared that attempting to capture Hansa Bay, and engaging in combat with the still-powerful 18th Imperial Army, would bog down the SWPA forces and delay MacArthur's timetable for his return to the Philippines. Instead, he suggested that if Admiral Nimitz's Pacific Fleet could provide carrier-based fighter cover, the Allies should bypass Hansa Bay and strike nearly 550 miles farther up the coast, at Hollandia. Despite opposition to the idea from more senior members of GHQ, Fellers took his suggestion directly to MacArthur, who immediately liked it.

Fellers quickly found himself in hot water with his own boss, Brigadier General Stephen J. Chamberlin. Committed to invading Hansa Bay, Chamberlin had rejected Fellers's suggestion to invade Hollandia. When Chamberlin discovered that Fellers had gone around him to MacArthur, he removed Fellers as chief of the planning section. MacArthur then demonstrated his gratitude to a man with a good idea by making Fellers his military secretary, thus rescuing Fellers's military carrier.[3]

Based at least in part on Fellers's suggestion and evaluation of the Hollandia defenses, MacArthur decided to bypass the more powerful and obvious targets at Wewak and Hansa Bay and instead reach all the way up to Hollandia. MacArthur sent his chief of staff, General Sutherland, to Washington to argue for approval of the change in plans. With the Joint Chiefs' approval, MacArthur then ordered his staff and commanders to begin planning for a dual invasion at Hollandia and nearby Aitape.

The order was accomplished in classic MacArthur fashion. The first thing he did was send what were called "warning instructions" to his air, naval, and ground commanders outlining in broad terms what their goals were. He then called them together to discuss each man's part in the planned operation, and appointed a coordinator. Although never a "control freak," he remained aware of what everyone was doing and rarely if ever interfered with the tactical execution of their plans once he had approved them. Samuel Eliot Morison described MacArthur's leadership in this way: "Here is the job to be done, these are the tools to do it with, and this is the time in which I wish it to be accomplished. You work out the details."[4]

Admirals Barbey and Kincaid and Generals Eichelberger, Kenney, and Krueger assembled their staffs to begin planning the invasions. MacArthur appointed Krueger to coordinate the plans developed by this group. With little knowledge of the terrain, they had to come up with how many troops were needed and how many ships were required. One of their first conclusions was that General Kenney's land-based fighter escort aircraft would be of little help since Hollandia was at the outer edge of their current range.[5]

Meanwhile, the successful isolation of Rabaul forced Imperial Headquarters to transfer control over General Adachi's Eighteenth Army, on New Guinea, to the Second Area Army. Commanded by General Korechika Anami, the Second Area Army, which had transferred from Manchuria, now assumed responsibility for the defense of Dutch New Guinea. Hollandia was the first Japanese base across the border in the Dutch section of New Guinea, while Aitape, 150 miles southeast, was the closest Japanese stronghold in Australian Papua New Guinea to the border.

As Adachi consolidated his forces at Hansa Bay and Wewak, where Japanese troops had built numerous bunkers and fortified tunnels into the rising coral, he did not lose sight of Hollandia—in January 1944, he had said the port was his army's "final base and last strategic point" in New Guinea. He also complained about the lax attitude of the Hollandia garrison, which for too long had been beyond the active combat zone. In March, General Anami, likely fearing envelopment of Madang by the American and Australian forces, ordered Adachi to begin withdrawing westward from Madang and other coastal strongpoints and consolidate his Eighteenth Army at Hollandia. These plans were placed on hold until July or August, however, since both Japanese generals believed that MacArthur would strike along the coast of Australian-governed New Guinea before crossing the border into the former Dutch territory. Adachi, especially, was convinced the next attacks would come at Hansa Bay and/or Wewak.[6]

The plan developed by MacArthur's GHQ called for three simultaneous landings. Two were in the Hollandia area: one at Humboldt Bay, the second about twenty-five miles west at Tanahmerah Bay. The third landing would be at Aitape.

Since occupying the Hollandia area in April 1942, the Japanese had constructed three airfields on the Lake Sentani plain between the two bays and behind the seven-thousand-foot-high Cyclops Mountains along the coast. Humboldt Bay was developed to serve as an anchorage for large ships that unloaded their cargoes there for transshipment by barge to the southeast as far as Wewak, 215 miles away. The town of Hollandia, which once served as the governmental seat of the region, was located on the western edge of Humboldt Bay. While the anchorage was important, MacArthur's main objectives were the three airfields. Capturing and improving them would extend the range of General Kenney's land-based bombers for future operations along the coast.

The area around Aitape was little more than a coastal plain covered mostly with wetlands and cut by numerous streams and rivers. Its primary value to the Allies was an airfield constructed by the Japanese eight miles east of Aitape near the Tadji Plantation. Two additional airfields were under construction, but were delayed by a combination of poor terrain and shortages of equipment for the engineers.

The landings at Hollandia, code-named Reckless, and at Aitape, code-named Persecution, presented MacArthur with an entirely new set of challenges. The three simultaneous invasions would be the largest operation so far undertaken by the Allies in SWPA. Nearly 220 ships would transport or escort eighty thousand men and their supplies and equipment over six hundred miles along enemy-occupied and -fortified coast. It would also be the first time he made a large-scale attack without being able to provide his troops the protection of land-based aircraft, both fighters and bombers. He was going to have to rely on the Navy for air cover by carrier aircraft, if Admiral Nimitz would agree to it.[7]

The issue of carrier-based air cover for the invasions was front and center when Nimitz and his deputy chief of staff, Rear Admiral Forrest Sherman, arrived in Brisbane on March 25. Just as MacArthur suspected, Nimitz was reluctant to commit any of his carriers to an operation in an area dominated by Japanese land-based aircraft. He was worried about the 351 aircraft that intelligence reports claimed were at the Hollandia airfields. General Kenney assured Nimitz that although his newer, long-range heavy fighters, the P-38 Lightnings, could not provide extended coverage for the invading troops, they could and would escort heavy bombers to attack the Hollandia airfields and decimate the enemy aircraft stationed there before the carriers arrived. As the naval officers looked on skeptically, Kenney boldly claimed he would wipe out the Japanese air units in Hollandia by April 5.

Still somewhat reluctant, Nimitz agreed to send his fast carriers to Hollandia in support of the assaults there, but stipulated they would remain only until the third day after the invasion, scheduled for April 22. He did agree to allow several of his smaller escort carriers to remain on station near the Aitape landings for as much as eight days to allow Kenney enough time to begin flying fighters out of the Tadji airfield.

As preparations proceeded for the landings at Hollandia and Aitape, MacArthur's headquarters devised a separate plan to reinforce General Adachi's opinion that Wewak and/or Hansa Bay were MacArthur's next targets. During late March and early April, Allied aircraft attacked both bases frequently, and American destroyers regularly made shore bombardment attacks at both locations. PT boats patrolled offshore nightly, several times leaving behind life rafts to convince the enemy that advance reconnaissance patrols had come ashore to prepare for landings.[8]

True to his word, Kenney began launching attacks on the Hollandia and Tadji airfields, as well as those at Wewak and Hansa Bay, on March 30. Reconnaissance photos of the three airfields at Hollandia taken that morning revealed just how unprepared the enemy was, as nearly three hundred aircraft sat on the ground, neatly parked. Later that day, sixty-five B-24 Liberator heavy bombers attacked. Among their first targets were antiaircraft guns, fuel dumps, and of course the idle aircraft. Eighty P-38s, retrofitted with external fuel tanks to extend their range, escorted the bombers and battled the few Japanese fighters that managed to become airborne. Kenney reported that the black smoke rising from the Japanese fuel dumps reached ten thousand feet and were visible 150 miles away.[9]

The following day, a second group of bombers and fighters attacked the three airfields. By day's end, at least 138 enemy planes lay destroyed on the ground, and over two dozen had fled the area, headed west for safety. The final bombing run was on April 3. Photoreconnaissance showed over 285 total planes destroyed in all three attacks. Both Nimitz and MacArthur were more than pleased with the results. The landings were on, with the fast carriers providing air cover, although there were not many enemy aircraft to protect against, thanks to Kenney's Fifth Air Force.[10]

Following the landings and capture of the badly damaged airfields, 340 enemy planes were found destroyed on or near the strips. Hidden in the jungle surrounding the Hollandia area were an estimated fifty more fighters that had dared to rise up to challenge the Americans and had been shot down in furious dogfights. When aircraft from the carriers of Rear Admiral Marc A. Mitscher's Task Force 58 arrived over the Hollandia airfields on April 21, they found few targets left unscathed by the Army Air Force bombers.[11]

Despite the destruction at Hollandia and Tadji, the Japanese, especially General Adachi, continued to believe that Hansa Bay and/or Wewak were MacArthur's next targets. In fact, many of the planes destroyed on the ground at Hollandia had been moved there to avoid expected Allied air assaults, and to prepare to attack enemy landings, at Hansa Bay and Wewak. Adachi had been ordered by Second Area Army headquarters to plan to send troops from Hansa Bay and Wewak to Hollandia in case the Allies landed there. He dragged his feet, however, finding one delaying excuse after another since he remained convinced that Wewak or Hansa Bay was next in the Allies' plan.[12]

MacArthur's plan of attack was straightforward. In command of Operation Reckless—the landings at Humboldt and Tanahmerah Bays—was Lieutenant General Eichelberger, who had spent his time since his success at Buna training troops for just such an operation. Under him were three U.S. Army generals. Humboldt Bay was to be taken by Major General

Horace H. Fuller's 41st Division (code-named Letterpress Landing Force), while Tanahmerah Bay was the target of the 24th Division (code-named Noiseless Landing Force) commanded by Brigadier General Frederick A. Irving. Once ashore, the 41st Division would circle around the Cyclops Mountains and head west toward the airfields. The 24th Division would do likewise, except it would head east. The two divisions were to link up on the Sentani Plain and take complete control of the airfields. Operation Reckless engaged 37,527 combat troops and 18,184 service and support troops, all of whom would be both transported to the landing sites and protected by more than two hundred naval vessels. Included among these were two cruiser forces, one Australian and one American, and eight escort carriers from Nimitz's Fifth Fleet.

Allied intelligence reports estimated between twelve thousand and sixteen thousand Japanese troops in the Hollandia area, but that most of these were service troops who did not even carry rifles. On the day of the landings, only about five hundred actual combat troops defended both bays and the airfields. Most of the military population consisted of air force personnel who no longer had any aircraft with which to fight, and construction and other support personnel.

The Japanese were clearly unprepared for what was coming. Prior to the landings on April 22, the senior officer in charge of all service personnel was Major General Toyozo Kitazono, who had previously commanded a field transportation unit at Wewak. Having been transferred from Adachi's Eighteenth Army, he evidently brought with him the latter's belief that the action was to be at Wewak or Hansa Bay, and that Hollandia was a backwater. He had no comprehensive plan to defend Hollandia. On the very day of the invasion, Kitazono would be replaced by an officer from the 6th Air Division, Major General Masazumi Inada. General Inada made a valiant effort to form a defense against the invading forces, but he had little to work with, and the Japanese forces quickly collapsed as many of the service troops fled into the nearby hills when the Allied ships began their shore bombardment.

Unable to find enough combat troops to form a decent defense, Inada as much as admitted defeat toward the end of the day of the

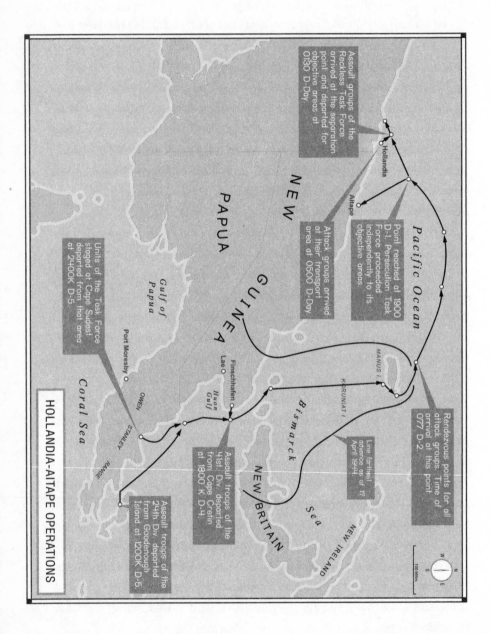

HOLLANDIA-AITAPE OPERATIONS

Assault groups of the Reckless Task Force arrived at the separation point and departed for objective areas at 0130 D-Day.

Point reached at 1900 D-1. Persecution Task Force proceeded independently to its objective areas.

Attack groups arrived at their transport area at 0500 D-Day.

Units of the Task Force staged at Cape Sudest departed from that area at 2400K D-5.

Assault troops of the 41st Div departed from Cape Cretin at 1800 K D-4.

Assault troops of the 24th Div departed from Goodenough Island at 1200K D-5.

Rendezvous points for all attack groups. Time of arrival at this point 077 D-2.

Line farthest advance as of 17 April 1944.

NEW GUINEA

PAPUA

Pacific Ocean

Hollandia

Aitape

Gulf of Papua

Port Moresby

Lae

Finschhafen

Huon Gulf

OWEN

STANLEY

RANGE

Coral Sea

Bismarck Sea

NEW BRITAIN

NEW IRELAND

MANUS I.

KORUNIAT I.

100 Miles

N
W   E
S

invasion, when he issued orders that his men should attempt to with-draw from the area during that night.[13]

The situation at Aitape was different. Of the 3,500 Japanese esti-mated to be there, over half were known to be combat troops who would be expected to mount a vigorous defense. Brigadier General Jens Doe commanded Operation Persecution and led the 163rd Regi-mental Combat Team, a Montana National Guard unit that had been detached from the 41st Division. An experienced unit, the 163rd had fought at Buna-Gona. Once the Allies were in control of the Aitape area, Major General William H. Gill's 32nd Infantry Division would relieve the 163rd for duties elsewhere.

All three simultaneous landings succeeded in completely surprising the Japanese. While there were the usual problems associated with amphibious assaults—some troops landing at the wrong beaches, others having to wade ashore because of the coral—what was absent was any serious opposition. Shore bombardments from the American and Aus-tralian cruisers and destroyers drove many of the enemy into the hills and nearby jungle. At both Humboldt Bay and Tanahmerah Bay, most of the enemy abandoned fixed positions without firing a shot. Troops from General Fuller's 41st Division found Japanese living quarters with half-eaten breakfasts and tea still brewing. At both bays, the Americans were happy to find pillboxes and other firing locations empty. The biggest obstacle encountered by the invading troops at Hollandia was the swamp. It proved to be mostly impassable to wheeled vehicles, and even several Marine Corps tanks on loan to the Army were bogged down with swamp water flooding their engines.[14] Staying on narrow pathways, the infan-trymen gradually made their way toward the three airfields.

Less than four hours after the landings began, General MacArthur, who had joined the invasion fleet aboard the cruiser *Nashville*, went ashore at both landing sites to inspect the situation. Admiral Barbey and Generals Krueger and Eichelberger accompanied him as the com-mander in chief, ignoring mud and swampy water, greeted shocked American soldiers. It was a classic MacArthur visit to the front. Stomp-ing around in the mud in his beat-up officer's cap with the gold braid while everyone else wore a helmet, he shook hands, chatted about the fighting, and complimented soldiers on the job they were doing. Author John Gunther described one of these trips: "He stalks a battlefront like a man hardly human, not only arrogantly but lazily."[15]

So pleased was MacArthur by what he found at Hollandia that, according to Admiral Barbey, the commander in chief suggested that the forty-five thousand reinforcements then on board ships en route to Hollandia be diverted to Wakde, 140 miles farther on, to surprise the Japanese there. Eichelberger thought it was not a good idea—they had no way of knowing if Japanese reinforcements were at that moment on their way to the Hollandia landing zones from bases farther west. MacArthur thought better of his impulsive idea.[16]

At Aitape, invading troops took less than six hours to reach and seize both airstrips at the Tadji Plantation. Australian RAAF airfield construction crews immediately started repairing the fighter airstrip, and two days later P-40 fighters began using the strip.[17]

At Humboldt Bay, American soldiers were shocked as groups of emaciated people emerged from the nearby jungle. They counted 120 Sikh soldiers who had been captured at Singapore and used as slave labor. Angered at the horrendous treatment they had received from their captors, many of the Sikhs begged for weapons so they could join in the search of their tormentors. Another group of more than one hundred soon came forward, mostly missionaries, including several nuns. All had been prisoners of the Japanese. Both groups were taken to ships offshore, where they were fed, clothed, and eventually transported to Australia.[18]

Over the next few days, as American troops made their way toward the airfields at the Sentani Plain between the bays, they encountered small groups of enemy soldiers willing to stand and fight, at least for a time. All the Japanese succeeded in accomplishing was to slow down an already slow-moving advance.

In addition to swamps, infantrymen had to endure a shortage of food. Supplies were stacking up on the beaches because the only means of transporting them to the front was by drafting soldiers into the role of porters. Everything had to be carried by hand. Adding to the difficulty, a lone Japanese plane had bombed one of the beaches at Humboldt Bay on D-Day plus one. One bomb struck a huge Japanese ammunition dump near the beach, causing a series of explosions that killed twenty-four Americans and injured one hundred others. The resulting fires raged for days, and were finally extinguished on the twenty-seventh, but by then 60 percent of the supplies on the beach had been destroyed.[19]

The situation went from bad to worse for both the movement of supplies to the troops in need of them, and the forward movement of those troops themselves. On March 24, several hours of heavy rain turned what passed for a road leading to the Sentani Plain into a virtual lake. The deluge ground nearly everything to a halt, including the airdrop of supplies. On the twenty-seventh, B-25s from Saidor were finally able to airdrop in badly needed ammunition. By then, all three airfields were in American hands while Japanese units continued to flee the area.

The 21st Regiment from General Irving's 24th Infantry Division captured Hollandia Drome on April 26. The same day, soldiers from the 186th Regiment of General Fuller's 41st Division took control of both Cyclops and Sentani Airdromes. Except for a few scattered groups, enemy soldiers had evacuated all three airfields.

The Hollandia landings cost the Americans 159 lives, including the men killed in the beach explosion. More than 600 Japanese surrendered, while a rough body count reported 3,300 dead enemy troops. The thousands of others who fled headed mostly toward the base at Sarmi, located farther up the coast opposite Wakde Island, but fewer than a thousand arrived. The rest were killed by Allied patrols, or died from disease, starvation, or infected wounds.

General Anami, commander of the Second Area Army, which included Hollandia, had wanted to send a reserve division to attack the Americans. His superior, General Hisaichi Terauchi, commander of the Southern Expeditionary Army, denied his request. Terauchi was more concerned about defending the Wakde-Sarmi area northwest of Hollandia.[20]

Meanwhile, a hundred miles east of Aitape at Wewak, General Adachi's concern about being surrounded and isolated by American and Australian forces had been heightened when he learned how quickly the defenses at Aitape and Hollandia had fallen. Fewer than three hundred men reached Wewak from Aitape, indicating that over six hundred had died of various causes, including enemy action. Another twenty-seven surrendered. The Aitape operation cost the Americans three deaths.[21]

At Hollandia, it quickly became clear to the Americans that the Japanese had intended to build a large base there. General Eichelberger reported the discovery of more than six hundred supply dumps loaded with thousands of tons of supplies left behind by the fleeing enemy. He wrote of "tarpaulin-covered hills of rice which looked like Ohio haystacks." There were tons of medical supplies, including quinine, thousands of canned goods, as well as sake and beer. Looking back on Hollandia, Eichelberger later wrote that he believed it was "the richest prize—supply-wise—taken during the Pacific War."[22]

Since the Japanese were monitoring Allied communications, in all likelihood General Adachi quickly understood what MacArthur's plan had been by assaulting Hollandia and what it meant for him and his troops when they translated a communiqué from his headquarters dated April 24, 1944. In it, MacArthur explained that the successful landings had thrown a "loop of envelopment" around Adachi's Eighteenth Army. He described the Imperial forces as "completely isolated."[23]

MacArthur departed the Hollandia area aboard the *Nashville* and headed back to Port Moresby, and then on to Brisbane to plan his next moves. Fighting around all three landing zones continued as small units of enemy soldiers attempted to die for their emperor or struggled to find their way to safety.

———————

Meanwhile, General Inada, commander of Japanese troops at Hollandia, made an effort to gather his surviving forces and organize a less chaotic withdrawal. He sent word that all Imperial soldiers should head toward a village fifteen miles west of Lake Sentani called Genjem. With most of their food supplies left behind, Genjem was an obvious gathering place, since the Japanese had begun growing a wide variety of foodstuffs in this agricultural center. If his men were going to make it to the safety of the Wakde-Sarmi area 125 miles through nearly untracked jungle, they would need all the food available at Genjem.

By April 30, Inada had managed to gather slightly more than seven thousand men at Genjem. They departed in ten separate groups and followed two routes toward their objective, without the benefit of their maps, which were now in the hands of the enemy. Japanese records estimate that only 7 percent of these men arrived at Sarmi. The rest fell victim to American patrols and roadblocks, or to disease and starvation. Inada was among the handful of survivors.[24]

At Aitape, General Gill's 32nd Infantry Division was reinforced by the 124th Regimental Combat Team from the Florida National Guard. Later the 112th Cavalry RCT was added. General Krueger was convinced that General Adachi, whom he knew to be an aggressive combat officer, was not about to wait around and allow his Eighteenth Army to be completely surrounded and isolated by the Americans. From MacArthur, Krueger requested and received additional troops, including the 43rd Infantry Division, waiting in New Zealand for assignment.

When the strength of the forces at Aitape reached the equivalent of three divisions, a corps headquarters was required for overall command. In late June, Major General Charles P. Hall and the XI Corps headquarters staff arrived. By that time, the Persecution Task Force, as it was known, had pushed its defense lines out in three directions. The most important of these was twenty-two miles to the east along the banks of the Driniumor River, facing the general direction from which enemy troops from Wewak might be expected.

At Wewak, General Adachi's Eighteenth Army remained a powerful force, with roughly fifty-five thousand men in three divisions and support units. Cut off from Japanese supply bases in western New Guinea, Adachi could not sit idly by and watch his army disintegrate as increasing numbers of units ran dangerously low on food supplies. Determined to take some positive action against the Americans, he ordered elements from each of his three divisions to begin the overland trek to Aitape. In early June, nearly twenty thousand men from the 20th, the 41st, and the 51st Infantry Divisions undertook the arduous task of a forced march through rain-soaked jungle. It took most of them a month to walk the ninety miles to the nearest American lines. With barge traffic all but eliminated by American PT boats, and wheeled vehicles unable to travel the narrow native paths, the men were required to carry everything they needed on their backs. Many of these men were already battle weary and weakened by disease before they started out. Meanwhile, Southern Expeditionary Army headquarters continued to be concerned about MacArthur moving farther along the coast to the Wakde-Sarmi area, so on June 17 they instructed Adachi to engage in only delaying actions at various locations throughout eastern New Guinea. By this time, it was too late to stop a Japanese attack at Aitape as portions of the 20th Division had already reached the outer edge of the Allied perimeter around Aitape, at the Driniumor River.

On June 21, Krueger's belief that Adachi was planning to attack at Aitape was confirmed when captured Japanese documents revealed much of Adachi's plans. American patrols throughout the perimeter area regularly engaged in action against enemy soldiers. These were considered to be mostly stragglers from various units, until a prisoner taken on July 10 revealed under interrogation that an attack from two directions was planned that very night. He told his questioners that one force would cross the Driniumor halfway between the village of Afua and the river's mouth into the sea.[25] Patrols along the western bank of the river, especially in the area assigned to 3rd Battalion of the 127th Infantry, had been regularly reporting sightings of Japanese soldiers on the east side of the river. Some of these involved large groups of well-armed troops. An attack was coming, and everyone knew it.

The action commenced at 11:45 p.m. on July 10, just as the prisoner had said. Samuel Eliot Morison would later describe the fighting along the Driniumor River as "the biggest and bitterest jungle battle in New Guinea since the Buna-Gona campaign of November–December 1942."[26] It began with a surprising artillery barrage on American positions across the river. Earlier, to maximize the effectiveness of their artillery fire, Japanese scouting units had mapped out where the Americans were located.

As many as ten thousand Japanese soldiers made the initial assault along the river. Many engaged in direct frontal attacks across the shallow water, resulting in considerable loss of lives from well-positioned American machine guns and artillery. Despite the appalling cost in lives, the Japanese continued attacking. In several places they were able to break through American lines and push the defenders back. On July 13, the American troops managed to reorganize themselves and counterattack. After daylight, American and Australian fighter-bombers supported the defending forces. In addition, Allied ships offshore bombarded enemy positions.

The fighting continued day and night as troops on each side fell from exhaustion. By the end of the month, the Japanese were running out of ammunition, which had been dangerously low when the attack began, and started falling back. On July 28, General Adachi considered the condition of his troops to be near total exhaustion. His staff estimated they would run completely out of food by August 3, even though the men were already on greatly reduced rations. On July 31, he sent word to the frontline units to begin preparations for withdrawal. Over the next two days, several desperate attacks were launched in an effort to drive the American defenders back and secure their food supplies, yet all failed. Early on August 4, Adachi ordered the 20th Division to begin withdrawing at noon. The 41st Division was to begin pulling back the following day.

Over the next few days and weeks the intensity of the fighting grew worse as Japanese troops attempted to drive American units away from their food supplies and at the same time withdraw under withering artillery, aircraft, and naval gunfire. Adachi tried to get badly needed food to his men using barges. Each time, the barges were destroyed or forced to return to Wewak by American PT boats and patrolling Allied aircraft. The fighting along the Driniumor River finally ended on August 25, 1944.

General Adachi's attempt to drive the Americans out of Aitape cost the lives of nearly half the twenty thousand men he committed to the effort. For the Americans, the price of defending Aitape was 440 killed and 2,560 wounded.

At Hollandia, American units had spread out and been engaged in mopping-up operations against groups of Japanese stragglers. By early June, when active patrolling ceased, it was determined that nearly 4,500 Japanese had died around Hollandia. Another 611 had surrendered to the invaders.

One hundred twenty-four Americans perished in Operation Reckless, and 1,100 were wounded. General Hugh Casey's construction crews wasted little time in repairing and extending the airfields on the Sentani Plain.

General MacArthur, ever planning the next phase of his relentless march back to the Philippines, informed his commanders that he intended to launch an invasion of Wakde Island on May 15, followed twelve days later by an assault farther up the coast on Biak Island. He would require air operations from the Sentani Plain airfields to support both assaults. General Eichelberger was given the job of overseeing the construction of badly needed roads from the coast to the three airfields, as well as the much-needed improvements to the three formerly Japanese airfields. Eichelberger had pointed out that Japanese airfields were not suitable for the larger and heavier American aircraft that would have to be stationed there to cover MacArthur's planned invasions. A fully loaded Mitsubishi Zero weighed 2,410 pounds, while a loaded American Lockheed P-38 twin-engine fighter weighed 17,500 pounds, and a B-25 Mitchell weighed nearly 20,000 pounds before its bombs were loaded.

Hollandia was to become an invaluable base for future air and naval operations. Eichelberger called the order to invade Hollandia "one of the great strategic decisions of the Pacific War." As Army engineers worked around the clock improving the airfields, it became apparent that their use would be limited to fighters and medium bombers such as the B-25. The ground was just too spongy and the drainage too poor to allow the heavy B-24s to land safely, even if steel matting was used on the runways. Despite this shortcoming, Hollandia grew into a major Allied base housing 140,000 soldiers. By the end of June, it had seven hospitals operating with 3,650 beds. Hollandia harbor, with dozens of docks constructed by American engineers, could anchor an entire battle fleet.[27]

Later in the year, Hollandia would serve as the jumping-off place for a fleet of hundreds of transports and warships that sailed thirteen hundred miles, taking tens of thousands of American soldiers to the landings at Leyte in the Philippines. Hollandia allowed MacArthur to achieve his goal of returning to the Philippines two months earlier than he had originally planned.[28]

CHAPTER 17

Next Stop: Wakde

General Kenney once described MacArthur as a leader who "believed in moving fast when he was winning."[1]

Even before the landings at Hollandia and Aitape on April 22, 1944, MacArthur's planners were working on the next step up the New Guinea ladder toward the Philippines: Wakde Island. Located 140 miles from Hollandia along the New Guinea coast near where it bends to the west, Wakde is actually two islands so close together that the Allies simply referred to them as one. A narrow waterway separates the islands, usable only by shallow-draft vessels. The larger island, Insoemoar, was the more important of the two because the Japanese had an airfield there. Its one drawback was that it was surrounded with thick coral, hindering an amphibious assault, except for a five-hundred-foot stretch of beach. That was where the landing would take place. The smaller, Insoemanai Island, was closer to the coast and not occupied by the enemy. Until the fall of Hollandia, the Japanese Second Army considered Wakde an important forward base for the defense of the Geelvink Bay, farther west. The bay served as protection for the southern flank of the large Japanese naval base at the Palau Islands located between New Guinea and the Philippines at the western edge of the Caroline Islands. This Japanese stronghold sat astride the southern route to the Philippines, and perhaps most important, guarded the oil and resource-rich Dutch East Indies.[2]

Less than three miles off the New Guinea coast, Wakde stood sentinel at the eastern end of Maffin Bay, a ten-mile-wide indentation in the mainland. On the western end of the bay was the village of Sarmi, which had become a refuge for Japanese troops who had fled from Hollandia. MacArthur's original plan was to conduct two landings in the area, one at Sarmi to capture the two Japanese airfields in the vicinity, and the other at Wakde Island. He changed his mind when he learned from General Willoughby, his intelligence chief, that as many as six thousand Japanese combat troops of the experienced 36th Division defended the Sarmi area. The fact that aerial photoreconnaissance revealed that the ground around the two airfields, Sawar and Maffin Airdromes, could not handle the weight of heavy American bombers, confirmed the decision. Fighters and medium bombers might use these fields, but the commander in chief wanted forward fields for his long-range heavies to enable them to attack the numerous enemy airfields then under construction in western New Guinea. This decision was supported when pilots engaged in Fifth Air Force bombing raids in the Sarmi area on April 28 and 29 reported strong antiaircraft fire that indicated the territory was well defended. Rather than risk an invasion, two days of raids effectively destroyed the two airfields and the tiny village of Sarmi itself.[3]

MacArthur turned his attention to Wakde, primarily the larger island of Insoemoar. Only 9,000 feet long and 3,000 feet wide, the island sported a 5,400-foot-by-390-foot runway built on coral. Photos revealed a series of barracks south of the runway where the Imperial troops occupying the island were housed. Several dispersal areas for parking aircraft were on the opposite side, some of which contained Japanese aircraft that had been destroyed on the ground by American raids. The island was home to a company of the 224th Infantry Regiment of the Japanese 36th Division, a mountain artillery platoon, several antiaircraft units, the 91st

Naval Garrison Unit—the airfield was used principally, but not solely, by the Japanese Navy—and a construction detachment to maintain the runway. Allied air officers convinced MacArthur that the Wakde field could be made to accommodate heavy bombers.[4]

On April 10 MacArthur ordered General Krueger to prepare for the invasion of Wakde, which he tentatively set for May 15. General Kenney instructed General Whitehead to throw everything he could against Wakde and the Maffin Bay area prior to the planned landing. During the first two weeks of May, the Fifth Air Force dropped fifteen hundred tons of bombs on the island and the Maffin Bay shoreline, as well as firing a half million rounds of machine-gun ammunition. In addition, Allied destroyers and PT boats cruised the bay, attacking targets of opportunity. Since the Japanese Army had pulled every available aircraft west to keep them safe from Allied attack, these vessels had little to fear from enemy air action.[5]

The Japanese were not blind to what was happening. The heavy bombardment, coupled with the successful amphibious landings at Hollandia and Aitape, convinced Lieutenant General Hachiro Tagami, commanding officer of the 36th Division, that the Allies planned an amphibious attack in his area. In fact, on May 16, one day before the landings took place, Tagami warned his unit commanders that it was "highly probable" that Wakde Island and Sarmi would soon be assaulted.[6]

To bolster the defenses of the Wakde airfield, Tagami had the service and air force troops on Wakde evacuated and replaced by eight hundred marines who could be expected to put up a stronger defense. This was done two days before the assault and remained unknown to the Allies until a prisoner revealed it following the successful invasion.[7]

In preparation for the Wakde assault, twenty thousand Americans boarded vessels of varying sizes at Hollandia and Aitape. Most were from the 41st Infantry Division, although members of the 542nd Engineer Boat and Shore Regiment were included. In overall command of the landings was Brigadier General Jens A. Doe, assistant division commander. Rear Admiral William Fechteler, Admiral Kenney's deputy, commanded the convoy taking the troops up the coast. At first glance, a twenty-thousand-man invasion force for such a small island might seem like overkill, but the

actual operation was to take place in two steps. General Krueger recognized that Wakde was too small to house all the troops he wanted to send
to the area, as well as the tons of supplies they would require. Therefore,
the first landing was scheduled two miles up the coast of the mainland
from Wakde near the village of Arara. Intelligence sources reported that
nearly eleven thousand Japanese troops were stationed along the coast
from Arare west to Sarmi, and could be activated in days to defend against
an amphibious landing. Most of the American troops were to be assigned
to protect the landing zone on the mainland while a battalion of the 163rd
Regimental Combat Team would conduct the invasion of Wakde from
the village of Toem, directly opposite Wakde.

Meanwhile, the troops on Wakde made preparations for a last-stand
defense of the island and airfield. They had constructed one hundred
pillboxes and bunkers made bombproof by layers of thick coconut logs
and coral overhead. Others took up positions in many of the caves that
dotted the island, while still others removed machine-gun turrets from
some of the many destroyed aircraft on the island and buried them up
to their muzzles. It was an impressive display of ingenuity by combat-
experienced men who realized they had nowhere to withdraw once the
enemy arrived. They waited patiently, hidden from spying enemy aircraft
whose pilots regularly reported seeing no human activity on the island.

In the rainy predawn hours of May 17, American and Australian
cruisers began pouring six-inch shells into Sarmi, Wakde, and all points
in between where Japanese troop concentrations were known or suspected. Ten American destroyers pulled in closer to shore to add to the
pounding. The firing stopped after one hour to allow several floatplanes to mark the mainland beach with smoke bombs to pinpoint the
locations for landing craft commanders to put their men and cargo
ashore. First ashore were the soldiers of the 3rd Battalion of the 163rd
Regimental Combat Team, landing, to their surprise, without opposition. They quickly established a defense perimeter. The 2nd and 1st
Battalions followed, along with a battalion of combat engineers. By nine
thirty a.m. the entire assault force was on the shore and had yet to
encounter any enemy resistance.[8]

The 1st Battalion moved through the perimeter and headed east toward Toem. The plan was to transport the battalion to Wakde the following day. In preparation, one company was quickly taken to Insoemanai Island after the tiny islet was determined to be undefended. Once there, men set up machine guns and mortars and began shelling Wakde.

Other than an occasional sniper, no Japanese opposition had yet been encountered. The consensus seemed to be that the Japanese had deserted Wakde. One story has it that the American company commander on Insoemanai claimed he could wade over to the big island and capture it with just his orderly. Luckily for him, he did not attempt it.[9]

That same day, General Eichelberger's chief of staff, General Clovis Byers, flew over the islands and reported no activity. He boasted he and his pilot would have landed on the airfield except for the numerous large bomb craters the Air Force had created.[10]

The Japanese, meanwhile, were waiting inside their bunkers, pillboxes, and caves, unseen by Allied eyes and unharmed by Allied bombs. One man who remained skeptical about the reported lack of defenses on Wakde was General Doe, who resisted attempts to move up the schedule for the invasion. He wanted to give the 218th and 67th Field Artillery Battalions that had come ashore with the 163rd a chance to continue the softening up of Wakde from their positions along the new beachhead at Arara.

At eight thirty the following morning, May 18, two destroyers opened a bombardment of Wakde with their five- and six-inch guns, focusing on the west side facing the smaller island since the assault craft would have to pass between the two islands to arrive at the landing beach. Overhead, several American fighter-bombers strafed the same area. This was followed by the arrival of three rocket-launching LCIs. Two of them led the landing craft in with the first of six waves of 1st Battalion troops. They laid down a barrage of rockets on the landing beach. The third LCI flanked the landing craft between it and the shore of Wakde, firing its rockets onto the shore. It was then that the Japanese machine gunners hidden along the shore opened a deadly fire on the landing craft. The LCIs quickly positioned themselves between the enemy shore and the troop landing craft to draw off the Japanese fire. The three rocket launchers suffered heavy casualties because of this courageous maneuver, with 20 percent of their crews killed or wounded.[11]

The first wave with Rifle Company B went ashore on the beach at 9:10. Succeeding waves with the remaining three companies, along with two Sherman tanks from the 603rd Tank Company of the 1st Cavalry Division, hit the beach by 9:25. One of the company commanders was killed by intense Japanese fire, and two others were wounded. The four companies fanned out and began clearing the area of enemy resistance. The two tanks proved invaluable in helping drive the Japanese from the relative safety of their bunkers. All four companies headed via different routes to the center of the island and the airfield. They found Japanese hiding in caves and coconut plantation homes that had been wrecked by the bombing and shelling. For the most part, the fighting was close in with rifles, grenades, and even bayonets as the enemy fought back desperately.

Shortly after noon, Company A's advance was halted by a group of Japanese firing from three pillboxes near what passed for the coast road. One tank eliminated the pillboxes and the infantry killed the troops staffing it and several foxholes behind it. The intense fighting continued in this vein for the rest of the day and all the following day. The Japanese were fighting to the death, as they had no means of escape. Near the eastern end of the airfield, the advance of three companies halted under relentless small-arms and machine-gun fire. The Americans were unable to gain control of the airfield as the enemy had positioned himself ideally for its defense. By nightfall, both sides took up defensive positions and waited for the return of daylight. The day's fighting cost the lives of twenty-one Americans, including seven officers and fourteen noncommissioned officers, as well ninety-four men wounded. The latter were taken back to the landing beach, where an LST serving as a frontline hospital had arrived. Along with it were three more LSTs bringing engineer construction crews and heavy equipment to begin work on the airfield as soon as it was taken. Japanese losses were estimated at two hundred dead and many more wounded. No Japanese surrendered that day.[12]

By the end of the third day, Wakde could be considered won. A few enemy stragglers remained hidden away, but were soon found and eliminated. The fight for Wakde cost the Americans 40 men killed and 107 wounded. Japanese losses were 759 killed and 4 captured, representing virtually the entire garrison. A few bodies remained buried inside caves that had been destroyed by demolition charges; the remains of several of these soldiers were uncovered in September 2005.[13]

The 836th Engineer Aviation Battalion began working on the airfield as soon as it was captured. The field was declared operational on the morning of May 20, and the first Allied planes arrived later that day. Soon, two fighter groups and two heavy bomber groups called Wakde Airdrome home. On May 27 B-24 Liberators stationed at Wakde were the first American warplanes to fly photorecon missions over the Philippine island of Mindanao. MacArthur and his army were on their way back.

With Wakde secured, American attention turned back to the mainland and focused on the eighteen-mile stretch from Toem to Sarmi and the ten thousand Japanese troops spread along the coast. The two remaining battalions of the 163rd RCT had formed and held a defensive perimeter around the Arara and Toem area, with only occasional contact with small enemy units during limited patrols. The western boundary of the perimeter was near the Tor River, just sixteen miles from Sarmi. When General Krueger learned from Allied code breakers that possibly two regiments of Japanese troops were planning to attack the Americans around Arara, he decided to move first. The attack was assumed to be coming from the direction of Sarmi to the west, where most enemy troop concentrations were located.

What Krueger did not know, and American intelligence had failed to detect, was that two battalions of the Japanese 223rd Infantry Regiment, along with their artillery support, were then in the process of crossing the Tor River about four miles inland. General Tagami, 36th Division commander, had ordered these troops, called the "Yoshino Force" after its commanding officer, Colonel Naoyasu Yoshino, to work their way around the American landing zone and prepare to attack the Americans from the rear.[14]

A second group of Japanese was also to the rear of the Americans. Called the "Matsuyama Force," after its commander, Colonel Soemon Matsuyama, it had been sent by General Tagami toward Hollandia to attack the Americans there. By May 17, when the landings at Arara took place, this force, made up of two battalions from the 224th Infantry and a battalion of mountain artillery, was halfway between Sarmi and Hollandia. It had taken nearly two weeks to reach this halfway mark. The same day, Tagami sent Matsuyama orders to halt and turn back toward a small coastal village named Masi-masi, about four and a half miles east of Toem. From there he was to prepare to attack the Americans.[15]

With troops to the east and the south of the enemy landing zone, Tagami positioned a third force west of the Tor River. This force was composed of at least one battalion of combat troops and a mix of construction and service units for approximately 2,500 men. He planned to trap the Americans within these three pincers. Both sides waited for the result of the fighting on Wakde before proceeding. Tagami could actually watch the extermination of his eight hundred men on the island from the vantage point of a hilltop near the Maffin airfield.[16]

On May 21, Brigadier General Edwin D. Patrick and his 158th Regimental Combat Team landed at Arara as replacements for the 163rd RCT. The 163rd was being withdrawn, along with its commander, Brigadier General Doe, to prepare for MacArthur's next planned assault, on Biak Island. Patrick had earlier served as Alamo Force chief of staff, but had locked horns with Krueger. When General MacArthur learned of the friction between the two, he suggested that Krueger assign Patrick command of the 158th RCT. This 3,100-man Arizona National Guard unit was one of the most unusual in the U.S. Army. Made up of members of the Maricopa and Pima Indian tribes, Mexican Americans, as well as whites, it was originally the 1st Arizona Volunteer Infantry, which had been an outgrowth of both the Arizona Rangers and a Confederate force called the Arizona Scout Companies. The regiment had received jungle warfare training in Panama, where it encountered the six- to ten-foot-long venomous pit viper snake commonly called the bushmaster, hence the nickname "Bushmasters" adopted by the regiment.

The regiment's new commander was a bit unusual himself. Born in Indiana, Edwin Patrick had joined the Indiana National Guard after college and served in World War I. Said to have mercurial mood swings that often made him reckless, he was bold and personally courageous in combat. His habit of wearing a green jumpsuit earned him the moniker "Green Hornet" by his men. He also attached a large, conspicuous star to the front of his helmet that many later suspected had resulted in his death during the Philippines Campaign in March 1945. By then he was commander of the 6th Division and one of only three American division commanders killed in combat during the war.[17]

General Krueger worried that the Japanese would attempt to retake Wakde, and that the small toehold he had on the mainland would offer little protection from a concentrated assault. He reversed an earlier decision concerning the size of the territory the Americans would hold in the Arara-Toem area and undertook to go on the offensive before the enemy did. Having been informed by Army intelligence that only about two thousand enemy soldiers were at Sarmi—a gross underestimate, as it turned out—he ordered Patrick to attack across the Tor River and head for Sarmi.

After relieving a battalion from the 163rd along the bank on the river, the 3rd Battalion of the 158th proceeded west toward its objective, a village located at the beginning of Maffin Bay that the Allies called Maffin No. 1. When the 3rd Battalion ran into increasing enemy resistance, the 1st Battalion was ordered across the river in support late that afternoon. By the end of the day, the advance elements of the 3rd Battalion had been forced by enemy fire to dig in four hundred yards short of the objective.

The following morning, the attack resumed, with the 1st Battalion advancing along the coast road and the 3rd Battalion on the left. Some progress was made, but Japanese resistance continued to increase. In addition, American artillery failed to silence Japanese artillery because the Japanese hid their weapons inside caves during the day, pulling them out after dark to bombard American positions. Assisted by several tanks, the Americans made slow progress over the next few days, finally reaching the Snaky River at the base of their next objective, Lone Tree Hill, on May 26.

One hundred seventy-five feet high, Lone Tree Hill was twelve hundred yards long and eleven hundred yards wide. Misnamed because someone drew a single tree atop the hill on an Allied map, it was actually covered in dense jungle growth and honeycombed with coral outcroppings, crevices, and caves that offered protection to the defending Japanese. The north side of the hill drops off precipitously to the shore of Maffin Bay. The fighting went badly for the Americans around Lone Tree Hill and they were forced to fall back first to the nearby Snaky River, then farther back to the Trifoam River near Maffin No. 1. The result was the relief of the 158th's field commander.

General Krueger became increasingly concerned about the safety of his beachhead when he learned of several poorly coordinated attacks from an unexpected quarter: the American eastern flank. These assaults were the work of the Matsuyama Force that had originally left Sarmi to attack Hollandia on May 2. One thing the Americans had in their favor was that the troops of the Matsuyama Force were now in extremely poor condition due to a lack of supplies and the exhaustion of the men who had been trampling through the jungle for weeks.

Adding to Krueger's worries was the return to the battlefield of the Yoshino Force, which had crossed and then recrossed the Tor River to attack from the south. Beginning at ten thirty p.m. on May 20, elements of this force struck isolated antiaircraft and machine-gun positions along the American perimeter west of Arara. Two gun positions fell to the enemy, who then turned the American machine guns against the other isolated positions. As the Japanese attempted to set ablaze the American supply dump, fighting during the night reached such ferocity that men struggled hand to hand, with rifle butts, bayonets, pistols, and knives, until the attackers were finally driven off at four thirty the next morning. The fighting around these gun positions and the supply dump resulted in twelve Americans dead and ten wounded. After daylight, the troopers counted fifty-two Japanese bodies. The fact that no wounded Japanese soldiers were found indicated that wounded men had apparently been taken away as the enemy retreated.[18]

Believing his own forces might be outnumbered, and that perhaps it had been a mistake to send the 158th RCT in with very little combat experience, Krueger decided a larger force was required, and ordered the entire 6th Infantry Division into the beachhead. In addition, Krueger needed to pull the 158th out of the current action because Patrick and his men were slated for an upcoming operation elsewhere. The unsuccessful fighting for Lone Tree Hill cost the 158th RCT 70 killed and 257 wounded. The one bright spot of the operation was that the Americans claimed to have killed nine hundred of the enemy, a figure that was never fully confirmed.[19]

Other than a few units that had fought during the New Britain invasion, the 6th Infantry Division was without real combat experience. Once again, Americans with little or no fighting background were thrown against hardened Japanese soldiers who had fought for several years in the bloodbath that was the war in China. The commanding officer of the 6th Infantry Division was Major General Franklin C. Sibert. The Kentucky native and West Point graduate was from a strong military family. His father had been a major general in the Army Engineers and commanded the 1st Infantry Division during the First World War, and his brother was a brigadier general on the staff of Omar Bradley in the European theater. Sibert had commanded a machine-gun battalion during World War I. When the Japanese attacked Pearl Harbor, he was serving on the staff of General Joseph "Vinegar Joe" Stilwell in the China-Burma theater. He accompanied Stilwell on his famous twenty-nine-day trek out of central Burma to India, a retreat that kept Stilwell barely ahead of the advancing Japanese.

The 20th Infantry Regiment of the 6th Division, along with a medical battalion and two field artillery battalions, arrived at Arara on June 11. They began relieving elements of the overwhelmed and exhausted 158th RCT. The latter had spent the previous three days solidifying its defensive position and eliminating several advance Japanese outposts. The remainder of the division, including General Sibert, who assumed command of

Tornado Task Force from the departing Patrick, soon joined them. Krueger wanted Sibert to begin immediate operations against Lone Tree Hill, as well as the two hills near it also occupied by enemy forces. General Krueger was determined to move against Sarmi, which he continued to believe, incorrectly, was lightly defended. He hoped to use the Maffin Bay area for staging operations against Biak and other islands to the west.

Once Sibert had his entire division and its equipment unloaded from landing craft, and his 1st Infantry regiment assigned the areas to the south and west from where the Yoshino and Matsuyama Forces had launched attacks, he moved against Lone Tree Hill. He was unaware that the remnants of both forces, badly mauled in their earlier attacks and suffering from food and ammunition shortages, as well as weakened by disease, had begun moving west, away from the Americans, in search of a place of safety. Colonel Matsuyama would eventually circle around and join the defense of Lone Tree Hill.[20]

Meanwhile, the Japanese were not idle. They were repairing and reinforcing their defenses on Lone Tree Hill and, from an observation post hidden deep behind branches of a tall tree atop the hill, keeping an eye on the activities of the Americans. Living quarters inside caves were expanded, and additional bunkers were built using mostly coconut logs and hunks of coral. Seven field artillery pieces were placed in advantageous positions on and around the hill. More than eight hundred combat troops from the 224th Infantry and the 36th Artillery waited for the Americans to try to capture the hill. Many remained well hidden inside the caves, under bunkers, and inside dugouts that kept them out of sight of the approaching enemy.[21]

In addition to the soldiers actually on the hill, there were another thousand Japanese troops on the two adjoining hills and in the surrounding area, focused on the approaches to the hill. These were mostly infantry, but also included men from artillery, antiaircraft, and construction units.

General Sibert launched his attack against Lone Tree Hill on June 20, using his division's 20th Infantry Regiment. In the vanguard were the 1st and 3rd Battalions. Halted by automatic-weapons fire, the men in several companies spent that night pinned down and isolated from the rest of the battalions. On the twenty-first, all three battalions spent the day patrolling and reconnoitering Japanese positions.

On June 22, the entire regiment struck from two directions. The 1st Battalion attacked from the beach, aided by several tanks. The tankers could not leave the coast road due to marshy soil, limiting their help. The 2nd and 3rd Battalions attacked from the jungle-covered south, but ran into problems with the muddy terrain. Help soon arrived in the form of eighteen P-47 Thunderbolt fighter–ground attack aircraft from the newly opened airfield on Wakde Island. Yet even this was less than satisfactory, as the Japanese had buried themselves deep into the hill in many places.

By midafternoon on the twenty-second, most of the 3rd Battalion troops had fought their way to the very summit of Lone Tree Hill, helped by an intense artillery barrage. What they did not realize was that the Japanese had offered only minor resistance to their advance. While the Americans struggled uphill, most of the enemy, hidden inside their caves and bunkers, allowed them to pass. Once the 3rd Battalion reached the top, the Japanese emerged and opened fire, cutting off any hope of escaping what was essentially a well-laid trap.

With the 3rd Battalion pinned down and calling for help, the 2nd Battalion rushed to the rescue until it was caught exposed in a gully and was itself trapped by concentrated enemy fire. Meanwhile at the top, the 3rd Battalion was relentlessly attacked by mortars, automatic weapons, and even small mountain artillery pieces the enemy had successfully hidden. After dark, Colonel Matsuyama and two companies of his 224th Infantry attacked in a banzai charge that resulted in six excruciating hours of hand-to-hand combat. Finally driven back by the desperate Americans, Matsuyama's men returned to their bunkers and caves. The fighting resulted in the deaths of thirty members of the 3rd Battalion and the wounding of nearly one hundred others. The number of Japanese dead and wounded could not be determined because the enemy dragged their casualties back to their hiding places. Among their wounded was Colonel Matsuyama, whose injury did not keep him from remaining in command of his troops.[22]

Both American battalions were isolated from each other and from the troops at the bottom of the hill. Their lines of communications cut, they were unable to inform their regiment that they were in desperate need of food, water, and ammunition. While the Americans waited for the next inevitable attack, Matsuyama received reinforcements in the form of three fresh companies that had made their way up the hill undetected.

Unable to dig into the coral, most of the men of the 3rd Battalion had to satisfy their need for protection from enemy fire by lying prone next to logs and trees felled by the earlier shelling and bombing. A nighttime torrential rainstorm made life for these men even more miserable, although it did have the positive effect of reducing Japanese attacks and providing them with some drinking water.[23]

The assault came just before dawn the next morning, June 23. It was not against the 3rd Battalion at the top, however, but the 2nd Battalion in and around the gully. The advancing troops did not engage with the usual Japanese battle cry, but approached the battalion silently. Somehow, they had acquired various pieces of U.S. Army uniforms and American weapons. If this was part of a plan to get in close to the 2nd Battalion, it mostly worked. The Americans at first held their fire, thinking the approaching men might be a patrol from another battalion. Since it was still before dawn, the Japanese could not be seen clearly until they were a mere fifteen yards away, when they were recognized as the enemy. In the hand-to-hand fighting that ensued, both sides suffered heavy casualties. After an hour, the Japanese once again withdrew to their bunkers and caves.

At eight a.m. the men of the 2nd Battalion were ordered to make every possible effort to reach the surrounded 3rd at the top of Lone Tree Hill. They were just four hundred yards from the 3rd, but realized there was no way they could go directly to the top. The enemy was too numerous and too well placed. It would be a suicide mission for most if not the entire battalion. Instead, they made their way back down and moved north around the hill, and then over the next few hours fought their way up to the crest. At two p.m. the lead units of the 2nd Battalion reached the men of the 3rd, but this only increased the number of Americans trapped atop Lone Tree Hill.

Efforts to get food, ammunition, and medical supplies to the trapped men were thwarted. Then, on June 24, an incredible act of heroism succeeded in opening a supply line to the trapped battalions. Company L of the 1st Infantry Regiment of the 6th Infantry Division attempted to force its way through the Japanese blockade. Loaded down with food and other badly needed supplies, the men finally fought their way to the top. Unfortunately, they had been unable to bring much ammunition, and now they, too, were trapped. It was then that Private First Class Carl H. Parsiola, a twenty-four-year-old construction machinery operator from Michigan, decided to take action. Dashing through machine-gun fire to get back down the hill, Parsiola organized a group of volunteers who attacked the Japanese positions with rocket launchers, hand grenades, and flamethrowers. The overwhelming and relentless assaults killed dozens of enemy soldiers, and more important, opened a route by which supplies, especially ammunition, could reach the beleaguered soldiers at the top. For his courageous action, Parsiola was awarded the Distinguished Service Cross.[24]

Fearing the loss of the men trapped atop Lone Tree Hill, General Sibert resorted to a maneuver that he had rejected when he took command of the task force: an amphibious landing to reach the back side of the hill. The operation involved two companies from the 3rd Battalion of the 1st Regiment, ten landing craft to ferry the troops, and thirteen other landing craft armed with 37mm guns to act as escorts and transport heavy equipment. The plan was to have these troops capture the beach and surrounding territory to the west of Lone Tree Hill. Unfortunately, the plan failed on at least two points. The planners were unaware the area directly inland was too swampy for the four tanks the escort vessels brought along, or even for the men to advance more than a few yards from the beach. They also failed to consider that the entire beach-landing zone was well within range of the 75mm artillery pieces the Japanese had in the hill. No progress was made through this maneuver.[25]

While it is true the Americans could have bypassed Lone Tree Hill

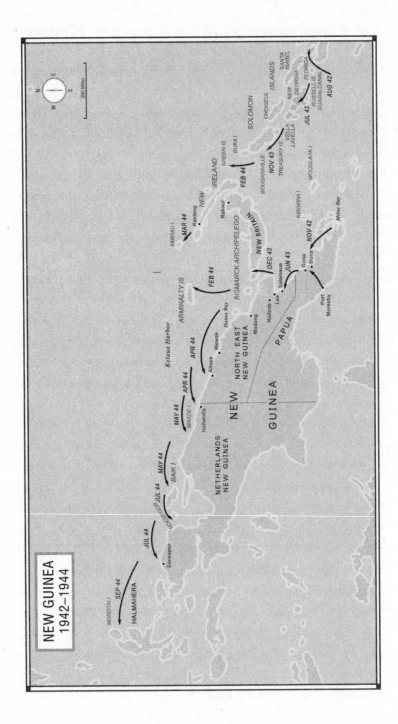

NEW GUINEA
1942–1944

and left the Japanese stationed there to starve or die trying to escape, the enemy's control of the hill gave them an ideal location from which to launch artillery barrages along the nearby shore of Maffin Bay. Since both MacArthur and Krueger saw the bay as an important staging area for five future operations—the invasions of Biak, Noemfoor, Sansapor, Morotai, and Leyte—they had no choice but to annihilate the Japanese on the hill who refused to surrender.[26]

On June 25 General Tagami, recognizing the futility of continuing the defense of Lone Tree Hill, ordered the troops to withdraw. By nightfall all that could slip away had done so. Others fell victim to search parties using flamethrowers and demolition charges to seal them inside their caves. Japanese body counts by the Americans vary widely, from five hundred to a thousand, with an unknown number buried in the caves. Approximately 150 Americans died taking Lone Tree Hill, and another 550 were wounded. The exhausted 6th Division was replaced by the 31st Division, whose soldiers continued mopping up remnants of the hill's defenders who remained behind. The division would record killing nearly three hundred more Japanese before it, too, was relieved at the end of August.

Of the two primary goals General Krueger hoped to achieve by expanding the original landing site, Maffin Bay Airdrome fell to the Americans quickly. His other objective, Sarmi, would remain in Japanese hands until the end of the war.

CHAPTER 18

Bloody Biak

The news from Wakde was not very good. Poor drainage made it nearly impossible for heavy bombers such as the B-24 to land on the airfields. This would be especially true during the rainy season, which would begin in September, roughly two months away. The airfields around Hollandia had the same problem. Fighters and B-25s might be able to use these fields, but MacArthur needed airfields from which to launch his heavies. He had promised Admiral Nimitz that his heavy bombers would be available to support the Navy's invasion of Saipan, scheduled for June 15.

General Kenney kept up his pressure on MacArthur to keep pushing forward in search of airfields from which he could launch his B-24s. The next obvious target for Allied planners—as well as for enemy planners—was Biak Island, 180 miles northwest of Wakde.

The largest of the Schouten Islands that dominate the approach to Geelvink Bay, Biak is roughly forty-five miles long and twenty-five miles wide. The official U.S. Army history of the war describes it as looking, from the air, similar to an old-fashioned high-topped shoe. Lying off its northwest corner, separated by a narrow strait that was little more than a small creek, and about one-third the size of Biak, is Soepiori Island. To the southeast, below the shoe's sole, is a group of small islands and islets known as the Padaido Islands. Mostly uninhabited, the Padaidos would play no role in the coming fighting, with the exception of the largest, Owi Island, which would earn a reputation among Army engineers as an "island of death."

Biak itself was like a coral fortress that had pushed up from the ocean floor during prehistoric times and dared an enemy to attempt to capture it. Most of the island is composed of rough-cut piles of sharp-edged coral that built upon itself, forming hundreds of caves, many with connecting corridors, high ridges that reached nearly 2,500 feet in height, and flat terraces. Japanese commander Colonel Naoyuki Kuzume used all these natural formations to build what MacArthur later described as a "brilliant defense structure." Unlike other coral islands, Biak was covered with thick rain forest and tangled undergrowth that often grew more than four feet high. The island's major drawback was an almost complete absence of freshwater. Rainwater quickly ran down to underground streams, leaving very little moisture on the surface.[1]

Biak had no natural anchorages or even a decent harbor. The island's perimeter was a coral reef that made landing troops dangerous and in some areas impossible. What made the island so valuable to both the Allies and the Japanese were the three airfields Japanese engineers had constructed along the southern shore, where the terrain was flat for several miles. A fourth airfield had been surveyed but work had not yet begun on it. The largest and most important was Mokmer Airfield. Two and a half miles west was Sorido Airfield. Both were near the coast. Between them and nearly one mile inland was Borokoe Airfield. All three names derived from nearby villages. Built on the coral, all three were capable of handling heavy bombers such as the B-24.

Allied intelligence was of mixed value to the invasion planners. Air recon photos revealed the presence of antiaircraft guns around the airfield at Mokmer, and possibly coastal guns near the Japanese supply base at Bosnek, the planned site for the American landings. Navy planners considered this and planned for a heavy shore bombardment before any landing craft went into action.[2]

The one piece of missing information was the number of enemy troops defending Biak. Photos showed hardly any, probably because they remained inside their caves and caverns during the daytime, when planes were overhead taking photographs. General Krueger decided not to send in his Alamo Scouts before the landings because he did not want to reveal to the Japanese how soon the invasion was coming. Some at MacArthur's headquarters were estimating the defenders at no more than two thousand. General Willoughby, MacArthur's intelligence officer, was apparently uneasy with the low estimates, even though he himself had put the number at 4,400. Willoughby's second thoughts concerning the number of defenders on Biak are clear in an intelligence summary he issued on May 22, in which he wrote that it was "probable that it will be defended very strongly."[3]

At the time of the American invasion, May 27, 1944, there were roughly thirty-six thousand people on Biak. The local population was about twenty-five thousand, while the Japanese forces consisted of eleven thousand men making up the Biak Detachment. Over one-third of these men were experienced combat veterans of three battalions from the 222nd Infantry Regiment of the 36th Infantry Division. Others included a company to crew nine Type 95 Ha-Go light tanks, a Formosan Special Labor Group, and several Imperial Navy base units. Immediately following the invasion of Wakde, Kuzume had terminated all construction work and turned every man he had into a combat soldier. He ignored orders he had received during April that he was to stop an invading force at water's edge, deciding instead to allow the Americans to come ashore and catch them in traps as they made their way to the airfields. The Allied control of the air and sea made halting assault troops on the beaches highly unlikely in the face of offshore bombardment and aircraft attacks.[4]

Kuzume concentrated his defenses in the hills overlooking the airfields. Inside their large caves, many of which could house over a thousand men, he installed machine-gun emplacements, mortars, and field artillery pieces that could be rolled out, fired, and retracted inside, safe from attacking enemy planes and shells fired from ships offshore.

Extensive supplies of ammunition, food, and freshwater were stored inside. Several caverns even had electric generators in use. Kuzume had wisely focused his defenses so that his forces could dominate the airfields and their approaches, and turn them into killing fields.[5]

Biak represented a new defense strategy for the Imperial Japanese Army. Until then, it had relied heavily on massed banzai attacks. The high casualty rate and lack of genuine success in dislodging American forces during these attacks resulted in this new strategy, called *fukkaku*. It was defined as making extensive use of underground, honeycombed defensive positions such as the caves and caverns on Biak. By the spring of 1944, with many ranking Imperial Army officers recognizing that Japan could not win the war, this new strategy was designed to prolong each battle as long as possible and increase the American casualties so that at some time in the near future Japanese negotiators could get better terms from the victors. They also referred to them as "endurance engagements." It was to prove successful on Biak.[6]

Control of Biak was as important to the Imperial Japanese Navy as it was to MacArthur and Kenney. Vice Admiral Matome Ugaki, commander of the battleships of the powerful Combined Fleet, wrote in his diary on the very day the American landings took place that "Biak Island is the most critical crossroad of the war."[7]

Evidently, the Imperial Navy had not learned the lesson from Midway— once again, it was seeking a "decisive battle" with the U.S. Pacific Fleet. Since it was likely this confrontation would be within bomber range of Biak, Japanese naval brass were seriously concerned that the Biak airfields would fall into American hands and their ships would be subject to attack by land-based bombers flying from there. If the island remained in Japanese hands, Imperial naval aviation could use the airfields in support of the hoped-for naval battle code-named Operation A-Go. Both sides had a lot riding on the outcome of the impending amphibious assault on Biak.[8]

Preparatory Allied air strikes against Biak began on May 17, 1944. B-24 Liberators flew hundreds of miles each way from the Admiralties and

Nadzab almost every day. Douglas A-20 Havoc light bombers flew out of Hollandia in the few days just before the landings, which were scheduled for May 27. Their raids had little effect on the enemy, since the bombing was mostly along the shore, where the landing would take place, and those further inland could not penetrate the coral caves the Japanese now called home. Some antiaircraft fire responded to the attacks, but remained minimal, as the Japanese planned on staying in safety until the enemy troops arrived. Kuzume had by now rounded up almost all the troops on the island and concentrated them in the hills overlooking the airfields.

The Biak invasion force was code-named Hurricane Task Force. Comprising most of the 41st Infantry Division—less the 163rd Regimental Combat Team, which was still in the Wakde-Arara area—all ground elements fell under the command of Major General Horace H. Fuller. A West Point graduate, class of 1909, Fuller had served two years as a cavalry officer in the Philippines prior to World War I. During that war, he commanded a field artillery unit in several battles, earning a promotion to colonel. In December 1941, Fuller was appointed to command the 41st Infantry Division on the sudden death of the division's previous commander.[9]

In addition to the division's regular complement, supporting the 41st were two antiaircraft batteries, two field artillery batteries, three aviation engineer battalions for airfield construction, and a tank company driving twelve Sherman M4 medium tanks that mounted a 75mm gun and several Browning machine guns. The Shermans would prove far superior to the nine light tanks Colonel Kuzume had available.

Rear Admiral William M. Fechteler, Admiral Barbey's deputy, commanded the Hurricane Task Force, the naval and amphibious component of the invasion. Fechteler's ships and craft had the dual role of escorting the ground troops across the open waters from Hollandia, shelling the enemy at Biak prior to the landings, and putting the troops and their equipment safely ashore. One of his primary concerns was the coral reef around the island. Although the site selected for the landing, east of the airfields, appeared to have the least reef, he warned his officers to prepare for a sudden and radical change of direction if more was learned about the condition of the reef.[10]

Fechteler's force consisted of two heavy cruisers, three light cruisers, and twenty-one destroyers. They escorted an array of APDs, LSTs, and other landing ships. Several of the larger landing ships carried smaller vessels to the scene, such as LVTs and DUKWs, the latter being a craft with wheels that, it was hoped, could make its way over the coral reef and onto the beach to discharge its passengers. An all-black unit from the Army's Quartermaster Corps that usually drove trucks was assigned to drive the DUKWs. Finally, there was a Special Service Unit composed of four sub-chasers, three LCIs equipped with rocket launchers similar to those used at Wakde, and a seagoing tug. Since, as was the policy in SWPA, the Navy was in charge until the ground forces were all ashore, there was a naval beach party to control the landings and get the men and equipment off the beach as quickly as possible to make room for each succeeding wave.[11]

Admiral Fechteler had been warned earlier that a large Japanese fleet believed to comprise six battleships, nine aircraft carriers, eleven heavy cruisers, two light cruisers, and thirty destroyers had been sighted by both the U.S. submarine *Bonefish* and an Australian Coastwatcher stationed on the remote southern Philippine island of Tawi-Tawi. Fechteler's instructions were that if this force headed to Biak, which it could reach in thirty-one hours, and he was confronted by a superior force, he should engage in a fighting retreat in order to draw the Japanese warships within range of Allied land-based bombers from the Admiralties and Nadzab. As it happened, this large naval force was intended for the "decisive battle" with the U.S. Pacific Fleet that the Imperial Navy was so fond of seeking.[12]

Air support for the Biak invasion came from General Kenney's planes at Hollandia and Wakde, with additional support from Australian and Dutch aircraft flying long-range reconnaissance and strategic bombing missions.[13]

The landing zone selected by General Krueger himself, in consultation with the naval and air commanders, was near a village named Bosnek, where they thought the coral would be the least destructive. The village was between seven and ten miles east of the airfields. At six thirty on the bright, clear morning of Saturday, May 27, designated Z-Day by MacArthur's headquarters, Admiral Fechteler gave the signal that all ships were in their assigned positions, and forty-five minutes of bombing and shelling began. Allied planes dropped 317 tons of bombs along Biak's southern coast, and the ships fired more than six thousand shells into the island. By the time the shelling and bombing ceased, the smoke blotted out the sunlight, hindering the boat drivers' attempts to locate their assigned landing places.[14]

The landing zone encompassed four locations identified as Green Beach 1, 2, 3, and 4. These landing sites stretched from about five hundred yards east of two stone jetties that crossed the coral reef in front of Bosnek to three hundred yards west of the jetties. Eight LSTs and five APDs positioned themselves offshore and began disembarking their cargoes of amphibious vehicles such as DUKWs and LVTs, which carried their own cargoes of tanks, artillery, and wheeled vehicles for use ashore, as well as some troops. Soon the entire area filled with dozens of landing craft of all shapes and sizes moving toward the beaches.

When Japanese lookouts on the island first spotted the approaching warships in the distance, they reported to Colonel Kuzume that the Imperial Navy was bringing the army reinforcements it had promised. The men were soon shocked when they realized their error.[15]

Kuzume was expecting the assault, but both the Imperial Japanese Navy and Army had put the date at mid-June, not late May. In fact, the surprise was so great that two high-ranking officers were caught on Biak at the time of the invasion. Lieutenant General Takazo Numata, chief of staff of the Second Area Army, had arrived on May 25 to warn Kuzume of the impending June invasion and to inspect his defense arrangements. Numata planned to fly out of Biak on May 27, but the preinvasion shelling from the American destroyers had closed the airfields. Also present was Rear Admiral Sadatoshi Senda, commanding officer of the 28th Naval Base Force at Manokwari, on the western end of New Guinea. The admiral, who had arrived to inspect the naval defenses of Biak, would perish in the coming battle for the island.[16] Allied intelligence radio interceptors later that day picked up a message from Numata to his headquarters demanding it find some way to evacuate him from Biak. It was not until June 10 that he would be rescued from the same fate that befell Senda.[17]

At first it appeared that the landings would be accomplished with few problems other than those caused by the coral reef, especially since there was no defense firing from the beaches. Yet as the sixteen landing craft carrying the 2nd Battalion of the 186th Infantry Regiment made their way toward their objectives, which were the two stone jetties fronting Bosnek, a powerful westerly current drove them off course. The situation grew worse when the dense smoke caused by the bombings and shelling blinded the coxswains driving the craft, so they had no idea they had drifted astray. As a result, the battalion went ashore at a mangrove swamp two miles west of its assigned beach. A few minutes later, the 3rd Battalion landed several hundred yards to the east of the 2nd, also at the wrong site. Despite the incorrect landing sites, the troops quickly moved inland to secure a road leading from Bosnek to Mokmer.

The original plan was that the 186th would land and secure the beaches, to be followed by the 162nd Regiment that was assigned to rush toward the airfields. Now the situation was thoroughly confused. The battalions of the 186th were closer to the airfields than the 162nd, so Colonel Oliver P. Newman, the commanding officer of the 186th, radioed General Fuller, the task force commander, requesting that the roles of the two regiments be reversed. Fuller refused to alter the original plan, so as Japanese soldiers watched from their hiding places in the caves high above, the two regiments crossed through each other's lines.[18]

While valuable time was lost sorting out the two regiments, the correct beaches had been located and additional troops and supplies, including the tanks and artillery, began coming ashore. The fact that the landings encountered little opposition fooled the Americans—from the lowliest soldier wading through the surf to the commanding general himself—into thinking that the enemy had in all likelihood abandoned Biak. They learned differently that night when Colonel Kuzume launched an attack using two battalions from the 22nd Infantry against what he hoped would be the entire beachhead. The overwhelming force of the Americans, who were still bringing men and equipment to shore, drove off the attackers.[19]

After the landing-site foul-up was corrected, the 3rd Battalion of the 162nd Regiment moved west along the coastal road toward Mokmer. As it approached a place where the coral and limestone cliffs reached

almost to the sea, about seven hundred yards west of Bosnek, the soldiers were forced into a narrow passage called the Parai Defile on
American army maps, where they came under heavy fire from enemy
troops. The defile was only five hundred yards wide and one and a half
miles long. The ridgeline above it reached to over two hundred feet
high and accommodated numerous caves and other places for Japanese
troops to hide and fire down on the Americans.

One company of American soldiers got within two hundred yards of
the Mokmer Airfield on May 28, but was driven back by a powerful attack
by Japanese infantry. As the Americans withdrew, they came under intense
fire from the caves to their north. Soon, most of two American battalions
were pinned down from both directions by fire that included a great
number of machine guns, mortars, and even field artillery pieces. Several
companies were cut off and isolated from their battalions. The Japanese
had an unobstructed view of the Americans below, while they themselves
were both protected and concealed by thick undergrowth. Return fire
from American field artillery units and even shelling from destroyers
stationed offshore failed to penetrate the caves and halt the firing.[20]

Four Sherman tanks from the 603rd Tank Company rescued the
isolated men, including Colonel Harold Haney, commander of the
162nd Infantry Regiment. A second Japanese attack at two p.m. included
several of the Japanese light tanks, but their 37mm guns and thin armor
proved no match for the Shermans' 75mm cannons and heavy armor.
This was the first tank-versus-tank battle fought in the SWPA. When the
ships offshore added to their misery, the Japanese tank drivers decided
they had had enough and retreated toward the airfield where they had
been hidden. Two hours later, 41st Division commander General Fuller
ordered all American troops to pull back as enemy infantry attempted
to cut off their escape. Eighty-seven Americans had been wounded in
the fighting, and sixteen killed. Enemy losses were unknown but suspected to be greater.[21]

Frustrated in his efforts to drive the Americans out of the Mokmer
area, Colonel Kuzume ordered a more powerful attack just after dawn
the following morning, May 29. Led by nine tanks, the Japanese suc-

ceeded in driving the remaining Americans east toward their beachhead. Although Kuzume's attack succeeded in regaining control of Mokmer village and nearby Parai, both of which the Americans had occupied, seven of his tanks were destroyed by Allied aircraft and artillery.[22]

General Numata and Admiral Senda, who were still on the island, realized the Biak Detachment was not going to drive the invaders out as long as the Allies dominated the air and sea. Several air raids by Japanese army bombers and navy fighters had inflicted only minor damage on the Americans at a high cost of planes and pilots. Following the loss of the tanks, they sent a jointly signed message to their respective navy and army headquarters asking for "the immediate commitment of our air forces and, if possible, some fleet units," to turn the tide against the enemy.[23]

By now, the invasion of Biak had done just what MacArthur expected: caught the enemy off guard and created confusion. While the island and its three operational airfields were of high importance to the Imperial Navy, the Imperial Army had already written it off and moved the Empire's defense line back, leaving Biak as a sacrificial lamb whose primary use was to delay the Allied advance. Now two ranking army and navy officers were requesting additional support for the Biak defenders from both services. The result was several attempts over the next two weeks to deliver reinforcements to Biak, using warships, but each was turned back by either Allied air attacks or the unexpected arrival of a U.S. Navy task force.

A final attempt to land reinforcements in support of Colonel Kuzume and his Biak Detachment was grand in design. The world's two largest and most powerful battleships ever constructed at the time, *Yamato* and *Musashi*, were to lead an armada of Imperial warships to attack Allied naval forces off Biak and to put several thousand troops ashore on June 15. Three days before the planned attack, the entire fleet was diverted to the Marianas, where the U.S. Pacific Fleet under Admiral Raymond Spruance was engaged in a large-scale bombardment that was an indication the Americans were soon to land there. Japanese admirals were still hoping for their decisive battle, and were expecting it would occur off the Marianas. The two large battleships and their armada turned in that direction. Biak was now without hope of reinforcement.

The same was not true for the Americans. Troops, including artillery units and two battalions from the 163rd Regiment, poured into the island on May 28, 29, and 30. Unfortunately, little real progress was made. The Japanese defenders were determined to drive out the enemy or die trying. Surrender and withdrawal were not options for most. Meanwhile, General Krueger was having second thoughts about General Fuller's leadership. He believed, as he later wrote, that sending the battalions from the 162nd along the narrow coastal corridor under the cliffs without "adequate reconnaissance" was "imprudent to say the least."[24]

Krueger was beginning to feel pressure from MacArthur. The commanding general was unsatisfied with the level of progress on Biak, and made those feelings known to the Alamo Force commander. Fuller was anxious to capture Biak's airfields so that MacArthur could bring in his heavy bombers, but then another option became available. Three miles south of Biak, located roughly between Bosnek and Mokmer, was a small, three-mile-long-by-one-and-a-quarter-mile-wide island called Owi. Although covered with jungle and undergrowth, the island's interior was mostly flat, with what appeared to be enough space for engineers to quickly build an airstrip. Fuller sent a patrol from the 163rd Regiment to the island to search for signs of Japanese troops. The men reported that no enemy was present. The island's sole inhabitants were two families who lived in homes constructed on stilts six feet above the beach. One lived on the north end and the other on the south end. Both families soon departed for their own safety.

On June 1, a survey party of eight men from the 864th Aviation Engineers was transported to the island by an LCI, which then quickly left so that Japanese aircraft, which occasionally bombed and strafed Biak from the nearly two dozen airfields within flying distance, would not detect the American interest in Owi. For the next three days, Captain Per R. Rosen and his men walked the perimeter of the island and mapped a location for a landing strip. With no means of contacting their battalion at Bosnek, they waited to be picked up. It seems, in the confusion caused by the news of the approaching enemy fleet with the two large battleships, the survey party was forgotten. When the enemy fleet turned away on June 12, someone remembered the men on Owi and they were picked up.

Over the next week, engineers bulldozed trees, bushes, and six-foot-high kunai grass to prepare a landing strip. On June 17, with the strip partially completed, a B-25 with a dead engine made a smooth emergency landing. Later that same day, a flight of six P-38s that had been forced to jettison their belly tanks during a dogfight and hadn't enough fuel to make it to Hollandia touched down safely. Owi was on its way to becoming an Allied airfield.[25]

Meanwhile, still stymied in his attempt to reach and capture at least the airfield at Mokmer, Fuller decided to send Colonel Oliver Newman's 186th Regiment in a roundabout direction to the north of the enemy cliffs to seize the high ground overlooking the airfield. As Newman's men rested and prepared to attack the Japanese who were preventing the 162nd Regiment far below from reaching the airfield, Fuller altered their mission and instructed Newman to attack the airfield directly and capture it. Colonel Newman objected strenuously to the change. The enemy in the caves along the cliffs, he told Fuller, would decimate his men if they moved against the airfield and did not wipe them out first. The division's assistant commander, Brigadier General Jens A. Doe, agreed with Newman, but Fuller would have none of it. He wanted that field taken quickly. He would only agree to allow Newman to reconnoiter the enemy positions on the cliffs for one day.[26]

The limited reconnaissance undertaken by the 186th failed to discover a large force of Japanese troops who were lying in wait for the Americans. On June 7, two battalions of the 186th Regiment succeeded in capturing the airfield, killing a small number of Japanese troops nearby. Then suddenly they realized they had walked into a trap as the Japanese in the cliffs opened fire down on them with artillery, mortars, and machine guns. American artillery units attempted to silence the enemy, but the Japanese were almost invisible—until a gun flash gave a position away. Over two thousand rounds of artillery shells were fired at the hidden enemy, but had less than their desired effect, as the Japanese continuously moved their guns around or simply withdrew them into caves until they were ready to fire again.

As the day was ending, Colonel Newman reported that his men were running dangerously low on food and water, and even more ominously, on ammunition. Since it was virtually impossible to reach the 186th over land because of the lethal fire from the cliffs, several attempts to bring supplies were made using landing craft, but these were driven off by heavy fire. During the night, landing craft did succeed in bringing in supplies and took off sixty-eight seriously wounded men and fourteen who had been killed during the day's fighting. The airfield was now in American hands, but it could not be repaired or used by Allied planes until the cliffs had been cleared of Japanese troops.[27]

Little real progress was made to put the three airfields under Allied control. General Fuller blamed the situation on a lack of manpower. He felt that he had gone in with fewer men than the job required. On June 13, he informed General Krueger that he needed another regiment to complete his mission. Although Krueger agreed to send the 34th Infantry Regiment from the 24th Division, he decided that Fuller was carrying too large a burden by remaining as both task force commander and division commander. Now that he was sending troops from another division, Krueger believed it was time to place the task force in the hands of a corps commander. He instructed General Eichelberger, who had performed a similar task at Buna, to proceed to Biak and assume the role of task force commander, leaving Fuller as division commander to deal with the ongoing tactical situation.[28]

As Eichelberger was leaving Krueger's headquarters at Hollandia after being given the Biak assignment, Krueger, whom Eichelberger was not fond of, told the corps commander, "Now don't go and get yourself killed." It was a play on the instructions MacArthur had given Eichelberger when he sent him to Buna in November 1942.[29]

Eichelberger arrived at Biak on June 15, three days ahead of his corps headquarters. Fuller took what he considered his demotion badly and immediately resigned as commander of the 41st Division. He blamed Krueger for what had happened and vowed never to serve under him again. One of Eichelberger's staff officers attempted to dissuade Fuller from resigning, explaining that the battle for Biak now involved more than one division, and it was natural for a corps to take over the task force. Fuller told him he had been begging for one additional regiment, and with that regiment, he claimed he could have taken all three airfields a week earlier.[30]

Fuller left Biak and met with MacArthur a few days later. The commander in chief awarded him a Distinguished Service Medal. Fuller later transferred to the South East Asia Command of British admiral Lord Mountbatten, where he served as a deputy chief of staff.[31]

Eichelberger moved quickly to appoint Fuller's assistant, Brigadier General Jens A. Doe, as division commander. Doe was an aggressive combat officer with whom Eichelberger had worked earlier in the war. The new task force commander quickly became acquainted with the same pressure from Krueger that his predecessor had suffered, but resisted the Alamo Force commander and ordered a halt to all offensive action to allow time for his exhausted men to rest and recuperate. He also toured the battle areas to get a clear understanding of the combat terrain and the location of Japanese units. It soon became clear to him that many of the caves were connected with underground corridors, allowing the Japanese to move quickly from one site to another without detection.

The key, as Eichelberger saw it, was not in direct frontal attacks on the cliffs, but in getting as many men as possible around back of the enemy to cut off his supply lines and attack from the rear. He then planned a three-pronged assault on the caves, using three battalions from the 163rd Regiment. The newly arrived troops of the 34th Regiment from the 24th Division moved farther west, where they easily captured the other two operational airfields that were only lightly defended.[32]

The new American strategy worked so well that Colonel Kuzume reportedly burned the 222nd Regiment's colors in a ceremony in one of the caves during the night of June 21–22. He followed this by committing ritual suicide, but before doing so he ordered all soldiers capable

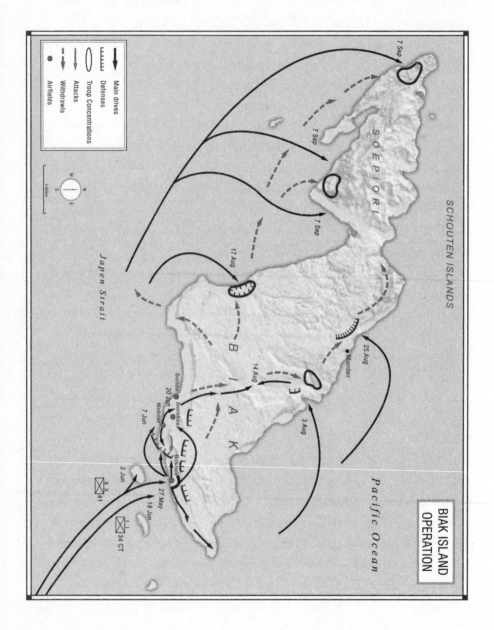

of fighting to launch a final attack on the Americans outside the cave at daylight. Those unable to participate were given grenades to end their lives.

The following morning, the soldiers stormed out of the cave in a screaming banzai attack and ran into twelve Americans standing guard near Colonel Newman's tent headquarters. Using rifles, machine guns, and grenades, the troops from the 186th Infantry stood their ground and mowed down 109 Japanese. One American died when an enemy soldier leaped into his foxhole and detonated a grenade that killed them both. General Eichelberger, touring the area, arrived minutes later to witness the results of the carnage. Learning what had just occurred, he awarded ten Bronze Stars and two Silver Stars to the twelve men, one posthumously.[33]

Although several hundred and possibly several thousand Japanese soldiers remained alive on the island, they were mostly disorganized stragglers who were hunted down in the coming months. Eichelberger and his corps headquarters were ordered to return to Hollandia on June 28. Seven days earlier, U.S. fighter planes had landed at Mokmer Airfield. Army engineers had worked around the clock to clear debris from the runway and make required repairs.

Fighting would continue on Biak for weeks. Finally, on August 20, General Krueger officially declared an end to the Hurricane Task Force operation. Biak had cost the lives of four hundred Americans, while another two thousand suffered battle-related wounds. The horrific conditions in which these soldiers fought is exemplified by the fact that nearly 7,500 were treated for malaria, dengue fever, and typhoid. The Japanese garrison was virtually wiped out. Over 4,700 bodies were counted and 200 taken prisoner. The rest died inside caves sealed up by detonation teams or assaulted by flamethrowers. Nearly six hundred Indian and Javanese POWs who had been used as slave laborers were liberated by the Americans.[34]

To General MacArthur's great disappointment and anger, the Biak airfields were not available for his bombers to support the Pacific Fleet's invasion of Saipan, despite his promise to provide such assistance. However, they would be valuable for his future operations on New Guinea and the Philippines.

CHAPTER 19

The General, the President,
and the Admiral

In July 1944, MacArthur made his one and only trip outside the SWPA
theater of war.

On June 17, while the fighting raged on Biak and MacArthur planned
his next moves, he received a disturbing message from Washington.
The Joint Chiefs, under pressure from Admiral King, were considering
bypassing the Philippines and targeting either Formosa, off the Chinese
coast, or even the Japanese Home Islands themselves. MacArthur
understood the implications of this strategy. The United States government would once again ignore his beloved Philippines and its people, as
he believed it had when the Japanese invaded the islands in December 1941.[1]

Asked for his views and recommendations, MacArthur replied that
either of the proposed operations would prove exceptionally risky since
they would have to be conducted without land-based air cover. To some,
this might have seemed an unusual answer from the man who as Army
chief of staff had belittled the airplane. His experience battling the Japanese on and around New Guinea, however, had convinced him of the

foolhardiness of fighting without powerful air support, especially from land-based bombers. There was a limit to what fighters and dive-bombers from the Pacific Fleet's carriers could accomplish on their own.[2]

MacArthur laid out his objections to bypassing the Philippines and leaving thousands of American and Filipino POWs in Japanese prison camps, and a population he referred to as "loyal Filipinos" at the mercy of the enemy. He closed by requesting that he be invited to Washington to present his views in person.[3]

General Marshall replied on June 24, advising MacArthur not to allow personal feelings to weigh too heavily on vital military strategic decisions. It was clear to MacArthur that Admiral King, who had been pushing for a strictly naval campaign against the Japanese Empire, had a convert in the Army chief of staff. Marshall told the SWPA commander he would speak to the president about MacArthur's coming to Washington to present his case personally, and expressed the opinion that Roosevelt would have no objection.[4]

It seems almost everyone in official Washington, including the Joint Chiefs, agreed with King and his planners that the Philippines must be bypassed and that the Pacific Fleet should instead spearhead an attack against Formosa. Secretary of War Stimson was one exception. After reading MacArthur's argument against the plan, Stimson told Marshall that the absence of large land-based aircraft to support the invasion was an important factor.

Out in the Pacific, opinions were different. Admirals Halsey and Spruance reportedly told Nimitz that they favored an invasion of Luzon over Formosa. Admiral King had no patience with naval officers who sided with MacArthur's views, so most kept their opinions to themselves. One who did not was Rear Admiral Robert Carney, Halsey's chief of staff. When King, who was visiting Nimitz's headquarters at Pearl Harbor, became angry at Carney and asked if he wanted to turn Manila into a London with all its bomb wreckage, Carney replied, "No, sir, I want to make an England out of Luzon." His implication was that hundreds of thousands of American troops could use the main Philippine island as a jumping-off point against the enemy, similar to the way

England served as the base for American forces invading Axis-controlled North Africa and Europe.[5]

Carney was not alone among the ranking admirals in the Pacific to oppose King's position on future strategy and support the view of MacArthur. Yet the general, in semi-isolation far out in the SWPA, was unaware that many of the leaders of the Navy he regularly railed against actually agreed with him. In a memo to Nimitz, Vice Admiral John H. Towers, deputy commander in chief of the Pacific Fleet and Nimitz's top aviation adviser, wrote that the Navy should forgo the central Pacific islands in favor of the Philippines. Two others who were close to Nimitz, Rear Admiral Charles McMorris and Rear Admiral Forrest Sherman, endorsed Towers's memo. After reading their arguments, Nimitz wrote "Concur" on the document and sent it to King.[6]

To King's great surprise, he learned that President Roosevelt himself was coming to Honolulu, scheduled to arrive shortly after King was scheduled to depart. Even more shocking, the Joint Chiefs, including King and Marshall, had not been invited to join him. The president wanted to meet personally with his theater commanders, Admiral Nimitz and General MacArthur. It has never been clear, then or now, why Roosevelt, whose health was rapidly deteriorating, made the trip, but in King's opinion, referring to the upcoming election, "he had to show the voters he was commander in chief."[7] Even after the war, King continued to fume about the president's meeting with Nimitz and MacArthur. In his autobiography, published in 1952, he titled the section dealing with the meeting, "President Roosevelt Intervenes in Pacific Strategy."[8]

Before leaving Hawaii, King wrote a letter to MacArthur, which he left behind to be hand-delivered to the general when he arrived. In it, King warned his adversary that the British military chiefs were planning to intrude in MacArthur's theater and possibly take control of Australia and the oil-rich Dutch East Indies once the Americans advanced to the Philippines. They were suggesting that Lord Mountbatten take over as SWPA theater commander.[9]

Quite suddenly and unexpectedly, on July 19 MacArthur received instructions from Marshall to be in Honolulu on July 26. MacArthur was unaware, as was almost everyone else in the Pacific, that the president of the United States had boarded the heavy cruiser *Baltimore* in San Diego on Saturday, July 22, the same day the Democratic Party convention in Chicago nominated Senator Harry Truman of Missouri as its vice presidential candidate. The ship waited until just after midnight to leave port, escorted by several destroyers and a flight of aircraft overhead. The president was evidently superstitious about beginning a long sea voyage on a Friday.[10]

MacArthur tried several times to beg off leaving SWPA, but to no avail. Marshall insisted he go to Honolulu. For security reasons, he could not divulge FDR's attendance but he did give MacArthur to understand that Admiral William Leahy would be present. MacArthur knew that Leahy, Roosevelt's closest military adviser, would not travel to Hawaii without his boss. It was clear the meeting was with the president.

MacArthur realized that with Marshall apparently siding with King, this might be his only opportunity to win over the most important decision maker in Washington to his strategic view that the Philippines should be taken before American forces moved farther north or west to Formosa or the Home Islands. Yet even with the possibility of a big payday, and after requesting permission to go to Washington himself, he was angry about being taken away from his war. He grumbled, "In the First War, I never for a moment left my division. Even when wounded by gas and ordered to the hospital."[11]

MacArthur left Brisbane for the nearly twenty-six-hour and almost three-thousand-mile flight on July 26—it was still July 25 in Hawaii. His plane made two stops for fuel, once after nearly a thousand miles at New Caledonia, then after another two thousand miles at Canton Island, before the final leg to Oahu. Since he had not been told the reason for the meeting, but that he would not require a staff, MacArthur traveled without notes or plans of any kind, and with only three other Army officers. One was Brigadier General Bonner Fellers, who served as his military secretary, and was reportedly well liked by the president since his pre–Pearl Harbor service gathering intelligence in Egypt. The others were an aide and an Army doctor.[12]

As MacArthur's plane made its approach to Hickam Field on Oahu in the early afternoon of July 26, the sky was filled with fighters and bombers on display for the president, whose ship soon rounded Diamond Head and headed into Pearl Harbor. It docked alongside pier 22-B, greeted by cheers and applause from the hundreds of sailors and civilians who had made their way to the pier after learning the president was arriving. It was a grand entrance, and Roosevelt enjoyed every minute of it. Once the gangway was in place, some four dozen flag and general officers, all looking smart in their best dress uniforms, went aboard to greet their commander in chief on the cruiser's quarterdeck. After all the introductions were made and the president had brief conversations with many of his officers, he turned to Nimitz and asked where MacArthur was. The admiral responded that he was not sure if MacArthur had yet arrived.

After landing at the Army airfield, MacArthur went directly to the quarters of Lieutenant General Robert Richardson at Fort Shafter, a short ride from Hickam. Richardson, an old friend from West Point, had invited MacArthur to stay with him, and the general gladly accepted. Richardson was not in his quarters, for as commanding officer of all Army and Air Corps forces fighting in the central and South Pacific theaters under Admiral Nimitz, and as military governor of Hawaii, he had joined Nimitz in welcoming President Roosevelt. MacArthur bathed, shaved, and dressed in a fresh khaki uniform under the worn Air Corps pilot's leather jacket General Kenney had given him, then donned his trademark rumpled Filipino field marshal's hat. Now he was ready to meet the president, whom he had not seen since retiring as chief of staff and shipping out to the Philippines in 1935. He climbed into the long, open car that General Richardson had provided and, accompanied by a military police motorcycle escort, made his way to the pier.

A short while later MacArthur made his own grand entrance dockside, as described by presidential speechwriter Samuel I. Rosenman, who had accompanied his boss on the trip. "Just as we were getting ready to go below, a terrific automobile siren was heard, and there raced onto the dock and screeched to a stop a motorcycle escort and the longest car I have ever seen. In the front was a chauffeur in khaki, and in the back one lone figure—MacArthur. When the applause died down, the General strode rapidly to the gangplank all alone. He dashed up the gangplank, stopped to acknowledge another ovation, and soon was on deck greeting the President."[13]

Rosenman reported that the president greeted MacArthur by first name and asked why he was wearing a leather jacket when the day was so hot. MacArthur explained he had flown from Australia and, pointing skyward, that it was cold flying across the ocean. The general made no mention of the fact he had taken time out for a bath and shave. The president and his two theater commanders sat for several official photographs, then said their good-byes after planning to meet the following morning. Roosevelt wanted both MacArthur and Nimitz to join him on an inspection of the island's defenses as well as other military installations, including hospitals.

Returning to Fort Shafter for dinner with General Richardson, MacArthur complained about being called away from the war for what appeared to amount to little more than a political picture-taking junket. He is also said to have told Richardson that Roosevelt's physical appearance had shocked him. Less than nine months later, President Roosevelt would be dead from a massive stroke.[14]

The following morning, July 27, Roosevelt, MacArthur—now wearing a regulation summer Army jacket—squeezed alongside Nimitz into the backseat of a red open car belonging to the Honolulu fire chief. Admiral Leahy sat in the front with the driver. At ten a.m., they set off on a whirlwind six-hour tour of the military facilities. General Richardson had devised the itinerary and wanted the president to see everything possible. Everywhere they went, cheering crowds greeted them, and Roosevelt responded with smiles and waves.

What transpired during this tour and on subsequent days was not officially recorded. This was the only presidential wartime conference for which no minutes were kept. What is known draws on the memories and agendas of the participants and those around them at the time. Biographers for both officers report that Nimitz and Leahy were virtually left out of the conversation during the entire day of touring as "Douglas" and "Franklin," as they addressed each other despite their longtime rivalry, discussed what they observed, and even engaged in some reminiscence about life in Washington before the war.[15] The president invited all three to dinner at his temporary residence, a cream-colored stucco mansion with a beautiful view of the surf crashing on Waikiki beach below.

After dinner, the officers followed the president into the home's living room, where the Navy had erected a large map of the Pacific. The room also contained other maps and paraphernalia that indicated that the Navy had come fully equipped to state its case, while MacArthur had just himself. It was evident to MacArthur that he would have "to go it alone."[16]

The president rolled his wheelchair up to the map, grabbed a bamboo pointer, and slapped it against the map. Turning to the general, he asked, "Well, Douglas, where do we go from here?" MacArthur immediately responded, "Mindanao, Mr. President, then Leyte—and then Luzon."[17]

MacArthur and Nimitz each took turns presenting his case for how to fight the future of the Pacific war, especially which route to take to Japan. Admiral Leahy reported that the president listened carefully to both men, stopping each periodically to ask questions or to point the conversation in a specific direction.

Nimitz presented what was in truth Admiral King's position, since he had already indicated to King that he agreed with the men on his own staff that the Philippine route was best. Admiral Leahy noted that Nimitz not only lacked the eloquence of MacArthur, but it was obvious he was arguing King's position, not necessarily his own. When the president asked him if having the Navy in Manila Bay would contribute to a successful conclusion to the war, he admitted it would. When MacArthur asked how they would neutralize the three hundred thousand Japanese troops in the Philippines if the islands were bypassed, he had no answer.

As for MacArthur, he spoke of the seventeen million Filipinos who he claimed remained loyal to the United States. He took the opportunity to discuss the Navy's use of Marines in massed frontal assaults on enemy-held islands, which he said was wasteful of American lives. When the president, who remained neutral throughout, pressed MacArthur about what many in Washington said would be the high cost in American lives of a Philippines invasion, the general denied it, claiming his losses would be no greater than they have been in his other amphibious assaults. He told Roosevelt that modern infantry weapons made frontal attacks outdated, and that only mediocre commanders engaged in them. Finally, he claimed the Filipino people would rise up to support an invasion by U.S. troops, while the loyalty of the population of Formosa, which had been under Tokyo's rule for fifty years, was an open question.

MacArthur argued the strategic and tactical importance of Luzon. He told the president that the massive Japanese forces in the islands would be able to attack American ships trying to bypass them by using their heavy bombers based there. He questioned how American voters would react to allowing four thousand American POWs to continue starving in Japanese prison camps while the Navy went elsewhere. MacArthur knew the condition of the prisoners because he maintained regular contact with American and Filipino guerrilla leaders in the Philippines throughout the war.

According to Nimitz, MacArthur emphasized that Americans would condemn Roosevelt for abandoning "17 million loyal Filipino Christians . . . in favor of first liberating Formosa and returning it to China."[18]

Even before the final day of the conference, Nimitz concluded that MacArthur had won his case. He was correct. The admiral did not know whether the president was won over by MacArthur's strategic arguments, his emphasis on the United States' moral obligation to liberate the Filipinos, or a desire to avoid a political scandal just before the next election.[19]

When MacArthur returned to his headquarters in Australia, he told his staff that the president had given him permission to proceed with planning the invasion of the Philippines. He gave the assembled officers details of the conference and spoke highly of the president's support. For his part, Roosevelt told a Honolulu press conference, "We are going to get the Philippines back, and without question General MacArthur will take a part in it." SWPA press releases for the remainder of the war would speak highly of Washington's support for the victories MacArthur's forces were achieving. It is almost as if two men who clearly understood each other had made a "scratch my back and I will scratch yours" deal. Their Honolulu conference helped the general move ahead with his war and the president to proceed to victory in the November elections without the specter of an angry MacArthur, who remained a favorite of the American public, in the background.[20]

The president left Honolulu and sailed first to Alaska, and then to the shipyard at Bremerton, Washington, where he addressed ten thousand workers in a speech broadcast nationwide. He spoke of the close cooperation between himself and "my old friend General MacArthur." While traveling, he wrote to MacArthur to confirm his support for the general's plan: "Some day there will be a flag-raising in Manila—and without question I want you to do it."[21]

Although the president had the power, he did not want to tell the Joint Chiefs what their decision should be between the Philippines and Formosa. Instead, he had Admiral Leahy, who was never truly convinced of King's Formosa-first strategy, make the case for him. Under pressure from King and his war plans chief, Rear Admiral Charles M. Cooke, the Chiefs would not reach a final decision for months, although in the meantime they did authorize MacArthur to occupy Leyte, an island in the central Philippines, which could then be used to reduce the effectiveness of the enemy's air strength on Luzon.[22]

Such moves were all in the near future, however. For now, MacArthur, who firmly believed he had the president's support, or at least acted as if he had it, had to continue his victorious march up the New Guinea coast before he could turn to the Philippines and fulfill his pledge to the Filipino people.

CHAPTER 20

Breakout from Wewak

MacArthur's policy of isolating powerful Japanese positions, allowing them to choose between surrender or death by starvation and disease, paid an important dividend. It permitted him to move along the New Guinea coast with unexpected speed, destroying smaller enemy units along the way. The largest of those isolated Japanese forces was the Eighteenth Army, commanded by Lieutenant General Hatazo Adachi.

Hunkered down along a seven-mile-wide corridor of jungle and swamp in and around the coastal town of Wewak, Adachi's force of sixty thousand soldiers had waited two months for either a relief force or orders from higher authorities. Neither came. With supplies running low and hundreds of men dying from malnutrition and disease each day, the army had resorted to confiscating the fields of local farmers and planting its own crops in hopes of survival. Rain pounded Adachi's troops almost daily while patrols regularly brought back news of Allied successes all around them. They were surrounded by Australian troops to their east, virtually impenetrable mountainous jungles to the south, the Allied-controlled sea to the north, and American forces in the west. Periodic bombing by Allied planes compounded their misery.

The plight of General Adachi and his men was widely known around the globe. *Time* magazine referred to him as the "Jap in a Trap."[1] They were on the minds of virtually everyone associated with the war. The Sixth Army's Alamo Scouts devised a plan to kidnap Adachi and bring him back as a prisoner of war. A Scout team leader, John McGowen, witnessed a Japanese-American interrogator questioning a Japanese sergeant who had been involved in building Adachi's headquarters building. Using diagrams of the building and surrounding area, based on information provided by the prisoner, the Scouts devised an operation to get the general, using both a submarine and a PT boat. On May 24, they submitted the plan to General Krueger, who refused to endorse it, saying that capturing Adachi was not worth the life of one Alamo Scout.[2] General MacArthur had already decided that Adachi was a nuisance who could be dealt with after Japan surrendered.

Adachi needed food and medical supplies for his troops, and an escape from the trap. His only recourse was to march the one hundred miles up the coast toward Aitape and attack the Americans. If he could break through their defenses, his men could find the food they so desperately needed.

During the early part of June Adachi began preparations for an attack on the American lines along the Driniumor River, twenty miles east of Aitape. The width of the river varies from thirty to ninety yards, and except for short periods when heavy rain turns it into a muddy torrent, it is easily crossed by troops on foot, especially using the numerous rocks, downed trees, and sandbars that dot the river. The Driniumor runs down from the Torricelli Mountains through the tiny village of Afua at the foot of the mountains, and then meanders its way roughly seven miles to the sea.

Japanese reconnaissance patrols reported that the river was lightly defended along its west bank, and that there were numerous Allied supply dumps containing large quantities of food in the area. This food was the main attraction for many of the starving Japanese soldiers. For some, it would prove their undoing as they exposed themselves to enemy fire in desperate attempts to get something to eat. Stretched in a thin line along the river were American troops, mostly from the 32nd Infantry Division.

General Adachi did not know that American code breakers had intercepted radio communications between him and Anami that revealed his plan for a major assault at Aitape. They were even able to keep bearings on his transmitter location as he moved his headquarters from Boikin, twenty miles west of Wewak, farther west to be closer to the planned action.[3]

Then, to Adachi's surprise, on June 20 Imperial Headquarters transferred the Eighteenth Army from Anami's command to that of General Hisaichi Terauchi, commander in chief of the Southern Expeditionary Army, which was superior to Anami's Second Area Army. On June 21, Terauchi sent Adachi orders to limit his forces to "delaying action at strategic positions in Eastern New Guinea."[4]

The change in the chain of command for Adachi's army and the order to engage in delaying actions were in part the result of a May 6 U.S. submarine attack on a convoy sailing from the Philippines to New Guinea. On board the ships were the 32nd and 35th Infantry Divisions, intended to reinforce Anami and his Second Area Army. Anami was to use these two divisions to attack Hollandia and Aitape from the west, while Adachi attacked Aitape from the east, the aim being to pin the Americans at Hollandia and Aitape inside a powerful pincer. The torpedo attack, however, cost the two divisions most of their artillery and infantry weapons. Imperial General Headquarters rejected a request by Anami that the survivors from the two divisions continue with the original plan to join him. Instead, the troops were sent elsewhere and, to add insult to injury, a new defense line was established that left most of New Guinea, except for the Vogelkop Peninsula at its very western end, and the island of Sansapor, on the wrong side of the line, with instructions to hold out against the enemy "as long as possible."[5]

The changed orders and the new primary defense line altered the equation for Adachi. His Eighteenth Army was now more than six hundred miles inside enemy territory. It was clear he had been written off by

Tokyo and no attempt could or would be made to reinforce, resupply, or evacuate his army. The nearly sixty thousand men—the number was declining daily, and MacArthur's headquarters put the remaining troops at between forty-five and fifty thousand—were left to die for their emperor.

If Adachi was no longer required to move into Dutch New Guinea in support of the Second Area Army, but to remain in place and engage in delaying actions, he could cancel the dangerous attack on Aitape. However, there was still the matter of providing for his sick and starving men. With no possibility of outside help, the Eighteenth Army was on its own in a struggle to survive. Adachi had no choice but to look on the planned Aitape attack as a "delaying action" and carry on with his plans. The alternative was to continue watching his army wither away as more men died or abandoned their posts and slipped off into the jungle in search of food and an escape route.

At first, General MacArthur believed that it was "improbable" that the abandoned Japanese Eighteenth Army could "seriously menace" his forces at Aitape. His staff estimated it would take the enemy weeks to trek through the jungle to reach the Driniumor, and those that did would not be fit for combat.[6]

Then MacArthur received a report from General Willoughby concerning a decrypted message from the Japanese Southern Expeditionary Army to Tokyo, asking that a submarine be rushed to Wewak with supplies that were needed by the Eighteenth Army for its planned attack on Aitape. Coupled with air-reconnaissance photos, PT boat patrol reports, and information provided by the local native population, it was clear that General Adachi was indeed planning a major assault on Aitape.[7]

Adachi's plan was to engage slightly over half his force in a concentrated attack at Aitape, leaving a smaller number behind to defend Wewak. He told his soldiers, "I am determined to destroy the enemy in Aitape by attacking him ruthlessly with the concentration of our entire force in that area. This will be our final opportunity to employ our entire strength to annihilate the enemy." It was an act of desperation, but he could not "find any means or method which will solve this situation strategically or tactically."[8]

In late May, more than twenty thousand Japanese began making their way along narrow jungle trails toward the Driniumor River. Their lines stretched for miles as they trudged through swamps and mud while under the occasional driving rainstorm. Despite their physical condition, they remained a determined and powerful force. The two main units for the attack were the 20th Division and the 41st Division. Added to their number was one regiment of the 51st Division. The total number of troops is deceptive, however, since few of these were actually infantry troops with combat training. Surviving records indicate that the force Adachi sent to Aitape contained fewer than eight thousand trained infantry soldiers. Another 2,500 were members of various field artillery units who somehow managed to drag along their 70mm and 75mm guns. Roughly five thousand more were to engage in support and supply roles for the infantry and artillery soldiers and fight when called on. The remaining 4,500 were a mix of maintenance men, headquarters clerks, and soldiers in other noncombat jobs who were to fight when it was required. Adachi left twenty thousand men to defend Wewak against harassing attacks by the Australian 5th Division, which had fought its way to within sixty miles of Wewak. Another fifteen thousand Japanese troops were to follow behind the attacking force with whatever supplies could be gathered in the Wewak area.[9]

During the weeks of marching, the Eighteenth Army remained in regular radio contact with the Southern Expeditionary Army headquarters, allowing American radio interceptors to keep track of its progress. General Willoughby reported that at the beginning of the march the Japanese were making about six to seven miles per day, whereas weeks later they were making less than half that number.[10]

Reconnaissance patrols Adachi had sent far ahead of the main troops reported that he could expect only two regiments of Americans defending the west bank of the Driniumor River. This was correct, but then, in anticipation of the impending attack, General MacArthur ordered the 43rd Division under Major General Leonard F. Wing to

Aitape. This New England National Guard division was rushing from New Zealand. Concerned it would not arrive in time, General Krueger sent in the 112th Cavalry Regiment and the 124th Infantry Regiment from the 31st Division in support of the 32nd Division, which was the main line of defense on the scene. With two divisions and elements of a third at Aitape, the defending force came under the command of Major General Charles Hall's XI Corps.[11]

In late June, American patrols began reporting the presence of Japanese soldiers on the opposite side of the river. At first they appeared to be reconnaissance patrols, but then they were revealed as combat units. Firefights ensued.

On July 17, the regiments of the U.S. 43rd Division started arriving from New Zealand to support the Aitape defense line. One of its four regiments was the 169th, from Connecticut. Tokyo Rose announced the arrival of the 169th in New Guinea, calling the regiment the "Butchers of Munda," a reference to the ferocious fighting it had engaged in to capture Munda, on New Georgia, in July and August 1943.[12]

As small-unit engagements increased and grew in intensity around the Driniumor River, MacArthur pressed Krueger to end the fighting and send the enemy troops fleeing. Krueger ordered two large-scale reconnaissance forces across the river to ascertain exactly where the enemy was and the size of their force. On July 10 a battalion from the 128th RCT and a squadron from the 112th Cavalry crossed to the east side of the river at separate locations and began a surprisingly fruitless search for the enemy's main force. The thick jungle limited visibility, and despite the fact that there were thousands of Japanese troops nearby, the Americans never caught sight of them. Unfortunately, these men were so far east they would not be available to defend the river line when Adachi launched his main attack at eleven thirty that night.

The attack began with a ten-minute artillery barrage, which surprised the Americans, who were unaware the enemy had dragged some of their heavy weapons through the jungle. Near the mouth of the river, a battalion from the Japanese 78th Regiment began crossing the river, expecting only light resistance. Well-prepared American artillery and mortars decimated them. Of the four hundred emperor's soldiers who entered the river, barely ninety survived. Farther upriver, another battalion suffered a similar fate, although some men were able to get to the opposite shore and work their way around back of the defenders.[13]

At the northern end of the river, Japanese troops from the 237th Infantry regiment and the 20th Division attacked across the river on a seventy-five-yard-wide front. Although they, too, suffered heavy losses, they were able to establish a beachhead on the American side and drive the defenders to a second line of defense at the River X-Ray, some three thousand yards back. Adachi took advantage of this small breakthrough by pouring every available unit through the area abandoned by the Americans. Thinking success was within his reach, the Japanese general decided to commit his reserve units to the fight as quickly as possible. Unfortunately, most of these units were still marching through the jungle and had not reached the front.[14]

In spite of their losses, the troops of the 78th Regiment continued to pour across the river near its mouth, pushing the Americans back. General Krueger ordered a halt to withdrawal and instructed General Hall to mount a counterattack and regain the Driniumor River line. Both sides kept sending more troops into the many skirmishes and battles up and down the river. The fighting was especially intense around the village of Afua, at the foot of the Torricelli Mountains where the river begins its push toward the sea, with control of the area changing hands several times over the next two weeks.

On July 31, General Hall ordered three battalions from the 124th Regimental Combat Team across the river near its mouth with orders to move south along the east side of the river toward Afua. By then, the Americans had reoccupied all the areas where the Japanese had crossed the river, and numerous Japanese units found themselves isolated behind enemy lines. With American units now on what had been his side of the river, and his losses mounting, Adachi was forced to rethink his plans. His troops were running dangerously low on ammunition, and many were completely out of food rations, forced to live off jungle plants and the small amount of food they recovered from temporarily abandoned

American positions. Several regiments reported they were down to fewer than one hundred men, with several as low as thirty soldiers accounted for. Finally, on August 4, Adachi ordered a halt to all attacks and instructed his surviving officers to begin the trek back toward Wewak. Although the actual number of Japanese casualties has never been determined, the fighting along the Driniumor cost the Eighteenth Army between nine thousand and thirteen thousand dead.[15]

Combat continued for several more weeks as Japanese troops attempted to fight their way from behind American lines and return across the river. The battle for Driniumor River cost fewer than six hundred American lives, and approximately 170 men wounded. Another eighty-five remained missing in the dense jungle. The official U.S. Army history acknowledges that the fighting along the river constituted a "major battle," but it was incidental to the progress of MacArthur's drive toward the Philippines.[16]

Pursued by American long-range patrols, the Japanese Eighteenth Army limped back to where it had come from, losing thousands more men along the way. General Adachi himself later described the story of his Army as "tragic."[17]

CHAPTER 21

Island-Hopping to Victory

By the late spring of 1944, the war in New Guinea was beginning to wind down for General Douglas MacArthur and the fifteen U.S. Army divisions he commanded, along with the American air and naval forces he planned to take with him to the Philippines.[1]

MacArthur's primary need, as his forces battled the enemy at various locations in New Guinea, was to keep the momentum going and to build additional airfields that could accommodate long-range heavy bombers and fighters, all the while avoiding massed Japanese concentrations. His next target was the area around the Vogelkop, or Bird's Head Peninsula, at the northwestern end of New Guinea. The name derives from the shape of the peninsula, which resembles the head of a large bird. The 8,500-square-mile jungle- and mountain-filled stretch was home to tens of thousands of Japanese troops. Their two main concentrations were at Sorong, at the front of the bird's head, facing west, and Manokwari, at the rear of the bird's head, facing east. The Vogelkop was, in MacArthur's words, "the last enemy stronghold in New Guinea." His plan was to bypass both locations and capture, instead, offshore islands that could help isolate the enemy troops and provide additional airfields for General Kenney's forces.[2]

First on the list was Noemfoor Island. Located approximately seventy-five miles west of Biak, and sixty-five miles east Manokwari, where twenty-five thousand Japanese troops would soon be bottled up with no means of escape, it was the obvious first step to surrounding the Vogelkop. Almost circular in shape, Noemfoor is eleven miles in diameter at its narrowest. It is roughly fifteen miles north to south and twelve miles east to west. When the first Japanese arrived in December 1943, the local population of approximately five thousand who lived in coastal villages must have sensed the danger they represented, as they fled to the dense forests of the island's interior.[3]

Unable to use locals as construction workers, the Japanese imported three thousand Javanese men, women, and children to toil as slave laborers, building the three airfields they planned. Only four hundred of these people would be found alive by the Allies, the rest having died from mistreatment, starvation, disease, and injuries. It was these airfields that made the island so attractive to General Kenney, who first suggested capturing Noemfoor to MacArthur. To the Allies, the most important of these was the completed Kamiri Airfield near the village of the same name and very close to the northwest coast. The strip was five thousand feet long and equipped with dispersal areas for storing aircraft. Built on the coral foundation of the island, it was expected to handle Kenney's medium bombers. The other airfields were Kornasoren, a few miles east of Kamiri, along the north coast, and Namber, on the southwest coast. The latter two were not yet completed, but well on the way to completion and could quickly be made serviceable for Allied fighters by American and Australian engineers.[4]

On June 4, 1944, MacArthur ordered his staff to quickly develop plans for the invasion of Noemfoor. One reason for the rush was that he had learned the Japanese were moving troops in small craft, such as luggers, from Manokwari to Noemfoor during the night hours to avoid Allied ships and planes. Once on Noemfoor, they stayed close to shore for the entire day, hidden from reconnaissance aircraft and PT boats.

During the following night, they made the seventy-five-mile run to Biak, bringing in reinforcements and supplies. Allied intelligence agents believed this was how the entire Japanese 221st Infantry Regiment arrived at Biak to battle the American invaders.[5]

Among the first questions the planners had to answer was, "How many Japanese were there to defend Noemfoor?" This was also one of General Krueger's first questions when MacArthur confirmed on June 17 that he was to invade, occupy, and defend the island against potential counterattacks, as well as ensure that all three airfields were able to receive Allied bombers and fighters as quickly as possible. Krueger was also instructed to find some way to build an anchorage to handle small naval ships. At the time, Noemfoor contained nothing resembling an anchorage for ships of any size since the island had never engaged in any sort of commerce.[6]

From reports he was receiving through ULTRA, General Willoughby estimated there were about 1,750 Japanese soldiers on the island, of whom 700 were actually combat troops. The remainder was from airfield construction and transport units, as well as other noncombatants. The Allies did not consider the Indonesian slave laborers or the nine hundred men from a Formosan auxiliary labor force as possible island defenders since they were not expected to fight on behalf of their cruel masters. While Krueger accepted these numbers, he remained concerned about earlier estimates regarding Biak, which had reported numbers of Japanese defenders far less than what his men had encountered there. He suspected that reinforcements were even then slipping into Noemfoor, given that it should be obvious to the Japanese that the island was the next Allied target. Krueger decided to send in the Alamo Scouts for a definitive answer.[7]

Adding to Allied worry about the planned amphibious invasion of Noemfoor was a coded Japanese message dated June 19 that revealed the shipment of nine coastal defense guns to the island.[8]

Air reconnaissance photos revealed the island surrounded by a coral reef, with only a few openings through which small craft could reach the beach. One of these was directly opposite the Kamiri Airfield, a contributing factor to that field's attractiveness as the initial target of MacArthur's proposed amphibious landings.

During the second half of June, Kenney's B-25s and P-38s pounded Noemfoor, as well as the airfields at Sorong and Manokwari, destroying as many as sixty enemy aircraft, many while still on the ground. They also sank ten thousand tons of shipping by attacking small craft trying to sneak supplies and reinforcements to New Guinea from the Philippines.[9]

On June 21, two teams of Alamo Scouts landed on Noemfoor with orders to estimate the number of Japanese combat troops, as well as both their physical condition and their morale—the latter based on their appearance, since an unkempt look might reveal low morale and poor discipline. Scouts were also to determine the caliber of the troops staffing the coastal defense guns. Finally, and perhaps most important, they were to report on the condition of the eight-hundred-foot beach fronting the Kamiri Airfield where the Americans planned to land.

The two teams, each totaling six men, arrived aboard a PT boat in the dark of night. Their first mission was to identify the exact location and size of the break in the coral reef offshore of the landing beach. They did so, and then found that the beach—now called Yellow Beach—was ideal for a landing, since it had only a gradual slope up from the water's edge. Searching the area around the airfield, they discovered that the enemy appeared rather shabby, and many walked around unarmed. They reported seeing three Japanese tanks, each sporting a 47mm gun and two 7.7mm machine guns. The PT boat picked the teams up during the night of June 23. Their estimate of the number of enemy troops on the island was five thousand, which turned out to be too high.[10]

Unknown to the scouts, they had been spotted by Japanese soldiers, who reported their presence to the island's commander, Colonel Suesada Shimizu. The colonel was the commanding officer of the 219th Infantry Regiment of the 35th Division, who on arriving at Noemfoor on June 8, had assumed command of the newly created Noemfoor Defense Detachment. Expecting an enemy assault in the near future, Shimizu established fourteen strongpoints to defend. The Kamiri Airfield was the primary defensive position, and the others were strung out along the coast in both directions toward the other airfields.[11]

The reports of enemy reconnaissance confirmed Shimizu in his conviction that the Kamiri Airfield would be the Allies' primary target and the beach just to its west would be their entry point. Meanwhile, radio intercepts warned General Krueger that the enemy commander on Noemfoor was anticipating an attack and moving troops from other sections of the island to the Kamiri Airfield area. Having already suspected that the enemy might be trying to reinforce the Noemfoor Defense Detachment, Krueger now sped up preparations to conduct the landing on June 30, the date MacArthur had recommended.[12]

The commander in chief had originally suggested to Krueger that he use units from the 6th Infantry Division for the Noemfoor invasion, but Krueger decided against that because the division was still heavily engaged in fighting in the Wakde area around Lone Tree Hill. Instead, he selected the 158th Regimental Combat Team, commanded by Brigadier General Edwin D. Patrick, the "Green Hornet." Unsure of the number of enemy combat troops his men would face, Krueger also prepared the 503rd Parachute Infantry Regiment as a reserve. If the eight thousand combat troops of the 158th RCT and the five thousand service personnel—mostly Australian engineers assigned to work on the airfields—became bogged down, the two thousand paratroopers would drop in to help. While they waited in the Hollandia area, the paratroopers studied maps and photos of Noemfoor and attended orientation lectures on the terrain and known enemy positions on the island.[13]

Both Admiral Barbey, whose ships would deliver the assault team, and General Kenney, whose aircraft were assigned to soften up the island's defenses prior to the invasion, pressured Krueger to delay the invasion by at least two days. Barbey insisted the infantrymen needed more practice at amphibious landings, and said several of the ships assigned to escort the invasion fleet were still at the Admiralties, refueling and rearming. Kenney wanted to be able to bring additional aircraft to the fight and needed the time to get them into the area. Reluctantly, knowing the delay would annoy MacArthur, Krueger agreed to postpone the invasion to Sunday, July 2. MacArthur gave the change his approval.[14]

In addition to the normal preinvasion bombardment by the Air Force's B-24s, B-25s, and A-20s around the entire landing zone at dawn on July 2, Noemfoor was treated to something special. Ten minutes before the troops hit the beach, three hundred thousand-pound bombs fused to detonate simultaneously "crunched along the line of beach defenses," as Kenney described the scene.[15]

Meanwhile, a mixed American-Australian fleet consisting of one heavy cruiser, two light cruisers, eighteen destroyers, and several rocket ships had fired eighteen thousand shells and eight hundred rockets at the landing zone and surrounding area, beginning at four thirty a.m. The naval bombardment was heavier than any that had ever taken place in the SWPA previously, and especially so for an invasion that many suspected might be only lightly resisted.[16]

Fifteen minutes before the scheduled eight a.m. landing, thirty-three Army Air Force B-24s attacked a coral ridge and hill line behind the airfield, from which enemy resistance was expected. They dropped five-hundred-pound bombs that shattered the coral. At eight, the landing craft passed through the opening in the reef, or in the case of tracked LVTs, climbed over it, and brought the first wave of troopers from the 1st and 2nd Battalions of the 158th RCT onto the sandy beach near the Kamiri Airfield.

Opposition was minimal, with only a few Japanese firing their weapons. Most had been so stunned by the massive bombardment that there was no fight left in them. At one point, about three dozen Japanese soldiers spilled out of a cave in the coral terrace just beyond the landing strip, which had quickly fallen to the Americans without resistance. The dazed enemy troops at first just milled around as if they were unsure what had happened and how they should respond. They had little chance for that, as the advancing Americans poured rifle and machine-gun fire into their midst, killing them all.[17]

The 1st Battalion of the 158th headed toward the western end of the airfield while members of the 2nd Battalion headed east. Everyone had to move as quickly as possible to make room for troops and tanks landing behind them. Both battalions were soon joined by the 3rd, and all troops engaged in clearing caves and other prepared defensive positions that had been mostly abandoned or were occupied by Japanese who put up little or no resistance. By nightfall, with thousands of combat and support troops ashore or soon to be, the beachhead extended beyond the airfield. Despite rumors, which later proved to be substantially false, of numerous enemy snipers in the area, the Americans began moving some of the partially destroyed thirty Japanese aircraft from the field as they waited for the Australian engineers of the RAAF's 62 Works Wing to arrive and begin repairing the landing strip.

The only serious opposition the invading forces encountered were some 70mm artillery and mortar shells fired onto the beach landing zone and the coral reef beyond from distant enemy positions. They succeeded in killing one American and injuring several others. In addition, several vehicles, including a truck filled with ammunition, were destroyed. The enemy shelling continued intermittently for about two hours until gunners aboard the naval escort ships found their targets and silenced them.[18]

The original plan for the 503rd Parachute Infantry Regiment called for a battalion to drop onto the Kornasoren Airfield once the Americans seized it, a milestone expected to be achieved on July 3. Yet when General Patrick was informed that a captured Japanese soldier had mentioned that between 3,500 and 4,000 enemy troops had been recently brought to the island to support its defense, he became concerned. He questioned if he might be facing a situation similar to that on Biak, where the enemy laid low during the actual landings, then later launched surprise attacks from well-fortified positions. Now he was unsure how many enemy combat troops he faced, especially when he recalled how Allied intelligence had greatly underestimated the number of Japanese at Sarmi.[19]

Patrick decided he did not want to wait for the reinforcements; instead, he radioed Krueger asking that the entire parachute regiment be sent right away, and changed its landing zone to the Kamiri Airfield, which was under his control. These troopers' presence at the airfield would relieve his infantrymen of defense duties so that they could prepare to fight whatever enemy was waiting for them in the nearby jungles and hills. General Krueger responded quickly that the 1st Battalion of the 503rd PIR would drop in at eleven the next morning, July 3. It would be followed over the next two days by the 2nd and 3rd Battalions. By midday on July 5, the entire regiment was scheduled to be at Kamiri Airfield to support the 158th RCT. This would give Patrick an additional two thousand combat troops to accomplish his mission.[20]

Meanwhile at Biak, another 2,700 men of the 34th Infantry Regiment of the 24th Division were preparing for the possibility that they might have to lend their support to the troops on Noemfoor. Having assembled on the Biak beach on June 30, they were prepared to load into LCIs in less than twenty-four hours for the nine-hour trip if they were needed. On Noemfoor, the Americans and Australians settled in for a relatively quiet night, although everyone remained on alert for a possible enemy attack.

At six thirty the following morning, July 3, a C-47 transport carrying paratroopers from the 1st Battalion took off from Hollandia and headed out over Humboldt Bay. Another followed every thirty seconds until all thirty-eight transports, along with three B-17s loaded with ammunition and other supplies, were airborne. Once all forty-one planes were over the water, they assembled into formation and headed toward Noemfoor. Unknown to the men aboard the transports, General Patrick had radioed Alamo Force headquarters with specific instructions on the approach the C-47s should use at Kamiri. A Canadian paratroop officer attached to Patrick's headquarters had warned him that the condition of the runway was such that it would be dangerous for the paratroopers to drop on it from their normal two-plane, side-by-side formation. Instead, the C-47s should fly in single file so that the men aboard would have a better chance of landing in the center of the airstrip. Although Kamiri Airfield was 250 feet wide, the Canadian's inspection of the drop zone revealed that the sides of the strip were covered with wrecked Japanese aircraft, as well as bulldozers, trucks, and other heavy equipment used by the engineers. The presence of all this equipment narrowed the usable air-

strip to just one hundred feet. The Canadian was worried the men dropping from the sky faced serious injury and even death if they landed
among all the obstacles. For some unknown reason, Patrick's instructions, and the reason for them, never reached the pilots of the C-47s or
the regiment's commander, Lieutenant Colonel George M. Jones, who
was aboard the first aircraft in formation.[21]

Just about everything that could go wrong with an insertion of paratroopers into a war zone—with the exception of enemy action, of which
there was still none—did go wrong at Kamiri Airfield on July 3. First,
the C-47s approached the drop zone two abreast instead of single file
as General Patrick had requested. This alone guaranteed at least some
of the paratroopers would land amid the equipment and debris on the
sides of the landing strip. This failure was compounded when the pilot
of the lead plane, carrying Colonel Jones, forgot to reset his craft's
altimeter from sea level to ground level, leading to his approaching at
an altitude of about 150 feet, far below the minimum 400 feet required
for the parachutes to open and the troopers to land safely. When the
green jump light signaled the men to go, they leaped out of the plane
without realizing how close to the ground they were. The following
C-47s had locked onto the first aircraft and approached the same way,
but the pilots of a few farther back realized the error and quickly
attempted to increase their altitude before the jumpers went out.

Once out of the aircraft, the parachutes had only a few seconds to
deploy before the troopers hit the ground harder than they should
have. As a result, they smashed onto the crushed and compacted coral
surface. Others crashed into various pieces of heavy equipment, and
several landed in trees or on tree stumps. Of 739 paratroopers who
jumped that morning, 72 officers and men were injured, many with
serious bone fractures, including broken ankles and legs. Colonel Jones
very nearly suffered a serious head injury, but was saved by his steel
helmet. He would complain of a throbbing headache for eight days
after. The battalion's commander, Major Cameron Know, suffered a
broken foot. The 1st Battalion of the 503rd PIR suffered a ten percent
casualty rate before ever encountering an enemy soldier.[22]

The injured soldiers received minimal first aid at the strip. Instead, they were taken to aid stations on the beach and eventually boarded ships for Finschhafen, where breaks and fractures were repaired. Some of these men would never be able to jump again. Despite his throbbing head, Jones reported to Patrick and received orders to relieve the infantrymen guarding the airstrip. By midafternoon, the 2nd Battalion of the 158th RCT had turned over defense of Kamiri Airfield to the paratroopers, who quickly established their own defense perimeter.[23]

On July 4, the 3rd Battalion was dropped onto Kamiri Airfield. By then, General Patrick had the construction equipment used to repair the landing strip moved as far away as possible, and the wrecked Japanese planes dragged off. This time, the C-47s came in at four hundred feet and in single file before the jump light turned green. The lucky jumpers managed to land in the sand along the sides of the runway, now cleared of vehicles. The unlucky ones landed on the crushed coral of the runway, which proved as hard as concrete. This time, 8 percent of the men suffered injuries that removed them from duty. By now, Colonel Jones had had enough of his troopers being injured, and prevailed on General Patrick to bring the 2nd Battalion to Noemfoor by ship. It arrived a few days later with no serious injuries.[24]

Once security for the Kamiri Airfield was in the hands of the paratroopers, Patrick resumed his advance across the island, with his focus on capturing the two other airfields. At about five a.m. on July 4, soldiers from the 1st Battalion of the 158th RCT forded the nearby Kamiri River and were attacked while crossing a small hill by three Japanese companies. The fighting lasted for several hours until the enemy withdrew, leaving behind the bodies of 201 comrades. The Americans suffered only two wounded. The Americans would henceforth know the place where the battle occurred as "Hill 201."

On the same day, the 3rd Battalion's troops moved east along the coastal road toward Kornasoren Airfield. Although they saw numerous signs of enemy activity in the area, including minefields and fixed defensive positions, they found no Japanese soldiers. They occupied the airfield without opposition, set up a perimeter defense, and began patrolling the area the following day, after calling in the engineers to work on the landing strip.[25]

Next, General Patrick turned his attention to Namber Airfield, along the island's west coast. Concerned about the location of the still substantial Japanese force on Noemfoor, Patrick decided against sending his 2nd Battalion, having been relieved of perimeter defense duty by the paratroopers, up the coast road to seize the airfield. Instead, he had them board landing craft and—escorted by three destroyers, an LCI rocket vessel, and six B-25s—on July 6, they landed on the coast and took control of the airfield with no enemy opposition. They had the airstrip ready to receive Allied aircraft within hours. One can only assume that Colonel Shimizu, the island's Japanese commander, had decided that since he did not have any aircraft, and the chances of Imperial Army or Navy airplanes coming to his rescue were nonexistent, he saw no reason to expend his force defending landing strips for which he had no use.[26]

Throughout the area occupied by the Americans, enemy activity was confined to a few stragglers who wanted to die for their emperor, or conversely, decided they were so hungry they just surrendered. On July 11, Patrick, aware that there remained some enemy force hidden in the jungle, divided Noemfoor into two sectors. The 158th RCT was to patrol and engage in mopping-up operations in the southern half of the island, while the 503rd PIR did the same in the northern half.

With the island being searched by, and mostly under the control of, friendly Americans, the native population emerged from hiding places in the jungle. Some waved Dutch flags to signal the Americans. With the help of Dutch civil authorities, they were resettled into their coastal villages, protected by American troops. In late July, the village chiefs called a meeting at which they declared war on Japan and began actively seeking out Japanese soldiers, who were either killed or captured and turned over to the Americans. By the end of August, they had taken fifty enemy soldiers prisoner and killed a similar number.[27]

Meanwhile, soldiers from both American regiments continued their search for the remaining Japanese on the island. Following a series of skirmishes, paratroopers discovered an enemy force hidden near a map location called "Hill 670." On July 16, the 1st Battalion of the PIR attacked the hill, killing 116 Japanese and seizing the high ground. The rest of the enemy, an unknown number, melted away into the jungle. Throughout the next weeks, the diminishing enemy force attempted to find a safe haven, but it was not to be. During the middle of August, patrolling Americans found clear signs that the enemy had turned to cannibalizing their own dead as well as slave laborers and even a few Americans.

Despite the fact that Colonel Shimizu and a handful of his men, probably his personal bodyguard, were never found, General Krueger declared the Noemfoor operation over on August 31, 1944. The American forces had suffered 63 men killed, 343 wounded, and 3 reported missing; Japanese deaths exceeded 1,700, and 180 were taken prisoner.

MacArthur's decision to invade and capture Noemfoor had two goals. One was to eliminate the small island as a staging area for Japanese troops being transferred from the large enemy base at Manokwari on New Guinea to reinforce the defenders on Biak. The second was to activate the enemy-built airfields for use by General Kenney's bombers and fighters as the Allies moved west along the Vogelkop Peninsula and even across the sea to the Philippines. Achieving the first was simple. With the Americans in control of Noemfoor, not only did the transfers to Biak halt, but also troops began to move out of this now clearly vulnerable base farther west to Sorong.

As for the three airfields, aviation engineers decided to abandon the idea of using Namber when they discovered it was badly graded and the base soil too rough. Kamiri, on which work began the day after it was captured, received its first aircraft, a squadron of Australian P-40 fighters, on July 6. The jewel of the three fields was Kornasoren. Australian group captain William Dale, the engineer in charge of construction, put every engineer and work party, including combat soldiers and native laborers on the island and nearby ships, to work twenty-four hours a day at what quickly became two seven-thousand-foot runways, complete with dispersal areas. The massive effort was able to meet MacArthur's instructions that Kornasoren be able to accommodate fifty P-38s by July 25. American B-24 Liberator heavy bombers soon arrived and began the first bombing attacks against Japanese petroleum-producing facilities on Borneo.[28]

The speed and low cost in casualties of the Noemfoor operation, as well as quick airfield construction, earned General Patrick, who personally oversaw everything, a commendation from MacArthur as well as an Oak Leaf Cluster of the Legion of Merit. On Krueger's recommendation, the "Green Hornet" was soon appointed commanding officer of the 6th Infantry Division.[29]

General MacArthur's final target in the conquest of New Guinea was the Vogelkop Peninsula and several of its offshore islands. If his engineers could find locations to build airfields, he could neutralize the large Japanese forces at Manokwari and Sorong, and even reach across the sea to the southern end of the Philippines, his ultimate objective.

There was some talk and even early planning at MacArthur's headquarters for an amphibious assault on one of the two Japanese bases on the peninsula. The problem was, the enemy was believed to have some fifteen thousand combat and service troops at Manokwari on the peninsula's east end, and seventeen thousand at Sorong on the western end. The commander in chief was unwilling to attack such well-defended locations. Relying instead on his "hit them where they ain't" theory of conquering the Japanese, he decided to find a place between the two bases that might be suitable for the building of a major airfield and possibly even a naval base. Using air reconnaissance photos, he focused his attention on two small coastal villages, Sansapor and Mar, located roughly halfway between the two large bases. In order to make a final decision, his planners needed to know much more about these two villages and the area around them than could be learned from photos. On June 23, a U.S. Navy submarine put a scouting party ashore near Mar. The group included members of the Alamo Scouts, Fifth Air Force terrain experts, hydrographic experts from the Seventh Amphibious Force, and Allied Intelligence Bureau agents.

After a week of scouting the area, the men reported there were good beaches for use by amphibious landing forces, and there were good locations on the coastal plane for the construction of airfields. They also reported that the nearest Japanese, no more than one hundred troops, were at a small barge station at Sansapor. That was all MacArthur needed to know. He ordered General Krueger to prepare his Sixth Army for a landing near Mar on July 30. Air Force and Naval headquarters received instructions to plan to support the landings.[30]

Operation Globetrotter, as it was called, took place right on schedule, on July 30, 1944. Major General Franklin C. Sibert, commanding officer of the 6th Infantry Division, was chosen to command the 7,300 troops who made simultaneous landings a few miles east of Mar, as well as on two islands, Middelburg and Amsterdam, directly offshore. The following day, a battalion landed a Sansapor just as the Japanese troops stationed there fled into the jungle. Each landing began at seven a.m. and took about two hours to complete. There was no opposition, and there were no Japanese soldiers to be seen.

Because airfield construction was the main objective of the landings, the 7,300-man invasion force had an unusually high percentage of service troops, especially engineers. Work began on airfields almost immediately. By August 17, a new landing strip on Middelburg Island was ready for fighters. On September 3, a six-thousand-foot steel-mat runway near Mar was reported ready to receive medium bombers. Construction was also completed on 2,800 feet of taxiways, and seven dispersal lanes. Too small for an airfield, Amsterdam Island became home to a PT boat base and a flying boat base, and Sansapor Point, just east of the village of Sansapor, housed a new air warning radar station. Patrols periodically engaged small numbers of Japanese, killing some and taking others prisoner.

The first Japanese air reaction to the landings did not take place until August 27. In the weeks before the landings, the Fifth Air Force, aided by Dutch and Australian aircraft, had neutralized most of the enemy airfields throughout the peninsula. Three enemy planes made a night raid in the Mar area, but caused little damage.

The airfield at Mar was soon home to the 347th Fighter Group and the 419th Night Fighter Squadron. The 418th Night Fighter Squadron and 18th Fighter Group were based at Middelburg. These airfields helped further isolate the large enemy forces at Manokwari and Sorong, leaving them little to do but attempt to survive.[31]

When Operation Globetrotter was officially declared over, fourteen Americans had died, several from scrub typhus, and thirty-five had been wounded. Enemy dead were estimated at 385, while 215 had surrendered.[32]

The occupation of the Mar-Sansapor area marked the end of MacArthur's offensive operations in New Guinea, a campaign that had spanned nearly three years and fifteen hundred miles. From Milne Bay at the east end of New Guinea to Sansapor at the west end, the Allies killed an estimated fifty thousand Japanese, and left nearly two hundred thousand more isolated and starving in their fortified defensive positions. MacArthur's "hit them where they ain't" policy resulted in fewer Americans being killed throughout the New Guinea campaign than died during the battle for tiny Iwo Jima in the central Pacific. Yet he had one more stop to make before heading to the Philippines: the island of Morotai.

Halfway between Sansapor and the southernmost territory of the Philippines are a group of several hundred islands named the Maluku Islands. During the sixteenth and seventeenth centuries, Dutch, Spanish, and Portuguese traders had called them the Spice Islands because they produced large quantities of nutmeg, mace, clove, and other spices. The largest of these islands was Halmahera, while the most northern, and closest to the Philippines, was Morotai. General MacArthur required one more island from which his aircraft could reach the Philippines and provide land-based air support for his planned invasion of Mindanao, which he had tentatively scheduled for November 15.

Halmahera was MacArthur's first selection, based on its location and the nine airfields the enemy had constructed there. That changed when intelligence reports estimated that at least thirty thousand Japanese

combat troops of the 32nd Infantry Division, supported by a large number of service troops, defended the seven-thousand-square-mile island.
Another drawback was that reconnaissance indicated that there were
only a few beaches to serve as landing zones, and all appeared to be well
defended by strong enemy fortifications.

Just six miles northeast of Halmahera was Morotai, a much more
attractive target that intelligence analysts believed contained fewer than
a thousand enemy soldiers. The actual number turned out to be closer
to five hundred. Less than seven hundred square miles in area, Morotai, like most islands in the New Guinea area, was blanketed in heavy
forests and had a rugged, mountainous interior. A special attraction to
the commander in chief was the single airfield the Japanese had built
on the Doroeba Plain, a large tract of relatively flat territory on the
island's southeast coast. Japanese engineers had abandoned the airfield
because they found the soil throughout the area too soft to support
aircraft operations.

The Morotai defenses were the responsibility of the 2nd Raiding Unit,
a commando force composed mostly of Formosan soldiers under Japanese officers. The unit's commander was Major Takenobu Kawashima,
who along with most of his officers had been trained at the Imperial
Army's Nakano School, which was used to develop intelligence and guerrilla warfare specialists. Since arriving on Morotai in late July, Kawashima,
who suspected the Allies might invade his little island along with the
larger target, Halmahera, had constructed a series of dummy gun positions and empty campsites at which he had fires lit at night, as if Japanese
soldiers occupied them.[33]

MacArthur informed Krueger that his next target was Morotai, and
set September 15 as the D-Day. Krueger selected Major General Charles
P. Hall, then at Aitape, to head up what he called the Tradewind Task Force,
with overall responsibility for the operation. Nearly sixty one thousand
troops were assembled for the task force. Approximately forty thousand
were combat troops from Major General John C. Persons's 31st Infantry
Division, and the 126th Regimental Combat Team from the 32nd Division. Supporting these were American and Australian air force personnel

assigned mainly to quickly build an airfield on the island as the combat units moved forward. The 6th Infantry Division, stationed at Sansapor, was designated as a reserve in case additional troops were required.[34]

Admiral Barbey's Seventh Amphibious Force picked up most of the 31st Division, less the 124th Regiment that was at Aitape, at Maffin Bay. The 124th loaded aboard the ships at Aitape and headed to Wakde Island, where it rehearsed the planned landings on September 6. Once the training was completed, the ships of Task Force 77 assembled and headed to Morotai. This fleet, commanded by Admiral Barbey, numbered over a hundred ships. Escorting the troop-carrying convoy was a support group of eight Australian and American cruisers and ten destroyers. Escort carriers and destroyer escorts searching for enemy submarines offered an outer ring of protection. Overhead, American and Australian aircraft flew wide-ranging patrols. The entire trip to Morotai went off without a hitch.[35]

Rear Admiral Russell S. Berkey commanded the support group aboard his cruiser *Phoenix*. Also aboard was General MacArthur, who made it clear he was not in command of the invasion, just along as an observer.

To reduce enemy air action against the landings, Allied aircraft bombed and strafed Japanese airfields on Halmahera and other nearby islands, reportedly destroying several hundred aircraft while most were still on the ground. No bombing raids were made on Morotai. In fact, Morotai suffered no attacks until the morning of the landings, when destroyers bombarded the Gila Peninsula, a long finger of land sticking out of the south coast of the island a short distance from the abandoned airfield. Several of General Kenney's bombers joined in, including some that dumped DDT behind the beaches to eliminate mosquitoes and other insects carrying malaria and scrub typhus, diseases that had caused a high casualty rate in the Sansapor-Mar landing areas.[36]

Aside from some accidents caused by large areas of dead coral covered in slime, beginning on the morning of September 15, the landings at two beach sites went off with only a few major problems. Engineers found the beaches too muddy for heavy equipment, and coral ridges

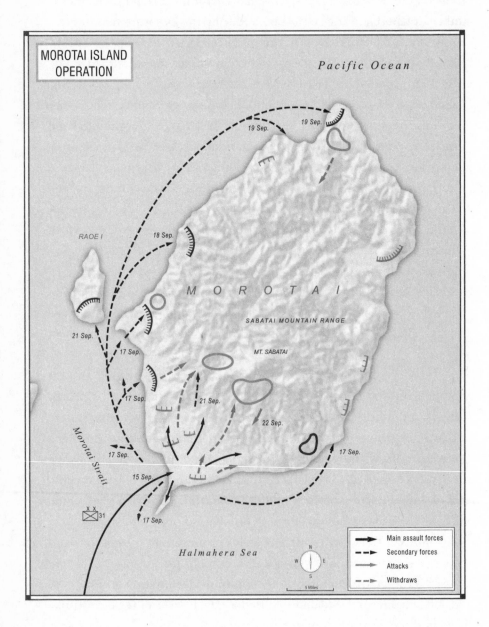

MOROTAI ISLAND
OPERATION

Pacific Ocean

19 Sep.

19 Sep.

RAOE I

18 Sep.

M O R O T A I

SABATAI MOUNTAIN RANGE

21 Sep.

17 Sep.

MT. SABATAI

17 Sep.

21 Sep.

22 Sep.

17 Sep.

17 Sep.

Morotai Strait

15 Sep.

17 Sep.

XX 31

Halmahera Sea

N
W   E
S

5 Miles

Main assault forces
Secondary forces
Attacks
Withdraws

just below the sea surface made it difficult for many of the landing craft to even approach the beaches. The coral reef grew clogged with vehicles and craft whose engines had been drowned in the four feet of surf or simply could not climb over the ridge. As a result, soldiers discharged at the reef had to wade through chest-high water to reach the muddy beaches. A survey party found a more acceptable beach less than a mile away, and it became the primary unloading site the next day.[37]

The men struggling to get to shore were fortunate that no Japanese snipers were lying in wait. In fact, the few enemy troops stationed near the landing beaches fled as soon as they saw the size of the invading force.

Sporadic small-unit fighting continued on Morotai for some time, but the Japanese on Halmahera were never able to reinforce the island's small garrison as Allied aircraft and PT boats blocked the Halmahera Strait between the two islands. American and Australian engineers ignored the partially built Japanese airfield and, as soon as the combat troops established a defensive perimeter around the Doroeba Plain, began construction on what would eventually be three airfields. The Wawama Airfield received fighters on October 4, and heavy bombers on October 19. Soon after, a flying boat anchorage and a PT boat base were operating.

The invasion of Morotai cost thirty-one American lives, along with eighty-five wounded. Enemy dead, those who could be found and counted, were 117, and another 200 are believed to have perished when the barge they were using to evacuate the island was attacked and sunk by PT boats.[38]

When MacArthur's troops landed on the Philippine island of Leyte on October 25, 1944, the airfields on Morotai would be the closest in Allied hands and able to contribute land-based bombers and fighter escorts to the invading forces.

Shortly after one p.m., following the successful landings on Morotai, the *Phoenix* headed south to MacArthur's headquarters at Hollandia, where he resumed planning his invasion of the Philippines and the fulfillment of his promise to return. Before leaving Morotai, however, the commander in chief had one final act to perform.

Less than two hours after the initial landings, MacArthur went ashore with a small party that included Admiral Barbey. From some fifty yards offshore, the general and his group waded through treacherous water up to their waists to reach the muddy beach.[39]

Once ashore, they met briefly with General Persons. Then MacArthur did something he always enjoyed: he stopped to chat with soldiers. An Australian journalist accompanying the party reported that he congratulated his men on a job well done. It is widely recounted that at one point, while standing on the beach with some officers, he suddenly stopped talking and looked off to the north, where the nearest of the Philippine islands lay less than three hundred miles away. "They are waiting for me there," he said quietly. "It has been a long time."[40]

EPILOGUE

General MacArthur considered the Philippines part of the United States, and as such, he believed Americans and Filipinos together should liberate the country. He broke this news to General Blamey on July 12, 1944, explaining that on November 1 Australian forces were to take full responsibility for military operations throughout New Guinea and New Britain, excluding the Admiralties, which the U.S. Navy now controlled. By then, American forces, without Australians, would be substantially out of New Guinea and engaged in fighting in the Philippines. This news disappointed Blamey, who had expected that at least two of his Australian divisions would go to the Philippines with the Americans.[1]

MacArthur expressed his view of the future of the Japanese forces he had bypassed and isolated on New Guinea and New Britain when he responded to a related question from General Marshall. He told the Army chief that the isolated enemy troops did not present a threat to existing operations or threaten those to come. He was confident that their ability to undertake successful operations was negligible. For the Allies to initiate offensives against them would "involve heavy loss of life," and those Japanese troops should be left alone to eke out their food supplies until the war ended.[2]

With the Americans' exit from the New Guinea area almost complete, General Blamey was in a difficult situation. He was struggling with some members of the Australian parliament who felt that since MacArthur had moved on to the Philippines and Australia was no longer directly threatened, the war was nearly over for Australia and it was time to reduce the size and cost of her army. Instead, Australian forces started offensive operations against the trapped enemy troops in New Guinea, in what some Australian politicians called "unnecessarily aggressive operations."[3]

In December 1944, the Australian II Corps attacked the Japanese concentrations on Bougainville. In February the Australian 6th Division launched a campaign against General Adachi's Eighteenth Army around Wewak, while the 5th Division developed a perimeter across the neck of the Gazelle Peninsula, further isolating Rabaul from the rest of New Britain. Following Emperor Hirohito's announcement on August 15, 1945, instructing his forces to lay down their arms, and the formal surrender signing ceremony on board the USS *Missouri* in Tokyo Bay on September 2, 1945, the bypassed garrisons each surrendered in turn.

On September 6, the Imperial Army and Navy forces at Rabaul, represented by Lieutenant General Hitoshi Imamura and Vice Admiral Jinichi Kusaka, surrendered to Lieutenant General V. A. H. Sturdee, commanding officer of the First Australian Army. The ceremony took place aboard the Royal Navy carrier HMS *Glory*. Three days later, General Blamey accepted the surrender of Lieutenant General Fusataro Teshima, commander of the 126,000 men of the Japanese Second Army. That event took place on Morotai Island. Lieutenant General Hatazo Adachi surrendered the thirteen thousand surviving soldiers of his Eighteenth Army to Major General H. Robinson, commanding officer of the Sixth Australian Army, at a small airstrip on September 13. Similar smaller ceremonies took place at Japanese outposts throughout the South Pacific and southwest Pacific until October 1, 1945.

The war in New Guinea took the lives of slightly more than two hundred thousand Japanese soldiers, sailors, and aviators. The United States and Australia each lost approximately seven thousand members of their military forces.

President Roosevelt's decision, prompted by Churchill and Australian prime minister John Curtin, to send MacArthur to Australia in command of all Allied forces in the theater gave him the win he and the American people so desperately wanted: victory over the nation that attacked Pearl Harbor. Could another American general have achieved the same result at so little cost in lives?

Assessing MacArthur's leadership, Lieutenant General Ryozo Sakuma, chief of staff of the Imperial Second Army, said, "I think that they were excellent tactics. I say this without prejudice. If any other plans had been used, the Americans would have had a very difficult time."[4]

On October 16, 1944, more than seven hundred vessels of all sizes sailed from the New Guinea coast and headed northwest. Their objective was the waters around Leyte Island in the Philippines, thirteen hundred miles away. One of the warships in the vast armada was the cruiser *Nashville*, with the commander in chief aboard. Douglas MacArthur was going home. A dozen battleships, nearly two dozen aircraft carriers, and almost one hundred cruisers and destroyers surrounded and protected a huge array of assault vessels carrying more than 150,000 men whose assignment was to liberate the Philippines. Overhead, nearly one thousand aircraft flew in wide-ranging patrols, watching for enemy ships and submarines. One historian contrasts the fleet to the cross-channel invasion of Normandy the previous June, calling the latter a ferry operation by comparison.[5]

On October 18, two days before the planned invasion—MacArthur called it A-Day to distinguish it from the D-Day at Normandy—six U.S. Navy battleships passed into Leyte Gulf under the command of Rear Admiral Jesse Oldendorf and began shelling Japanese shore installations.

At ten a.m. on October 20, the first wave of four U.S. Army divisions— all part of General Walter Krueger's Sixth Army—began hitting the beaches of Leyte along a ten-mile-wide front. MacArthur watched anxiously through his field glasses as soldiers and supplies pushed inland against less enemy resistance than he had expected. Finally, at one p.m. he had had enough waiting. He left the *Nashville*'s bridge, rounded up several of his staff, and ordered a landing craft to take them to the beach. Unable to get close enough to shore due to the number of craft unloading troops, supplies, and equipment, the commander in chief climbed out of the craft, dropped into nearly knee-deep water and trudged to the beach.[6]

A few minutes before two p.m. MacArthur stepped up to a group of microphones that would broadcast his message across the Philippines and eventually around the world. "People of the Philippines," he began, "I have returned. By the grace of Almighty God our forces stand again on Philippine soil—soil consecrated in the blood of our two peoples." He then asked the island nation's population to rally to him and use every opportunity to strike against their common enemy.[7]

Months of fierce fighting lay ahead before the Japanese forces surrendered, prompted only by the atomic bombing of two Japanese cities and the emperor's decision to stop the destruction. As Supreme Commander for the Allied Powers, MacArthur accepted the Japanese surrender aboard the battleship *Missouri* on September 2, 1945. He then went on to administer Japan and transform it into a modern, Western-style democracy.

ACKNOWLEDGMENTS

In his recent book, *A Disease in the Public Mind,* noted author and historian Thomas Fleming wrote, "My favorite metaphor for writing a history book is the image of an author standing on the shoulders of dozens of previous scholars." For me, this is especially true with the writing of this book. I am in debt to a number of historians who have written or researched various aspects of the war in New Guinea. These include, especially, Peter Williams in Australia, whose book *The Kokoda Campaign 1942: Myth and Reality* was an invaluable source, as was his help and advice; and Bruce Gamble, an American author who has written extensively about the Japanese invasion of Rabaul and its later recapture by the Allies, who also provided valuable assistance.

I owe a special thank-you to James W. Zobel of the MacArthur Memorial in Norfolk, Virginia, for his kindness and generosity. Also a thank-you to Lance Zedric, historian of the Alamo Scouts Historical Foundation, for his expertise.

Several people helped with the writing and editing over the past several years, including my wife, Kathy; my daughters, Alexandra and Olivia; and my close friend Michele Del Monte. Roger Labrie read and commented on the entire manuscript with professional expertise and understanding. Thanks to you all.

My appreciation goes to my agent, Deborah Grosvenor, who liked the idea for this book the moment we discussed it and kept after me to write it. Finally, thanks to my editor, Brent Howard, who saw the value of this project and wanted to publish it, and had the patience to allow me the extra time I needed to complete it. His contribution to improving the manuscript in many ways earned my lasting respect. To the many people who helped along the way but whose names do not appear above, please once again accept my gratitude for your assistance and my apology for the absence of your name.

BIBLIOGRAPHY

OFFICIAL HISTORIES

Australian Government Documents and Publications

Brown, Gary, and David Anderson. *Invasion 1942: Australia and the Japanese Threat.* Canberra: Parliamentary Research Service, 1992.

Bullard, Steven, trans. *Japanese Army Operations in the South Pacific Area: New Britain and Papua Campaigns, 1942–1943.* Canberra: Australian War Memorial, 2007.

Dexter, David. *The New Guinea Offensives.* Canberra: Australian War Memorial, 1961.

Gill, G. Hermon. *Royal Australian Navy 1939–1942.* Canberra: Australian War Memorial, 1957.

Gillison, Douglas. *Royal Australian Air Force 1939–1942.* Canberra: Australian War Memorial, 1964.

Long, Gavin Merrick. *Australia in the War of 1939–1945.* Canberra: Australian War Memorial, 1963.

McCarthy, Dudley, *Australia in the War of 1939–1945.* Vol. 5, *South-West Pacific Area—First Year.* Canberra: Australian War Memorial, 1959.

Yoshihara, Lt. Gen. Kane. *Southern Cross: Memories of the War in Eastern New Guinea.* Translated by Doris Heath. Canberra, Australia: Australian War Memorial, Manuscript MSS0725, 1955.

U.S. Government Documents and Publications

Beckman, Kyle B., LCDR, USN. *Personality and Strategy.* Fort Leavenworth, KS: U.S. Army Command and General Staff College, 2002.

Casey, Major General Hugh J. *Amphibian Engineer Operations.* Washington, D.C.: Office of the Chief Engineer, 1959.

————. *Engineer Memoirs*. Washington D.C.: U.S. Army Corps of Engineers, 1993.

Coakley, Robert W. *World War II: The War Against Japan*. Washington, D.C.: Center for Military History, United States Army, 1989.

Dod, Karl C. *Technical Services, the Corps of Engineers, the War Against Japan*. Washington, D.C.: Department of the Army, 1966.

Drea, Dr. Edward J. *Defending the Driniumor: Covering Force Operations in New Guinea, 1944*. Fort Leavenworth, KS: Combat Studies Institute, 1984.

Fowle, Barry W. *Builders and Fighters: U.S. Army Engineers in World War II*. Washington, D.C.: Office of History, U.S. Army Corps of Engineers, 1992.

Frierson, Maj. William C. *The Admiralties: Operations of the 1st Cavalry Division (29 February–18 May, 1944)*. Washington, D.C.: Center for Military History, U.S. Army, 1990.

Hough, Lt. Col. Frank O., and Major John A. Crown. *The Campaign on New Britain*. Washington, D.C.: U.S. Government Printing Office, 1952.

Maneki, Sharon A. *The Quiet Heroes of the Southwest Pacific Theater*. Washington, D.C.: National Security Agency, 2007.

Milner, Samuel. *U.S. Army in World War II: Victory in Papua—The War in the Pacific*. Harrisburg, PA: National Historical Society, 1993.

Morton, Louis. *The War in the Pacific: Strategy and Command: The First Two Years*. Washington, D.C.: Office of the Chief of Military History, Department of the Army, 1962.

Papuan Campaign: The Buna-Sanananda Operation, 16 November 1942–23 January 1943. Washington, D.C.: U.S. Government Printing Office, 1989.

Parker, Frederick D. *A Priceless Advantage: U.S. Navy Communications Intelligence and the Battles of Coral Sea, Midway, and the Aleutians*. Washington, D.C.: National Security Agency, 1993.

Reports of General MacArthur: The Campaigns of MacArthur in the Pacific. Vol. 1, Prepared by his General Staff, Washington, D.C.: 1950.

Reports of General MacArthur: Japanese Operations in the Southwest Pacific Area. Vol. 2, Compiled from Japanese Demobilization Bureau Records, Washington, D.C., 1950.

Shaw, Henry I., and Major Douglas T. Kane. *History of U.S. Marine Corps Operations in World War II*. Vol. 2. Washington, D.C.: Historical Division, U.S. Marine Corps, 1963.

Smith, Robert Ross. *The Approach to the Philippines: The War in the Pacific*. Harrisburg, PA: National Historical Society, 1994.

Vego, Milan. "The Port Moresby–Solomons Campaign and the Allied Reaction, 27 April–11 May 1942." *Naval War College Review* 65 (1) (Winter 2012).

Wigmore, Lionel. *The Japanese Thrust*. Canberra, Australia: Australian War Memorial, 1957.

PUBLISHED WORKS

Alexander, Larry. *Shadows in the Jungle: The Alamo Scouts Behind Japanese Lines in World War II*. New York: NAL Caliber, 2009.

Alexander, Joseph H. *Storm Landings: Epic Amphibious Battles in the Central Pacific*. Annapolis: Naval Institute Press, 2009.

Ambrose, Stephen. *Eisenhower: Soldier, General of the Army, President-Elect*. Vol. 1. New York: Simon & Schuster, 1983.

Aplin, Douglas. *Rabaul 1942*. Melbourne: 2/22 Battalion A.I.F. Lark Force Association, 1980.

Archer, Jules. *Front-Line General: Douglas MacArthur*. New York: Julian Messner, 1963.

———. *Jungle Fighters: A G.I. War Correspondent's Experiences in the New Guinea Campaign*. New York: Julian Messner, 1985.

Arnold, H. H. *Global Mission*. New York: Harper & Brothers, 1949.

Astor, Gerald. *Crises in the Pacific*. New York: Donald I. Fine Books, 1996.

Barbey, Daniel E. *MacArthur's Amphibious Navy: Seventh Amphibious Force Operations 1943–1945*. Annapolis: United States Naval Institute, 1969.

Bentley, Caitlin T. *Disease and Destitution: Malaria and the Liberation of New Guinea and the Philippine Islands*. Research Thesis, Ohio State University, 2013.

Berg, A. Scott. *Lindbergh*. New York: G. P. Putnam's Sons, 1998.

Bergerud, Eric. *Touched with Fire: The Land War in the South Pacific*. New York: Penguin Books, 1996.

———. *Fire in the Sky: The Air War in the South Pacific*. Boulder, CO: Westview Press, 2000.

Bernstein, Marc D. *Hurricane at Biak: MacArthur Against the Japanese, May–August 1944*. Xlibris, 2000.

Black, Conrad. *Franklin Delano Roosevelt: Champion of Freedom*. New York: Public Affairs, 2003.

Black, David. *In His Own Words: John Curtin's Speeches and Writings*. Bentley, Australia: Paradigm Books, 1995.

Borneman, Walter R. *The Admirals: Nimitz, Halsey, Leahy, and King—The Five-Star Admirals Who Won the War at Sea*. New York: Little, Brown, 2012.

Bradley, John H. *The Second World War: Asia and the Pacific*. Wayne, NJ: Avery Publishing Group, 1989.

Bradley, Phillip. *The Battle for Wau: New Guinea's Frontline*. Port Melbourne, Australia: Cambridge University Press, 2008.

———. *To Salamaua*. Port Melbourne, Australia: Cambridge University Press, 2010.

Breuer, William B. *MacArthur's Undercover War: Spies, Saboteurs, Guerrillas, and Secret Missions*. New York: John Wiley & Sons, 1995.

Brooks, Victor. *Hell Is Upon Us: D-Day in the Pacific, June–August 1944*. New York: Da Capo, 2005.

Brune, Peter. *Those Ragged Bloody Heroes*. St. Leonards, Australia: Allen & Unwin, 1992.

———. *A Bastard of a Place: The Australians in Papua*. St. Leonards, Australia: Allen & Unwin, 2005.

Bulkley, Robert J. *At Close Quarters: PT Boats in the United States Navy*. Annapolis: Naval Institute Press, 2003.

Caidin, Martin, and Edward Hymoff. *The Mission*. Philadelphia: J. B. Lippincott Company, 1964.

Campbell, James. *The Ghost Mountain Boys: Their Epic March and the Terrifying Battle for New Guinea—The Forgotten War of the South Pacific*. New York: Three Rivers Press, 2007.

———. *The Color of War: How One Battle Broke Japan and Another Changed America*. New York: Crown, 2012.

Catanzaro, Francis B. *With the 41st Division in the Southwest Pacific*. Bloomington: Indiana University Press, 2002.

Collie, Craig, and Hajime Marutani. *The Path of Infinite Sorrow: The Japanese on the Kokoda Track*. Crows Nest, Australia: Allen & Unwin, 2009.

Collier, Peter, and David Horowitz. *The Roosevelts: An American Saga*. New York: Simon & Schuster, 1994.

Collingham, Lizzie. *The Taste of War: World War II and the Battle for Food*. New York: Penguin Press, 2012.

Connaughton, Richard. *MacArthur and Defeat in the Philippines*. New York: Overlook Press, 2001.

Cortesi, Lawrence. *The Deadly Skies*. New York: Zebra Books, 1982.

———. *Operation Cartwheel: The Final Countdown to V-J Day*. New York: Zebra Books, 1982.

———. *Pacific Hellfire*. New York: Zebra, 1983.

———. *Gateway to Victory*. New York: Zebra Books, 1984.

Costello, John. *The Pacific War 1941–1945*. New York: Harper Perennial, 2009.

Cowdrey, Albert E. *Fighting for Life: American Military Medicine in World War II*. New York: Free Press, 1994.

Coyne, Kevin. *Marching Home: To War and Back with the Men of One American Town*. New York: Viking, 2003.

Davis, Donald A. *Lightning Strike: The Secret Mission to Kill Admiral Yamamoto and Avenge Pearl Harbor*. New York: St. Martin's Press, 2005.

D'Este, Carlo. *Warlord: A Life of Winston Churchill at War, 1874–1945*. New York: HarperCollins, 2008.

Devlin, Gerard M. *Paratrooper!: The Saga of U.S. Army and Marine Parachute and Glider Combat Troops During World War II*. New York: St. Martin's Press, 1979.

Drea, Dr. Edward J. *MacArthur's ULTRA: Codebreaking and the War Against Japan, 1942–1945*. Lawrence: University Press of Kansas, 1992.

Drury, Bob, and Tom Clavin. *Halsey's Typhoon: The True Story of a Fighting Admiral, an Epic Storm, and an Untold Rescue*. New York: Atlantic Monthly Press, 2007.

Dull, Paul S. *A Battle History of the Imperial Japanese Navy (1941–1945)*. Annapolis: Naval Institute Press, 1978.

Egeberg, Roger Olaf. *The General: MacArthur and the Man He Called "Doc."* New York: Hippocrene Books, 1983.

Eichelberger, Robert L. *Our Jungle Road to Tokyo*. Nashville, TN: Battle Classics, 1989.

Ferrell, Robert H., ed. *The Eisenhower Diaries*. New York: W. W. Norton, 1981.

Feuer, A. B. *Coast Watching in World War II: Operations Against the Japanese on the Solomon Islands, 1941–43*. Mechanicsburg, PA: Stackpole Books, 2006.

Flynn, Errol. *My Wicked, Wicked Ways: The Autobiography of Errol Flynn*. New York: Cooper Square Press, 2002.

Frank, Richard B. *Guadalcanal: The Definitive Account of the Landmark Battle*. New York: Penguin Books, 1992.

———. *MacArthur*. New York: Palgrave Macmillan, 2007.

Frei, Henry P. *Japan's Southward Advance and Australia: From the Sixteenth Century to World War II*. Honolulu: University of Hawaii Press, 1991.

Fuchida, Mitsuo, and Masatake Okumiya. *Midway: The Battle That Doomed Japan*. Annapolis: Naval Institute Press, 1992.

Gailey, Harry A. *Bougainville 1943–1945: The Forgotten Campaign*. Lexington: University Press of Kentucky, 1991.

———. *MacArthur Strikes Back: Decision at Buna, New Guinea, 1942–1943*. Novato, CA: Presidio Press, 2000.

———. *MacArthur's Victory: The War in New Guinea, 1943–1944.* New York: Presidio Press Books, 2004.

Gamble, Bruce. *Fortress Rabaul: The Battle for the Southwest Pacific, January 1942–April 1943.* Minneapolis: Zenith Press, 2014.

———. *Invasion Rabaul: The Epic Story of Lark Force, the Forgotten Garrison, January–July 1942.* Minneapolis: Zenith Press, 2014.

General Staff, GHQ. *Reports of General MacArthur.* Vols. 1 and 2. Washington, D.C.: U.S. Army, 1966.

Gilbert, Martin. *Winston S. Churchill: Road to Victory 1941–1945.* Boston: Houghton Mifflin, 1986.

Greenfield, Kent Roberts. *Command Decisions.* New York: Harcourt, Brace and Company, 1959.

Griffith, Thomas E., Jr. *MacArthur's Airman.* Lawrence: University of Kansas Press, 1998.

Groom, Winston. *The Aviators: Eddie Rickenbacker, Jimmy Doolittle, Charles Lindbergh, and the Epic Age of Flight.* Washington, D.C.: National Geographic, 2013.

Guard, Harold. *The Pacific War Uncensored: A War Correspondent's Unvarnished Account of the Fight Against Japan.* Havertown, PA: Casemate Publishers, 2011.

Gunther, John. *The Riddle of MacArthur: Japan, Korea, and the Far East.* New York: Harper & Brothers, 1951.

Hall, Gwedolyn Midlo, ed. *Love, War and the 96th Engineers (Colored).* Urbana: University of Illinois Press, 1995.

Hall, Timothy. *New Guinea 1942–1944.* Sydney: Methuen Australia, 1981.

Harries, Meirion, and Susie Meirion. *Soldiers of the Sun: The Rise and Fall of the Imperial Japanese Army.* New York: Random House, 1991.

Harris, Brayton. *Admiral Nimitz: The Commander of the Pacific Ocean Theater.* New York: Palgrave Macmillan, 2012.

Hastings, Max. *Retribution: The Battle for Japan, 1944–1945.* New York: Alfred A. Knopf, 2008.

———. *Inferno: The World at War, 1939–1945.* New York: Alfred A. Knopf, 2011.

Heefner, Wilson A. *Twentieth Century Warrior: The Life and Service of Major General Edwin D. Patrick.* Shippensburg, PA: White Mane Publishing Company, Inc., 1995.

Henebry, John P. *The Grim Reapers: At Work in the Pacific Theater.* Missoula, MT: Pictorial Histories Publishing Company, Inc., 2002.

Hersey, John. *Men on Bataan.* New York: A. A. Knopf, 1943.

Holmes, W. J. *Double-Edged Secrets.* Annapolis: Naval Institute Press, 1979.

Holzimmer, Kevin C. *General Walter Krueger: Unsung Hero of the Pacific War.* Lawrence: University Press of Kansas, 2007.

Hough, Richard. *The Longest Battle: The War at Sea, 1939–45.* New York: William Morrow, 1986.

Howarth, Stephen. *Morning Glory: The Story of the Imperial Japanese Navy.* London: Arrow, 1985.

Hoyt, Edwin P. *Blue Skies and Blood.* New York: Paul S. Erickson, Inc., 1975.

———. *MacArthur's Navy: The Seventh Fleet and the Battle for the Philippines.* New York: Orion Books, 1989.

Huff, Sid. *My Fifteen Years with General MacArthur.* New York: Paperback Library, 1964.

Hunt, Frazier. *The Untold Story of Douglas MacArthur.* New York: Devin-Adair Co., 1954.

Hutchinson, Garrie. *Pilgrimage: A Traveller's Guide to Australia's Battlefields.* Melbourne: Black, Inc., 2006.

Ienaga, Saburo. *The Pacific War, 1931–1945: A Critical Perspective on Japan's Role in World War II.* New York: Pantheon, 1978.

Ito, Masanori, and Roger Pineau. *The End of the Imperial Japanese Navy.* New York: McFadden Books, 1965.

James, D. Clayton. *The Years of MacArthur.* Vol. 1, *1880–1941.* Boston: Houghton Mifflin Company, 1970.

———. *The Years of MacArthur.* Vol. 2, *1941–1945.* Boston: Houghton Mifflin Company, 1975.

James, D. Clayton, and Anne Sharp Wells. *From Pearl Harbor to V-J Day: The American Armed Forces in World War II.* Chicago: Ivan R. Dee, 1995.

Johnson, Forrest Bryant. *Phantom Warrior: The Heroic True Story of Pvt. John McKinney's One-Man Stand Against the Japanese in World War II.* New York: Berkley Caliber, 2007.

Johnston, George. *War Diary 1942.* Sydney, Australia: William Collins Pty. Ltd., 1984.

Johnston, George H. *The Toughest Fighting in the World: The Australian and American Campaign for New Guinea in World War II.* Yardley, PA: Westholme Publishing, 2011.

Johnston, Stanley. *Queen of the Flat-Tops.* Garden City, NY: Nelson Doubleday, Inc., 1979.

Kahn, E. J., Jr. *G.I. Jungle: An American Soldier in Australia and New Guinea.* New York: Simon & Schuster, 1943.

Kenimer, Harkness. *General MacArthur at Port Moresby.* Atlanta, GA: Harkness Kenimer, 1997.

Kennedy, Paul. *Engineers of Victory: The Problem Solvers Who Turned the Tide in the Second World War.* New York: Random House, 2013.

Kenney, General George C. *General Kenney Reports.* New York: Duell, Sloan and Pearce, 1949.

———. *The MacArthur I Know.* New York: Duell, Sloan and Pearce, 1951.

Keogh, Eustace. *South West Pacific 1941–45.* Melbourne: Grayflower Publications, 1965.

Kidston, Martin J. *From Poplar to Papua: Montana's 163rd Infantry Regiment in World War II.* Helena, MT: Farcountry Press, 2004.

Lardner, John. *Southwest Passage: The Yanks in the Pacific.* New York: J. B. Lippincott, 1943.

Larrabee, Eric. *Commander in Chief: Franklin Delano Roosevelt, His Lieutenants, and Their War.* New York: Touchstone, 1987.

Layton, Rear Admiral Edwin T. *And I Was There.* New York: William Morrow & Co., 1985.

Leary, William M., ed. *We Shall Return! MacArthur's Commanders and the Defeat of Japan.* Lexington: University Press of Kentucky, 1988.

———. *MacArthur and the American Century: A Reader.* Lincoln: University of Nebraska Press, 2001.

Lee, Clark, and Richard Henschel. *Douglas MacArthur.* New York: Henry Holt, 1952.

Lewin, Ronald. *The American Magic.* New York: Farrar, Straus and Giroux, 1982.

Lindbergh, Charles A. *The Wartime Journals of Charles A. Lindbergh.* New York: Harcourt Brace Jovanovich, Inc., 1970.

Livingstone, Bob. *Under the Southern Cross: The B-24 Liberator in the South Pacific.* Nashville, TN: Turner Publishing, 1998.

Lord, Walter. *Incredible Victory.* New York: Harper & Row, 1967.

———. *Lonely Vigil: Coastwatchers of the Solomons.* New York: Viking Press, 1977.

Lovell, Mary S. *The Sound of Wings: The Life of Amelia Earhart.* New York: St. Martin's Press, 1989.

Lowe, James P. *Nadzab (1943): The First Successful Airborne Operation.* M.A. thesis, Louisiana State University, 2004.

Lundstrom, John B. *The First Team: Pacific Air Combat from Pearl Harbor to Midway.* Annapolis: Naval Institute Press, 1984.

———. *Black Shoe Carrier Admiral: Frank Jack Fletcher.* Annapolis: Naval Institute Press, 2006.

MacArthur, General Douglas. *Reminiscences.* New York: McGraw-Hill, 1964.

Manchester, William. *American Caesar: Douglas MacArthur 1880–1964*. Boston: Little, Brown, 1978.

———. *Goodbye, Darkness: A Memoir of the Pacific War*. Boston: Little, Brown, 1979.

Martin, Charles A. *The Last Great Ace: The Life of Major Thomas B. McGuire, Jr.* Fruit Cove, FL: Fruit Cove Publishing, 1998.

Mayo, Lida. *Bloody Buna*. Garden City, NY: Doubleday & Company, Inc., 1974.

McAulay, Lex. *Battle of the Bismarck Sea*. New York: St. Martin's Press, 1991.

———. *MacArthur's Eagles: The U.S. Air War over New Guinea, 1943–1944*. Annapolis: Naval Institute Press, 2005.

———. *We Who Are About to Die: The Story of John Lerew—A Hero of Rabaul 1942*. Queensland, Australia: Banner Books, 2007.

McEnery, Jim, and Bill Sloan. *Hell in the Pacific: A Marine Rifleman's Journey from Guadalcanal to Peleliu*. New York: Simon & Schuster, 2012.

Mercado, Stephen C. *The Shadow Warriors of Nakano: A History of the Imperial Japanese Army's Elite Intelligence School*. Lincoln, NE: Potomac Books, 2002.

Miller, John, Jr. *Cartwheel: The Reduction of Rabaul*. Harrisburg, PA: National Historical Society, 1993.

Miller, Merle. *Ike: The Soldier as They Knew Him*. New York: G. P. Putnam's Sons, 1987.

Morelock, Jerry, and Faculty Staff, Combat Studies Institute. *Studies in Battle Command*. N.p.: Military Bookshop, 2011.

Morgan, Ted. *FDR: A Biography*. New York: Simon & Schuster, 1985.

Morison, Samuel Eliot. *Breaking the Bismarcks Barrier July 1942–May 1944 (Vol. VI)* Edison, NJ: Castle Books, 2001.

———. *Coral Sea, Midway and Submarine Actions, May 1942–August 1942 (Vol. IV)*. Edison, NJ: Castle Books, 2001

———. *Leyte, June 1944–January 1945 (Vol. XII)*. Edison, NJ: Castle Books, 2001.

———. *New Guinea and the Marianas, March 1944–August 1944 (Vol. VIII)*. Edison, NJ: Castle Books, 2001.

———. *The Struggle for Guadalcanal, August 1942–February 1943 (Vol. V)*. Edison, NJ: Castle Books, 2001

Mosley, Leonard. *Marshall: A Hero for Our Time*. New York: Hearst Books, 1982.

Murphy, James T. *Skip Bombing*. Westport, CT: Praeger Publishers,1993.

Paull, Raymond. *Retreat from Kokoda: The Australian Campaign in New Guinea 1942*. Richmond, Australia: William Heinemann Australia, 1983.

Perret, Geoffrey. *Old Soldiers Never Die: The Life of Douglas MacArthur*. New York: Random House, 1996.

———. *There's a War to Be Won: The United States Army in World War II*. New York: Random House, 1991.

Perry, Mark. *The Most Dangerous Man in America: The Making of Douglas MacArthur*. New York: Basic Books, 2014.

Polsky, Andrew J. *Elusive Victories: The American Presidency at War*. New York: Oxford University Press, 2012.

Pogue, Forrest C. *George C. Marshall: Organizer of Victory 1943–1945*. New York: Viking Press, 1973.

Potter, E. B. *Nimitz*. Annapolis: Naval Institute Press, 1976.

Prados, John. *Islands of Destiny: The Solomons Campaign and the Eclipse of the Rising Sun*. New York: NAL Caliber, 2012.

Prange, Gordon W. *God's Samurai: Lead Pilot at Pearl Harbor*. Washington, D.C.: Brassey's, 1990.

Prefer, Nathan. *MacArthur's New Guinea Campaign*. Conshohocken, PA: Combined Books, Inc., 1995.

Ramsey, Edwin Price, and Stephen J. Rivele. *Lieutenant Ramsey's War*. New York: Knightsbridge Publishing Co., 1990.

Rems, Alan. *South Pacific Cauldron*. Annapolis: Naval Institute Press, 2014.

Renehan, Edward J., Jr. *The Lion's Pride*. New York: Oxford University Press, 1998.

Rickenbacker, Edward V. *Rickenbacker*. Englewood Cliffs, NJ: Prentice-Hall, 1967.

Riegelman, Harold. *Caves of Biak: An American Officer's Experiences in the Southwest Pacific*. New York: The Dial Press, 1955.

Roberts, Andrew. *Masters and Commanders: How Four Titans Won the War in the West, 1941–1945*. New York: HarperCollins, 2009.

Robinson, Pat. *The Fight for New Guinea: General Douglas MacArthur's First Offensive*. New York: Random House, 1943.

Roscoe, Theodore. *United States Destroyer Operations in World War Two*. Annapolis: Naval Institute Press, 1953.

Rothgeb, Wayne P. *New Guinea Skies*. Ames: Iowa State University Press, 1992.

Rottman, Gordon L. *Japanese Army in World War II: The South Pacific and New Guinea, 1942–43*. Oxford: Osprey Publishing, 2005.

———. *World War II Pacific Island Guide*. Westport, CT: Greenwood Press, 2001.

Ryan, Peter, ed. *The Encyclopedia of Papua and New Guinea*. Melbourne: Melbourne University Press, 1972.

Sakai, Saburo. *Samurai*. New York: Time-Life Books, 1990.

Salecker, Gene E. *Blossoming Silk Against the Rising Sun: U.S. and Japanese Paratroopers at War in the Pacific in World War II*. Mechanicsburg, PA: Stackpole Books, 2010.

————. *Fortress Against the Sun: The B-17 Flying Fortress in the Pacific.* New York: Da Capo Press, 2001.

————. *Rolling Thunder Against the Rising Sun: The Combat History of U.S. Army Tank Battalions in the Pacific in World War II.* Mechanicsburg, PA: Stackpole Books, 2008.

Sandler, Stanley. *World War II in the Pacific: An Encyclopedia.* New York: Garland Publishing Inc., 2001.

Schmitz, David F. *Henry L. Stimson: The First Wise Man.* Lanham, MD: Rowman & Littlefield, 2001.

Schweikart, Larry, and Dave Dougherty. *A Patriot's History of the Modern World.* Vol. 1, *From America's Exceptional Ascent to the Atomic Bomb: 1898–1945.* New York: Sentinel, 2012.

Selby, David. *Hell and High Fever.* Sydney: Currawong Publishing Co. Pty. Ltd., 1956.

Sherwood, Robert E. *Roosevelt and Hopkins: An Intimate History.* New York: Harper & Brothers, 1948.

Siegel, Craig. *Righteous Might: One Man's Journey Through War in the Pacific.* Portland, OR: Rochelle Publications, 2012.

Sloan, Bill. *Undefeated: America's Heroic Fight for Bataan and Corregidor.* New York: Simon & Schuster, 2012.

Smith, Michael. *The Emperor's Codes: The Breaking of Japan's Secret Ciphers.* New York: Penguin Books, 2002.

Smith, Rex Alan, and Gerald A. Meehl. *Pacific War Stories: In the Words of Those Who Survived.* New York: Abbeville Press, 2004.

Spector, Ronald H. *Eagle Against the Sun: The American War with Japan.* New York: The Free Press, 1985.

Steinberg, Rafael. *Island Fighting.* Alexandria, VA: Time-Life Books, 1978.

Stephenson, Michael, ed. *Battlegrounds: Geography and the History of Warfare.* Washington, D.C.: National Geographic, 2003.

Stimson, Henry L., and McGeorge Bundy. *On Active Service in Peace and War.* New York: Harper & Brothers, 1948.

Stoelb, Richard A. *Time in Hell.* Sheboygan Falls, WI: Sheboygan County Historical Research Center, 2012.

Taaffe, Stephen R. *MacArthur's Jungle War: The 1944 New Guinea Campaign.* Lawrence: University Press of Kansas, 1998.

Taylor, Jay. *The Generalissimo.* Cambridge, MA: Harvard University Press, 2009.

Thienel, Phillip M. "Engineers in the Union Army, 1861–1865." *Military Engineer.* March/April 1955.

Thomas, Evan. *Sea of Thunder: Four Commanders and the Last Great Naval Campaign 1941–1945*. New York: Simon & Schuster, 2006.

Thompson, Peter. *Pacific Fury: How Australia and Her Allies Defeated the Japanese Scourge*. North Sydney, Australia: William Heinemann Australia, 2008.

Toland, John. *But Not in Shame: The Six Months After Pearl Harbor*. New York: Random House, 1961.

———. *The Rising Sun: The Decline and Fall of the Japanese Empire, 1936–1945*. New York: Random House, 1970.

Toll, Ian W. *Pacific Crucible: War at Sea in the Pacific, 1941–1942*. New York: W. W. Norton, 2012.

Trefalt, Beatrice. *Japanese Army Stragglers and Memories of the War in Japan, 1950–75*. New York: Routledge, 2003.

Tugwell, Rexford G. *The Democratic Roosevelt*. Garden City, NY: Doubleday & Co., 1957.

Ugaki, Admiral Matome. *Fading Victory*. Pittsburgh, PA: University of Pittsburgh Press, 1991.

Vader, John. *New Guinea: The Tide Is Stemmed*. New York: Ballantine, 1971.

Van der Vat, Dan. *The Pacific Campaign: The U.S.–Japanese Naval War 1941–1945*. New York: Touchstone, 1992.

Veale, Lionel. *The Wewak Mission: Coastwatchers at War in New Guinea*. Ashmore City, Australia.: L. P. V. Veale, 1996.

Watson, Robert Meredith, Jr., *Seahorse Soldiering: MacArthur's Amphibian Engineers from New Guinea to Nagoya*. Xlibris, 2003.

Weise, Selene H. C. *The Good Soldier: The Story of a Southwest Pacific Signal Corps WAC*. Shippensburg, PA: Burd Street Press, 1999.

Whan, Major Vorin E., Jr., ed. *A Soldier Speaks: Public Papers and Speeches of General of the Army Douglas MacArthur*. New York: Frederick A. Praeger Publishers, 1965.

Whitney, Major General Courtney. *MacArthur: His Rendezvous with History*. New York: Alfred A. Knopf, 1956.

Williams, Peter. *The Kokoda Campaign 1942: Myth and Reality*. New York: Cambridge University Press, 2012.

Williford, Glen. *Racing the Sunrise: Reinforcing America's Pacific Outposts, 1941–1942*. Annapolis: Naval Institute Press, 2010.

Willoughby, Maj. Gen. Charles A., and John Chamberlain. *MacArthur: 1941–1951*. New York: McGraw-Hill, 1954.

Wilson, Paul C. *The Sunset War*. Bloomington, IN: 1st Books Library, 2003.

Winters, Harold. *Battling the Elements: Weather and Terrain in the Conduct of War.* Baltimore: Johns Hopkins University Press, 1998.

Wukovits, John. *Admiral "Bull" Halsey: The Life and Wars of the Navy's Most Controversial Commander.* New York: Palgrave Macmillan, 2011.

Zedric, Lance Q. *Silent Warriors of World War II: The Alamo Scouts Behind the Japanese Lines.* Ventura, CA: Pathfinder Publishing, 1995.

Zuckoff, Mitchell. *Lost in Shangri-La: A True Story of Survival, Adventure, and the Most Incredible Rescue Mission of World War II.* New York: Harper, 2011.

SOURCE NOTES

When I read a book, I generally use two bookmarks: one for the last page I've read, and one for the page housing the corresponding source notes. I do this because I often want to know more about a person, a quote, or an incident mentioned by the author, but not discussed in depth in the book I am reading. Examining the author's cited source enables me to dig deeper into questions and events that interest me, such as what was said before or after the quoted passage, how others responded to the incident, and the background of the person mentioned. That information may not be appropriate for inclusion in the present work, but may be interesting and often results in my purchasing another book. This becomes difficult when the sources identified are located in an archive that is not easily accessed. Because of this, I have endeavored as often as possible to select sources that are available to readers who wish to learn more about the events about which I have written.

Prologue

1 Manchester, p. 146; Taylor, pp. 92–93.
2 Harries, pp. 201–9.
3 MacArthur, p. 106.
4 Coakley, pp. 502–3.
5 Milner, p. 3.

Chapter 1: "This Is War, Not a Sunday School Picnic"

1 Collie, p. 5.
2 Ibid.
3 Vego, p. 94.
4 Bullard, p. 14.
5 Gamble, *Invasion Rabaul*, p. 66.
6 Selby, pp. 7–8.
7 Gamble, *Invasion Rabaul*, pp. 56–57.
8 Ibid., p. 60; Selby, p. 24.
9 Gillison, p. 313.
10 Ibid., p. 314.
11 Aplin, p. 278.
12 Selby, pp. 15–16.
13 Aplin, pp. 25–26.
14 Gillison, p. 321.
15 Ibid., p. 363.
16 Ibid, p. 364; *Time,* February 15, 1943.
17 Gamble, *Invasion Rabaul*, p. 70.
18 Ibid.
19 *World War II Database,* www.ww2db.com.
20 Bullard, p. 22.
21 Gamble, *Invasion Rabaul*, p. 74.
22 Selby, p. 27.
23 Ibid.
24 Gamble, *Fortress Rabaul,* p. 5.
25 *Sun-Herald,* Sydney, Australia, October 3, 2002.
26 Prange, p. 54.
27 Ibid.
28 http://www.warsailors.com/singleships/herstein.html.
29 McAulay, *We Who Are About to Die,* p. 118; Gillison, pp. 356–57.
30 Gillison, pp. 356–58.
31 McAulay, *We Who Are About to Die,* p. 121.
32 Gillison, p. 358.
33 Bullard, p. 24.
34 Gamble, *Invasion Rabaul*, p. 81; Aplin, p. 3.
35 http://asopa.typepad.com/asopa_people/2009/07/the-herstein-mens-fateful-decision-to-stay.html.
36 http://www.warsailors.com/singleships/herstein.html.
37 Bullard, p. 23.

38 Ibid., p. 16; http://kokoda.commemoration.gov.au/war-in-papua/japanese-intelligence-on-kokoda.php.
39 McAulay, *We Who Are About to Die*, p. 123.
40 Gamble, *Invasion Rabaul*, p. 84.
41 Selby, pp. 35–36.
42 Lorna (Whyte) Johnston interview with Dr. Barbara M. Angell, May 5, 1998. www.angellpro.com.au.

Chapter 2: "Every Man for Himself"

1 Bullard, p. 24.
2 Ibid., p. 25.
3 Selby, p. 38.
4 Wigmore, p. 403.
5 Bullard, p. 26.
6 Wigmore, p. 653.
7 Prange, p. 54.
8 Hall, p. 18.
9 Selby, p. 43.
10 *New York Times*, January 25, 1942, p. 26.
11 Roscoe, pp. 88–92.
12 Hall, pp. 24–25.
13 www.info.dfat.gov.au/info/historical/HistDocs.nesf.
14 Costello, p. 180.
15 www.info.dfat.gov.au/info/historical/HistDocs.nesf.
16 Black, pp. 194–95.
17 Manchester, p. 214.
18 McAulay, pp. 144–45.
19 Gamble, *Invasion Rabaul*, pp. 235–42.
20 Selby, pp. 183–96.
21 Gamble, *Fortress Rabaul*, pp. 54–62.
22 Bergerud, *Touched with Fire*, p. 213.
23 Ibid., p. 38; Lundstrom, pp. 88–108; Johnston, *Queen of the Flat-Tops*, pp. 67–79; Gamble, *Fortress Rabaul*, p. 68.
24 Johnston, *Queen of the Flat-Tops*, p. 77.
25 Ugaki, p. 92.
26 Bergerud, *Touched with Fire*, p. 39.

Chapter 3: First Landings in New Guinea

1 Dull, p. 102.
2 Lovell, p. 273.
3 Bullard, pp. 38–39.
4 Ibid., p. 47.
5 Lundstrom, p. 124; Gillison, p. 454.
6 Flynn, pp. 81–82.
7 Gamble, *Invasion Rabaul*, p. 113; Gillison, p. 455.
8 Ibid.
9 Gamble, *Fortress Rabaul*, p. 112.
10 Gamble, *Invasion Rabaul*, p. 163; McCarthy, p. 57.
11 Bradley, *Wau*, p. 6.
12 McCarthy, p. 57.
13 Lundstrom, pp. 125–31.
14 Bradley, p. 10; Gillison, p. 455.
15 Bradley, p. 10; Johnston, *Queen of the Flat-Tops*, p. 89.
16 Sakai, pp. 164–65.
17 Gillison, p. 456; Johnston, *Queen of the Flat-Tops*, pp. 91–92.
18 Bullard, p. 48.
19 Ibid.
20 Spector, p. 150.
21 Bullard, p. 58.

Chapter 4: A General in Search of an Army

1 Black, p. 320.
2 Manchester, pp. 73–76; James, pp. 115–27.
3 Manchester, p. 110.
4 Manchester, p. 160; Hunt, p. 171; Perret, p. 227.
5 Perret, p. 187.
6 James, *The Years of MacArthur*, vol. 2, p. 97.
7 Perret, p. 272.
8 Ibid., p. 269.
9 Schmitz, pp. 41–42.
10 Miller, p. 334.
11 Manchester, p. 273.
12 Ambrose, p. 93.
13 Schweikart, p. 405.
14 Ferrell, p. 49.
15 Schmitz, pp. 145–46.

16 James, *The Years of MacArthur*, vol. 2, p. 87.

17 D'Este, p. 446.

18 Manchester, p. 251.

19 Sherwood, p. 508.

20 Manchester, p. 251.

21 Sherwood, p. 509.

22 Salecker, p. 158.

23 Manchester, p. 267.

24 MacArthur, p. 145.

25 Manchester, p. 271; Willoughby, p. 13.

26 Lee and Henschel, p. 160.

27 Manchester, p. 268.

28 Lardner, p. 14.

29 Manchester, pp. 267–68.

30 James, *The Years of MacArthur*, vol. 2, p. 84.

31 *New York Times*, March 18, 1942, p. 1.

32 Ibid.

33 Ibid.

34 Bergerud, *Touched by Fire*, p. 43.

35 Hunt, pp. 271–72; Manchester, p. 270; Perret, p. 283; James, *The Years of MacArthur*, vol. 2, pp. 297–98.

36 Lee and Henschel, pp. 160–61.

37 Manchester, p. 272.

38 Hastings, *Inferno*, p. 218.

39 *New York Times*, March 21, 1942, p. 1.

40 Hersey, pp. 306–8.

41 Leary, *MacArthur and the American Century*, p. 110.

42 Ibid.

43 Whan, pp. 115–16.

44 Lardner, p. 73.

45 Johnston, *The Toughest Fighting in the World*, p. 52.

46 *Melbourne Herald*, March 18, 1942, p. 1.

47 MacArthur, p. 151.

48 Perret, p. 285.

49 www.HomeofHeroes.com.

50 Whan, pp. 117–18.

51 Manchester, p. 146.

52 *New York Times*, May 10, 1932, p. 17.

53 Manchester, p. 280.

54 *Saturday Review*, September 26, 1964, pp. 42–43.

55 Ferrell, pp. 48, 50.

56 Stimson and Bundy, p. 507.

57 Manchester, p. 283.

58 Beckman, p. 20.

59 Sherwood, p. 455.

60 Manchester, p. 283.

61 Lear, *MacArthur and the American Century*, p. 147.

62 Morton, pp. 251–52.

63 MacArthur Memorial Archives RG-4: USAFPAC.

64 Ibid., Box 7, Fol. 1.

65 Drury, pp. 49–50; Wukovits, p. 205.

66 Hunt, p. 280.

67 Perret, p. 288.

68 Manchester, p. 282.

69 James, *The Years of MacArthur*, vol. 2, p. 123; Whitney, p. 67.

70 Ibid., pp. 120–21.

71 Leary, p. 147.

72 Morison, *Breaking the Bismarcks Barrier*, p. 32.

73 Spector, p. 145.

74 Sherwood, pp. 603–5.

75 Morgan, p. 639.

76 Black, *Franklin Delano Roosevelt*, pp. 750–51.

77 Tugwell, p. 349.

78 *The War with Japan, Part 1. (7 December 1941 to August 1945).* United States Military Academy Department of Military Arts and Engineering. Part 1, 1950, p. 112.

Chapter 5: To Port Moresby by Sea

1 Bullard, pp. 1–2; Vego, pp. 94–95.

2 Dull, p. 118.

3 Johnston, *War Diary 1942*, p. 18.

4 Bullard, p. 50.

5 Johnston, *War Diary 1942*, p. 18.

6 Vego, p. 94.

7 Frei, p. 166.

8 Ibid, pp. 162, 166.

9 Vego, p. 95; Frei, p. 168.

10 Toland, *Rising Sun*, p. 54.

11 Brown and Anderson, p. 8.

12 Frei, p. 173.

13 Holmes, p. 65.

14 www.pacificwar.org.au/CoralSea.

15 Holmes, p. 70.

16 Bullard, p. 56.

17 James, *The Years of MacArthur*, vol. 2, p. 157; *Reports of General MacArthur*, vol. 1, pp. 45–46.

18 Ugaki, p. 75.

19 Spector, p. 157.

20 Feuer, pp. 36–37.

21 Ibid., p. 15.

22 James, *The Years of MacArthur*, vol. 2, p. 159.

23 Hoyt, *Blue Skies*, p. 25.

24 Ibid.; Dull, p. 121.

25 Morison, *Coral Sea*, p. 27.

26 Dull, p. 122.

27 Ugaki, p. 121.

28 Lundstrom, p. 192; Ugaki, p. 121; Bullard, p. 72.

29 Lundstrom, p. 192.

30 Extract from the report of Commander John S. Philips, downloaded from http://ibiblio.org/hyperwar/USN/ships/logs/AO/ao23-Coral.html.

31 Lundstrom, p. 195; Hoyt, p. 52; Vego, p. 134.

32 Lundstrom, *Black Shoe Admiral*, pp. 1166–71.

33 Morison, *Coral Sea*, p. 40.

34 Lundstrom, *Black Shoe*, p. 169.

35 Ibid.; Morison, *Coral Sea*, p. 42.

36 Vego, p. 135.

37 Lundstrom, pp. 206–7.

38 Ibid., p. 205.

39 Hoyt, pp. 63–67.

40 Ugaki, p. 23

41 Vego, p. 135; Lundstrom, pp. 209–18.

42 Dull, p. 126.

43 Hough, pp. 192–93.

44 Lundstrom, pp. 222–23.

45 Ibid., p. 228.

46 Hoyt, pp. 81–84; Hough, pp. 194–95; Dull, pp. 126–28.

47 Dull, p. 128.

48 Hoyt, pp. 88–99; Dull, p. 128; Spector, pp. 161–62.

49 Dull, p. 128.

50 Lundstrom, pp. 279–82; Hough, pp. 198–99. Hoyt, pp. 127–61.

51 Morison, *Coral Sea*, p. 63.

52 General Staff, *Reports of General MacArthur*, vol. 6, chapter 3, endnotes.

53 *Pittsburgh Post-Gazette*, May 22, 1942, p. 2.

54 Gamble, *Fortress Rabaul*, pp. 174–75.

55 James, *The Years of MacArthur*, vol. 2, pp. 162–63.

Chapter 6: Second Landings in New Guinea

1 Maneki, p. 90; Drea, *ULTRA*, p. 24.

2 Maneki, p. 90.

3 Ibid., p. 79.

4 Lewin, pp. 182–83.

5 Drea, *ULTRA*, p. 37.

6 Costello, p. 276.

7 Dull, pp. 133–36.

8 Morison, *Coral Sea*, p. 81.

9 Harris, p. 91; Parker, p. 52; Fuchida, p. 161.

10 Fuchida, p. 161.

11 Lewin, p. 100.

12 *Manila Tribune*, June 12, 1942, p. 4.

13 Lord, *Incredible Victory*, p. 286.

14 Ibid.

15 Ito, p. 56.

16 Bullard, pp. 100–1.

17 Ibid., p. 107.

18 *Reports*, vol. 2, part 1, pp. 138–41.

19 McCarthy, p. 120.

20 Ibid., pp. 121–22.

21 Johnston, *The Toughest Fighting in the World* p. 50; *Sydney Morning Herald*, March 23, 1942, p. 5.

22 Milner, p. 48.

23 Gillison, p. 538.

24 James, *The Years of MacArthur*, vol. 2, pp. 190–91.

25 Gill, p. 51.

26 Milner, pp. 51–52

27 Ibid., p. 51.

28 Dod, p. 156; www.pacificwrecks.com/airfields.png/dobodura/index/html.

29 Milner, p. 53.

30 Holmes, p. 118.

31 James, *The Years of MacArthur*, vol. 2, pp. 191–92; Milner, pp. 52–53; Spector, p. 188.
32 Collie, p. 55.
33 Bullard, p. 112.
34 *Reports*, vol. 2, part 1, p. 142.
35 Dull, p. 176; Bullard, pp. 116–17; *Reports*, vol. 2, part 1, p. 142.
36 Milner, pp. 54–55; *Reports*, vol. 2, part 1, pp. 142–43.
37 Dull, p. 176.

Chapter 7: Death Along the Kokoda Track

1 Williams, p. 52.
2 McCarthy, p. 108.
3 Milner, pp. 56–57.
4 Collie, pp. 65–66.
5 Milner, pp. 62–63.
6 Campbell, p. 46.
7 James, *The Years of MacArthur*, vol. 2, p. 182.
8 Mayo, p. 11; Milner, p. 63.
9 Mayo, p. 21.
10 Australian Military Medal citation.
11 Bullard, p. 131.
12 Brune, p. 40.
13 Mayo, p. 21.
14 Williams, p. 52.
15 Brune, p. 41.
16 Williams, p. 51, from the 39th Battalion war diary.
17 Paull, p. 55.
18 Collie, p. 67.
19 Paull, p. 57.
20 Brune, p. 45.
21 Collie, p. 72.
22 Brune, p. 47.
23 Paull, p. 62.
24 Ibid.
25 Collie, p. 70.
26 Williams, p. 55.
27 Paull, p. 70.
28 Williams, p. 60; Mayo, p. 26.
29 Morison, *The Struggle for Guadalcanal*, vol. 5, p. 53; Milner, p. 68; Dull, pp. 187–94; Toland, *The Rising Sun*, p. 362.

30 Bullard, pp. 153–54; Milner, p. 68.

31 Frank, *Guadalcanal,* pp. 143–47.

32 Harries, p. 400.

33 Collie, pp. 81–83.

34 Bullard, p. 151.

35 James, *The Years of MacArthur,* vol. 2, p. 192.

36 Perret, p. 301.

37 Griffith, pp. 51–55.

38 James, *The Years of MacArthur,* vol. 2, p. 197; Perret, p. 302.

39 Griffith, p. 56.

40 Kenney, *The MacArthur I Know,* p. 36; Perret, p. 302.

41 Griffith, p. 46.

42 James, *The Years of MacArthur,* vol. 2, p. 198.

43 Manchester, p. 301.

44 Griffith, p. 57.

45 Kenney, *The MacArthur I Know,* p. 43.

46 Kenney, *General Kenney Reports,* pp. 30–31.

47 Ibid., p. 62.

48 McCarthy, pp. 194–95.

49 Ibid.

50 Collingham, pp. 293–94.

51 Collie, pp. 92–93.

52 Williams, p. 69.

53 *Reports of General MacArthur,* vol. 1, p. 70.

54 Paull, p. 222.

55 Harries, p. 404.

56 Collie, p. 136.

57 Bullard, p. 166.

58 Kenney, *General Kenney Reports,* p. 106.

59 Campbell, *The Ghost Mountain Boys,* pp. 109–110.

60 Collie, p. 137.

61 Ibid., p. 139.

62 Paull, p. 270.

63 Ibid., p. 85.

Chapter 8: First Defeat at Milne Bay

1 Milner, p. 39.
2 Morison, *Breaking the Bismarks Barrier*, p. 27.
3 McCarthy, p. 155.
4 *Sydney Morning Herald*, August 28, 1942, p. 5.
5 Morison, *Breaking the Bismarcks Barrier*, p. 36.
6 Dr. Peter Londey, Presentation at the Australian War Memorial, September 5, 2002, taken from Clive Baker and Gregg Knight, *Milne Bay 1942* (Loftus, NSW: Baker-Knight Publications, 1991), p. 5.
7 Peter Londey, *Australian Dictionary of Biography* (Canberra: Australian National University, 1996).
8 Milner, p. 42.
9 "Australian Story," transcript of ABC broadcast January 4, 2002, interview with Barr.
10 Ryan, pp. 1028–29.
11 Drea, p. 44.
12 A. J. Hill, *Australian Dictionary of Biography* (Canberra: Australian National University, 2002).
13 Keogh, pp. 189–90.
14 Milner, p. 77.
15 Drea, p. 45.
16 Milner, p. 79.
17 Kenney, *General Kenney Reports,* pp. 82–83.
18 Brune, *Bastard of a Place,* p. 289.
19 http://www.combinedfleet.com/kusentei.htm.
20 Quoted in Brune, *Bastard of a Place,* p. 290.
21 Collie, pp. 112–13.
22 GHQ Operation Instruction No. 19 of 1 Oct., quoted in McCarthy, p. 260.
23 Yokota Shigeki interrogation report, Australian War Memorial.
24 Brune, *Bastard of a Place,* p. 289.
25 Hutchinson, p. 333.
26 Thompson, p. 340.
27 Bergerud, *Touched by Fire,* p. 257.
28 Milner, p. 84.
29 James, *The Years of MacArthur,* vol. 2, p. 208.
30 Collie, p.106.
31 Ibid.
32 Bullard, p. 175.
33 Ibid.
34 Gilbert, p. 217.

Chapter 9: "Take Buna, or Not Come Back Alive"

1 Perret, p. 310.

2 James, *The Years of MacArthur*, vol. 2, pp. 210–11.

3 Arnold, pp. 336–49.

4 James, *The Years of MacArthur*, vol. 2, p. 212.

5 Morison, *Breaking the Bismarks Barrier*, pp. 31–32.

6 MacArthur, p. 157.

7 Milner, p. 102.

8 Milner, pp. 106–7.

9 Kahn, pp. 87–88; Milner, p. 108.

10 Milner, pp. 115–16.

11 Bergerud, *Touched with Fire*, p. 33.

12 Mayo, p. 91.

13 Perret, p. 319.

14 Mayo, p. 87.

15 Kahn, pp. 121–22.

16 Ed Drea, "World War II: Buna Mission," *World War II* (September 2002.)

17 Mayo, p. 92.

18 Campbell, *The Ghost Mountain Boys*, pp. 167–69.

19 Bullard, p. 211.

20 Kenney, *General Kenney Reports*, pp. 150–51.

21 Milner, pp. 202–3.

22 McCarthy, pp. 450–51.

23 Groom, p. 348.

24 Rickenbacker, p. 332.

25 Ibid., pp. 332–33.

26 Eichelberger, pp. 20–22.

27 Kenney, *General Kenney Reports*, p. 158; Milner, p. 205 fn.

28 Eichelberger, p. 22.

29 Ibid.

30 Mayo, p. 93; Milner, p. 135.

31 Morlock, p. 123.

32 Johnston, *The Toughest Fighting in the World*, p. 216.

33 Campbell, *The Ghost Mountain Boys*, p. 272.

34 Keogh, p. 270.

35 Milner, p. 347.

36 Eichelberger, p. 62.

37 Perret, p. 330.

38 Mayo, p. 188; Bergerud, *Touched with Fire*, p. 225; Willoughby, p. 107; Manchester, p. 337.

Chapter 10: Sailing the Bismarck Sea

1 James, *The Years of MacArthur*, vol. 2, p. 239.
2 Morison, *Breaking the Bismarcks Barrier*, p. 47.
3 Ibid., p. 50.
4 James, *The Years of MacArthur*, vol. 2, p. 239.
5 Leary, *We Shall Return!*, p. 208.
6 Barbey, pp. 8–9.
7 Ibid., pp. 21–24.
8 Bullard, pp. 243–44.
9 General Staff, *Reports of General MacArthur*, vol. 2, p. 189.
10 Perret, pp. 331–32; Drea, *ULTRA*, p. 64.
11 McCarthy, p. 544.
12 Ibid., p. 545.
13 Phillip Bradley, p. 22.
14 McCarthy, pp. 94–96.
15 Dull, p. 268.
16 Phillip Bradley, p. 75.
17 Gamble, *Fortress Rabaul*, pp. 281–84.
18 Bradley, p. 79.
19 Ibid., pp. 76–84; Kenney, *General Kenney Reports*, p. 177; McCarthy, pp. 674–75.
20 Gillison, p. 675.
21 Bradley, p. 122.
22 McCarthy, pp. 575–76.
23 Ibid., p. 545.
24 Bradley, p. 196.
25 General Staff, *Reports of General MacArthur*, vol. 2, p. 193; McCarthy, p. 576.
26 Gamble, *Fortress Rabaul*, p. 289.
27 Drea, *ULTRA*, p. 67.
28 Ibid., p. 68.
29 Kenney, *General Kenney Reports*, p. 198.
30 Ibid., p. 199.
31 Perret, p. 333.
32 McAulay, *Battle of the Bismarck Sea*, pp. 44–45; Gamble, *Fortress Rabaul*, p. 304.
33 Livingstone, pp. 52–53.
34 Gillison, p. 691.
35 Morison, *Breaking the Bismarcks Barrier*, p. 58; McAulay, *Battle of the Bismarck Sea*, pp. 46–48; Gamble, *Fortress Rabaul*, pp. 304–5.
36 McAulay, *Battle of the Bismarck Sea*, p. 49.
37 Ibid., p. 54.
38 McAulay, *Battle of the Bismarck Sea*, p. 57.

39 Gillison, p. 692.

40 Ibid.

41 Gillison, pp. 691–98; Morison, *Breaking the Bismarcks Barrier*, pp. 54–61; McAulay, *Battle of the Bismarck Sea*, pp. 61–134; Gamble, *Fortress Rabaul*, pp. 288–315.

42 Bulkley, pp. 180–82.

43 Gillison, p. 694.

44 Kenney, *General Kenney Reports*, p. 206.

Chapter 11: Assault on Salamaua

1 James, *The Years of MacArthur*, vol. 2, p. 120.

2 Holzimmer, pp. 102–3.

3 Casey, *Amphibian*, p. v.

4 James, *The Years of MacArthur*, vol. 2, p. 311.

5 Holzimmer, p. 104.

6 General Staff, *Reports of General MacArthur*, vol. 1, p. 101 n3.

7 Morton, p. 412.

8 http://digital.library.wisc.edu/1711.dl/FRUS; *The Casablanca Conference, 1943*, pp. 774–75.

9 Holzimmer, p. 104.

10 James, *The Years of MacArthur*, vol. 2, p. 212.

11 Perret, p. 335.

12 Leary, p. 41.

13 Dexter, p. 222.

14 General Staff, *Reports of General MacArthur*, vol. 1, p. 107n11.

15 Holzimmer, p. 97.

16 Perret, p. 336.

17 Leary, p. 66.

18 MacArthur, p. 170.

19 Davis, p. 213.

20 Morison, *Breaking the Bismarcks Barrier*, p. 118.

21 Davis, p. 220.

22 Miller, *Cartwheel*, p. 43.

23 Kenney, *General Kenney Reports*, p. 227.

24 Morison, *Breaking the Bismarcks Barrier*, pp. 126–27.

25 Davis, p. 220.

26 Harris, p. 122.

27 Davis, pp. 249–66; Harris, p. 122; Morison, *Breaking the Bismarcks Barrier*, pp. 128–29.

28 General Staff, *Reports of General MacArthur*, vol. 1, p. 100.

29 Morton, p. 401.

30 Borneman, p. 311.

31 Ibid., p. 312.

32 Ibid., p. 313.

33 MacArthur, pp. 173–74.

34 Bradley, *To Salamaua*, pp. 42–45.

35 Ibid., p. 47.

36 Miller, *Cartwheel*, p. 201.

37 Dexter, p. 20.

38 Yoshihara, n.p.

39 Miller, *Cartwheel*, p. 211.

40 Wukovits, p. 155.

41 Holzimmer, p. 111.

42 Miller, *Cartwheel*, p. 55.

43 Ibid., pp. 58–59.

44 James, *The Years of MacArthur*, vol. 2, p. 323.

45 Bulkley, pp. 188–89.

46 Casey, *Amphibian Engineer Operations*, p. 66.

47 Renehan, p. 175.

48 Collier, pp. 408–10.

49 Ibid., pp. 429–30.

50 General Staff, *Reports of General MacArthur*, vol. 1, p. 121.

51 James, *The Years of MacArthur*, vol. 2, pp. 323–24.

52 Kenney, *General Kenney Reports*, pp. 252–53.

53 Perret, *Old Soldiers Never Die*, p. 352.

54 Kenney, *General Kenney Reports*, p. 253.

55 Ibid., pp. 276–79.

56 General Staff, *Reports of General MacArthur*, vol. 2, p. 215.

57 Ibid., vol. 1, p. 122.

58 Ibid., p. 121; MacArthur, p. 178.

Chapter 12: Pincers Around Lae

1 Lovell, pp. 273–74.

2 Miller, *Cartwheel*, p. 191.

3 Morison, *Breaking the Bismarcks Barrier*, p. 259.

4 Ibid., p. 260.

5 Griffith, pp. 133–34.

6 Dexter, p. 268.

7 Salecker, *Blossoming Silk Against the Rising Sun*, pp. 110–11.

8 Barbey, pp. 74–75.

9 Ibid., p. 76.

10 Dexter, p. 328.

11 Kenney, *General Kenney Reports*, p. 290.

12 Ibid.

13 Barbey, p. 71.

14 Roscoe, p. 257.

15 Miller, *Cartwheel*, pp. 203–4.

16 Morison, *Breaking the Bismarcks Barrier*, pp. 263–64.

17 Dexter, p. 332.

18 Barney, p. 79.

19 Miller, *Cartwheel*, p. 207.

20 Lowe, p. 52.

21 Kenney, *The MacArthur I Know*, p. 107.

22 Kenney, *General Kenney Reports*, p. 289.

23 Ibid., pp. 293–94.

24 Devlin, p. 262.

25 MacArthur, p. 179.

26 Salecker, *Blossoming Silk Against the Rising Sun*, p. 120.

27 Gailey, *MacArthur's Victory*, p. 61.

28 Kenney, *The MacArthur I Know*, pp. 108–9.

29 Willoughby, p. 130.

30 Kenney, *General Kenney Reports*, p. 294.

31 Dexter, p. 381.

32 Morison, *Breaking the Bismarcks Barrier*, p. 265, Miller, *Cartwheel*, p. 205.

33 Dexter, p. 325.

34 Miller, *Cartwheel*, p. 211.

35 Dexter, p. 324.

36 Gailey, *MacArthur's Victory*, p. 70.

Chapter 13: War on the Huon Peninsula

1 Miller, *Cartwheel*, p. 212.

2 Ibid.

3 General Staff, *Reports of General MacArthur*, vol. 2, part 1, pp. 223–24.

4 Miller, *Cartwheel*, p. 214.

5 Gailey, *MacArthur's Victory*, p. 83.

6 Barbey, pp. 88–89.

7 Ibid.

8 Miller, *Cartwheel*, p. 218.

9 Dexter, p. 447.

10 *Sydney Morning Herald*, Oct. 3, 1947, p. 2.

11 Morison, *Breaking the Bismarcks Barrier*, p. 269.

12 Watson, p. 147; Miller, *Cartwheel*, p. 220.

13 Fowle, p. 359; *Pittsburgh Press*, March 28, 1945, p. 21; Dod, pp. 253–54; Watson, p. 148; Spector, pp. 241–242.

14 Miller, *Cartwheel*, p. 221.

15 www.2esb.org/04_History/Book/Chapter_05.htm; Dexter, p. 618 fn.

16 Gailey, *MacArthur's Victory*, p. 92; Dexter, p. 648.

17 *Courier-Mail* (Brisbane), November 29, 1943, p. 1.

18 http://www.2esb.org/04_History/Book/Chapter_05.htm.

19 Barbey, p. 130.

20 Miller, *Cartwheel*, pp. 296–300.

21 Gailey, *MacArthur's Victory*, p. 138.

22 Watson, pp. 149–50; Dexter, p. 727; Steinberg, p. 137.

23 Drea, *ULTRA*, pp. 92–93.

24 Steinberg, p. 137.

25 Trefalt, pp. 51–52.

26 Gailey, *MacArthur's Victory*, p. 138.

27 James, *The Years of MacArthur*, vol. 2, p. 347.

28 Gailey, *MacArthur's Victory*, p. 139; Miller, *Cartwheel*, pp. 303–4.

29 *Time* 42 (14) (October 4, 1943), pp. 34, 37.

Chapter 14: Invasion Across the Straits

1 Drea, *ULTRA*, p. 89.

2 Griffith, p. 140; Kenney, *General Kenney Reports*, p. 314; Drea, *ULTRA*, p. 89.

3 Griffith, pp. 139–140.

4 Ibid., p. 141.

5 Kenney, *General Kenney Reports*, p. 317.

6 Miller, *Cartwheel*, p. 248; Dull, p. 290.

7 Drea, *ULTRA*, pp. 89–90; Kenney, *General Kenney Reports*, pp. 318–19.

8 Morison, *Breaking the Bismarcks Barrier*, pp. 324–25.

9 Dull, pp. 291–92; Morison, *Breaking the Bismarcks Barrier*, pp. 327–28.

10 Kenney, *General Kenney Reports*, p. 323.

11 Dull, p. 294.

12 Bergerud, *Touched with Fire*, p. 647.

13 James, *The Years of MacArthur*, vol. 2, pp. 331–32.

14 Griffith, p. 144.

15 Gailey, *MacArthur's Victory*, pp. 104–5.

16 Perret, p. 357.

17 Holzimmer, p. 115; Alexander, pp. 44–68.

18 Morison, *Breaking the Bismarcks Barrier*, p. 374.

19 Barbey, p. 107.

20 Gailey, *MacArthur's Victory*, p. 113; Morison, *Breaking the Bismarcks Barrier*, p. 113; Miller, *Cartwheel*, pp. 285–86.

21 Bulkley, pp. 217–19.

22 Shaw, p. 342.

23 Hough, *The Campaign on New Britain*, p. 144.

24 Mosley, pp. 264–67.

25 Pogue, p. 323.

26 MacArthur, pp. 183–84.

27 James, *The Years of MacArthur*, vol. 2, pp. 372–73.

28 http://www.mhric.org/fdr/chat27.html.

29 *Canberra Times*, December 28, 1943, p. 1; Kenney, *General Kenney Reports*, p. 334.

30 Barbey, p. 120; Perret, p. 358.

31 Shaw, p. 349.

32 Hough, *The Campaign on New Britain*, p. 49.

33 Shaw, p. 370.

34 Ibid., p. 428.

Chapter 15: The General and the Admiralities

1 Morrison, *Breaking the Bismarcks Barrier*, p. 433.

2 http://www.dutcheastindies.webs.com/manus.html.

3 Griffith, p. 151.

4 MacArthur, p. 188.

5 Holzimmer, p. 134; Alexander, p. 72.

6 Zedric, pp. 99–100; Alexander, pp. 77–80.

7 Miller, *Cartwheel*, p. 319.

8 MacArthur, p. 188

9 Walter Krueger, "Report on the Brewer Operation," 8/2/44. Series 4, box 3/14, Walter Krueger Papers, Cushing Memorial Library and Archives, Texas A & M University.

10 Taaffe, pp. 60–61.

11 Barbey, p. 152.

12 James, *The Years of MacArthur*, vol. 2, p. 382.

13 Miller, *Cartwheel*, pp. 328–29.

14 Egeberg, p. 30.

15 James, *The Years of MacArthur*, vol. 2, p. 385.

16 Drea, *ULTRA*, pp. 100–101.

17 Morison, *Breaking the Bismarcks Barrier*, p. 439.

18 Ibid., p. 437.

19 Frierson, p. 33.

20 Miller, *Cartwheel*, p. 330.

21 Frierson, p. 37.

22 Miller, *Cartwheel*, p. 331.

23 Taaffe, p. 66.

24 Morison, *Breaking the Bismarcks Barrier*, pp. 442–43.

25 Frierson, p. 56.

26 Drea, *ULTRA*, p. 104.

27 Greenfield, ed., *Command Decisions*; Miller, "MacArthur and the Admiralties," p. 223; Morrison, *Breaking the Bismarcks Barrier*, p. 448.

Chapter 16: Reckless and Persecution

1 Drea, *ULTRA*, p. 97.

2 Costello, p. 456.

3 Taaffe, pp. 77–78.

4 Morison, *New Guinea and the Marianas*, p. 48.

5 Barbey, pp. 158–59.

6 Smith, *The Approach to the Philippines*, pp. 97–98.

7 Drea, *ULTRA*, p. 105; Perret, p. 379.

8 James, *The Years of MacArthur*, vol. 2, pp. 447–48.

9 Kenney, *General Kenney Reports*, p. 380.

10 Gailey, *MacArthur's Victory*, p. 173.

11 Morison, *New Guinea and the Marianas*, p. 36.

12 Spector, p. 286.

13 Smith, *The Approach to the Philippines*, p. 99.

14 Gailey, *MacArthur's Victory*, pp. 179–80.

15 Gunther, pp. 28–29.

16 Barbey, pp. 172–73.

17 Gailey, *MacArthur's Victory*, p. 177.

18 Barbey, p. 176.

19 Gailey, *MacArthur's Victory*, p. 185.

20 James, *The Years of MacArthur*, vol. 2, p. 449.

21 Ibid.

22 Eichelberger, p. 114.

23 James, *The Years of MacArthur*, vol. 2, pp. 449–50.

24 Smith, *The Approach to the Philippines*, p. 101.
25 Morison, *New Guinea and the Marianas*, pp. 72–73; Rems, pp. 204–5; Smith, *The Approach to the Philippines*, p. 143.
26 Morison, *New Guinea and the Marianas*, p. 73.
27 Eichelberger, p. 122; Smith, *The Approach to the Philippines*, p. 83; Taaffe, p. 99.
28 Perry, p. 284; Taaffe, p. 99.

Chapter 17: Next Stop: Wakde

1 Kenney, *General Kenney Reports*, p. 395.
2 Drea, *ULTRA*, p. 123.
3 Holzimmer, pp. 149–50; Barbey, p. 186; Drea, *ULTRA*, p. 127.
4 General Staff, *Reports of General MacArthur*, vol. 2, p. 277.
5 Kenney, *General Kenney Reports*, p. 397.
6 General Staff, *Reports of General MacArthur*, vol. 2, p. 278.
7 Kenney, *General Kenney Reports*, p. 398.
8 Prefer, p. 56; Morison, *New Guinea and the Marianas*, pp. 97–98.
9 Prefer, p. 57.
10 Eichelberger, p. 137.
11 Morison, *New Guinea and the Marianas*, p. 100.
12 Smith, *The Approach to the Philippines*, pp. 226–28.
13 *Jakarta Post*, November 10, 2005.
14 Heefner, p. 95.
15 Smith, *The Approach to the Philippines*, pp. 234–35.
16 Ibid.
17 Taaffe, p. 130.
18 Smith, *The Approach to the Philippines*, pp. 257–58.
19 Sandler, p. 1031.
20 Smith, *The Approach to the Philippines*, p. 259.
21 Prefer, p. 92.
22 Ibid., pp. 94–95; Smith, *The Approach to the Philippines*, pp. 270–71.
23 Taaffe, p. 138.
24 Bentley, p. 40.
25 Gailey, *MacArthur's Victory*, pp. 204–5.
26 James, *The Years of MacArthur*, vol. 2, p. 456.

Chapter 18: Bloody Biak

1 MacArthur, p. 291; Smith, *The Approach to the Philippines*, pp. 280–81; Steinberg, p. 146.

2 Morison, *New Guinea and the Marianas*, p. 104.

3 Taaffe, p. 147.

4 Bernstein, pp. 51–53.

5 Morison, *New Guinea and the Marianas*, p. 108.

6 Alexander, *Storm Landings*, p. 110.

7 Ugaki, p. 376.

8 Dull, pp. 302–4.

9 Prefer, pp. 108–9.

10 Morison, *New Guinea and the Marianas*, p. 106.

11 Smith, *The Approach to the Philippines*, p. 284.

12 Gill, pp. 415–16.

13 Prefer, p. 108.

14 Kenney, *General Kenney Reports*, p. 399; Taaffe, p. 144.

15 Drea, *ULTRA*, p. 137.

16 General Staff, *Reports of General MacArthur*, vol. 2, p. 285.

17 Bernstein, p. 91.

18 Smith, *The Approach to the Philippines*, pp. 291–92.

19 General Staff, *Reports of General MacArthur*, vol. 2, p. 285.

20 Smith, *The Approach to the Philippines*, p. 306.

21 Salecker, *Rolling Thunder Against the Rising Sun*, pp. 146–48.

22 General Staff, *Reports of General MacArthur*, vol. 2, pp. 286–87.

23 Ibid.

24 Holzimmer, p. 158.

25 *Charlotte Sun*, Port Charlotte, FL, August 23, 2010; http://engineersvietnam.
com/engineers/WWII/owi.htm.

26 Holzimmer, pp. 158–59.

27 Smith, *The Approach to the Philippines*, pp. 321–24.

28 James, *The Years of MacArthur*, vol. 2, pp. 459–60.

29 Eichelberger, p. 144.

30 Riegelman, pp. 138–39.

31 James, *The Years of MacArthur*, vol. 2, p. 460; Taaffe, p. 168.

32 Eichelberger, p. 146.

33 Ibid., pp. 151–52.

34 Smith, *The Approach to the Philippines*, pp. 392–93.

Chapter 19: The General, the President, and the Admiral

1   Whitney, p. 120.
2   Perret, pp. 400–1.
3   James, *The Years of MacArthur*, vol. 2, pp. 523–24.
4   Whitney, p. 123.
5   Perry, p. 268.
6   Potter, pp. 280–81.
7   Perry, p. 269.
8   Borneman, p. 382.
9   Potter, p. 315; Hunt, p. 332.
10   Black, p. 975.
11   Manchester, p. 364.
12   Perret, p. 402.
13   Tugwell, p. 655.
14   Potter, p. 317.
15   Ibid.
16   James, *The Years of MacArthur*, vol. 2, p. 530; MacArthur, p. 197.
17   Manchester, p. 368.
18   Black, p. 978.
19   Pogue, p. 452.
20   James, *The Years of MacArthur*, vol. 2, pp. 534–35.
21   Black, p. 981; James, *The Years of MacArthur*, vol. 2, p. 535.
22   Potter, p. 321.

Chapter 20: Breakout from Wewak

1   *Time*, July 24, 1944.
2   E-mail from Lance Zedric, Alamo Scouts Association historian, July 29, 2014.
3   Drea, *ULTRA*, p. 144.
4   General Staff, *Reports of General MacArthur*, vol. 2, p. 299.
5   Drea, *Defending the Driniumor*, pp. 25–26.
6   James, *The Years of MacArthur*, vol. 2, p. 483.
7   Willoughby, p. 190; Drea, *ULTRA*, pp. 144–45.
8   Willoughby, p. 190.
9   Smith, *The Approach to the Philippines*, p. 147.
10   Drea, *ULTRA*, p. 144.
11   Holzimmer, p. 169.
12   Robert J. Conrad, "Back in Battle," *Courant*, Hartford, CT, July 10, 1994.
13   Gailey, *MacArthur's Victory*, pp. 236–37.

14 General Staff, *Reports of General MacArthur*, vol. 2, p. 300; Gailey, *MacArthur's Victory*, p. 237.

15 Ibid., pp. 301–3.

16 Smith, *The Approach to the Philippines*, p. 205.

17 MacArthur, p. 194.

Chapter 21: Island-Hopping to Victory

1 James, *The Years of MacArthur*, vol. 2, p. 480.

2 MacArthur, p. 194.

3 Smith, *The Approach to the Philippines*, p. 421.

4 Gailey, *MacArthur's Victory*, p. 244; Smith, *The Approach to the Philippines*, p. 420.

5 Prefer, p. 186.

6 Holzimmer, p. 161.

7 Drea, *ULTRA*, p. 40.

8 Ibid.

9 Kenney, *General Kenney Reports*, p. 407.

10 Alexander, *Shadows in the Jungle*, pp. 98–99.

11 General Staff, *Reports of General MacArthur*, vol. 2, p. 297.

12 Taaffe, p. 179.

13 Salecker, *Blossoming Silk Against the Rising Sun*, p. 159;

14 Holzimmer, p. 161.

15 Kenney, *General Kenney Reports*, p. 407.

16 Taaffe, p. 180; Gill, p. 443.

17 Morison, *New Guinea and the Marianas*, p. 138.

18 Smith, *The Approach to the Philippines*, pp. 409–10.

19 Heefner, p. 106.

20 Salecker, *Blossoming Silk Against the Rising Sun*, pp. 160–61.

21 Prefer, pp. 190–91.

22 Devlin, pp. 426–27.

23 Salecker, *Blossoming Silk Against the Rising Sun*, p. 164.

24 Devlin, p. 429.

25 Heefner, p. 108.

26 Taaffe, p. 185.

27 Smith, *The Approach to the Philippines*, p. 421.

28 Ibid., p. 423.

29 Heefner, p. 112.

30 Morrison, *New Guinea*, p. 141.

31 Gailey, *MacArthur's Victory*, p. 256.

32 Smith, *The Approach to the Philippines*, p. 445.

33 Mercado, p. 93; Rottman, *World War II Pacific Island Guide*, p. 253.

34 James, *The Years of MacArthur*, vol. 2, p. 486.

35 Morison, *Leyte*, pp. 21–23.

36 Taaffe, p. 219.

37 Smith, *The Approach to the Philippines*, p. 487.

38 Morison, *Leyte*, p. 24.

39 Barbey, p. 227.

40 James, *The Years of MacArthur*, vol. 2, p. 489.

Epilogue

1 James, *The Years of MacArthur*, vol. 2, p. 481.

2 General Staff, *Reports of General MacArthur*, vol. 1, p. 161.

3 Long, pp. 55–72.

4 General Staff, *Reports of General MacArthur*, vol. 2.

5 Perret, p. 418.

6 Costello, pp. 502–3.

7 Perry, pp. 288–89.

INDEX